THE EDUCATION OF CHILDREN WITH SEVERE LEARNING DIFFICULTIES

THE EDUCATION OF CHILDREN WITH SEVERE LEARNING DIFFICULTIES

Bridging the Gap between Theory and Practice

Edited by JUDITH COUPE and JILL PORTER

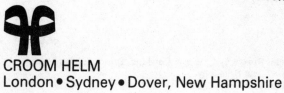

CROOM HELM
London • Sydney • Dover, New Hampshire

© 1986 Judith Coupe and Jill Porter
Croom Helm Ltd, Provident House, Burrell Row,
Beckenham, Kent BR3 1AT
Croom Helm Australia Pty Ltd, Suite 4, 6th Floor,
64-76 Kippax Street, NSW 2010, Australia

British Library Cataloguing in Publication Data

The Education of Children with Severe Learning
    Difficulties: bridging the gap between theory
    and practice.
    1. Handicapped children — Education
    I. Coupe, Judith   II. Porter, Jill
    371.9   LC4015

    ISBN 0-7099-3445-9
    ISBN 0-7099-3446-7 pbk

Croom Helm, 51 Washington Street, Dover,
New Hampshire 03820, USA

Library of Congress Cataloging-in-Publication Data
Main entry under title:

The Education of children with severe learning
    difficulties.

    Includes index.
    1. Mentally handicapped children—Education—Addresses,
essays, lectures.   2. Handicapped children—Education—
Addresses, essays, lectures.   I. Coupe, Judith D.
II. Porter, Jill.
LC4601.E3   1986   371.92′8   86-929
ISBN 0-7099-3445-9
ISBN 0-7099-3446-7 (pbk.)

Typeset in 10pt Times Roman by Leaper & Gard Ltd, Bristol, England
Printed and bound in Great Britain by
Biddles Ltd, Guildford and King's Lynn

CONTENTS

Acknowledgements   vii
List of Contributors   viii
Foreword *Peter Mittler*   1
Introduction *Judith Coupe and Jill Porter*   6

Part One: Curriculum Method and Organisation   9

1. The Curriculum Intervention Model (CIM)
   Judith Coupe   11

2. Beyond a Simple Behavioural Approach *Jill Porter*   44

3. Classroom Management *Peter Sturmey and Tony Crisp*   70

Part Two: Factors Influencing Learning and Development   85

4. The Development of Personality and Emotion
   Sarah Sandow   87

5. The Development of Cognition and Perception
   Nigel Carden   101

6. Motor Competence in Children with Mental Handicap
   James Hogg   128

7. The Development of Language and Communication
   Juliet Goldbart   153

8. The Learning Process *Peter Evans*   183

9. Sensory Handicap
   A. Hearing Impairment *Chris Williams*   214
   B. Visual Impairment *David Ellis*   224

Part Three: The People Involved   237

10. Parents as Partners
    A. The Changing Scene *Philippa Russell*   239
    B. Parents' Contribution to the Education of their Child
        Helen McConachie   253

11. The Role of the School Staff *Mike Johnson*   269

12. The Role of the Linked Agencies
    A. The Educational Psychologist *Peter Farrell*   291

B. The Speech Therapist *Sue Roulstone*   300
C. The Remedial Therapists: Professions Allied to
    Medicine *Ann Grimley*   312
D. Support Services for the Hearing-Impaired
    Angela Foulkes and Richard Fitzsimons   326
E. Support Services for the Visually Impaired
    Alison Frankenberg   336
F. The Peripatetic Teacher for the Deaf-Blind *Jim Dale*   348
G. The District and Community Mental Handicap Team
    Richard Cotmore   359
H. The Support Unit *Jim Buggy*   375
I. The Consultant Paediatrician *Ian McKinlay*   382

Index   391

ACKNOWLEDGEMENTS

To John, Mike, Simon and Martin for their patience, to Margaret Walker, Ann Fitzmaurice, our colleagues at Melland School and the Special Education Team at West London Institute of Higher Education, and in particular our thanks go to James Hogg for his invaluable support.

LIST OF CONTRIBUTORS

JIM BUGGY is a senior specialist social worker for the City of Manchester with responsibility for residential placement and respite fostering of children.

NIGEL CARDEN, M.Phil., is the head of the Junior Department at Wedgwood School for pupils with severe learning difficulties. Previously he was psychologist on the Anson House Project, Hester Adrian Research Centre, University of Manchester.

RICHARD COTMORE is a social work assistant on the Community mental handicap team, Central Nottinghamshire. Prior to this he was a research worker at Nottingham University.

JUDITH COUPE is an experienced teacher and spent three years at the Hester Adrian Research Centre on a Schools Council project. She was an advisory teacher with Cheshire and is now Headteacher, Melland School, Manchester.

TONY CRISP is a clinical psychologist working with both mentally handicapped and elderly people. He has previously carried out research on dressing, self injurious behaviour, toilet training and goal planning.

JIM DALE, M.Ed., is a qualified teacher of the deaf and the blind. Also he has the diploma for teaching Deaf-Blind from Perkins School, USA. Up to his retirement in 1985 he was peripatetic teacher for Deaf-Blind, Inner London Education Authority.

DAVID ELLIS is Principal Clinical Psychologist with the Mental Handicap Service of N.E. Essex Health Authority based in Colchester. He is a member of the National Committee on the Multi-Handicapped Blind (CMHB).

PETER EVANS, PhD, is a Senior Lecturer and Senior Research Officer on curriculum research for Pupils with Moderate Learning Difficulties Project at the University of London, Institute of Education.

PETER FARRELL is tutor to the M.Sc Educational Psychology Training Course at the University of Manchester. As a practising Educational Psychologist with Manchester Education Committee he has regular contacts with special schools.

RICHARD FITZSIMONS has additional training as a teacher of the deaf and as an audiologist. A former deputy head of Shawbrook School, Manchester, he is now responsible for Assessment and Audiological support in the Service for Hearing Impaired Pupils, Manchester LEA.

ANGELA FOULKES is a trained teacher of the deaf who worked in the Department of Audiology, University of Manchester where she specialised in Pre-school Assessment and Parent Guidance. She now leads a team of Manchester Education Authority Support Teachers specialising in work with under fives and with multiply handicapped children.

ALISON FRANKENBERG, B.A (Hons), has the Diploma in Special Education (Visual Handicap). She is visiting teacher for pre-school children in Manchester Education Service for Visually Impaired Children and Students.

JULIET GOLDBART, PhD, is a lecturer in the Department of Psychology and Speech Pathology at Manchester Polytechnic. Her research interests include the development and facilitation of communication in children and adults with severe learning difficulties.

ANN GRIMLEY worked in paediatrics in Salford, Manchester and Delaware, USA. Currently she is District Physiotherapist in Preston. Having held the post of Registration Education Spokesman she is now Chairman for the Paediatric Chartered Physiotherapists.

JAMES HOGG, PhD, is Deputy Director of Hester Adrian Research Centre, University of Manchester. His research has incorporated early education and development of children with severe learning difficulties with special reference to motor competence, profound retardation and multiple impairment and, at present, ageing. He has also been involved in the development of staff training and established the Education of Developmentally Young In-service training Course (EDY).

MIKE JOHNSON, M.Ed., was an Educational Psychologist and is now a Senior Lecturer in the Special Educational Needs Centre at Manchester Polytechnic.

HELEN McCONACHIE trained as a clinical psychologist. She worked in the Hester Adrian Research Centre, University of Manchester and for the Speech Pathology and Therapy Section at Manchester Polytechnic. She is now lecturing in Psychology at the Wolfson Centre, Institute of Child Health, London.

Dr IAN McKINLAȲ is Consultant Paediatric Neurologist and clinical lecturer in child health at the Manchester Children's Hospital.

JILL PORTER is Lecturer in Special Education, West London Institute of Higher Education. Prior to this she obtained an MA in the psychology of mental handicap at Keele University and taught children with severe learning difficulties in Leeds and Manchester.

SUE ROULSTONE is the Chief Speech Therapist for Bristol and Weston Health Authority with responsibility for organising community speech therapy services.

PHILIPPA RUSSELL is Senior Officer, Voluntary Council for Mentally Handicapped Children, National Childrens Bureau. She is a parent member of the DHSS Development team for mentally handicapped children and of the Fish Committee on Special Educational Needs in ILEA.

SARAH SANDOW, PhD, is Principal Lecturer in Special Education, West London Institute of Higher Education. She has strong research interest in Parent-Professional relations.

PETER STURMEY, PhD, is a Clinical Psychologist working with nursing staff in Olive Mount Hospital for mentally handicapped adults, Liverpool. His research interests involve various applied aspects of organised teaching to mentally handicapped adults.

CHRIS WILLIAMS, PhD, is Director of Psychological Services (Learning Disability), Exeter Health Authority. He is Senior Lecturer for the British Institute of Mental Handicap and honorary lecturer for the Department of Psychology at the University of Exeter.

FOREWORD

Peter Mittler, Professor of Special Education, University of
Manchester

This book reflects the radical transformation which has been
taking place in the education of children with severe learning difficulties in the past 15 years.

In the first place, the book has been planned and edited by
teachers. This in itself should occasion no surprise until one recalls
that almost all earlier books on the subject were written by psychologists and before that by doctors, often with a background in
research and university teaching. It is fitting that more teachers
should now be writing about their work and taking their rightful
place as leaders in their field. At the same time, the book reflects a
strong spirit of partnership with the many other disciplines whose
contribution is indispensable. These include research workers, as
well as other practitioners, and the parents themselves.

The rapid growth in the skills of teachers in this field is one of
the most remarkable success stories in the development of special
education and of education itself. During and prior to the 1960s,
the work of a small band of teachers and teacher trainers was
largely unrecognised by society as a whole or by educationalists in
particular. It took years of political pressure and lobbying to secure
from governments the undertaking to transfer responsibility for the
education of children with severe learning difficulties from health
to education authorities, at both national and local levels. Even
then, many people initially doubted whether the work of the
former Junior Training Centres could be regarded as educational,
and the government of the day was only with difficulty persuaded
at the last moment to include profoundly and multiply handicapped children in the legislation. A number of teachers in the
'new special schools', as well as many parents, were initially appre-
hensive about the proposed change and doubted whether the
education service had the training or the motivation to meet its
new responsibilities.

Looking back to 1971 in the light of 1985 and the level of
professionalism reflected in this book, the pace of change has
indeed been impressive. Historians will one day analyse the rapid

development of this sector of the education service and try to weigh the relative importance of the many different influences at work.

But our task now is to look ahead, not backwards, and to ask ourselves how the work of special schools and the staff who work in them can and should adapt to the needs of the twenty-first century?

Imagine a young, newly qualified teacher taking up a post in a special school today. What kind of changes will take place before that teacher reaches retirement in the 2020s? Will we in Britain still have some 500 special schools for children with severe learning difficulties? What will we be saying then about the 1981 Education Act, about the work of schools and teachers, the role of parents and of other professionals? Will the children be very different from those we know today? Will public attitudes be markedly different? What kind of society will our children be learning to live in? Where and how will they live, what work will they do and how will they spend their leisure time?

Unless we begin now to ask and answer at least some of these questions, we risk the danger of stagnation and burn-out. These risks are all the greater when professionals have as many achievements to their credit as those who work in special schools for children with severe learning difficulties. There is still plenty of scope for growth and development, no shortage of ideas on better practice, plenty of enthusiasm and motivation to improve skills. It is the very success of the work that carries the greatest dangers of complacency. The present structure of special schools has provided a secure and highly reinforcing framework for the rapid progress made in the past 15 years. But is it the right structure for progress in the next 15, 25, 55 years? If not, when and how are we going to begin to modify the structure?

Despite all their positive achievements, special schools are under attack from many quarters and for many different reasons. They are under attack not so much for what they do but for what they represent — a segregated service which isolates children from their peers and which almost by definition provides an inadequate preparation for living in an integrated adult community. Special schools are now being asked to justify their existence. What is it that they do that can be done only in the setting of the special school? How much of the teaching and of the interdisciplinary work could be transferred to ordinary schools? Now that we are developing individual educational programmes, what would be needed for the specific and unique needs of individual children to be met in the setting of an ordinary school?

These are challenging questions which are also being asked in other services. Staff working in hospitals for the mentally handicapped were among the first to point out that there was no reason why many, if not all, of the 'services' which they provided could not be provided in community settings. Most of their residents were admitted, not because they needed a hospital as such, but because there were no community services which could meet their needs for residential care combined with daytime occupation and health supervision. Money is now being transferred from health to local authorities to provide for their individual needs on the basis of an individual service plan in the community. Some hospitals are working for total closure within 10 to 15 years, and the size of most others will be reduced drastically.

The analogy with hospitals may seem inappropriate because innumerable official reports, enquiries and research studies have shown that living conditions in hospital are generally poor, that training and rehabilitation facilities are inadequate and that hospitals are generally too isolated from community facilities to provide a basis for rehabilitation. This is true in general, although there are many exceptions to such a stereotype. But because hospitals are, in principle, thought to provide an unsatisfactory environment for people with mental handicaps, their staff are now beginning to work with colleagues in local authorities to answer the question of how the specific needs of each individual currently in hospital could be met more satisfactorily by community services.

We have no hesitation in asking the reverse of that question for people living in the community. What would be needed to make it possible for a person with mental handicap to continue to live in an ordinary house in a known neighbourhood? What adaptations to the house, what kinds of support services to the family or substitute family, what kinds of day and community services are needed by this particular individual to prevent hospital admission? In other words, how can the specific needs of a named individual be met in ordinary settings? Such questions have been asked and answered for an increasing number of people with physical impairments and disabilities. Why are we not asking them as often for people with intellectual disabilities?

All special schools would agree that preparation for leaving and for living in the adult community is one of their primary aims. The school-leaving review provides, in theory at least, an ideal framework for different professionals and parents to share ideas and to draw up plans for the future, hopefully with the participation of the young person directly involved. In practice, the available options for most young people today, and probably for some time to come, are far narrower than the range of needs and possibilities found in a group of school leavers. In the last analysis, the special school will be judged by the skills and abilities of its leavers and by their subsequent achievements and life histories. No matter how skilled the staff, how good the level of interdisciplinary co-operation, how well the school works with its parents or how satisfied they are, no matter how highly the school is rated by advisers or inspectors, or how frequently it is seen as a model of good practice by visitors from all over the world, the ultimate criterion of its success must lie in the pupils themselves.

Special schools are well equipped to respond to these challenges. The high level of knowledge and skill reflected in this book is a tribute to the professionalism of the staff who work in them. But the challenges they face in the future are different from those that they have successfully confronted in the past. In particular, they will need to develop much closer working links with ordinary schools and work for a true educational integration for a greater number of pupils. The challenge here is not simply one of loca-tional integration — the mere placement of children into ordinary schools — but also of ensuring that high quality, relevant and realistic individual educational programmes are designed, imple-mented and reviewed in ordinary schools, and in full partnership with specialist teachers and other professionals, as well as with parents and the young people themselves.

But there is a bigger and more long-lasting challenge. If educa-tion is defined in terms of everything which helps an individual to learn and to develop, then education is clearly much broader than what goes on within the school, whether that school is called special or ordinary. This principle has already been recognised by bringing educational services to young children long before it is time for them to attend school. It has also found expression in the greater partnership developed with families. Nor do educational needs cease at 16, 19 or any other age. People with intellectual disabilities need opportunities for life-long education, long after they have left schools and colleges of further education. Teachers in special schools will therefore have to find ways of sharing their expertise with staff of a wide range of community agencies who are well placed to help all of us to continue to learn and to develop our knowledge, understanding and skills.

In short, the challenge for special education is to push aside the four walls of the school and become a resource for the whole community.

INTRODUCTION

Judith Coupe and Jill Porter

The book was conceived because of the frustration at the limitations in the current state of literature concerning the education of
pupils with severe learning difficulties. We are conscious of an
ever-present gap between research and practice. Hence, the need
for a book which relates to 'experimental evidence' and makes it
accessible to the teacher. By providing a background in the necessary aspects of psychology and development we wish to aid
teachers to interpret the information, critically examine and assess
the findings and, of even more importance, to see the relationship
of this to her own work in the classroom.

Through Warnock (DES 1978) and the subsequent 1981
Education Act we have been introduced to the notion of identifying the individual educational needs of the pupil. The mandatory
process of statementing and reviews has brought about a welcomed
move towards the schools' accountability in planning, monitoring
and maintaining pupil progress. This concept is, by necessity,
reflected in courses for teacher training, both initial and in-service,
where they, too, are under scrutiny to produce professional expertise and uphold academic standards. To meet these changes we
wish to stimulate interest in reading, interpreting, questioning and
evaluating the important current developments concerning aspects
of education for pupils with severe learning difficulties.

This book is divided into three sections which relate the 'how',
the 'what' and the 'who' of education — Part 1 : Curriculum
Method and Organisation, Part 2 : The Process of Learning and
Development, Part 3 : The People Involved. Despite this division
there is a strong theme that runs throughout.

Of central importance is our emphasis on enabling a child to be
capable of setting his own goals and having the necessary flexible
adaptive behaviours to achieve them. We are concerned with the
child's ability to create order from the chaos of the real world. A
world which, unlike the classroom, is inconsistent and which brings
a wide variety and differing intensity of stimuli and consequent
demands on the child. The key skills required by the child are
discrimination and generalisation. Only through discrimination will

6

the child be able to see the critical sameness and differences that will enable him to organise his thoughts and experiences and store them in a meaningful, flexible manner, providing him with a basis for rational action.

The child must not be encouraged to view himself as completely dependent on other people, but to make choices and decisions and, hence, control his own environment. Because we cannot, and would not, wish to account for every situation that the child will encounter, achievement of the skill of generalisation is crucial. This is reflected in the need to avoid placing undue emphasis on the learning of specific skills, or indeed, even in sequences of behaviour, and instead to concentrate on providing learning strategies and opportunities for their use.

There can be no absolute compartmentalism. We must acknowledge the complexity of human behaviour and learning and be aware of the pitfalls of viewing a child only in terms of developmental areas. Because our concern lies with the whole child, we acknowledge that the curriculum, its philosophy and intervention process reflects the interactive nature of learning. Of paramount importance is the contribution made by the parents, school staff and linked agencies — the roles of individuals with different skills working as a team towards a common goal.

PART ONE: CURRICULUM METHOD AND ORGANISATION

At the heart of any purposeful education lies the curriculum. When it is accompanied by an agreed strategy for assessment, programme planning recording and evaluation, Judith Coupe shows how the school can account for meeting the needs of individual pupils. An effective curriculum should provide guidance for a balanced selection of priority target behaviours and all those experiences and activities which promote the continual development of the whole child.

In this context, Jill Porter in Chapter 2 provides a rationale for the use of a behavioural approach to teaching the child with severe learning difficulties. She emphasises the need to think beyond simple contingency manipulations to the role of errors in learning. Centring on the major problems — that of achieving maintenance and generalisation, she considers the nature of reinforcement and that of stimulus control and setting conditions. Fundamental to the generalisation process is the need to teach discrimination and to build up sequences of behaviour.

Peter Sturmey and Tony Crisp in Chapter 3 cite evidence to show that learning in small groups is possible and may even facilitate learning by imitation — an important learning to learn skill. They discuss the problems of small group teaching, for example, the need for entry requirements to the group, and the tendency for teaching to be on one particular task (usually language, imitation or table-top activities), in addition to the perennial problem of how to provide for the remainder of the class. Guidelines are given for small group teaching. The authors then go on to discuss assigning particular roles to staff and compare this method of classroom management with small group and individual teaching. There is no doubt, in the evidence provided, that assigning roles and small group teaching lead to high levels of activity and compare favourably with traditional one-to-one teaching.

1 THE CURRICULUM INTERVENTION MODEL (CIM)

Judith Coupe

Introduction

The 1981 Education Act states that all pupils in need of any special educational input are referred to as pupils with special educational needs. Under Section 5, notice of intention to assess is served on parents whose child may have special educational needs. Subsequent assessment is a multi-disciplinary process which requires the advice of the parents, teacher, school medical officer and educational psychologist. The latter three component personnel must be involved, but at the same time other advice may be sought. Advice reports are collated and summarised in the educational statement. Highlighted in this document is the necessity to identify the pupil's abilities in terms of strengths and weaknesses and to plan for the immediate and long term needs. Obligatory reviews, held at least annually with parents, ensure continual evaluation of these needs and how they are being met. In order to make certain that the prescribed changes are occurring, a monitoring system must be built into the school's curriculum. In this way an evaluation can be made of whether or not the intended outcomes are, in fact, being obtained. A well-documented objectives curriculum should enable a school to fulfil this requirement to assess, programme plan, record and evaluate.

DES Circular 6/81 refers to the necessity for all schools to produce curriculum statements. Four obligatory areas are identified:

1. each school is to write a statement on what it intends to do for its pupils, i.e. aims;
2. information is to be made available as to how these aims will be achieved;
3. information is to be made available as to how the school will monitor and evaluate its success in achieving what it sets out to do, i.e. curriculum;
4. information is to be made available as to how the school will inform parents, governors, professional colleagues and the community of its philosophy and curriculum emphasis.

11

It is important for the school to see the value in preparing a structured curriculum document based on an agreed philosophy and methodology. The curriculum is seen as an instrumental device through which the school mobilises and organises its professional and material resources to achieve specified ends. It involves those activities and experiences which are directed by the school or influenced by other societal agencies so that its avowed purposes will be fulfilled. It is a mechanism through which it is hoped to produce continuous and cumulative changes in pupil behaviour which would only emerge at different rates, if at all, in the absence of intervention. It is essentially a means through which planned modifications in pupil behaviour are produced progressively.

Traditionally headteachers have been left with almost total responsibility for planning the curriculum in their schools (Wilson 1981). However, it is increasingly recognised that, alongside the school staff, parents, governors, etc. have a legitimate interest. What is taught must reflect fundamental values in our society and is 'largely a measure of the dedication and competence of the headteacher and the whole staff and of the interest and support of the governing body' (Welsh Office, DES 1981). The quality of a pupil's education is dependent on the expertise of teaching, the resources available and in particular, the curriculum. Ultimately, it is the teacher who ensures that the individual needs of each pupil are met. However, it is the curriculum that provides the direction and relevant information from which these decisions can be made. It needs constantly to be open to evaluation and change.

The Warnock Committee (DES 1978) claimed that staff involvement and commitment are necessary for a curriculum to succeed. Indeed, all staff should have a vested interest in its continuing development, and teachers should feel justified in seeing themselves as a source of expertise. The Warnock Report also stressed that the curriculum will be determined by four inter-related elements: 1. setting of objectives; 2. choice of materials and experiences; 3. choice of teaching and learning methods to attain the objectives; 4. evaluation. In turn, this is sanctioned by the enactment of the 1981 Education Act and Circular 6/81.

Establishing a Framework of Curriculum

A curriculum must never be imposed on a school (DES 1978); staff must have a sincere interest in its development, and their skills must be utilised appropriately. The qualities and skills required from staff will incorporate commitment, motivation, teamwork, communication of ideas, analytical evaluation of self and others and also acceptance of change. Essentially, it is necessary for all staff to work closely together to share ideas, support each other, teach consistently and meet the needs of each individual pupil. In this way curriculum development leads to a consensus of agreement, hence consistency and continuity of teaching. Nine important considerations are expressed by Burman, Farrell, Feiler, Heffernan, Mittler and Reason (1983).

1. The whole school must agree the need to look at curriculum, and parents should be asked about their priorities.
2. The roles of linked agencies need to be clarified in terms of how much commitment they can offer.
3. All staff who will implement the approach need to be included.
4. Once core areas are defined, staff need to organise themselves into groups and decide on the compartments.
5. Decide on the frequency of meetings and target dates for work to be submitted from groups.
6. Identify and agree on the level of skill components so that objectives are sequenced consistently.
7. Try out sequences of objectives regularly and discuss.
8. Discuss and utilise the school's existing curriculum.
9. Decide when to involve parents:
   (a) inform them and explain the new curriculum;
   (b) share planning and recording with them;
   (c) communicate when targets are realised.

Selecting and developing a particular type of objectives-based curriculum is not a matter of superiority, i.e. one model is not better than another. The main concern is using the strengths of the staff and resources to suit the needs of an individual school in defining what behaviours are considered necessary to teach. Once the objectives-based approach is worked out, it is efficient and simple to run because the teachers know exactly where they are and where they are going. It leads to clear methodology, but at the same time certainly demands a high level of expertise from the teacher (Ainscow and Tweddle 1979). For the benefit of the school and each individual pupil, it is worth all the investment of time and energy so that all pupils can be assessed via precise behavioural objectives. From this, a programme of intervention can be designed for the individual pupil and carried out using target behaviours, task analysis and recording. The school policy on methodology can be incorporated alongside the teacher's own style and the resulting child performance evaluated.

The objectives framework ensures continuity throughout the school. Access to information is gained easily, and there is a considerable amount of freedom and autonomy for teachers in selecting and implementing programmes. The teacher controls for the success and complexity of individual pupils' learning. Within the framework of curriculum development it is vital to take a balanced account of all the experiences offered to pupils. To facilitate the development of attributes such as values and attitudes, curricular activities can be planned deliberately. Yet it is necessary to be aware of the complex nature of these experiences so as to 'avoid the danger of seeking to measure the unmeasureable' (Wilson 1981). The essence of curriculum planning should be to achieve purposeful activities whenever teaching takes place. 'Balance has to be achieved between direct skills teaching and all those other activities which widen horizons, arouse interest and give purpose to learning' (Wilson, 1981).

Part One: The Curriculum Document

Inspired by its educational aims the curriculum provides a philosophical framework which promotes a sense of purpose to the work of the school. It provides a rationale and a foundation for subsequent goals and objectives. To teach a pupil according to an agreed philosophy, the school will need to produce a curriculum document which provides detailed, structured information which is available to all teachers and which is concerned with what to teach — the 'what' of education. This will be developed and continually evaluated and adapted by school staff, parents, governors and all interested agencies. However good this document is, it will be of little use unless, alongside it, the school has identified an agreed procedure of teaching intervention which incorporates assessment, programme planning, recording and evaluation: APRE — the 'how' of education. Ainscow (1984) also makes this important distinction between the 'what' and 'how' of education.

Figure 1.1: Curriculum Intervention Model

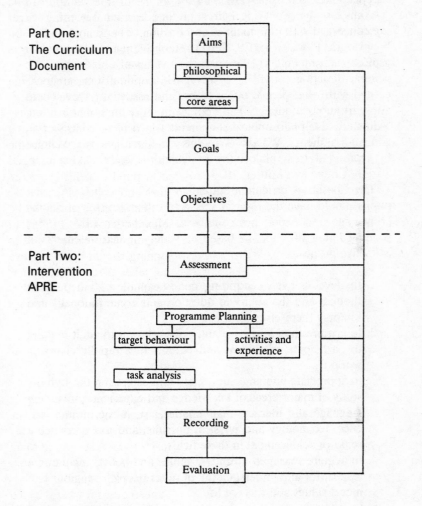

Source: Judith Coupe 1985

Aims

'First to enlarge a child's knowledge, experience and imaginative understanding, and thus his awareness of moral values and capacity for enjoyment; and secondly, to enable him to enter the world after formal education is over as an active participant in society and a responsible contributor to it, capable of achieving as much independence as possible' (DES 1978).

Aims essentially provide a direction for educational intent. They are concerned with potentialities and possibilities and not concrete behaviours. Plowden (DES, 1967) refers to them as 'benevolent aspirations', and Peters (1966) uses the analogy of aims as giving the general direction in which to travel. Educational aims are concerned with what people ought to be, and essentially they should apply to pupils of all ages and abilities in all sectors of education. 'Aims are also philosophical statements which form a basis of an educational theory. We ask "Why this aim?" and justify the choice by relating it to a philosophy to which we adhere' (Leeming, Swann, Coupe and Mittler, 1979).

The Cheshire Curriculum Statement (1982) makes it clear that pupils should have the right of access to different areas of human knowledge and experience. Similarly, Manchester LEA (1984) produced aims of schooling based on widely agreed statements of collective purpose:

1. to develop lively, enquiring minds capable of independent thought and the ability to question and argue rationally and to apply themselves to tasks;
2. to acquire the knowledge and skills relevant to adult life and to participate as citizens and parents in a rapidly changing world;
3. to appreciate human achievement and aspiration through the study of major areas of knowledge and experience, including language and literacy, mathematics, art, music, drama, science, technology and physical pursuits, and to experience a sense of achievement in these fields;
4. to acquire reasoned attitudes, values and beliefs including a respect for and understanding of other people's religious and moral values and ways of life;
5. to understand the world in which they live and the interdependence of individuals, groups and nations;
6. to experience responsibility, develop negotiating skills and exercise judgement;
7. to experience the school as a caring, supportive, learning environment where there is equal opportunity regardless of sex, race, culture or disadvantage;
8. to foster enjoyment of the learning process which encourages

them to take advantage of educational opportunities throughout life by the development of social, economic and political awareness.

Without exception aims need to be stated so that they can be examined, understood and followed. For all schools the selection and emphasis of an aim should embrace a philosophy such that each individual pupil is able to achieve the maximum degree of autonomy and efficiency of functioning as a happy and participating member of his community. For a working curriculum to develop an aim and philosophy such as this will necessitate more detailed breakdown into core areas, i.e. curriculum areas and experiences. Generally, areas of competence such as communication, fine and gross motor, perceptual and cognitive skills, life and social skills, etc. are encompassed. In addition, areas of human development which are harder to influence such as aesthetic development, moral development and personality should be identified and incorporated. These core areas and experiences will be the initial step in identifying what we ought to be teaching our pupils.

It is a challenging task but essential for schools to promote actively attitudes and values such as: self-confidence, social competence, curiosity and enthusiasm; make reasoned judgements, moral judgements; have aesthetic appreciation, consideration for others, etc. In Wilson (1981) and Schools Council Paper 70 (1981) this is discussed in detail. 'Personal adjustment and socially co-operative attitudes have been considered as vital as the growth of knowledge or skills' (Wilson 1981). In general, the development of values and attitudes are only referred to as aims. How they are to be achieved is seldom made explicit in the curriculum document. In essence a balance between direct skill teaching and all those other activities which widen horizons, arouse interest and give purpose to learning must be achieved.

Goals

For most schools the age range of pupils with severe learning difficulties is 2 to 19 years, although some education authorities have opted for separate primary- and secondary-age schools. Inevitably, individuals will vary greatly in terms of their ability and additional sensory or physical handicaps, and the curriculum must cater for the educational needs of all.

Guided by models of development, a wealth of information can be gained concerning all areas of learning. This developmental approach is especially valuable as an assessment device and is particularly appropriate for use with chronologically or developmentally young pupils. By using the developmental model a teacher is offered detailed guidance for teaching sequences or selected patterns of behaviour. However, a school exists to educate all pupils and to prepare them for their future lives. Many would argue that a developmental approach is restrictive, assumes that our pupils follow a delayed pattern of normal development and is an inadequate guide for teaching adolescents.

Gardner and Murphy (1980) highlight disadvantages of adopting a developmental approach. They strongly emphasise skills. Their skills analysis approach is still based on an objectives model, but is more concerned with what skills the pupil needs and what actual behaviours are involved for that particular skill. In practice, the skills analysis model can prove problematical when a child's developmental level is not sufficiently well developed for entry behaviours — in which case a developmental model is necessary. However, these two models are in essence combined and complementary from the start. We do not know how the stages do come together, but logically we cannot get away from a progressively developmental model: as part of the educational process we must try it out and evaluate. Whichever approach is used, it is important for the curriculum to be accessible to the user. Goal areas are the logical, organisational breakdown between aims and objectives.

When used as part of a curriculum, a traditional developmental approach will be organised into goal areas which will take the form of sequences of developmental checklists, e.g.:

Core area: motor development
Sub core area: fine motor development
Goals: 1. fine motor checklist 1 to 12 months
      2. related fine motor activities 1 to 12 months
      3. fine motor checklist 12 to 30 months
      4. fine motor checklist 30 to 60 months
      5. pre-writing 1 to 7 years

A skills analysis approach for this same area of motor development will result in re-organisation of the content into skill areas such as:

Core area: motor development
Sub core area: fine motor development
Goals: fixating and focusing
  tracking
  grasping and gripping
  early hand/eye co-ordination
  threading
  drawing
  holding a writing implement
  stacking and building
  shape drawing
  painting
  screwing
  cutting
  handwriting

HM Inspectors (DES 1979a) stress that curriculum areas should incorporate 'some checklist of important knowledge or skills to be acquired, or of essential areas of understanding or experience to which all pupils need access, within their capacities'. Wilson (1981) recognises that 'most school subjects or areas of experience have their developmental aspects: a hierarchy of skills, a broadening and enrichment of concepts, increasing complexity of information and understanding'. Brown, Branston, Hamre-Nietupski, Pumpian, Certo and Gruenewald (1978) considered that most curricula failed to incorporate appropriate content for adolescents. They saw many restrictions with using developmental checklists or skills analysis, and they present a 'Strategy for developing chronological age appropriate and functional content for severely handicapped adolescents and young adults'. Basically, they provided the idea of selecting teaching content according to the appropriate and future use of the environment, e.g.:

Core area: life and social skills
Sub core area: to use appropriately kitchen facilities
Goals: 1. Survival Cookery.
   (a) mechanics of kitchen equipment
   (b) drink preparation
   (c) food preparation
  2. Living Skills
   (a) washing up

(b) cleaning equipment
(c) laundry washing
(d) ironing
(e) repairing
(f) shoe cleaning

For each individual pupil the school must at some time consider consolidation of existing skills and then must utilise these to the full in order to apply them to life demands. Living involves the application of existing skills: the school must ensure that the curriculum content distinguishes between acquisition of new behaviours and skills and application of existing behaviours and skills to the real life environment.

Goals, therefore, involve a combination of developmental behaviours, skills analysis and appropriate environmental influences. They require a distinction between acquisition and application of skills. They will also reflect Ainscow and Tweddles's notion of the closed curriculum which incorporates those behaviours which teachers consider to be essential learning (Ainscow and Tweddle 1979). This involves core areas which all teachers identify as vital for pupils' education and which are considered essential for providing structured control and opportunities for pupils to learn basic skills. In contrast, their open curriculum involves what we refer to as experiences — less structured opportunities to learn from the environment. Brennan (1979) refers to a 'core curriculum' which stresses 'education for mastery' and 'education for awareness'. Those areas where learning for awareness is necessary are not less important to the pupil than the areas where thoroughness is essential. Rectory Paddock staff also identify two areas (Rectory Paddock 1983). Their developmental core curriculum purports to get at the general learning and development and, in turn, weaknesses and delays. It succeeds in blending development with skills. These core skills are then generalised to numerous social and vocational purposes, so that their applied curriculum is concerned with the all-round personal development of each pupil.

There are few curricular materials available which have been designed specifically for adolescents and young adults with severe learning difficulties. The outcome is often that developmentally appropriate content is taught which is often non-functional, artificial and inappropriate for the actual chronological age. Whelan and Speake (1979) produced the Copewell System for these very pupils. It is up to the schools to concern themselves with the reality of age and functionally appropriate content in natural, realistic environments. Brown *et al.* (1978) propose a model which encompasses both systematic structure and controlled, realistic opportunities.

Important skills are often taught in an artificial or simulated environment. As we cannot assume that the skills learned will generalise to 'real' environments, it seems more appropriate to conduct initial teaching in the real environment. Teachers and parents should join in partnership to direct this aim. Educational programmes, even from an early age, should focus on preparing pupils to function as independently and productively as possible in non-school and post-school environments. The environments familiar to the pupil's home, peer group and wider community have a strong influence, and priority of emphasis should be given to these. In supporting the notion of teaching age-appropriate skills, it is vital to identify the relevant age-appropriate needs of each pupil. In turn, these should be reflected in the equipment, materials and environments for the pupils.

The environmental model is certainly not only relevant to adolescents. It would be of great value if taught from two years, e.g. what should a two-year-old, seven-year-old or 18-year-old be able to do in a kitchen, lounge or garden that is age-appropriate and functionally appropriate? The selection of environmental goals will incorporate the application of existing skills to the appropriate environment. In many instances it will incorporate skills analysis and developmental progression of behaviours. By providing a wide range of experiences for pupils, teachers can ensure that they are in a setting which potentially facilitates generalisation of skills, in particular, those skills and behaviours which are not so easily taught through a more structured approach — for instance, singing, instrument playing, leisure skills, outings, dance, etc.

Objectives

Educational objectives refer to knowledge, skills and attitudes: objectives involve antecedents, behaviour and consequences (Kiernan and Jones 1977). They consist of newly acquired behaviours which should generalise to other situations. The curriculum needs to be concerned with descriptions of observable behaviours which identify the end product of learning. They need to be specific, precise statements of intent which refer to any child. We must also take care to use behavioural objectives for the pupil which must not be confused with objectives for the teacher which relate to the method of teaching.

Whereas an aim is a statement which refers to the direction for working and is essentially unobtainable, an objective refers to precise changes in behaviours — which are often observable. Mager (1972) consistently outlines the differences between aims and objectives. He is primarily concerned with ensuring that objectives are 'performances' and not 'fuzzies' and his 'Hey dad test' offers virtually foolproof guidance as to what is and is not an objective. 'Hey dad, let me show you how I can develop my potential' is clearly a fuzzy objective.

Objectives must be concerned with skills, values, attitudes, relationships etc. Ainscow (1984) states that, to facilitate a balance in the curriculum, use can be made of three different forms of objectives: 1. behavioural objectives — 'learning outcomes written in terms of pupil behaviour that can be observed and measured'; 2. experience objectives — 'situations designed to engage children in a problem experience or task without specifying in advance what the particular learning outcome will be'; 3. affective objectives — 'interests, values and attitudes to be developed'. Depending on the nature of the goals the actual objectives can assume a sequence of development.

Core area: cognitive development
Goal: early cognitive development 0 to 12 months
Objectives:
will linger with glance on point where moving object slowly disappears;
will mouth;
will attempt to keep mobile in motion by repeated hand, arm, leg movements;
will use repetition of action with interesting result;
will visually inspect new objects;
will produce selected responses to adult familiar body movement;
will hit toys;
will search for partially hidden object;
will touch adult hand after demonstration of mechanical toy;
will shake toys;
will examine toys;

will find object under single screen;
will make same gesture as response to familiar gesture;
will lean forward to search for fallen object;
will use complex exploratory behaviours with toys;
will return eyes to starting point when moving object disappears;
will drop one or both toys to reach for another, when hands full;
will find objects hidden openly under one of two screens;
will pull support to get toy;
when shown two bricks hit together, child will hit brick on table or hits adult's hand;
will drop and throw;
will use locomotion to retrieve toy needed in play;
will imitate two bricks hit together, after initial groping;
will use container, and other relational play;
will find object hidden under several superimposed screens;
will resist pulling support when toy just off it;
will imitate hitting two bricks together, directly;
will use self-pretend play;
will search in box top and under screen for object hidden by invisible displacement;
will imitate novel gesture, when he can see himself perform;
will use string to obtain object tied to it, object in sight;
will search in box top, then directly under screen, after invisible displacement under one of two screens;
will use string to retrieve object when not in direct view;
will hand mechanical toy back to examiner after demonstration to have it re-started

Alternatively, the objectives can facilitate a skills analysis approach which may or may not be developmental, but which must essentially involve a progression of complexity or skill.

Core area: cognitive development
Goal: object related scheme, 0 to 18 months (Coupe and Levy 1985)
Objectives:
glance — will regard object momentarily (2 secs);
touch — will make hand/finger contact with object;
hold momentarily — will hold object momentarily when placed in hand (ulnar side) (2 secs);

retain — will retain object placed in hand (ulnar side) (10 + secs);

alternating glance — will glance alternately at two objects — may be slow;

visual inspection — will regard object held by adult or on surface more than momentarily (44 secs);

mouths — will take object to mouth or mouths object in close proximity;

hold — will hold object intentionally (30 + secs) (object placed in hand can resist gravity and rotate hand to any position);

hit — will hit object with hand or bang object on surface;

two-handed scoop — will scoop up object using two hands;

grasp when in view with hand — will reach and grasp when object and hand in view;

look when holding — will look at object he is holding;

hand transference — will transfer objects from hand to hand;

visually directed reaching — will grasp object immediately when in view (shapes hand in anticipation of securing objects);

exploration — will explore object physically by feeling, poking, prodding;

shake — will shake object deliberately, moves it side to side;

examine — will peer at object intently, may turn over and around to examine visually;

let go — will release object voluntarily, but no visual monitoring of action;

one-hand grasp — will grasp object immediately, one hand leading;

complex — will differentiate between objects and may scratch, squeeze, pull along table, tear, crumple, rub, or slide, as appropriate;

view functional side — will turn mirror or three-dimensional object to view functional or more interesting side;

drop or throw — will drop or throw object deliberately, monitors action, looks where it lands;

combining objects — will place (drops) objects into container, bangs together, stacks, etc.;

functional use — will use objects appropriately, for example, builds with bricks, drinks from cup, etc.;

giving — will give object to adult to instigate social interaction or to get it activated;

showing — will show object to adult without giving it up;

naming — will give correct or approximate label of person, object or action.

Finally, the objectives section of a working curriculum document can highlight those skills and sequences of behaviours necessary for functioning in a variety of environments.

Core area: life and social skills
Sub core area: to use kitchen facilities appropriately
Goal: ironing
Objectives:
1. will put up ironing board;
2. will iron the following with adult selecting temperature:
    (a) teatowel
    (b) pillowcase
    (c) table cloth
    (d) duvet cover
    (e) T-shirt
    (f) skirt
    (g) trousers/jeans
    (h) short sleeved blouse/shirt
    (i) man's shirt/long sleeve
    (j) nightdress/pyjamas
    (k) dress
3. can select temperatures by self and iron items (a) to (k);
4. irons independently and safely.

Part Two: Intervention APRE

Assessment, Programme Planning, Recording, Evaluation

Having established the 'what' of education in the form of a written curriculum document, it remains to define the 'how'. Four main stages of intervention are identified: assessment, programme planning, recording, evaluation. The advantage of an objectives model is that it is, in essence, a curriculum related to assessment which is a useful model to evaluate and guide teaching (Cameron 1981). It implies clear specification of behavioural objectives relevant to the child which are appropriately broken down further and provides a medium through which recording and evaluation occur.

Assessment. Individual assessment can 'discover and understand the nature of the difficulties and the needs of the individual' (DES 1983). The concern is with what the pupils can do and what they need to know next. Parents of children with special educational needs have the right to be given information on assessment procedures, and it is of obvious advantage if assessment is an integral part of curriculum design. Assessment is of great value when based on criterion-referenced approaches, i.e. measuring the pupil's behaviour against a specified criterion on the selected task. It offers criteria against which to measure pupils' existing performance level and a baseline for instruction and is a means for selection of the next objective.

It is important for assessment to be carried out by the person who really knows the child, i.e. his class teacher. However, through assessing pupils on their mastery of objectives within the curriculum, the educational psychologist can also, when necessary, determine what the pupil has not yet mastered and the reason for the failure to learn (Winter 1981). In the light of Section 5 of the 1981 Education Act, this is an important consideration and can lead to identification of those skills which need to be taught.

In Figure 1.2, Gregory has been assessed as unable to achieve objectives 3, 5 and 6 in the goal area C of 'dressing and selection/care of clothing'. In the goal area of 'care of the bedroom', he failed to achieve objectives 4, 5 and 7 of 'bedmaking' and objective 1 of 'room management'.

For the objective 'looks after clothes properly — hangs them up, folds neatly, etc.', Greg was given a pair of underpants, a pair of socks, a pair of trousers and a jacket to put away in a wardrobe and chest of drawers. He proceeded to place underpants and socks on a clothes hanger, drape the jacket on the bed and drop the trousers on the floor of the wardrobe.

In Figure 1.3, Josie is assessed as achieving objectives 1-5 in the goal area Numbers, 1-3 in Time and 1-2 in Money.

Programme Planning

When the pupil has been assessed on the objectives in the curriculum document it remains for the teacher, in consultation with parents, to select the area or areas of future learning. The teacher needs to utilise the information concerning what the pupil can and cannot do to plan what to teach next and more importantly how to teach it thoroughly, systematically and successfully. Programme

Figure 1.2: Bedroom

Dressing

A. Getting dressed

✓	1. co-operates with dressing — lifts leg, holds out arms etc.
✓	2. pulling up/down — adult initiates, pupil completes action
✓	3. puts on one or two items, e.g. pants and vest only
✓	4. puts on most clothing, cannot zip, button or tie
✓	5. can fasten buttons — cardigan, coat, etc.
✓	6. can fasten cuff buttons
✓	7. can fasten hook and eye — skirt, trousers
✓	8. can fasten open-ended zip
✓	9. can fasten press studs
✓	10. can fasten buckle — belt and shoe types
✓	11. can fasten shoe laces

B. Getting undressed

✓	1. co-operates with undressing — lifts leg, raises arms, etc.
✓	2. pulling up/down — adult initiates, pupil completes action
✓	3. undresses self, needs help with fastenings
✓	4. undresses independently

C. Dressing and selection/care of clothing

✓	1. must be told to dress
✓	2. dresses by self at appropriate time
	3. chooses suitable clothing for different weather conditions, e.g. warm clothes on cold days, does not wear heavy clothing on hot days, etc.

Figure 1.2 continued.

✓	4. chooses appropriate clothes for specific occasions — party, beach, etc.
	5. aware of when clothes need washing or repairing
	6. looks after clothes properly — hangs them up, folds neatly, etc.
✓	7. changes clothing, e.g. socks, pants, regularly

Care of the bedroom

   A. Bedmaking

✓	1. helps an adult to strip and make the bed
✓	2. can strip bed independently
✓	3. can fit a fitted base sheet
	4. can fit a flat sheet, tucking it in appropriately
	5. can fit blanket, tucking it in appropriately
✓	6. can put pillow into pillow case properly
	7. can fit bedspread, smoothing out appropriately
✓	8. can arrange duvet on bed properly
✓	9. can fit duvet inside duvet cover

   B. Room management

	1. can tidy clothes into appropriate places, i.e. pants, T-shirts in drawer, jacket, dress on hanger in wardrobe
✓	2. can keep surfaces clean with duster/wet cloth/polish, etc.
✓	3. can use vacuum cleaner/carpet sweeper to keep carpet clean

Figure 1.3: Numbers

✓	1. can rote count to 5
✓	2. can count objects to 5
✓	3. can rote count to 10
✓	4. can count objects to 10
✓	5. can recognise written numbers, using matching cards, 1-10
	6. can name written numbers, 1-10
	7. can match 1-10 with objects
	8. can match 1-10 with pictures or dots
	9. can copy written numbers 1-10
	10. can write numbers 1-10 beside groups of pictures or dots, however they are arranged
	11. can sequence, using words first, second, etc.
	12. steps as above, numbers 11-20
	13. addition, exactly as in pink sheets
	14. subtraction, as in pink sheets

Time

✓	1. can use day, night, tomorrow, yesterday, morning, etc.
✓	2. can sequence. Can use before, after
✓	3. can name day
	4. can recognise special times on clock face
	5. can use quicker, slower. Can measure crudely with egg-timer, candle, etc.
	6. can name months
	7. can tell time of hour on clock
	8. can tell time: (a) $\frac{1}{2}$ hour, (b) $\frac{1}{4}$ hour
	9. can use calendar

Figure 1.3 continued.

Money

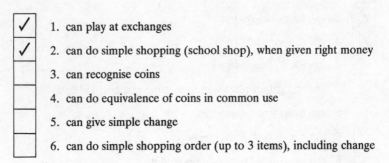

✓	1. can play at exchanges
✓	2. can do simple shopping (school shop), when given right money
	3. can recognise coins
	4. can do equivalence of coins in common use
	5. can give simple change
	6. can do simple shopping order (up to 3 items), including change

planning by necessity must account for all priority individual teaching as well as activities and experiences felt to be pertinent to the child's overall development and the method by which these can be achieved.

Target Behaviour.   Whereas the objective can apply to any child, the target behaviour is tailor-made for the individual pupil and specification of criterion for success is of paramount importance. Target behaviours involve the selection and statement of a particular objective to suit the individual needs of a pupil. They incorporate who will do what, when and under what conditions. Burman *et al.* (1983) identify three elements: 1. a statement of what the child should do after instruction; 2. a description of the important conditions under which this important behaviour should occur; 3. a precise description of what constitutes mastery of the behaviour that has been taught.

The teacher needs to know precisely what the individual pupil is expected to do at the end of a teaching session that could not be done before. This must be specified, and documentation is essential. It is up to the teacher to determine what the individual pupil will be required to do to achieve success. Obviously different behaviours and different pupils require individual consideration. Account needs to be taken of accuracy of response, consistency of response, frequency of response and generalisation and discrimination of that response. For a school-based assessment it may be satisfactory to specify only frequency, e.g. the pupil will perform the desired task on four out of five occasions.

Assessment of Gregory's skills for the goal 'dressing and selection/care of clothing' indicated which objectives he has and has not achieved. From this information, the following target behaviour was specified: Gregory will put the following items of clothing away in the appropriate places — socks in drawer, underpants in drawer, jacket and trousers on a coathanger in the wardrobe. To a criterion for success of 5/5.

Josie's assessment also highlighted her strengths and weaknesses. For her, a target behaviour for the goal area 'money' was considered to be a priority: Josie will identify 10p out of a selection of three coins: 2p, 5p and 10p when asked to 'show me 10p'. To a criterion for success of 6/6.

Task Analysis. For some pupils the selection of the objective and subsequent target behaviour will prove to be too big a step. To make the learning easier and the steps more reasonable and realistic for the individual pupil it may be necessary to break the target behaviour down into smaller steps of graded difficulty. Gardner and Murphy (1980) summarise task analysis by referring to 'learning hierarchies'. The EDY (education of the developmentally young) course (Foxen and McBrien 1981), provides thorough insight into this aspect of the behavioural objectives approach together with supporting theory and methodology. The two different examples highlight the need for differing complexities of task analysis to suit the needs of individual pupils.

Gregory had difficulties putting his clothes away appropriately, and, on assessment, he failed to achieve that objective. He put his underpants and socks on the hanger, trousers on the floor of the wardrobe and jacket on the bed. It is interesting to note that when this was discussed with his mother, she said that she usually put all his garments for the next day's wear onto the same coathanger when Gregory was in bed.

For Gregory it was considered necessary to break the target behaviour down into smaller steps of graded difficulty — task analysis:

Core area: life and social skills
Sub core area: to use the bedroom appropriately
Goal: dressing and selection/care of clothing

Objective: look after clothes properly — hang them up, fold neatly, etc.

Target behaviour: Gregory will put the following items of clothing away in the appropriate places: socks in drawer, underpants in drawer, jacket and trousers on a coathanger in the wardrobe. To a criterion for success of 5/5

Task analysis:

step 1: puts socks in sock drawer, criterion 3/3;

step 2: puts underpants in underpants drawer + step 1, criterion 3/3;

step 3: folds trousers over bar of hanger and puts in wardrobe + step 2, criterion 4/4;

step 4: puts jacket over coathanger with trousers and hangs in wardrobe + step 3, criterion 5/5.

For Josie:

Target behaviour: Josie will identify 10p out of a selection of three coins: 2p, 5p and 10p, when asked 'show me 10p'. Criterion for success 6/6.

A task analysis was considered necessary for Josie and the steps were specified as follows:

Task analysis:

step 1: 10p and 2p presented in the same position, 4/4;

step 2: 10p and 2p presented in random positions, 6/6;

step 3: 10p, 2p and 5p presented in the same position, 4/4;

step 4: 10p, 2p and 5p presented in random positions. 6/6.

A task should never have a standardised outcome. One target behaviour may be task-analysed into 5 steps, 15 steps or 50 steps, depending on the individual strengths and weaknesses of the child.

Activities and Experiences. It would be difficult and unrealistic to attempt to teach the child at target behaviour level throughout the school day. Not all teaching needs to be carried out in such detail. There are many other curriculum areas which provide essential and valuable educational experiences and opportunities for generalising learning in a less structured way. The teacher still needs to plan and account for pupils' development within them. To assist with classroom organisation and management it is advisable for the teacher to make a detailed weekly timetable in which the needs of each pupil in the class are balanced and adequately planned for.

Josie's priority target behaviours for one half term are:

Productive language — Josie will describe the action in four pictures using four element utterances: subject, verb, modifier, noun, e.g. Jim is riding the bike, criterion 5/5;

Life and social — Josie will wash her hair after having applied the shampoo and rinse it under supervision, criterion 5; observations;

Life and social — Josie will tie the bow of her shoelace, having first made the knot, criterion 6/6;

Pre-number — Josie will identify 10p out of a selection of three coins, 2p, 5p and 10p, when asked to 'show me 10p', criterion 6/6;

Pre-number — Josie will verbally identify the times 'quarter past' and 'quarter to', up to 12 o'clock, when presented in random order, criterion 4/4;

Fine Motor — On verbal request Josie will write her first and second name from memory, criterion 3/3.

For this same half-term Josie is also particularly involved in weekly swimming, flower arranging, horticulture, woodwork and ice skating. The nine pupils in her class are timetabled for individual and group work between the teacher and the nursery nurse, who each have a complementary weekly timetable. Figure 1.4 illustrates the carefully thought out balance between priority target behaviours for Josie and those activities and experiences considered important for her total development.

Recording

How do we know what each individual pupil does in a teaching session? We need to record their progress. The recording system is a cumulative record of the pupil's performance and will identify which steps are being taught. Schools often advocate guidelines but generally the scoring system must be simple and easy to use by the

Figure 1.4: Melland School Educational Programme

Week: 25th Feb-1st March, 1985

Class: 5
Teacher: Miss Ann Fitzmaurice
Nursery Nurse: Mrs Gill Lockett

	a.m.		p.m.
Mon	Fine motor Josie-1st & 2nd name DP-home address BR-1st name AC-home address AP, AH, DO, DG, LW See nursery nurse timetable.	Pre-number Josie-coin recognition DG-money addition AC-coin equivalents AH-coin equivalents BR, DP, LW, DO,AP See nursery nurse timetable.	Swimming professional instruction received at Miles Platting Baths (all class).

Tue	Educational outing
	(all class)
	Location: Stockport
	Purpose: to get cookery items for
	the class
	HR to get passport photo
	Each pupil to buy own drink in cafe
			Flower arranging
			Skills:
			1. select approx. 3 fresh
			   flowers (daffodils,
			   carnations, freesia)
			   with a variety of
			   foliage;
			2. arrange in wet oasis.
			   Josie, BR, DG, LW, AC.

Wed	Life & social skills
	Josie-hairwashing
	AH-ironing
	BR-dressing
	AC-hairbrushing
	LW-dressing
	
	DP, DG, DO, AP,
	See nursery nurse
	timetable.
		Survival cookery:
		toasted cheese
		sandwich.
		Skills:
		1. spreading
		2. cutting
		3. use of grill
		(all class)
			Woodwork:
			making spice racks
			Skills:
			1. sanding ready prepared
			   pieces of wood.
			2. tacking together with
			   pin tacks.
			3. varnishing.
			
			Josie, AH, DO, DG, DP.

Thu	Language
	Josie-5 element
	
	DP-3 element
	
	DG-final sounds
	LW-signing
	
	AC, AH, AP, DO, BR
	See nursery nurse
	timetable.
		Pre-number
		Josie
		AH
		AP Time
		DO
		BR
		
		DG, DP, LW, AC,
		See nursery nurse
		timetable.
			Horticulture
			Skills:
			1. preparation of seed trays;
			2. sowing of seeds in
			   trays;
			3. putting in greenhouse;
			4. planting seeds in
			   open ground;
			5. weeding and digging.
			
			Josie, AP, AH, DO, DG

	Life & social skills Josie-shoe laces	Completion of all priority	Ice Skating professional instruction received

	a.m.		p.m.
Fri	LW-teeth cleaning AC-hairwashing DP-shoe cleaning BR, AP, AH, DO, DG, See nursery nurse timetable.	target behaviours	at Altrincham Ice Rink. Josie, AP, AH, DO, DP.

N.B. Initials indicate other class 5 pupils.

teacher. The teacher and anyone directly involved in working with the child must feel at ease and be able to score, adapt and judge what is appropriate. All school staff must understand what is involved. It is crucial for the recording system to be thoroughly and systematically used with efficiency. The numerical scoring procedure used in EDY (Foxen and McBrien 1981) is of particular value:

0 = inappropriate response
1 = incorrect response
2 = achieved with strong physical (or strong verbal) assistance
3 = achieved with verbal or gestural prompts
4 = achieved spontaneously

Each number denotes the degree of assistance required by the child. This illustrates a quick, efficient and informative method of recording the child's performance in the individual teaching situation.

Gregory's target behaviour and subsequent task analysis are scored using this numerical system:

Target behaviour: Greg will put the following items of clothing away in the appropriate places — socks in drawer, underpants in drawer, jacket and trousers on a coathanger in the wardrobe. Criterion 5/5.
Task analysis steps:
step 1: put socks in sock drawer, criterion 3/3;
step 2: put underpants in underpants drawer + step 1, criterion 3/3;
step 3: put trousers over bar of hanger and hang in wardrobe + step 2, criterion 4/4
step 4: put jacket over coathanger with trousers and hang in wardrobe + step 3, criterion 5/5.

Date	Recording									
	Step 1									
6.11.84	2	3	4	3	4	4	4	(achieved)		
	Step 2									
13.11.84	3	3	4	4	3	4	4	3		
27.11.84	3	3	4	3	4	4	4	(achieved)		
	Step 3									
4.12.84	2	2	2	3	2	3	4	3		
10.12.84	2	2	3	3	3	3	3	4	3	
17.12.84	3	2	2	3	3	3	4	4	4	4	(achieved)
	Step 3 (recap)									
14.1.85	3	4	4	4	4					
	Step 4									
	2	2	2	3	2	3	3	2		
18.1.85	2	3	3	3	2	3	4	3		

The scoring is also efficient for noting Josie's performance on her Target Behaviour.

Target behaviour: Josie will identify 10p out of a selection of three coins: 2p, 5p, 10p when asked to 'show me 10p', criterion 6/6.
Task analysis steps:
step 1: 10p and 2p presented in the same position, criterion 4/4;
step 2: 10p and 2p presented in random positions, criterion 6/6;
step 3: 10p, 2p and 5p presented in the same position, criterion 4/4;
step 4: 10p, 2p and 5p presented in random positions, criterion 6/6.

Date	Recording									
	Step 1									
17.1.85	2	2	3	2	4	3	4	4	4	3	
22.1.85	3	4	3	3	4	3	4	4	4	4	(achieved)
24.1.85	4	4	4	4	(recap)					
	Step 2									
29.1.85	2	2	3	2	2	4	4	3	3	2	3	4

In addition to priority target behaviours Josie and Gregory have been involved in many other activities and experiences. It is most important that their progress is recorded. Again, the numerical system proves consistent, effective and easy to use. Figures 1.5 and 1.6 illustrate how much information can be obtained. Gregory takes part in — and obviously enjoys — five-a-side and crab football. The assessment shows that he has mastered five objectives. Staff continue to record and evaluate his level of mastery by observing him as he participates in the weekly game.

Flower arranging for Josie is also an enjoyable experience. In this she has mastered four objectives. Five other areas are currently being worked on, and the scores indicate that she requires little prompting to achieve these.

Evaluation

Evaluation plays a major role in the successful implementation of the school curriculum. Individual schools vary in the ways in which assessment, programme planning and recording of an individual pupil are evaluated. Evaluations could be carried out and written up twice per term on each pupil's progress. If a target behaviour is achieved then the child is re-assessed and new priorities are discussed, considered and specified as appropriate. Similarly, annual routine assessments ensure that a continual check is kept on all progress. A routine such as this can work well if it stems from an established procedure of assessment, programme planning and recording. If the pupil has not achieved the target behaviour, the evaluation must account for the following:

is the target behaviour the most appropriate objective to teach?
is the task analysis detailed enough?
is the reward strong enough, i.e. is the child sufficiently motivated?
is preparation for the teaching satisfactory?
is the presentation of the session clear enough in terms of materials and teacher style?

It is vital to assess whether target behaviours are achieved in order to determine what to teach next. Half-termly evaluations in pupils' record files can lead to effective accountability. To complement the detailed evaluation of the individual pupil it is important to be aware that in many areas of development 'particularly in attitudes

Figure 1.5: Integrated afternoons — evaluation Gregory

Pupil: Gregory   Melland School   Date: Jan 1985
Integrated afternoons activity: sports   Day: Tuesday
                                 five-a-side
                                 crab football

Objectives	Likes	Dislikes	Experienced	Working on	Mastered	Left
When stationary will catch large ball	✓		4		4	
When stationary will throw ball to partner	✓		3	3		
When stationary will throw ball to hit target	✓		3	3		
Will catch ball whilst moving	✓		3	3		
Will throw ball to partner whilst moving	✓		3	3		
Will throw ball to hit target whilst moving	✓		3	3		
Will kick ball to partner when stationary	✓		4		4	
When stationary will receive ball with feet	✓		4		4	
Will kick ball to partner whilst moving	✓		3	3		
Will receive ball with feet whilst moving	✓		3	3		
Will dribble ball in straight line	✓		3	3		
Will dribble ball round obstacles	✓		2	2		
Can move along playing surface on bottom	✓		4		4	
Knows own team members and remembers in heat of game	✓		3	3		
Knows which end own team attacking and remembers in heat of game	✓		3	3		

Co-operates in team situation	✓	3	3	
Observes simple rules	✓	3	3	
Behaves in sporting way whether won or lost	✓	4		4

Figure 1.6: Integrated afternoons — evaluation Josie

Pupil: Josie　　Melland School　　　　　　　　　　Date: Jan 1985
Integrated afternoons activity: Flower arranging　　　Day: Tuesday

Objectives	Likes	Dislikes	Experienced	Working on	Mastered	Left
Will name flowers	✓			3		
Will name colours	✓				4	
Will soak oasis	✓				4	
Will select container	✓				4	
Will place oasis in container	✓		3		4	
Will select approx. 6 flowers	✓		3		4	
Will select approx. 10 pieces of foliage	✓		3			
Will cut flowers to length required	✓			3		
Will cut foliage to length required	✓			3		
Will arrange foliage in oasis	✓			3		
Will arrange flowers in oasis	✓			3		

and values, objective evaluation is not possible' (Wilson 1981). This formality should certainly not discourage teachers from making written comment.

Evaluating the Curriculum

Evaluation of curriculum affects the direction and organisation of the whole school and Robson (1980) points to these aspects:

intrinsic evaluation. If it is felt that the behavioural approach is worthwhile, then build on it, adapt, amend, change the curriculum where necessary and have control over its results. Discuss with others so that any changes are for the better and suit the circumstances of individual teachers, schools and pupils. The school as a community has a role to play in evaluation. Use parents, governors, linked agencies, etc.

Performance Evaluation. An objectives-based curriculum enables the teacher to know about progress or lack of it. It can be an assessment for learning but also a means to identify strengths and weaknesses of the curriculum. 'The purpose of evaluation is not to prove but to improve.' The child's learning is related to intervention actively devised by the teacher.

Context Evaluation. Assess the general annual effects of staffing, allocation of resources, etc. When do programmes have to be adapted or abandoned? What do people feel about working the curriculum? Individual schools must account for the growing population of pupils with severe learning difficulties who have additional, complex disorders, e.g. social and emotional, combined sensory handicaps, physical handicaps. There is a core of pupils who are culturally different, where family attitudes may not necessarily place equal value on education, where English may not be a first language.

Further considerations must account for the changing nature of staff. The school curriculum might be excellent but without adequate in-service training teachers will not be able to use it satisfactorily. The issue of general economics must be considered. A school may invest time and resources on staff training but how viable is this to carry out?

Cameron (1982) points to numerous advantages which are to be gained from evaluating a curriculum:

additions, deletions, changes and clarifications necessary in the curriculum document are identified;
the assets and shortcomings in teaching methods are identified;
ongoing assessment is an integral part, and this leads to knowledge of the child;
programme planning, teaching and evaluation are closely linked;

not like psychometric tests or value judgements where all are separate procedures;

assessment has direct contact for teachers, parents, nursery nurses. All staff who come in contact with pupils can be involved in this procedure. It takes the emphasis of assessment away from the visiting professionals;

it facilitates hypothesis testing and consequent teaching. It promotes a developmental searching element. To search for what is best for the pupil.

Where Next? What Next?

There is so much good work going on in individual schools that it is vital to encourage dissemination and exchange of ideas between schools. Each must continue to excel in meeting the needs of its individual pupils. To continue and extend the development of curriculum, it is important for the school to stretch its resources and expertise to the full. Once a curriculum is established and being implemented the staff themselves can continue to develop by considering the following techniques.

Discuss relevant papers, articles and books. Perhaps appoint a reader to guide this.

Knowledge of current research findings can be of great benefit. Seek information and meetings with staff from establishments such as Hester Adrian Research Centre, Thomas Coram.

Subscribe to any relevant journals, e.g. BIMH Journal.

Subscribe to and attend meetings of any relevant societies or associations, e.g. NCSE (National Council for Special Education), MENCAP, Autistic Society.

Build up a thorough, up-to-date library.

Hold numerous in-service courses — use school staff as presenters, and also invite outside speakers in for seminars.

Set up working parties of interested staff to investigate areas of weakness or concern.

Write up and disseminate worthwhile information. It opens channels for communication of ideas.

Visit other schools, look for similarities and differences, strengths and weaknesses.

Make criticism constructive.

Observe one another teaching.

Constantly be aware of age and functionally appropriate life demands.

Encourage innovators of new ideas. Foster and discuss these ideas.

Share and communicate about all aspects of education.

Meet with individual parents and groups of parents on a regular basis to ensure that what they see as important for their child is considered.

Use videos.

Encourage students and their tutors — speech therapy, teaching, NNEB, nursing, etc. Exchange information and ideas.

Welcome and draw on the resources of all linked agencies.

The future, according to the Warnock Report (DES 1978), is for schools to become educational centres of excellence with practical research and resources. Many special schools have quickly and efficiently adopted principles that mainstream schools are turning towards. A policy of integration and sharing is to be encouraged whenever pupils with severe learning difficulties can gain benefits and widen their experience.

Curriculum development is a crucial element of a school for pupils with severe learning difficulties, but, in producing better curricula, tighter and more specific individual teaching programmes and methods, we must consciously prevent the outcome of a compartmentalised child. We are educating children and, as such, must maintain a realistic balance and continually strive to educate the whole child.

References

Ainscow, M. (1984) 'Curriculum Development in Special Schools. The Role of Management', in *Management and the Special School*, T. Bowers (ed.), Croom Helm.

Ainscow, M. and Tweddle, D.A. (1979) *Preventing Classroom Failure: An Objectives Approach*. Wiley.

Brennan, W.K. (1979) *Curriculum Needs of Slow Learners*. Schools Council Working Paper 63. Evans/Methuen Educational.

Brown, L., Branston, M.B., Hamre-Nietupski, S., Pumpian, I., Certo, N. and Gruenewald, L. (1978) *A Strategy for Developing Chronological Age Appropriate and Functional Curricular Content for Severely Handicapped Adolescents and Young Adults*. Draft paper, University of Wisconsin.

Burman, L., Farrell, P., Feiler, A., Heffernan, M., Mittler, H. and Reason, R.

(1983) 'Redesigning the School Curriculum'. *Special Education: Forward Trends, 10* (2).

Cameron, R.J. (1981) 'Curriculum Development 1: Clarifying and Planning Curriculum Objectives'. *Remedial Education, 16* (4).

Cameron, R.J. (1982) 'Curriculum Development 2: Teaching and Evaluating Curriculum Objectives'. *Remedial Education, 17* (3).

Cheshire County Council Education Committee (1982) *A Curriculum Statement.*

Coupe, J. and Levy, D. (1985) 'The Object Related Scheme Assessment Procedure'. *BIMH Jnl, 13.*

DES (1978) *Special Educational Needs.* Report of the Committee of Enquiry into the Education of Handicapped Children and Young People (The Warnock Report). HMSO.

DES (1979a) *Children and Their Primary Schools* (The Plowden Report). HMSO.

DES (1979b) *A View of the Curriculum.* HMI Matters for Discussion Series. HMSO.

DES (1981a) *Circular No. 6/81* HMSO.

DES (1981b) Welsh Office. *The School Curriculum.* HMSO.

DES (1983) *Circular No. 8/83.* HMSO.

Foxen, T. and McBrian, J. (1981) *Training Staff in Behavioural Methods.* Trainee Workbook, Manchester University Press.

Gardner, J. and Murphy, J. (1980) 'A curriculum model', in *Curriculum Planning for the ESN(S) Child,* vol. 1. N.B. Crawford (ed.), British Institute of Mental Handicap.

Kiernan, C. and Jones, M. (1977) *Behaviour Assessment Battery.* NFER.

Leeming, K., Swann, W., Coupe, J. and Mittler, P. (1979) *Teaching Language and Communication to the Mentally Handicapped.* Schools Council Curriculum Bulletin 8. Evans/Methuen Educational.

Mager, R.F. (1972) *Goal Analysis.* Fearon.

Manchester Education Committee (1984) *Curriculum 5-16 For Manchester Schools: A Consultative Document.*

Peters, R.S. (1966) *Ethics and Education.* Unwin University Books.

Rectory Paddock School (1983) *In Search of a Curriculum,* 2nd edn. Mere Publications.

Robson, C. (1980) 'Evaluation of curriculum for the severely mentally handicapped', in N.B. Crawford (ed.) *Curriculum Planning for the ESN(S) Child,* vol. 1. British Institute of Mental Handicap.

Schools Council Working Paper 70 (1981) *The Practical Curriculum.* Methuen Educational.

Whelan, E. and Speake, B. (1979) 'The scale for assessing coping scales', in *Learning to Cope.* Human Horizons Series, Souvenir Press.

Wilson, M.D. (1981) *The Curriculum in Special Schools.* Schools Council Programme 4.

Winter, S. (1981) 'Behavioural objectives and educational psychology'. *Jnl of Association of Educational Psychologists, 5* (7).

2 BEYOND A SIMPLE BEHAVIOURAL APPROACH

Jill Porter

Introduction

The literature on behavioural approaches and, in particular, on behaviour modification is prolific — the abundant number of journals that concentrate solely on aspects of theory and application make this easily apparent. Reviews of research (eg. Whitman, Scibak and Reid 1983; Matson and McCartney 1981) reveal the extent of its application not only to the severely mentally handicapped but also to the profoundly mentally handicapped. However, it is too often seen as an approach that rests in the domains of psychologists and, in particular, with clinical approaches to treatment rather than teaching approaches to education. Only 13 per cent of studies in the Whitman, Scibak and Reid (1983) review were carried out in the classroom, and only 9 per cent involved teachers. Bearing this in mind it is hardly surprising that the misconception exists that it is a technique primarily for dealing with inappropriate behaviours rather than for the teaching of new skills; or that it involves simply 'the continuous dispensing of edible reinforcers or the use of aversive methods, restriction of liberties or even electric shock' (McBrien and Foxen 1981).

The main concern of this chapter is to go beyond this initial level of approach and provide a deeper understanding and awareness of the principles that lie behind it and how they relate to the teaching of children with severe learning difficulties — why it is in fact a suitable approach. It will be argued that attention needs to be given, not just to changing behaviours, but to the maintenance and generalisation of that behaviour, if we are to use it effectively as a teaching approach. Behaviour modification involves more than simply manipulating reinforcement contingencies. We need to attend to setting conditions and stimulus control so that the child knows when and where to carry out new forms of behaviour, as well as how to perform the 'given' task.

It is not the concern of this chapter to provide the teacher with skills — realistically these cannot be produced by the mere reading of the written word and should ideally be taught in the classroom on an in-service course run by a suitably qualified instructor. Readers are referred to such training programmes as 'Education of the Developmentally Young' (EDY) and Project TASS. The intention is to provide the reader with a fuller appreciation of the techniques, together with an understanding of how learning occurs (see also Chapter 8), so that, having acquired mastery in the practice through an in-service course, the teacher can become proficient in programme design and arranging the environment to offset some of the limitations currently in evidence in the literature.

Evolution of the Behavioural Approach

The behaviourist approach evolved from the move in psychology away from the role of the unconscious and conscious in learning to a more empirical approach based on the study of overt behaviour, i.e. behaviour that could actually be seen rather than implied. The essential features therefore are the taking of baselines, the isolating of variables and the monitoring of change. This translates for the teacher into the importance of assessment, the exact descriptions of behaviour to be learned — breaking them down into component parts — and recording the progress of the child in learning.

An extension of this approach is behaviour modification which embodies these principles, but whose basis lies in behavioural learning theories — the most easily recognisable one being that of operant conditioning. This states that if a behaviour is reliably followed by the presentation of a reinforcing stimulus, the strength-probability is increased. Put more simply, behaviours are acquired, altered or maintained by their effect on the environment. The reinforcing stimulus, because it follows a piece of behaviour, can only have an impact on subsequent behaviour. Hence it affects the future probability of the behaviour, the likelihood of it happening again.

Behaviour may also be under the control of a stimulus that occurs prior to the behaviour, the discriminative stimulus, and this largely dictates in the first place which behaviour occurs. It can be viewed as a cue to the child, telling him what to do. Thus we have a situation whereby some stimulus in the environment becomes associated with a response, and if it is followed by reinforcement it is more likely to occur again. This assocation is probably brought about through classical conditioning. Classical conditioning occurs when an unconditioned stimulus is paired with another stimulus —

in Pavlovian tradition, food with the tone of a bell. Food on its own leads to a response of salivation, an unconditioned response because it is a reflex. When the two stimuli have occurred together on a number of occasions, the sound of the bell on its own now becomes a conditioned stimulus as it leads to salivation. The salivation in response to the bell is now called a conditioned response as it is generally a slower and weaker response than that to food. This is discussed more fully in Chapter 8.

These two types of conditioning need not be viewed as the distinct process they are usually set out to be (Thomas and O'Callaghan 1981). There are common features that they share. These include extinction — where the behaviour is no longer emitted after the reinforcement is withdrawn (the unconditioned stimulus in classical conditioning); spontaneous recovery where the response may make a sudden reappearance after extinction; and generalisation when both the stimulus may generalise and so may the response. These two forms of conditioning must be seen as complementary processes in learning and as major contributors to behaviour modification.

Reinforcement and its Effect on Behaviour

Reinforcement may be postive or negative, but *both* types lead to an *increase* in behaviour. Positive reinforcement involves presenting something pleasurable. Negative reinforcement involves removing something aversive. Skinner (1974) gives the following example of negative reinforcement. 'When we take off a shoe that is pinching, the reduction in pressure is negatively reinforcing, and we are more likely to do so again when the shoe pinches.' Punishment on the other hand is the opposite to reinforcement as it leads to a decrease in behaviour, this time by presenting an aversive stimulus. Thus putting tight shoes on a child is likely to lead to a decrease in walking.

Reinforcement can be delivered on a continuous schedule, i.e. every time the behaviour occurs, or on an intermittent schedule, sometimes when the behaviour occurs. If we stop the reinforcement, the behaviour will carry on for far longer if we have been reinforcing it sometimes when the behaviour occurred, rather than every time the behaviour occurred. Hence, the advantage of intermittent reinforcement is that it is more resistant to extinction.

Schedules of Reinforcement

There are four schedules of reinforcement: fixed ratio, variable ratio, fixed interval and variable interval. Ratio schedules are based on the number of times the behaviour occurs to reinforcement, interval schedules refer to the passage of time between reinforcement. Fixed ratio one (FR1) is continuous reinforcement. FR2 on the other hand, is where every second occurrence of the behaviour is reinforced, FR3 every third, and so on, and thus intermittent reinforcement. Variable ratio reinforcement is where we change the number of times the behaviour occurs before reinforcement. So sometimes we may reinforce on the second occurrence of the behaviour, sometimes on the fifth, sometimes on the third; the ratio keeps changing.

Fixed and variable intervals work in much the same way except now we are looking at the time between reinforcement. On a fixed interval we might reinforce every two minutes, provided the behaviour is occurring. On a variable interval we keep changing the time required between reinforcers. Variable interval schedules produce moderately high and steady rates of responding (Poling, Fugua and Miltenberger 1983), because the child has to persist with the behaviour as he never knows when the next reinforcer will occur. Fixed interval schedules on the otherhand, produce a low overall rate as the level of responses drop off after a reinforcer occurs and rise again when the next one is expected. Interval schedules are more important for the teacher when duration and frequency of the behaviour are important, such as attending behaviour, 'in-seat' behaviour (Yule and Carr 1980).

Other Essential Features of Behaviour Modification

Another essential feature of behaviour modification is task analysis — the breaking down of a task into small, manageable steps. Each step should involve the step before so that the final step of the task analysis is the child completing the whole target behaviour. The child's behaviour is in this way shaped by rewarding each successive approximation (or step) to the target behaviour. This shaping can take the form of backward or forward training, the latter where the task analysis works forward through the task starting at the beginning of the task, the former where we start teaching with the final piece of behaviour of the task and then teach the next to last piece of behaviour, and so on, working backwards through the task. In addition we can talk of backward and forward chaining where, for a complex task involving subsets of skills, we chain each skill together. We teach each skill separately; for example, in bathing we may teach the child the skills of undressing and then the skills of filling the bath with water, and when he is successful at both independently, we chain the two together by rewarding him when he has carried out both tasks. As with training, chaining may be carried out in a backward or forward direction. The example of bathing showed here was forward chaining, but we could have taught it backwards by starting with the child dressing himself and drying himself.

There are no set rules for when to follow backward or forward methods in shaping. It is often dependent on which part of the task is easiest for the child. If this is the first part, then forward methods might be used, but if it is the last part, then backward methods might be better. Backward methods do have some advantages. The child is always working into a learnt part of the task which can be encouraging in itself. In addition he is always being rewarded for the final stage of the target behaviour and this does not change. What does change are the demands on him to reach this final stage, but at least he knows what the task is about; what he is aiming for.

A criterion of success needs to be established prior to teaching, and this denotes the stage at which we will be satisfied that the child has actually mastered the task. Very often it states the number of times the child must carry out the task correctly and can be expressed as a fraction or percentage. We may for example state that the child has to reach criterion of 5/5, that is, he must carry it out correctly five times in a row; or, if it is a special needs child, we may feel that, due to the vagaries of responsiveness, a better criterion would be 3/5 or 60 per cent. For some tasks, the important factor may be how long it takes the child to do the task, or that it is done spontaneously. This may be included in the state-ment of criterion of success or included in the defining target behaviour. In addition to the task as a whole having a criterion of success, we must also state one for each step of the task that will be reached before we move onto the next step.

Inappropriate Behaviours

Although the emphasis throughout this chapter is on the teaching of positive skills, teachers are often concerned about inappropriate behaviours that are impeding learning. There are a variety of punishment techniques that can be used in the classroom but whichever method is selected, there are some pre-requisites to be followed:

1. They should only be carried out after consultation and agreement with parents and other members of staff and interested parties.
2. They must be acceptable to the members of staff/parents who will be using them.
3. They should be carried out in a non-emotional, 'businesslike' fashion, and in no instance should they be vindictive.
4. Where there are a number of problem behaviours, work should only be carried out on one at a time, and this behaviour should be clearly defined.
5. Baselines should be taken before any form of corrective procedure is used.
6. They should not be carried out over an extended period of time.

Extinction. A number of techniques for reducing inappropriate behaviour rest, in part or total, on the principles of extinction; that is, if the reinforcement is removed, the behaviour will be less likely to occur. It is therefore necessary to identify exactly what is reinforcing the child. Some inappropriate behaviours, such as self-stimulating ones, may be intrinsically reinforcing; the child gains pleasure from the behaviour itself. Others may be reinforced because they lead to a pleasant occurrence in the environment, such as increased attention from the teacher. Negative reinforcement may be the important factor, if, for example, the behaviour leads to the teacher no longer demanding that the child carry out a task that he doesn't want to do. Behaviours where the reinforcement has occurred intermittently will be more difficult to reduce with extinction than behaviours which are reinforced every time the behaviour occurs, such as with the intrinsically reinforcing behaviours — provided, of course, you can remove that reinforcement. Another problem of behaviours undergoing extinction is that the behaviour gets worse before it gets better. There is, therefore, the danger that the behaviour will reach such a pitch that the teacher reimposes the reinforcement and consequently ultimately reinforces a behaviour far worse than the child originally manifested.

Time-Out from Positive Reinforcement.   With time-out the child loses the opportunity for positive reinforcement, through one of two methods, either removing the reward from the child, or removing the child from the rewarding situation.

1. Removing the reward from the child. This is often the easier form to take if there is a single reinforcer and if it is easy to remove. It circumvents the problem of having to struggle to remove a child from the immediate environment, and it also avoids inadvertent negative reinforcement of the child (and the teacher). The child does not escape from the environment and the task (and the teacher does not escape from the presence of the child).

2. Removing the child from the reinforcing situation. Where there are a number of reinforcing factors, where the reinforcing agent is the attention of peers or where the child's continued presence is disruptive to the others, then it may be better for the child to be removed to an unstimulating corner of the room or be taken out of the room.

Whatever method is used, it is important that a release contingency is decided on as part of the programme. This release contingency may take the form of a specified period of time of not carrying out the inappropriate behaviour before 'time-in' resumes. The time requirement should not be very long, partly because the child is likely to forget what it was he did and partly because success lies in setting up response competition. The child has the choice of being rewarded for appropriate behaviour or timed-out for inappropriate behaviour; there can be no choice where he is timed-out for long periods of time. Success lies in providing the context of a highly rewarding situation from which to time him out.

Response Cost.   Response cost is similar to time-out but involves the loss of a positive reinforcer that is usually tangible and already in the child's possession. It is often used in token economies where the child has a pre-specified number of tokens earned for good behaviour and which are taken away when the misbehaviour occurs. It can also involve the loss of privileges (Whitman, Scibak and Reid 1983). This contrasts with time-out where the child loses the opportunity for positive reinforcement for a while.

Contingent Restraint.   Contingent restraint is another variation of extinction and, more directly, time-out; unlike the previously discussed techniques, it can be used when the behaviour is intrinsically reinforcing. It often takes the form of either physically holding the child or applying a restraining device such as splints. With self-injurious behaviours it has the advantage of stopping them quickly. Restraining must be withdrawn gradually to avoid the child becoming dependent on it to control behaviour. Release from restraint may well be followed by a high rate of inappropriate behaviours (Williams, Schroeder, Eckerman and Rojahn 1983).

Differential Reinforcement.   This is a technique whereby inappropriate behaviours undergo extinction and other behaviours are reinforced. Hence inappropriate behaviour is removed, the child is rewarded for not carrying out the behaviour, or in some instances, for not carrying out extreme forms of it. It can be used in conjunction with other techniques such as time-out (Woodward, Magim and Johnston 1983).

Over-correction.   This is a controversial technique (Foxen and McBrien 1981), whereby the child either has to practise over-correct forms of behaviour (positive practice over-correction), or restore the environment to a better than normal state (restitutional over-correction). A signal is given to the child that he is misbehaving, which takes the form of a verbal warning. Following this, the child is instructed to carry out an 'over-correct' behaviour; if he does not respond, graduated guidance is given whereby his limbs are physically moved, and faded as he starts to comply with demands. This may be inappropriate with some children who are either too large or to whom any physical contact/attention is rewarding. It has been recommended that the over-correction be carried out over an extended period of time (Foxen and McBrien 1981), although Cary and Bucher (1983) found short durations (30 seconds) of positive practice to be as effective as longer durations (3 minutes). If their findings generalise to other children and to restitutional over-correction, the technique will be less demanding on teacher time and energy.

The enforced effort demanded of the child in over-correction constitutes the presentation of an aversive stimulus (true punishment) and may be unpalatable to members of staff and parents. It also involves time-out, for while the child is engaged in over-correction procedures, he is unable to engage in any rewarding behaviour. Duker and Seys (1983) found this technique more effective in the long term than extinction on its own. This is because behaviours are being replaced, and hence it is important for teachers to focus on what they want the child to be doing instead. The aim should always be to replace behaviours rather than simply to eradicate them, and few successes will be gained without this. Punishment techniques on their own are not an effective control of behaviour. They must always be counteracted by the teaching of positive skills through reinforcement. Without this there are strong indications that punishment may well lead to maladaptive emotional responses and the replacement of one inappropriate behaviour by another equally inappropriate one!

The Behavioural Approach and the Child with Severe Learning Difficulties

A behavioural approach does not differentiate between the child with severe learning difficulties and the ordinary child. Behaviour is viewed as a continuum with no qualitative difference between normal and abnormal behaviour — they are governed by the same principles of learning (Whitman, Scibak and Reid 1983), and as such this accords with the fact that our aims in teaching are also not qualitatively different (Warnock Report 1978). In this sense it forms a very positive approach while also being essentially an individual approach to teaching. The child is carefully assessed and objectives formulated dependent on their level of functioning and analysed according to the learning difficulties and approach that the child uses. Rewards should be based on the teacher's experience of the child and assessed through presenting the child with a multiple-choice situation, or by presenting the rewards one after another (sequential sampling) and noting throughout the child's response. Finally, rewards must be tested by reward training to ensure that they are indeed 'something the child will work for' (Foxen and McBrien 1981).

In addition the environment for that particular child is an all important factor in shaping his behaviour. What evolves through a behavioural approach is therefore a 'detailed analysis of the individuals and the environment and the design of an individually tailored programme rather than an attempt to fit the subject ...' to some predetermined procedure (Cliffe, Gathercole and Epling 1974).

Learning is made a pleasurable experience for the child through the use of positive reinforcement. This contrasts strongly to the traditional approach of education which was characterised by children learning to escape or avoid unpleasant occurrences — caning, in the past; in the present, ridicule, criticism, detention, etc. — that is, through negative reinforcement i.e. positive reinforcement is not and was not used: approval, stars, marks, prize days can all provide positive reinforcement. However, if we consider the hierarchy of reinforcement, it will be apparent why these rewards may not be effective for many children with severe learning difficulties.

Merrett and Musgrove (1982) outline four levels in the hierarchy of reinforcement. Level 1: the first level is that of primary reinforcement where bodily sensations such as the need for food, drink, warmth, etc. control behaviour. Level 2 occurs when these primary reinforcers become associated with other events such as smiles, praise or tokens and through this association the 'other events' become sufficient on their own to teach and maintain new patterns of behaviour. These events then form Level 2 and are mainly social reinforcers. It is then only the systematic and repeated pairing of level 2 with level 1 reinforcers that leads the child with severe learning difficulties to work in order to gain such things as approval tokens. This emphasises the need to pair praise with a known (level 1) primary reward if the child is ever to progress to the stage whereby approval on its own will bring about learning. These two levels of reinforcement are extrinsic in that they come from outside the person, whereas levels 3 and 4 are intrinsic. Level 3: the activities themselves begin to be reinforcing, and the approval of others is slowly superseded by feelings of self-approval. Level 4: this self-approval is now clearly related to self-established standards of behaviour and expectations. The reinforcement is almost entirely intrinsic and gratification may well be postponed.

So we can see that reinforcement values develop — they are 'progressive and interdependent' (Merrett and Musgrove 1982) and must be seen as such to understand their function. Although one might wish otherwise, the child with severe learning difficulties cannot effectively be reinforced intrinsically if he has not reached that stage of development and passed through levels 1 and 2. A behavioural approach, through its emphasis on observation and assessment, enables the teacher to ascertain which particular event motivates the individual child and to apply it to develop the child's behaviour into more complex forms.

Reinforcement does not only make learning a pleasurable experience for the child, it also facilitates the learning process. Learning can be seen to involve attending to the correct stimuli (Zeaman and House 1979), making a response and forming an association between the two. Reinforcement may not only act as a response strengthener, i.e. making that response likely to occur again, it may also facilitate the association with the stimulus. 'If the correct object is selected, reward is given immediately which acts to strengthen both the instrumental response and whichever observing response immediately preceded it' (Zeaman and House 1963). If however the reward is not given immediately, then some intervening response may inadvertently be reinforced. The same holds true if the reward is not attention-getting as it effectively delays reinforcement.

For learning to be effective, the association must not only be formed with the correct response, but with the appropriate or correct feature of the stimulus, that is, the response must be under the correct stimulus control. For example, the child who correctly carries out a picture matching task should do so on the basis of the actual content of the picture and not by using the cues perhaps inadvertently provided by the background colour. Rather than let the child flounder in a wealth of incoming information, the relevant stimulus is often exaggerated or highlighted in some manner to direct their attention towards it. Likewise, to help the child perform the correct response he is helped through prompting — it may take the form of physically helping the child, giving gestural cues or verbal ones, or a combination. It is important, however, that both the prompts and the 'high-lighting' of features of the stimulus are faded so that the child can act independently in everyday circumstances.

The advantage of the behavioural approach can be seen, then, to lie in meeting the individual learning problems of children with severe learning difficulties in terms of both understanding and motivation. The emphasis is firmly on success rather than on failure and punishment, thus making learning a pleasurable experience. What remains unclear is the role of failure in learning.

Errorless Learning

Clearly, in the past, the child with severe learning difficulties experienced a high level of failure by being 'unable to meet the demands of the environment ... with detrimental intellectual and affective consequences' (Hogg and Mittler 1980). Indeed Weeks and Gaylord-Ross (1981) argue that difficulty in task may well relate to aberrant behaviour, as the child finds this behaviour negatively reinforcing if it leads to successful avoidance/escape from the task. Errorless learning creates a situation whereby the child is prevented from making mistakes and is in contrast to trial and error learning where the child learns the correct behaviour by systematically eliminating incorrect responses. The emphasis in the literature has been on discrimination learning where the child has to discriminate between two choices of stimuli — the correct one, S+, and the incorrect one, S−. Errorless learning can involve presenting only the correct simulus and gradually fading in the incorrect stimulus, with the aim that the child never responds to the incorrect stimulus. Trial and error learning, on the other hand, involves the presentation of both S+ and S−, the child being rewarded everytime he responds to S+, S− responses being non-reinforced, so that the latter will extinguish over time. Early research by Terrace (1963) and his work with pigeons found that the errorless technique was a much more effective way of promoting learning. It involves stimulus control changing from one characteristic of the stimulus to the correct discriminative one. So, for example, if the task was to discriminate between two words, so that, initially, one word was presented in a very large form and the incorrect word was faded-in by presenting it in very small form and the size gradually increased, the child would initially be responding on the basis of size rather than on the letter content. Stimulus control therefore has to shift from one aspect of the task (intensity) to a second functional aspect (form) at some point in the training — and this may well not take place until the last stages of training when responding can drop to a chance level. The child, in fact, has been hindered from defining the correct characteristics of the stimulus early in training.

Lambert (1980) gives a number of guidelines to the use of errorless training. He points out that success depends partly on a good task analysis of steps. The process of changing from one stimulus cue to another should be gradual, and ideally the incorrect stimulus should be introduced gradually from very near the beginning of training. In addition the child should not spend too long on each step; there should not be a high criterion of success for each step, as the shift in stimulus control from one dimension to a second dimension will be disencouraged with what could be viewed as over-learning. Lambert also suggests that, for the correct response to continue after training, the discrimination should be learned under intermittent reinforcement. This is supported by a study of coin recognition by McIvor and McGrinley (1983) where reinforcement was changed part-way through training from a continuous schedule to a variable ratio. Success was achieved with six out of seven children. Interestingly, the few errors that were made occurred at the point where the stimulus cues are increasingly refined — where the children had to discriminate between a 10p coin and a 50p coin.

Lambert comments on two other limitations in the use of errorless learning. The procedures are not effective if the child is already showing error perserveration before training, i.e. if the child consistently and repeatedly responds to the incorrect stimulus. Teaching of a task, therefore, cannot change effectively from trial and error methods to an errorless one. In much the same way, if the discrimination task involves reversal of previously learnt material or, if the material has to be responded to in certain contexts and not in others, errorless learning is not effective as it establishes strong stimulus control and prevents the child from attending to other relevant features of the task. A typical experimental procedure for reversal and relational learning might involve the child learning to respond to the circle, and not the triangle, when they are presented on a yellow background, and then to go on to respond to the triangle, and not the circle, when presented on a blue background. The relevance to school tasks could be seen by the child learning one-to-one correspondence for number work but then having to relearn that money does not always correspond one-to-one — the new cues are now size and colour.

Clearly then, errors do have a place in the learning of complex discrimination tasks but we cannot assume that this is true of other tasks. It may be that simple tasks, in particular motor tasks, which involve prompting so the child receives the correct sensation of the necessary movement, may well be better learned without mistakes. The question that remains unresolved is exactly when to introduce them in the learning process.

Going Beyond the Simple

Two key issues are important for effective teaching, firstly that the behaviour should continue over time and, secondly, that the behaviour should occur in different settings, that is to say, there should be maintenance and generalisation of skills taught. The question of generalisation forms one of the central problems of behaviour modification (Ward and Gow 1982), and the increasing failure to achieve this has become of fundamental concern (Borkowski and Cavannagh 1979).

Our concern in teaching is 'the child's strategy for dealing with his world' (Kiernan 1981). We need to know why we are teaching certain skills, what purpose this new skill is to be put to and how is it going to help the child in dealing with the world. Otherwise 'education may amount to little more than a series of loosely related intrusions upon their lives' (White and Haring 1978) and the teaching of splinter skills. We need to ask ourselves several important questions when formulating teaching programmes:

1. what actual *skills* is this task teaching?
2. how will the child use these skills in other tasks?
3. how do these skills relate to previously learned tasks?
4. what will control these behaviours — what are the antecedents, the setting conditions, the stimulus control and the reinforcement for these behaviours?

These issues all relate to the maintenance and generalisation of behaviour. Maintenace is concerned with the durability of a behaviour. Furthermore, it seems that, without maintenance, there can be no generalisation. 'It is fundamental to the generalisation process as it precedes it' (Ward and Gow, 1982); both processes therefore clearly relate to the method and content of our teaching.

Factors Affecting the Maintenance of Behaviour

Reinforcement is one consideration. For behaviour to be durable, it must be maintained in some way that society would normally perpetuate that skill, i.e. by natural contingencies (Stokes and Baer 1977). The use of arbitrary reinforcers in the teaching situation should only be viewed as a means to an end (Wheldall 1982). Thus reinforcement must be faded by changing the nature of the reinforcement and the schedule on which it is delivered. Built into the task analysis should be details for changing from continuous reinforcement to intermittent reinforcement.

One procedure that can be very effective in maintaining behaviours, once they are established, is delaying reinforcement. In an experiment by Fowler and Baer (1981) reinforcement was delayed until the end of the day — a time-saving arrangement of contingencies for the teacher. Not only did behaviours maintain, they also occurred in new settings, possibly because the children could not discriminate the time or place in which performance must occur. Obviously, with a child with severe learning difficulties, delay may have to be increased gradually, for example at the end of a session, end of a morning, end of a day, etc.

Another technique suggested by Cullen, Hattersley and Tennant (1977) is to use naturally-occurring reinforcers wherever possible. They provide the example of the child who likes to go outside to play, and dressing skills are built in as a pre-requisite. Hence skills are not taught in isolation but in natural contexts using natural reinforcers and natural antecedents; the child sees others going out to play, and this becomes the controlling stimulus to put his coat on with the reward of going outside. There can be nothing less motivating than frequent practice of a dressing skill in an unnatural context, where the only behaviour that follows the task is to strip off and do it again!

The Controlling Stimulus. This brings us to another facet of maintenance — the need to pay attention to the controlling stimulus of an action as part of the setting conditions and antecedents of a behaviour. As Westmacott and Cameron (1981) point out, 'Daily life is a series of interlocking behaviours.' Behaviours are not carried out in isolation but form part of a chain whereby the response of one action forms the stimulus to another (how Watson saw learning as occurring). This is also a way of bringing delay to naturally-occurring reinforcers. Rather than teaching isolated skills, we need to build up chains of behaviour. For example, our objective might be that the child will push the car, the overall aim being to improve eye-hand control. Rather than just prompting the child to push the car and rewarding him every time he does it, we set the scene. We might build a bridge using large bricks, and the child guides the car through. Or, he misses, the bridge collapses — even better. As his skill progresses, the bridge becomes smaller, he builds the bridge and pushes the car, etc. The game is changed to pushing a train along a track under a bridge. Pushing a car then becomes a stimulus for brick-building, brick-building for building a rail track, 'castle', etc. The skills are all clearly related to eye-hand control but the setting is creating interest. In behaviourist terminology, the stimulus for the chain of responses serves a dual function: it may either be a reinforcing or a discriminative stimulus (Thevdt, Zane and Walls 1984), or both.

Setting Events

Some setting events, such as the sex and age of the child, are unchangeable, but others can be manipulated. They may in fact prove more important than contingencies of reinforcement (Glynn 1982). These can take the form of actual physical changes such as introducing new toys or equipment and may affect the child directly or indirectly if they affect the behaviour of other people who, in turn, affect the target child. Teachers may be 'inspired' by the arrival of new equipment or toys to try them out themselves, hence forming a model for the child. Incidental teaching can occur when the behaviour of an adult leads the child to initiate inter-action with the new materials. The effectiveness of an adult's presence cannot be under-rated, especially as a potential model carrying out a parallel activity — whether it is PE activities, picture-lotto games, gardening or role-playing in the Wendy House. Negative effects can also accrue, however, if the teacher/adult perhaps inadvertently restricts the child's opportunities to learn by 'providing the answers'. Halle, Baer and Spradlin (1981) found teachers were maintaining simple responses even though some children were capable of more complex ones. It was over-come by delaying the model prompt of asking for help in social situations. Often we respond to simple gestures and one word responses while, as Halle, Baer and Spradlin (1979) state, 'a time delay is a simple yet powerful method of manipulating the environment to increase opportunities for verbal responding'.

Previous learning history will also affect the child's response in a given situation, as we have seen in the learning of relational and reverse learning. The child's experience of a similar programme is the most frequently cited factor again relating to discrimination learning, but discrimination plays a part in all curriculum areas. For example, the child who has learned to complete a two-piece jig-saw by always manipulating the same half of the puzzle will have problems of generalising when faced later with a six-piece puzzle which demands manipulating pieces such as , where there is no 'prong' to fit in. Thus previous learning history is inhibiting new learning.

Setting events or stimulus events either facilitate or inhibit the link between stimulus and response (Wahler and Fox 1981), and much more emphasis should be placed on these by those concerned with the education of children with severe learning difficulties. They are important for eliciting behaviour, for maintaining it and for generalisation. Thus the environment, in the widest sense of the word, needs to be arranged to facilitate both behaviour change and the transfer and adaptiveness of the behaviour. The advantage to the teacher is that arranging the environment can be carried out in advance or concurrently with teaching and perhaps even obviate the need for reinforcement (Glynn 1982).

Generalisation

Turning to look in more detail at generalisation, it becomes evident that the approaches advocated differ considerably in complexity. At one level we have the suggestion of Kazdin (1983) that the range of stimuli during training should be expanded to include variations in who carries out the programme with the child and when and where it takes place. At another level is that of general case programming (Colvin and Horner 1983; Carnine and Becker 1982) which will be discussed later. Stokes and Baer (1977) review the technology of generalisation and argue that generalisation does not take place without special programming.

As Brown (1978) urges, we need to select skills for training that are general enough to fit different tasks in different settings, or to train the art of generalisation as a basic skill in its own right. What we need to avoid is the child following a 'blind-rule' procedure where he is not aware of the value of the strategy and the contexts in which it will prove useful. Situations should be avoided where a strategy is 'welded' to a particular task.

One important strategy or learning-to-learn skill that we can teach the children with severe learning difficulties, is that of imitation. Observational learning accounts for the acquisition of large, integrated patterns of behaviour (Bandura 1977) and results from observing other people's behaviour and the consequences for them. It is particularly important for the development of language skills. Bandura draws our attention to four important component processes: attending to the significant features of the model, remembering it, having the motor skills necessary to reproduce it and the necessary motivation. Teaching imitation should therefore pay attention to these four processes, all of which can provide problems for children with severe learning difficulties. Hence the model may need to be exaggerated or accentuated — to aid attention; imitation should immediately follow the model — to aid remembering; prompting should help the child to make the necessary movements, and he and the model should be reinforced. Kiernan (1977) has successfully demonstrated its applicability even with profoundly handicapped children, although some did have difficulties with responses which did not involve objects. Uzgiris and Hunt (1975) provide a scale of imitation for assessment purposes.

Processes Involved in Generalisation. There are a number of processes involved in generalisation, and not all may be available for the child with severe learning difficulties. Stimulus generalisation may occur where the child responds to a second similar stimulus as he responded to the first. Response generalisation involves the making of a second and associated response to the stimulus. The ultimate level of this is the transfer of a strategy where the strategies become free from the training context. This occurs in a period of formal operations and therefore is unlikely to be a process incurred by children with severe learning difficulties. Lastly, there may be generalisation of effects where behaviour generalises from one child to another, due to modelling and peer influence.

The fundamental feature of generalisation is discrimination learning as the child has to discriminate between situations in order to know which particular behaviour to perform and when to do so. Therefore as Carnine and Becker (1982) state, generalisation is a question of learning to discriminate critical sameness and differences. This forms the basis of general case programming where responses which share critical sameness are reinforced and other responses are not. Failure will be a result of over-generalising or under-generalising. In addition errors will be made if the stimulus control is restricted, or where behaviour is controlled by irrelevant stimuli or where there is response distortion (Colvin and Horner 1983). To minimise control by irrelevant stimuli, and hence over-generalising, we need to select non-examples to present, and careful selection and sequencing of examples to avoid under-generalising and response distortion.

Brown, Campione and Murphy (1977) suggest that the teaching of skills should concern their performance — in at least three different settings, in response to three different sets of instructional material, in the presence of at least three different people, and to at least three different appropriate language cues. As Ward and Gow (1982) point out, this could prove extremely time consuming and unnecessary; by using general case programming instead, instruction is improved so that concepts and operations are taught with a selection of materials and cues to ensure generalisation. The difference between the two approaches partly centres on the discriminative ability of the child in question, and it is quite credible that the approach recommended by Brown, Campione and Murphy is suitable for programming generalising with some children with severe learning difficulties. As Whitman, Scibak and Reid (1983) say, 'Ultimately it may be necessary albeit time-consuming, to programme generalisation by implementing training in an array of different situations in which a response is appropriate.'

General Case Programming.   General case programming involves providing a range of examples which are the same with respect to one and only one distinctive quality, but which show the limits of possible variations. In addition untaught examples — probes — are included to test for generalisation across the range. Colvin and Horner (1983) outline the following procedures:

1. isolate all the stimulus situations in which the response will occur, defining where behaviour will occur and the amount that needs to be taught;
2. determine the range of stimulus and response variation in these situations;
3. identify the minimum number of examples that illustrate the full range of stimulus variation. Ideally they should contain an equal amount of information and be paired with non-instances;
4. these should be sequenced. They suggest putting together, or one after another, maximally similar instances and non-instances. However, it could be hypothesised that, for children with severe learning difficulties, the degree of difference between the two should be gradually decreased, so that instances and non-instances are initially very different and gradually made more similar;
5. to avoid response distortion, juxtapose those that need the most difficult response with those that need less difficult responses;

6. include probes after a few examples have been taught to act as tests of generalisation and provide a guide towards errors.

Sprague and Horner (1981) illustrate the efficacy of this approach. The task was to teach six severely handicapped students to operate vending machines. When the students were trained on only one machine, there was minimal transfer to a second machine. Training was then carried out on three machines, but these did not illustrate the full range of variables — for example in the location of coin slot, selection apparatus, etc. — so again, generalisation was minimal. Training was then given on six machines which were maximally different in carefully selected ways, and generalisation was very high.

Colvin and Horner (1983) taught the generalised use of a screw driver so that students were trained on a number of response variations, using a variety of types and sizes of screws and screw drivers. They raise the question of whether easy to hard sequencing is most effective as there was some evidence that students would have progressed more rapidly through the programme if harder examples had been introduced earlier in training. They also suggest that repeated practice on a limited number and variety of examples should be avoided, and therefore as much diversity as possible should be introduced early on in training. This appears to facilitate stimulus and response generalisation and minimal response distortion by preventing the overlearning of stimulus-response connections.

Going beyond a simple approach leads us to conclude on a number of points of reference for the teacher. It suggests that careful attention needs to be paid to reinforcement, that ultimately, motivation should come from naturally occurring (intermittent) events. Hence we need to programme this into a task analysis. Setting conditions should be given just as much, if not more, consideration than reinforcement, not only in terms of eliciting new skills but also to achieve maintenance and generalisation.

Careful selection should be made of the skills to be taught to ensure that they are applicable in a wide range of situations. Although sequencing of easy to hard holds true for many teaching situations, it is not necessarily the correct procedure in generalisation. Methods of teaching should pay careful attention to stimulus control which ultimately must lie with some facet of the task, rather than a teacher imposed aspect. Highlighted in the study of generalisation is the importance of teaching discrimination skills to the child if we are to achieve the intention of providing the child with an enduring and adaptable set of strategies for meeting the world.

And the Limitations

The behaviourist approach is not, and should not be viewed as, a panacea for the learning problems of children with severe learning difficulties. There are notable exceptions that make the techniques less effective, for example, with children about whose particular learning problems we have insufficient knowledge. Failures also occur for other, and this time redeemable, reasons, including an inadequate understanding of what is required (Berger 1982). In addition it is not simply a question of teachers carrying out techniques effectively, but also of basing programmes on a thorough understanding of the learning processes involved. Thus we are guided towards these areas of limitation.

Obviously the effectiveness of the behaviour approach will not be maximal if the teacher is not taught how to assess the child's level of functioning, how to carry out the procedures of shaping, prompting task analyses, reinforcement and recording. There is a clear need for 'carefully prepared and closely supervised work with children in the real setting of the school' (Foxen and McBrien 1981). It is not enough that teachers are told to praise appropriate behaviour. As Berger (1982) points out it may not be a positive reinforcer at all! Such over-simplification leads to abuses or inappropriate uses, again a source of failure. However, a suitable training programme does not guarantee results. As 'a general rule as soon as training is terminated, behaviour reverts to pre-training levels' (Kazdin 1983); that is, unless steps are taken to avoid it, teachers' responses are extinguished after training. Their motivation to carry on will not, for example, be as high as research workers who design and carry out programmes correctly and consistently for reasons other than/or in addition to the desire to bring about learning. Built into the training programme must be motivation comparable to that of research workers (opportunities for advanced degrees, esteem, professional advancement, occupational requirement) (Ferguson and Cullari 1983).

The second area of limitations centres around the child himself, and in particular we may question the applicability of the techniques to the profoundly handicapped. Ellis, Deacon, Harris, Poor, Angers, Diorio, Watkins, Boyd and Cavalier (1982) came to the conclusion that 'we can infer some profoundly retarded individuals will learn extremely slowly if not at all'. The assumption cannot be made that the profoundly handicapped will not learn — in their teaching of a discrimination task they found no clear link between IQ and learning. Some of the most profoundly retarded (with mean IQ of 8) learned and remembered as well as some of the moderately handicapped (mean IQ of 43.8). The inconsistency of responses encountered in this study will be a very familiar problem to teachers. 'One day a subject would appear alert and attentive and responsive to the task, but on another it would seem as if the laboratory visit was an entirely new experience ...' (Ellis, *et al.* 1982; p. 5). Similarly, other problems outlined by Barrett and Lindsley (1962) are found in the teaching situation. These included very low response levels as well as periods of non-responding and very stereotyped patterns of response.

The outlook for generalisation and maintenance is not good. Ellis *et al.* (1982) found that mastery of a task on one day was no assurance of learning another similar problem or even of relearning the same problem. However, before we draw too heavily on their findings, we must recognise that he was using an adult population. One problem that can occur in maintenance is that, when the child moves onto an intermittent schedule of reinforcement, the behaviour can spontaneously extinguish (Rice, McDaniel, Stallings and Gatz 1967). Teachers may also find that they cannot move children from primary reinforcement by pairing reinforcers or establish stimulus control with the profoundly handicapped, as not all can be classically conditioned (Hogg, Remington and Foxen 1979). The question of reinforcers quite often poses the biggest headache with this group of children. Consumable rewards may be unsuitable but auditory stimulation has been found effective (Remington, Foxen and Hogg 1977) as has visual stimulation (Rice, McDaniel, Stallings and Gatz 1967). Some children clearly do not show the ability to discriminate pain from pleasure. 'Clearly more research is needed before we can say with any certainty that these techniques are effective for teaching skills' to the profoundly handicapped (Whitman, Scibak and Reid 1983).

Interestingly these very real limitations are rarely cited by the critics of behaviour modification, who tend to believe that behavioural principles should stay the concern of animal psychologists and whose main aversion seems to rest with the idea of reinforcement as a means of changing behaviour. In going beyond a simple approach, it becomes clear that reinforcement is just one facet of the environment. Reinforcers have been viewed as bribery, that the child should be rewarded for effort rather than success, that their use is tantamount to saying the task is not worthy of doing for its own sake. Clearly the more effort the child puts in, the longer he works, the more opportunities for reinforcement — and it is reinforcement at the appropriate level of hierarchy. As Kazdin (1980) points out, few people would work if they were not paid, given smiles, praise, approving gestures, or if their work did not match some self-established standard. A more plausible area of criticism stems from the use of terminology, described by Tibbits (1983) as ' moronic litany of cumbersome jargon — simplest issues reissued in a long-worded language adapted from a semi-literate mid-American sub-culture'. Others put it more briefly! Terminology, however, allows people to communicate effectively without ambiguity and without the need for long-hand descriptions.

Other criticisms apply to observed practice — Wheldall (1982) warns us about 'behavioural overkill' — the result of neglecting antecedents, and setting events in establishing an over-enthusiastic, often artificial approach to contingency management. What must be guarded against is the idea that there could be a catalogue of procedures for particular problems. Reviews of the literature provide good aids for directing teachers towards possible techniques, but because of the individual emphasis of behavioural approaches, there can never be 'methods inherently unable to fail' (Tibbits 1983). Each and every child must be viewed within his or her own context.

Lastly, to turn to the third area of limitations. There is the need to understand the learning process — by a good understanding of normal development — and from this an appreciation of why the child with severe learning difficulties will 'deviate'; but more important, there is the need to understand how skills interrelate, how skills build on one another and hence what will be appropriate goals for the individual child. Thus the behavioural approach should not be viewed as an eclectic approach, but one that provides the 'routes' to achieve the skills that a developmental approach suggests, providing we go beyond the simple.

As Wheldall (1982) says, 'We must replace the notion of a peanut pushing, Smarties-smothering, token-trafficking behaviour modification "enthusiast" with the concept of a skilled behaviour analyst.'

References

Bandura, A. (1977) *Social Learning Theory.* Prentice Hall.

Barrett, B.H. and Lindsley, O.R. (1962) 'Deficits in acquisition of operant discrimination and differentiation shown by institutionalised retarded children'. *Am. Jnl of Mental Deficiency, 67,* pp. 424-36.

Berger, M. (1982) 'Applied behaviour analysis in education: a critical assessment and some implications for training teachers'. *Educational Psychology, 2* (3 & 4), pp. 289-300.

Borkowski, J. and Cavannagh, J. (1979) 'Maintenance and generalisation of skills and strategies by the retarded' in N.R. Ellis (ed.). *Handbook of Mental Deficiency: Psychological Theory and Research,* 2nd edn. Lawrence Erlbaum.

Brown, A.L., Campione, J.C. and Murphy, M.D. (1977) 'Maintenance and generalisation of trained metamnemonic awareness by educable retarded children'. *Jnl of Experimental Child Psychology, 24,* pp. 191-211.

Brown, A.L. (1978) 'Knowing when, where and how to remember: a problem in metacognition', in R. Glaser (ed.). *Advances in Instructional Psychology,* vol. 1. Lawrence Erlbaum.

Carey, R.G. and Bucher, B. (1983) 'Positive practice over-correction — the effects of duration of positive practice on acquisition and response reduction'. *Jnl of Applied Behaviour Analysis, 16,* pp. 101-9.

Carnine, D.W. and Becker, W.C. (1982) 'Theory of instruction: generalisation issues'. *Educational Psychology, 2* (3 & 4), pp. 249-62.

Cliffe, M.J., Gathercole, C. and Epling, W.F. (1974) 'Some implications of the experimental analysis of behaviour for behaviour modification'. *Bull. Br. Psychological Society, 27,* pp. 390-7.

Colvin, G.T. and Horner, R.H. (1983) 'Experimental analysis of generalisation: an evaluation of a general case programme for teaching motor skills to severely handicapped learners', in J. Hogg and P. Mittler (eds.). *Advances in Mental Handicap Research,* Vol. 2. Wiley.

Cullen, C., Hattersley, J. and Tennant, L. (1977) 'Behaviour modification — some implications of a radical behaviourist view'. *Bull. of the Br. Psychological Society, 30,* pp. 65-9.

DES (1978) *Special Educational Needs.* Report of the Committee of Enquiry into the Education of Handicapped Children and Young People (The Warnock Report). HMSO.

Duker, P. and Seys, D. (1983) 'Long-term follow-up effects of extinction and over-correction procedures with severely retarded individuals'. *Jnl of Mental Subnormality, 19,* part II.

Ellis, N.R., Deacon, J.R., Harris, L.A., Poor, A., Angers, D., Diorio, M., Watkins, R.S., Boyd, B.D. and Cavalier, A.R. (1982) 'Learning, memory and transfer in profoundly, severely and moderately mentally retarded persons'. *Am. Jnl of Mental Deficiency, 87* (2), pp. 186-96.

Ferguson, D.G. and Cullari, S. (1983) 'Behaviour modification in facilities for the mentally retarded: problems with the development and implementation of training programmes', in S.E. Breuning, J.L. Matson and R.P. Barrett (eds.). *Advances in Mental Retardation and Developmental Disabilities.* JAI Press.

Fowler, S.A. and Baer, D.M. (1981) "'Do I have to be good all day?" The timing of delayed reinforcement as a factor in generalisation'. *Jnl of Applied Behaviour Analysis, 14*, pp. 13-24.

Foxen, T. and McBrien, J. (1981) *Training Staff in Behavioural Methods.* Trainee Workbook. Manchester Univ. Press.

Glynn, T. (1982) 'Antecedent control of behaviour in educational contexts'. *Educational Psychology, 2* (3 & 4), pp. 215-29.

Halle, J.W., Baer, D.M. and Spradlin, J. (1979) 'Time delay: a technique to increase language use and facilitate generalisation in retarded children'. *Jnl of Applied Behaviour Analysis, 12*, pp. 431-9.

Halle, J.W., Baer, D.M. and Spradlin, J. (1981) 'Teachers' generalised use of delay as a stimulus control procedure to increase language use in handicapped children'. *Jnl of Applied Behaviour Analysis, 14*, pp. 389-409.

Hogg, J., Remington, R.E. and Foxen, T.H. (1979) 'Classical conditioning of profoundly retarded, multiply handicapped children'. *Developmental Medicine and Child Neurology, 21* (6), pp. 779-86.

Hogg, J. and Mittler, P. (1980) 'Recent research in mental handicap: issues and perspectives', in J. Hogg and P. Mittler (eds.). *Advances in Mental Handicap Research*, Vol. 1. Wiley.

Kazdin, A.E. (1980) *Behavior Modification in Applied Settings*, revised edn. Dorsey Press.

Kazdin, A.E. (1983) 'Applying behavioral principles in school', in C.R. Reynolds and T.B. Gutian (eds.). *Handbook of School Psychology.* Wiley.

Kiernan, C. (1977) 'Towards a curriculum for the profoundly retarded, multiply handicapped'. *Child Care, Health and Development, 3* (4).

Kiernan, C. (1981) *Analysis of Programmes for Teaching.* Globe.

Lambert, J.L. (1980) 'Stimulus fading procedures and discrimination learning by retarded children', in J. Hogg and P. Mittler (eds.). *Advances in Mental Handicap Research*, Vol. 1. Wiley.

McBrien, J. and Foxen, T. (1981) *Training Staff in Behavioural Methods.* Instructor's Handbook. Manchester Univ. Press.

McIvor, M. and McGrinley, P. (1983) 'Teaching coin discrimination using an errorless learning procedure'. *Mental Handicap, 11* (3), pp. 110-13.

Matson, J. and McCartney, J. (eds.) (1981). *Handbook of Behavior Modification with the Mentally Retarded.* Plenum Press.

Merrett, F.E. and Musgrove, W.J. (1982) 'The hierarchy of reinforcement mainspring of the behavioural approach to teaching and learning'. *Educational Psychology, 2* (3 & 4), pp. 301-12.

Poling, A., Fugua, R. and Miltenberger, R. (1983) 'Basic operant research with the mentally retarded', in S.E. Breuning, J.L. Matson and R.P. Barrett (eds.). *Advances in Mental Retardation and Developmental Disabilities*, Vol. 1. JAI Press.

Remington, R.E., Foxen, T. and Hogg, J. (1977) 'Auditory reinforcement in profoundly retarded multiply handicapped children'. *Am. Jnl of Mental Deficiency, 82* (3), pp. 299-304.

Rice, H.K., McDaniel, M.W., Stallings, V.D. and Gatz, M.J. (1967) 'Operant behaviour in vegetative patients II'. *Psychological Record, 17*, pp. 449-60.

Skinner, B.F. (1974) *About Behaviourism.* Jonathan Cape.

Sprague, J.S. and Horner, R.M. (1981) 'Experimental analysis of generalised vending machine use with severely handicapped students'. Unpub. work cited in G.T. Colvin and R.M. Horner. 'Experimental analysis of generalisation: an evaluation of a general case programme for teaching motor skills to severely handicapped learners', in J. Hogg and P. Mittler (eds.). *Advances in Mental Handicap Research*, Vol. 2. Wiley.

Stokes, T.F. and Baer, D.M. (1977) 'An implicit technology of generalisation'. *Jnl of Applied Behaviour Analysis, 10* (2), pp. 349-67.

Terrace, H.S. (1963) 'Discrimination learning with and without errors'. *Jnl of the Experimental Analysis of Behavior, 6*, pp. 1-27.

Thevdt, J., Zane, T. and Walls, R. (1984) 'Stimulus functions in response chaining'. *Am. Jnl of Mental Deficiency, 88* (6), pp. 661-7.

Thomas, G. and O'Callaghan, M. (1981) 'Pavlovian principles and behaviour therapy', in G. Davey (ed.). *Application of Conditioning Theory.* Methuen.

Tibbits, J. (1983) 'Behaviourism and therapy'. *Mental Handicap, 11* (4), p. 153.

Uzgiris, I.C. and Hunt, J. McV. (1975) *Assessment in Infancy: ordinal scales of infant development.* Univ. of Illinois Press.

Wahler, R. and Fox, J. (1981) 'Setting events in applied behavior analysis: toward a conceptual and methodological expansion'. *Jnl of Applied Behaviour Analysis, 14*, pp. 327-38.

Ward, J. and Gow, L. (1982) 'Programming generalisation: a central problem area in educational psychology'. *Educational Psychology, 2* (3 & 4), pp. 231-48.

Weeks, M. and Gaylord-Ross, R. (1981) 'Task difficulty and aberrant behavior in severely handicapped students'. *Jnl of Applied Behaviour Analysis, 14* (4), pp. 449-63.

Westmacott, E.V.S. and Cameron, R.J. (1981) *Behaviour Can Change.* Globe.

Wheldall, K. (1982) 'Behavioural pedagogy or behavioural overkill?' *Educational Psychology, 2* (3 & 4), pp. 181-4.

White, O. and Haring, N. (1978) 'Evaluating educational programmes serving the severely and profoundly handicapped', in N. Haring and P. Bricker (eds.). *Teaching the Severely Handicapped,* Vol. 3. Columbus Ohio Special Press.

Whitman, T., Scibak, J. and Reid, D. (1983) *Behavior Modification with the Severely and Profoundly Retarded, Research and Applications.* Academic Press.

Williams, J.L., Schroeder, S.R., Eckerman, D.A. and Rojahn, J. (1983) 'Time-out from positive reinforcement procedures with mentally retarded persons an eclogical review and analysis', in S.E. Breuning, J.L. Matson and R.P. Barrett (eds.). *Advances in Mental Retardation and Developmental Disabilities,* Vol. 1. JAI Press.

Woodward, R.J., Magim, C. and Johnston, W.A. (1983) 'The reduction of self-stimulatory behavior using a differential reinforcement of other behavior (d.r.o.) schedule'. *Br. Jnl of Mental Subnormality, 19*, pp. 65-73.

Yule, W. & Carr, J. (eds.). (1980) *Behaviour Modification for the Mentally Handicapped.* Croom Helm.

Zeaman, D. and House, B. (1963) 'The role of attention in retardate discrimination learning', in N.R. Ellis (ed.). *Handbook of Mental Deficiency.* Lawrence Erlbaum.

Zeaman, D. and House, B. (1979) 'A review of attention theory', in N.R. Ellis (ed.). *Handbook of Mental Deficiency, Psychology Theory and Research,* 2nd edn. Wiley.

3 CLASSROOM MANAGEMENT

Peter Sturmey and Tony Crisp

Introduction

The efficient and effective use of classroom resources has been of concern to practitioners in a variety of educational settings, e.g. day nurseries (Herbert-Jackson *et al.* 1977), classes in primary schools (Galton and Simon 1980), remedial classes (Sewell 1982) and secondary schools (Beasley 1983). Likewise, in services for the mentally handicapped the optimal use of resources, particularly the use of staff has been explored. Again a variety of applied settings such as classrooms (McBrien and Weightman 1980), special needs units (Porterfield, Blunden and Blewitt 1980), hospital wards (Horner 1980) and adult training units (Crisp and Sturmey 1984a) have featured in this work. This growing volume of research reflects the increasing concern for accountability and effectiveness in human services of all kinds not just services for the mentally handicapped, a concern which has surfaced in the United States (Neigher and Schulberg 1982) but is now prevalent here also.

Much of this work has been undertaken within, or strongly influenced by, an applied behaviour analysis framework. In previous chapters the basic behavioural techniques have been described. The aim of this chapter is to describe some organisational approaches to implementing these techniques with students in micro-environments such as classrooms with a view to optimising staff and student performance. In the limited space available only a general overview of some of the basic procedures will be possible. However in each case we will describe the basic approach together with research bearing upon its strengths and limitations.

Small Groups and Individual Tuition

Almost all research into teaching mentally handicapped students has used a one-to-one teaching situation, that is one teacher working with one student, with no other students present. The literature reports considerable successes over a wide range of skill areas and problem behaviours with one-to-one teaching (Favell, Favell and McGimsey 1978). However in educational settings, whether for children or adults, teachers are most frequently teaching small groups of students who may manifest a wide variety of behavioural deficits and excesses. In these circumstances success does not come easily or rapidly. The gap between what is achieved by researchers with individual teaching and what is perceived to be realistically possible in service settings often leads to considerable frustration on the part of teachers and other direct care staff who feel that much research is not relevant to their situation since it is undertaken in a context of resources that they do not possess (Slama and Bannerman 1983).

Various arguments have been advanced on the relative merits of individual teaching and small group approaches. Individual teaching, for instance, allows the choice of goal, materials, prompts, reinforcers and other aspects of the teaching situation to be tailored to meet the individual needs of the person being taught. The teacher is enabled to direct attention exclusively to the student being taught and likewise the students need only attend to one set of materials and one teacher. Bijou (1966) has suggested that these arrangements should be in the room for all students not just those with special needs.

Other workers have advocated a small group teaching arrangement suggesting that it may offer several advantages over the individual approach. Brown, Holvoet, Guess and Mulligan (1980) suggest, for instance, that small groups may facilitate modelling between students and may increase generalisation of skills to other settings where groups of individuals are present. In a small group arrangement students may be encouraged to assist one another by prompting and reinforcing task completion. Hence communications and co-operative behaviour may be developed.

Several empirical studies have compared teaching in small groups and individual teaching across a variety of task situations. These will now be considered.

Studies have demonstrated that learning can occur as quickly in small groups as during individual training. Oliver and Scott (1981) trained eight severely mentally handicapped adults, aged 19-21 years, to point to hard or heavy objects by fading prompts and progressively increasing the number of objects from two to eight. Subjects in small groups took 50 trials to criterion and subjects in one-to-one training took 62 trials to criterion, a non-significant difference. That is, the rate of acquisition was equally rapid in both methods of teaching, and the presence of other students did not interfere with learning. Some students have suggested that small groups may facilitate learning by imitation. Biberdorf and Pear (1977) compared teaching pairs of mentally handicapped children a picture-naming task either separately or in pairs. Each child was assigned an individual list of pictures to name. Children who were taught in pairs learned nearly half of each other's picture names. Again this suggests that learning in small groups is possible and may even facilitate learning by imitation.

The attempt to provide students with individual tuition in a group situation may occasionally leave those individuals not being taught without materials or unoccupied, and these may go on to display disruptive or otherwise unacceptable behaviour (Sturmey, Crisp and Dearden 1983). In consequence staff may frequently have to 'turn-away' from the student receiving individual attention (Westling, Ferrell and Swenson 1982) to attend to these problem behaviours which, in turn, may increase in frequency and intensity. Several attempts have been made to solve this difficulty, that is to provide individual tuition while caring for a group of students. We shall be discussing research on room management and related procedures below. However Storm and Willis (1978), in a study comparing individual teaching and small group teaching, describe a variant of small group teaching termed the add-in method. During the add-in method one student was taught a series of motor imitation tasks. When criterion was reached, a second student joined the group and so on. Although skill acquisition was roughly equal in all three methods individual training provided only 20 hours occupation per individual, whereas the add-in method provided 62 hours and the small group provided fully 80 hours occupation per individual.

The problem of generalisation of skills from individual teaching to small group situations is illustrated by Koegel and Rincover (1974). These authors individually trained eight mentally handicapped, autistic children in a set of prelinguistic skills. The children did reach criterion during individual teaching but failed to perform these skills in their normal classroom when all eight children were present. In a second experiment Koegel and Rincover gradually faded in extra children into the individual teaching situation, thus increasing group size gradually to eight children. In this way seven out of eight children were able to perform the skills acquired during individual teaching in the regular classroom setting.

Teaching in small groups can be arranged in several ways. Mittaug and Wolfe (1976) investigated two ways of managing small groups to promote speech among four mildly and moderately handicapped children aged 10-12 years. The first condition was termed task independence when each child had his own puzzle pieces in front of him. The second condition was task interdependence when each child's puzzle pieces were distributed among the other children, and each child had to make requests for pieces from his partner. Mittaug and Wolfe found that speech among the four children increased greatly during the task interdependent condition and were almost absent during the task independent condition. Further, even when contingent sweets were available during the task independent condition this had no effect on speech between the children. This study suggests that staff can arrange materials in a variety of ways during small groups to promote social interaction among participants which may not be seen in other conditions.

Although most of this research appears to indicate that small group teaching is often successful, it does have limitations. Some further difficulties are these. Firstly, individuals require certain entry behaviours to benefit from small group teaching. Clearly some individuals are too disruptive or active for teaching in small groups, and their presence may make teaching in small groups less effective than individual teaching. Storm and Willis (1978) for example reported that performance in their small group teaching arrangement actually became worse than baseline at first. Only after five hours of small group teaching did performance begin to surpass baseline. During these initial stages subjects frequently walked away, sat down or turned away; and only after consistent correction of these initial problems did the group become readily manageable. Even though these individuals did eventually learn in small groups, some individuals may require extensive individual teaching in entry behaviours such as remaining seated for short periods, sitting down and attending before they can be taught in small groups.

A second problem is that, in all these studies, the students were taught the same task or tasks that were substantially similar. In settings for severely mentally handicapped students it may not always be possible to constitute groups of students who can be taught the same goal or task. Where this is not possible, one-to-one teaching is difficult to achieve (Crisp and Sturmey 1984a).

A final limitation is that most of the studies of small group teaching have focused upon tasks that appear to suit this arrangement such as desk-top activities, imitation and language skills. Alberto, Jones, Sizemore and Doran (1980) compared the individual and small-group teaching of three tasks. When teaching the understanding of prepositions and colour discrimination both methods of organisation were equally effective. When teaching dressing however individual teaching led to consistently better performance than when dressing was taught in small groups. It is unclear what the critical differences between these tasks were but Alberto, *et al.* suggested three possible reasons for the outcome. Firstly, modelling was easiest during desk-top activities since the students' view of correct responses was not obscured. Secondly, during dressing students progressed at different rates, and thus appropriate models were not always present. Thirdly, the first two tasks involved simple motor responses such as pointing whereas dressing is motorically far more complex.

It appears that teaching in small groups can be a viable strategy, although it is not completely clear from research to date under what circumstances. However conclusions that have been reached suggest that teaching in small groups can probably be most effective if the following conditions are observed: 1. selecting students who do not disrupt the smooth running of the group; 2. selecting students who can imitate to maximise modelling; 3. including peer models; 4. selecting goals that are shared by the group; 5. choosing tasks that can be observed easily to facilitate modelling; 6. choosing tasks which involve simple responses; 7. finally, consideration needs to be given to the size of the group. Surprisingly little attention has been given to the effect of varying the 'span of control', that is the number of students for whom a teacher is responsible, upon teacher and student performance. However, this is an important variable influencing both the content and duration of teacher-student interactions. In our studies (Crisp and Sturmey 1984a) we have used small groups of four or five severely handicapped students with one teacher. Even though it was possible to maintain a moderately high level of activity in these groups, very little individual teaching was possible. Since individual teaching will remain an important strategy, as it is often not possible to constitute a group of students who share the same teaching objectives or tasks, a span of control of 1:4 or 1:5 may be too large when individual tuition is contemplated.

Room Management and its Variants

In the previous section we indicated that research has shown that severely mentally handicapped students are able to learn new skills when behavioural programmes are designed and implemented to meet their specific needs. However we also indicated that, in practice, it is very difficult to provide individual tuition in service settings where resources are such that group teaching is of necessity the standard practice. Although various strategies have been developed in attempting to solve this difficulty, one approach that has attracted considerable interest in this country is Room Management.

Room management (Porterfield *et al.* 1980) is a procedure developed to promote both individual teaching and high activity levels in groups of students. The original procedure consisted of giving staff clearly defined roles. The room manager has responsibility for providing materials for almost all students who are seated — typically at tables arranged in a horseshoe shape. The room manager prompts appropriate use of materials in disengaged students, praises engaged students, and replaces completed materials. The room manager may thus occupy five to ten students in a high activity task which releases a second staff, the individual helper, who may then spend time with individuals, uninterrupted, in order to provide individual skills training.

Several variants of the basic room management procedure have been developed. McBrien and Weightman (1980) used a third staff role, the equipment mover, to move aids around a classroom for multiply handicapped children. Beswick (1984) developed another staff role, the special helper, to reduce excessive wandering in a group of active, severely mentally handicapped women. The special helper neutrally prompted out-of-seat individuals towards their seat, praised sitting down and provided an initial activity, and then the room manager took over responsibility for that person. Finally, Walter (1978) developed a modified individual helper role, termed the hygiene manager, at a special needs unit. While the room manager took responsibility for the majority of students, hygiene managers were responsible for meeting students who arrived at different times through the morning, helped them off with their coats, took them to the toilet and then let the room manager take responsibility for them. Once the hygiene manager had seated all trainees they could then begin individual training. Hence, as well as the basic room manager plus one individual helper, a variety of additional staff roles have been developed to meet the specific needs of students as they have arisen. Many staff roles developed in day care settings for toddlers have not yet been explored with mentally handicapped individuals (Doke and Risley 1972; Loos, Williams and Bailey 1977; LeLaurin and Risley 1972). The general principle of developing explicit staff roles may provide many other useful procedures broadly similar to room management (Gunstone, Hogg, Sebba, Warner and Almonds 1982).

Several studies have shown that room management can greatly increase the level of group activity (group engagement) compared to baseline conditions (Porterfield *et al.* 1980; Woods and Cullen 1983) as well as decreasing undesirable and disruptive behaviours (Spangler and Marshall 1983; Beswick 1984). For example Spangler and Marshall found that group engagement increased from approximately 10 per cent during baselines to approximately 75 per cent during room management. At the same time levels of inappropriate behaviour fell from approximately 13 per cent during baseline to 6 per cent during room management. Not all studies report such dramatic changes for all individuals (McBrien and Weightman 1980; Mansell, Felse, DeKock and Jenkins 1982). This variability of outcome reflects a number of factors such as the ability of the students (Crisp and Sturmey 1984a; Collins 1984) and choice of suitable materials (Breuning, *et al.*, 1981; Quilitch, Christopherson and Risley 1978). Other factors such as the level of disruption (shouting, throwing materials, self-injury, fighting and wandering) are also likely to reduce the effectiveness of room management in our experience.

Room Management Compared with Small Groups and Individual Teaching

Most of the research on room management discussed above made comparisons between room management and either no treatment baselines (Spangler and Marshall 1983) or slightly modified baselines such as providing trainees with extra materials (Mansell, *et al.*

1982). In this section we describe a series of studies comparing room management with alternative strategies such as small groups and individual teaching. This research took place in an adult training unit located in a small hospital for young adult severely and profoundly mentally handicapped (Sturmey, Crisp and Dearden 1983).

In the first of these studies room management was compared with teaching in small groups (Crisp and Sturmey 1984a). The subjects were three nursing assistants and 13 students. The students had an average age of 25 years (range 21-32 years) and had a mean Vineland Social Age (Doll, 1947) of 2.3 years (range 0.9-4.5 years). All were ambulant (i.e. could climb stairs), six had epilepsy, one was blind. There were no frequent, major behaviour problems in this group. The staff had worked in this setting for 16 years, nine months and three months, and one had been trained in goal planning techniques (Houts and Scott 1975). During the room management condition one staff worked as room manager and two staff worked as individual helpers training students on their goal plans. During small groups each staff was assigned to work with a group of four or five students. Again individual goal plans were in operation.

The two procedures were in many ways equivalent. Students spent nearly 90 per cent of their time with materials available, just over 40 per cent of their time using materials appropriately, remained in seat nearly all the time and received interaction from staff for about 15 per cent of the time. They differed in that, during room management, students received individual training for an average 14 per cent of the time whereas, in small groups, each received training for only 2 per cent of the time. Thus in this study, a group of normally active, ambulant, severely and profoundly mentally handicapped adults could be kept sitting down and using materials equally well by either a room management or small groups arrangement. However working in small groups did not enable the staff to spend much time teaching individually according to goal plans as they had frequently to attend to the needs other members of the group.

A second study was carried out to compare room management with individual training (Crisp and Sturmey, 1984b). This experiment was carried out with a similar group of students. There were three staff (of whom only two participated at any one time) and twelve students. The average age of students was 25.7 years (range

21-32 years) and their average social age 2.6 years (range 1.1-6.8 years). All subjects were ambulant. The staff were one state-enrolled nurse and two nursing assistants who had worked in this setting for six years, two years and for four months. In this study the room management was carried out by one room manager and one individual helper. During the 'individual training' condition the trainees were initially seated, provided with activity materials and prompted to use them and then left alone. The two staff then worked individually with students on their goal plans. Once all students had received training, the process began again, hence some students could receive additional training if time was available. In this condition, then, the role of room manager was abolished, staff devoting their time wholly to individual training.

The differences between 'individual training' and room management were quite distinct in this study. During 'individual training' an average of 14.4 students were trained which occupied on average 11 per cent of students' time. During room management only nine students were trained, and this occupied on average only 3 per cent of their time. Although 'individual training' provided more training than room management, room management provided prompting and reinforcement for performance on a holding activity that 'individual training' did not. During room management students had materials available for 81 per cent of the time, had finished materials in front of them 7 per cent of the time, had no materials in front of them for 12 per cent of the time, used them appropriately for 29 per cent of the time and were out of seat for only 4 per cent of the time. In contrast, during individual training students had materials available for 41 per cent of the time, had finished materials in front of them for 11 per cent of the time, had no materials in front of them for 47 per cent of the time were on task for 16 per cent of the time and were out of seat for 14 per cent of the time. Finally during room management students received staff interaction for 8 per cent of the time and during individual training received staff interaction for only 3 per cent of the time. Clearly, room management provides less individual training than an individual training arrangement but produces higher activity levels and greater staff-student interaction. A third experiment (Crisp and Sturmey 1984b) broadly replicated these findings with a group of non-ambulant, multiply handicapped adults.

This group of experiments indicated that both room management and small groups produced high levels of activity in the group as a whole. 'Individual teaching', while providing an increased opportunity for individual tuition, does so at the expense of other activities and is clearly not a suitable organisational arrangement to use with the groups of students we used in the study. It may be, however, that 'individual teaching' as we have used it might be a viable option for use with those students who are 'high engagers' (Mansell, *et al.* 1982), that is, students who can maintain a high level of activity on holding activities without frequent prompting and reinforcement from staff. Group composition as well as task/goal variables must then be considered when determining which organisational arrangements to use in a particular setting.

Complementary Pairing of Students

In the previous sections we examined various approaches to organising staff. Teachers and other care staff, however, indicate that they often attempt to organise their students, taking care in arranging who sits next to whom in the classroom, both to maximise the time spent on task, increase co-operation and minimise disruption. One of the more common strategies is to pair a student who is on task much of the time with one who is not. This may have several advantages. The student who spends little time on task may observe the one who is on task longer being reinforced by the instructor's praise and thereby increase his time on task. Observational learning was first systematically reported in normal children by Bandura (1965). Although this effect has been observed with the mentally handicapped it does not always occur, and when it does, may even have unplanned, negative side effects. Many severely mentally handicapped students may not possess observational learning skills. A recent series of studies by Ollendick and his colleagues, however, have suggested that, in both normal and mentally handicapped children, observing reinforcement does increase on task behaviour initially. However, after a few trials the performance of the non-reinforced child decreases to a level below baseline (Ollendick, *et al.* 1983) and is often accompanied by signs of boredom and 'emotional' behaviours (Ollendick and Shapiro 1984). A further study suggested that these problems could be overcome and high levels of on-task behaviour reinstated by intermittently reinforcing the child for correct modelling (Ollendick, *et al.* 1983). In sum, pairing students together is probably not an effective strategy on its own. The student who is supposed to learn by modelling is effectively extinguished, and verbal and other forms of aggression may ensue. The procedure may be effective if it is supplemented by intermittent reinforcement of the on-task behaviour emitted by the modelling child.

A second strategy for complementary pairing has been developed by Bakke and Milan (1983) in an industrial setting for mentally handicapped adults, some of whom were also physically handicapped. In this setting the task involved packing items into envelopes. Some of the mentally handicapped people worked very slowly, and although they were paid in proportion to their productivity the pay did not arrive until the end of the week. Thus reinforcement was not delivered immediately. In the same setting were several individuals with cerebral palsy who were physically unable to perform the task. Bakke and Milan devised a strategy whereby one able-bodied, mentally handicapped person was paired with one physically handicapped person. The physically handicapped person used a coin change machine fitted with a handle that they could operate to dispense a coin for every ten envelopes his partner completed. In this way production was greatly increased from approximately 50 to 130 envelopes per 30 minutes, and the physically handicapped person could participate in the workshop's activities. Bakke and Milan (1983) suggested that there may be other ways of pairing individuals with different, complementary handicaps to promote purposeful activity. Such a strategy may be useful in other settings such as classrooms although specific examples have not yet been demonstrated.

Concluding Remarks

One-to-one teaching is usually the strategy employed in research into teaching mentally handicapped students (Storm and Willis 1978). However, this strategy is not always viable in applied settings due to the low levels of activity observed in students not currently being trained (Sturmey and Crisp 1984a). In this chapter we have outlined a number of alternative strategies — small groups, room management and its variants, and complementary pairing of students — which may be of value to practitioners in applied settings. A wide range of other procedures may be developed in the future using the general principle of describing explicit staff roles to meet the needs and resources of particular settings.

As yet research does not provide clear guidelines for the selection of optimal strategies of classroom organisation. Reports suggest that both student and task characteristics may influence the selection of the ideal organisational strategy as well as the resources made available. Each method of classroom organisation has both advantages and limitations which should be recognised if the optimal strategy of classroom organisation is to be selected from the range currently available to practitioners.

References

Alberto, P., Jones, N., Sizemore, A. and Doran, D.A. (1980) 'A comparison of individual and group instruction across response tasks'. *Jnl of the Association for the Severely Handicapped, 5*, pp. 285-93.

Bakke, B.L. and Milan, M.A. (1983) 'Complementary pairing of handicapped workers with compensatory skills: a strategy to increase independence'. *Behaviour Research and Therapy, 21*, pp. 575-7.

Bandura, A. (1965) 'Influence of models' reinforcement contingencies on the acquisition of imitative responses'. *Jnl of Personality and Social Psychology, 1*, pp. 589-95.

Beasley, W. (1983) 'Teacher management behaviours and pupil task involvement during small group laboratory activities'. *Jnl of Research in Science Teaching, 20*, pp. 713-19.

Beswick, J.A. (1984) 'Evaluation of a room management "package"'. Paper presented at Hester Adrian Research Centre, 23 March 1984, a part of the symposium 'Organising environments for mentally handicapped people'.

Biberdorf, J.R. and Pear, J.J. (1977) 'Two-to-one versus one-to-one student teacher ratio in the operant verbal training of retarded children'. *Jnl of Applied Behaviour Analysis, 10*, pp. 5-6.

Bijou, S.W. (1966) 'A functional analysis of retarded development', in N.R. Ellis, (ed.). *Intl Review of Research in Mental Retardation,* Vol 1. Academic Press.

Breuning, S.E., Davis, V.G. and Lewis, J.R. (1981) 'Examination of methods of selecting goal-directed activities for institutionalised retarded adults'. *Education and Training of the Mentally Retarded, 16*, pp. 5-12.

Brown, F., Holvoet, J., Guess, D. and Mulligan, M. (1980) 'The individualized curriculum sequencing model III: small group instruction'. *Jnl of the Association of the Severely Handicapped, 5*, pp. 352-67.

Collins, G. (1984) 'Implementing a room management procedure on a day unit for mentally handicapped people: some methodological issues and individual effects'. Paper presented at Hester Adrian Research Centre, 23 March 1983, a part of the symposium 'Organising environments for mentally handicapped people'.

Crisp, A.G. and Sturmey, P. (1984a) 'Organising staff to promote purposeful activity in a setting for mentally handicapped adults: an evaluation of alternative strategies — small groups and room management'. *Behavioural Psychotherapy, 12*, pp. 281-99.

Crisp, A.G. and Sturmey, P. (1984b) 'Models of organisational functioning in training settings for the mentally handicapped'. Paper presented at the symposium 'Organising environments for mentally handicapped people', Hester Adrian Research Centre, University of Manchester.

Doke, L.A. and Risley, T.R. (1972) 'The organisation of day-care environments: required vs optional activities'. *Jnl of Applied Behaviour Analysis, 5*, pp. 405-20.

Doll, E.A. (1947) *Vineland Social Maturity Scale*, American Service, Minnesota, USA.

Favell, J.E. and McGimsey (1978) 'Relative effectiveness and efficiency of group vs individual training of severely retarded persons'. *Am. Jnl of Mental Deficiency, 83*, pp. 104-9.

Galton, M. and Simon, B. (1980) *Progress and Performance in the Primary Classroom*. Routledge and Kegan Paul.

Gunstone, C., Hogg, J., Sebba, J., Warner, J. and Almonds, S. (1982) *Classroom Provision and Organization for Integrated Pre-school Children*. Anson House Preschool Project Paper 2. Dr Barnardo's.

Herbert-Jackson, E., O'Brien, M., Porterfield, J. and Risley T. (1977) *The Infant Centre*. University Park Press.

Horner, D. (1980) 'The effect of an environmental "enrichment" programme on the behaviour of institutionalized profoundly retarded children'. *Jnl of Applied Behaviour Analysis, 13*, pp. 473-91.

Houts, P.S. and Scott, R.A. (1975) 'Goal planning in mental health rehabilitation'. *Goal Attainment Review, 2*, pp. 23-32.

Koegel, F.L. and Rincover, A. (1974) 'Treatment of psychotic children in a classroom environment: I. learning in a large group'. *Jnl of Applied Behaviour Analysis, 7*, pp. 45-59.

LeLaurin, K. and Risley, T.R. (1972) 'The organisation of day-care environments: "zone" vs. "man-to-man" staff assignments'. *Jnl of Applied Behaviour Analysis, 5*, pp. 225-32.

Loos, F.M., Williams, K.P. and Bailey, J.S. (1977) 'A multi-element analysis of the effect of teacher aides in an "open"-style classroom'. *Jnl of Applied Behaviour Analysis, 10*, 3, p. 437.

Mansell, J., Felce, P., DeKock, U. and Jenkins, J. (1982) 'Increasing purposeful activity with severely and profoundly handicapped adults'. *Behaviour Research and Therapy, 20*, pp. 594-604.

McBrien, J. and Weightman, J. (1980) 'The effect of room management procedures on engagement of profoundly handicapped children'. *Br. Jnl of Mental Subnormality, 26*, pp. 38-53.

Mittaug, D.E. and Wolfe, M.S. (1976) 'Employing task arrangements and verbal contingencies to promote verbalizations between retarded children'. *Jnl of Applied Behaviour Analysis, 9*, pp. 301-14.

Oliver, R.B. and Scott, T.L. (1981) 'Group versus individual training in establishing generalization of language skills with severely handicapped individuals'. *Mental Retardation, 19*, pp. 285-9.

Neigher, N.D. and Schulberg, H.C. (1982) 'Evaluating the outcome of human service programs ... A reassessment'. *Evaluation Review, 6*, pp. 731-52.

Ollendick, T.H., Dailey, D. and Shapiro, E.S. (1983) 'Vicarious reinforcement: expected and unexpected effects'. *Jnl of Applied Behaviour Analysis, 16*, pp. 485-91.

Ollendick, T.H. and Shapiro, E.S. (1984) 'An examination of vicarious reinforcement processes in children'. *Jnl of Experimental Child Psychology, 37*, pp. 78-91.

Ollendick, T.H., Shapiro, E.S. and Barrett, R.P. (1982) 'Effects of vicarious reinforcement in normal and severely disturbed children'. *Jnl of Consulting and Clinical Psychology, 50*, pp. 63-70.

Porterfield, J., Blunden, R. and Blewitt, E. (1980) 'Improving environments for profoundly handicapped adults using prompts and social attention to maintain high group engagement'. *Behaviour Modification, 4*, pp. 225-41.

Quilitch, H.R., Christopherson, E.R. and Risley, T.R. (1977) 'The evaluation of children's play materials'. *Jnl of Applied Behaviour Analysis, 10*, pp. 501-2.

Sewell, G. (1982) *Reshaping Remedial Education.* Croom Helm.

Slama, K.M. and Bannerman D.J. (1983) 'Implementing and maintaining a behavioural treatment system in an institutional setting'. *Analysis and Intervention in Developmental Disabilities, 3*, pp. 171-91.

Spangler, P.F. and Marshall, A.M. (1983) 'The unit play manager as facilitator of purposeful activities among institutionalized profoundly and severely retarded boys'. *Jnl of Applied Behaviour Analysis, 16*, pp. 345-9.

Storm, R. and Willis, J. (1978) 'Small groups training as an alternative to individual programmes for profoundly retarded persons'. *Am. Jnl of Mental Deficiency, 83*, pp. 283-8.

Sturmey, P. and Crisp, A. (1984a) 'Different methods of organizing training for mentally handicapped young adults'. *Intl Jnl of Rehabilitation Research, 7*, pp. 429-31.

Sturmey, P. and Crisp, A. (1984b) 'The effects of room management on stereotyped and self-injurious behaviour in six profoundly mentally handicapped young adults'. *Bull. of the Br. Psychological Society, 37*, p. A22.

Sturmey, P., Crisp, A. and Dearden, B. (1983) 'Room management with profoundly handicapped young adults by nurses in a hospital adult training unit'. *Mental Handicap, 11*, pp. 118-20.

Walter, A. (1978) 'Intervention strategies with a group of profoundly mentally handicapped adults'. Unpublished BPS diploma thesis: British Psychological Society, Leicester.

Westling, D.L., Ferrell, K. and Swenson, K. (1982) 'Intraclassroom comparison of two arrangements for teaching profoundly mentally retarded children'. *Am. Jnl. of Mental Deficiency, 86*, pp. 601-8.

Woods, P.A. and Cullen, C. (1983) 'Determinants of staff behaviour in long-term care'. *Behavioural Psychotherapy, 12*, pp. 4-17.

PART TWO: FACTORS INFLUENCING LEARNING AND DEVELOPMENT

There is an almost arbitrary division of aspects of development. The first four chapters in this section highlight the interrelationship between the major developmental achievements of the child. These chapters are not intended as a simple, rationalised checklist of skills but as a way of perceiving the relationship between curriculum areas. In this vein Sarah Sandow in Chapter 4 draws together the meeting points of the 'grand' theories of development. She views the development of personality and socialisation within the context of the child's overall development, and through the application of social learning theory shows how the personality of the child may have been shaped.

Chapter 5 looks at the place of cognition in the curriculum and the interrelationship with action and perception. Nigel Carden traces the key cognitive tasks of the child using the Uzgiris and Hunt scales as a basis and goes on to take a positive view of the pre-operational skills, relating then to curriculum demands.

The importance of cognitive development, and in particular means-end behaviour, is a theme which is continued by James Hogg in Chapter 6. He takes an information processing approach to motor development, and in so doing illustrates how teaching may be fragmented and non-functional if the child is not viewed as a whole. In this chapter we clearly see the value of input from psychology to developing effective teaching strategies.

Communication is a crucial factor in the child's success within society. In Chapter 7 Juliet Goldbart promotes the importance of teaching language within a communicative context. The chapter highlights the ways in which the rule systems of language and communication offer a variety of approaches to intervention.

85

Peter Evans argues that a deficit approach to learning is unhelpful, and that one can view the problems of learning within a developmental context, that is, in terms of how the child takes in and organises information. In Chapter 8 he proposes that a cognitive information processing approach is in keeping with a behaviourist approach in that 'behaviour modification techniques represent sound ways of achieving' a goal. He demonstrates the need for a memory system that is structured and organised but flexible. Because the child is not efficient in structuring knowledge it rests with the teacher to bridge the gap by organising the environment to require the child to make active interactions with it.

Chapter 9 outlines the nature of auditory and visual impairment and discusses their effect on the development of the child with severe learning difficulties. The authors question the implicit assumption that the fundamental problem is always one of mental handicap and point to the spiralling of dual handicaps without accurate assessment and efficient intervention.

4 THE DEVELOPMENT OF PERSONALITY AND EMOTION

Sarah Sandow

Introduction

This chapter will take a developmental approach to personality and social behaviour in the handicapped child. It will be argued that 'grand' theories such as those of Freud and Piaget are inappropriate in view of the combination of delay and deficit experienced by the child with severe learning difficulties, and that structural approaches to personality such as those of Eysenck are similarly unproductive, leading to a stereotyping of characteristics which does not help us to understand the child's behaviour. A more useful approach is found in social learning theory and the recognition that personality and social behaviour are part of a transactional process of development. This transaction is as much a part of the experience of the child with severe learning difficulties as it is for the 'normal' child.

Approaches to the Study of Personality

A major characteristic of twentieth-century psychology has been the formulation of 'grand theories' originated by important thinkers, often elaborated by their students and occasionally changed in the process. Science (and social science) has developed through a series of paradigm changes (Kuhn 1961), and each successive theory has attempted to 'explain' more comprehensively the phenomena under study. Even more than in the natural sciences, it is hard to fit all the subject-matter of psychology into one giant theoretical approach, but that has not stopped us trying to do so. In turn, Freud and the psychoanalysts, Binet and the psychometricians, Piaget and the cognitive theorists, gestaltists, behaviourists, psycholinguists, personality structuralists, have all been seized upon as major leaders of psychological thought. Because a principal concern of psychology has been the study of human development, it is in this area above all that the debate has centred.

The theories all have some things in common and have successively included those elements of each other theory which seemed useful. The most important of these elements have been: the idea of progression, where a child is described as passing through a series of age-related stages; the idea of the inheritance of relatively stable characteristics; and the idea of learning through interaction with the environment.

Age stage-related progression was adopted by Binet and the psychometricians, who found it useful to describe a child in terms which related the infant to the ten-year-old in stages, each conveniently one year long (Baer 1970). Binet devised tests which could be performed by the average seven-year-old, eight-year-old, etc., and by relating each child's performance to this, he could establish a 'mental age' which could be compared with his chronological age at that time. It was after Binet's death that others extended his idea by expressing the relation between mental and chronological age as a quotient of intelligence ('IQ') and linking this with another grand theory, that of stability of inherited human characteristics, suggested that this quotient was fixed and immutable. We can see how, while Binet was concerned merely with describing a child's performance at a specific time, these followers became interested in predicting it. This had a dramatic effect on their expectations of children's behaviour, particularly of the less able (Clarke and Clarke 1974). (The popularity of this adaptation at a time when universal education was in its infancy, was partly due to its social and political usefulness.)

Not all age-related stages were thought of as one year long. Freud, for example, proposed that the stages of emotional development succeeded each other at longer, but still relatively fixed and predictable, intervals, and Piaget, 'the giant of developmental psychology' (Hunt 1969), adopted a similar framework for cognitive development; a series of age-related stages characterised by certain interactions with the environment which in duration almost mirror those of Freud, while they are concerned with intellectual rather than with emotional development. It may be useful to look at these analyses side by side.

Crucial to Freud's approach is the idea that successful passage through each stage is a pre-requisite for the next and that failure to experience fully each stage and to negotiate the passage to the next

Figure 4.1: Framework for Development

Age	Freud	Piaget
0 — 2	Oral	Sensory — motor
2 — 4	Anal	Pre-operational
4 — 6	Phallic	
6 — 8		
8 — 10	Latent	Concrete operations
10 — 12		Formal operations
13 +	Genital	

will cause neuroticism in adult life. Piagetian theory also incorporates the principles of preparation and transfer; each stage depends
on the previous one, and there are elaborate explanations for the
process of transfer from one to another. It is not appropriate in this
chapter to explore this theory in detail; it is cited here merely as
another example of the way in which we are accustomed to
describe the passage through childhood as a series of interdependent stages which we must negotiate successfully in order to arrive
as successful adults; something we are taught as children will occur
at some pre-determined age — 18 or 21, or 24? In practice most of
us are aware that this is a concept we do not apply to ourselves. A
quick survey of adult opinion in any circle will reveal very different
views of when each person actually 'grew up', and 35, 40, or even
60 may be cited as the age of maturity.

As well as developmental approaches to the study of human
characteristics, there are also structural ones. Indeed the former
approach may implicitly accept the latter, suggesting that when we
'arrive' as adults we may fully express a particular structure of
personality which remains more or less stable for the rest of our
lives. Piaget and Freud proposed that we arrived there due to a
process of interaction with the environment; other theorists have
suggested that the environment has had little to do with it, and that
we mature according to the genetic blueprint laid down for us
before birth. Gesell took this view: 'Environmental factors
support, reflect and modify, but they do not generate the progres-

sions of development ... maturation is so fundamental that it cannot be transcended' (Gesell 1948; p. 8).

Studying one of the major developmental processes, Chomsky (1957) also proposed that linguistic development took place along pre-programmed lines which were largely unaffected by environmental factors. Lenneberg (1964; 1967) hypothesised a biological basis for language, which he saw as a specific example of the process of differentiation and categorisation which characterises the infant's response to his environment. Speech, like any other behaviour, will not occur in the absence of an 'environmental trigger'. This echoes the approach of the ethological school, who drew parallels with animal behaviour and saw the environment as instrumental in the release of certain behaviours at critical periods. These ideas accord well with Piaget's and Freud's age-related stages, although the actual role of the environment varies in different theoretical constructs.

One way in which we validate theories in psychology is to measure them against one another, and we tend to express ideas in a language already laid down by earlier theorists. Thus, for example, Chomsky's gradual unfolding of language from a genetically pre-programmed base was more comprehensible and acceptable in the light of the findings of ethologists about pre-programming in other developmental areas. Hess (1964) described a process in the early life of nidifugous birds (ducks, geese, etc.) when 'following' behaviour was elicited by a moving stimulus, usually the mother bird. This behaviour did not occur at any other developmental stage, but was triggered at a particular point in the fledgling's life. If the mother was not present, it could be elicted by some other moving object, such as a cardboard duck, a toy on the end of a piece of string, or even a human being walking past. Chomsky's ideas on the emergence of language by the environmental triggering of a pre-programmed genetic mechanism at a critical period seemed an obvious parallel. Similarly, we have seen how Freud's successive interdependent stages have made it easier to encompass Piagetian ideas. We have learned to see childhood as a process of travelling towards some adult goal of complete if not perfect personality formation, and this enabled us to accept the idea of standard types of personality which would be fully attained at maturity. Eysenck identified these through a process of factor analysis. This revealed two major dimensional axes, 'extravert-introvert' and 'stable-neurotic'. These were to become part of the language and Eysenck's maps of personality succeeded and echoed the medieval division of temperaments into choleric, phlegmatic, sanguine and melancholic (Eysenck 1981).

The 'Handicapped' Personality

Early attempts at classifying those with severe learning difficulties began with an acceptance of this kind of typology. Langdon-Down's 'ethnic classification of idiocy' deliberately linked intellectual and social characteristics with body-type, and superficial facial similarities with different races. The identification of 'mongoloid idiocy' is the only one of his definitions which has survived, but it was in fact one of a series in which (of course!) the Western European caucasian type was seen as the most superior. Down's work must be seen in the context of the ideas, then just published, of Morel, who proposed a theory of degeneracy in which mild general debility or 'immorality' in one generation was linked causatively with alcoholism, prostitution and tuberculosis in the next, leading inevitably to venereal disease, madness and idiocy in the third and fourth generation. (This theory may cause us to see the nineteenth-century best sellers, such as Jane Eyre, La Dame aux Camellias and East Lynne in a new light.) This, and the newly emerging study of heritability of Galton and others, encouraged the Victorians to regard the handicapped as a separate, probably degenerate, species, whose behaviour was governed by special rules and could be predicted in accordance with them.

Tredgold, in the 1949 edition of his standard work (Tredgold and Soddy 1949) concentrated entirely on such superficial aspects of the subnormal personality, observing either placidity and unresponsiveness or restlessness and excitability. Tredgold, in the tradition described above, regarded these 'abnormal reactions' as constitutional and therefore encouraged the establishment of stereotypes which can, unfortunately, still be encountered today. The two stereotypes are equally destructive. The placid type (which was seen to include most of those with Down's Syndrome) is supposed to be 'no trouble', 'easy going', a 'vegetable', a picture which suggests and encourages a lack of stimulation, social isolation and few learning opportunities. By contrast the 'hyperactive type' is regarded as being incapable of control and is therefore excluded from meaningful activity, merely being presented with objects of no value which can be destroyed without loss. Deviations of this stereotypic thinking can be observed in the descriptive 'theories' of different types of handicapped individuals, such as athetoid children who are reputed to be friendly and sociable, children with cerebellar lesions 'clinging', microcephalics quick, active, bird-like and distractible, and Down's Syndrome children happy, musical, easy going, affectionate and excellent mimics. The characterisation of autistic children (Creak 1951) in terms of symptom clustering is a particular example, and it is notable that advances in the education of these children have only been made since the abandonment of such stereotyping in favour of a developmental model.

The adoption of any static model of personality places the responsibility for learning squarely on the child, and absolves the teacher from failure. When the child as we observe him fails to conform to the 'normal' age-related development we associate with the rest of the population, it is easy to revert to the Victorian habit of seeing him as a member of a different species, following rules of behaviour which differ from those which apply to the 'normal' child to which, briefly, we now turn.

Socio-perceptual Development in the Young Child

Perceptually, the first 18 months of life have been described by Kagan (1971) as a 'critical period' in which four main experiences are paramount. While we may not (see above) accept the idea of 'critical periods' (and Kagan later modified his views) (Kagan and Klein 1973), the significance of the four perceptual phenomena described by him are acceptable as a foundation for later developments. During this period, the child acquires, according to Kagan; 1. perceptual representations of particular objects, and people; 2. feelings of attachment to those individuals; 3. conditional associations of pleasure and displeasure with those objects and people; 4. expectations of gratification in distress.

Taking these one at a time, we may consider what is involved in 1. Perception is more than sensation; it is less than comprehension. It may be visual, auditory or be mediated by taste, smell or touch. It involves the registration, recall and recognition of sensory data. It requires neurological organisation at a very sophisticated level; a level which is now known to be possessed by the normal neonate (Bower 1977; Bryant 1974; Salapatek and Kessen 1966; Salapatek 1975; Wertheimer 1961).

It is clear that 2., the development of attachment, is entirely dependent upon 1. We cannot become attached to something or someone we do not recognise, be it the smell of milk or the face of a caring person. If we do not develop this attachment, there is no opportunity to experience the pleasure of their presence and the displeasure of their absence often enough for the associations 3. to become conditioned. Finally, the expectation of regularities in perceptual and cognitive experience culminates in the certainty of comfort; the confidence that gratification in distress will be mediated by those individuals who have become conditioned positive reinforcers. The infant is thus developing a pattern of expectations and responses to his environment which in later life we term 'personality', and this pattern is dependent entirely on the efficiency of his perceptual processes.

During the period from 18 months to 3 years the developing perceptual sophistication is accompanied by increasing motor skill, which enables the child to encounter more objects, people and events with which to enlarge his understanding. The parallel acquisition of language enables him to question, label, demand and interpret these experiences. The child begins to understand that he can have an effect on his environment, and that his behaviour is more or less constrained by that environment. Socialisation involves three stages: first, the acquisition of desired behaviours and the suppression of undesired behaviours by a process of reinforcement and observation; second, the acquisition of desired values and suppression of undesired values; finally, the interpretation of these values as rules which at first are seen as external, specifically cited to sanction or forbid individual actions, and then become automatic codes of conduct which are followed without specific reference, eventually becoming the standards of behaviour we recognise as adults. This beginning of socialisation is dependent upon the earlier establishment of percepts, attachment to those percepts, conditioned pleasure and displeasure and the expectation of gratification (Kagan 1971).

At the same time, the child's emotional development becomes more sophisticated. In infancy, emotion, or 'affect' consists of more or less generalised excitement, but later the child is able to distinguish in himself happiness, joy, misery and anxiety. The degree to which this process is subject to uncertainty is illustrated by the ease with which the young child passes from pleasure to hysteria.

Socio-perceptual Development in the Handicapped Child

We may consider the handicapped child in the light of this discussion, attempting to pursue the same developmental path. However, his sometimes bizarre and illogical behaviour may be understood if we consider which of the processes may be incomplete. A child who is 'delayed' is often described in terms of the 'milestones' of development he is late in achieving. These are seen mainly as motoric and linguistic in character, but the underlying processes are significant. In the young normal child, myelination, the process whereby the insulating Schwann cells develop around the axons of individual neurones to facilitate neuronal transmission, is not complete until age 4; in the delayed child it may be later. Perceptual organisation and experiential storage are dependent upon an adequately-developing central nervous system. Not only may the child not walk or crawl until a late age, but the perceptual processes on which his relationship with the environment are built may also be delayed. A child who cannot form perceptual impressions both within and across modalities, cannot remember and recognise them.

An unrecognised stimulus is unlikely to lead to attachment. Without the continuity which is a necessary concomitant of attachment, the child's expectations of gratification will be haphazard in the extreme. As these perceptual skills underpin the socialisation process, this too is likely to be disrupted, and the child will acquire approved and inhibit disapproved behaviours inconsistently and unpredictably. The rules he devises for his behaviour (at a later chronological age than normal) will appear bizarre and perverse. This process is most clearly seen in the catastrophic reactions to trivial events, determination to maintain sameness in the environment and retreat into stereotypy characteristic of autistic children (Wing 1966). Many other children, not identified as autistic, also exhibit these behaviours, which are mysterious and frightening to parents. This often results in confused and inconsistent management which reinforces the child's determination to impose a series of inappropriate restructurings on the environment (Sameroff 1975).

A further complication is that 'delay' is rarely a complete description of a handicapped child. Specific deficits in the motor, language or sensory system add special problems. An immobile, cerebral palsied child who has retained the neonatal reflexes exemplifies this. The tonic-neck reflex actively prevents such a child from regarding what he holds in his hand. The 'startle' (Moro) reflex prevents him from responding to parental approaches, and his general immobility interferes with his ability to explore actively his environment. Held and Hein (1963) found that only active practice facilitated the adaptation of subjects to new perceptual experiences. There are obvious parallels in the experience of the visually or auditorily handicapped.

In the case of language, Eisenson (1972) has proposed that in order to comprehend, an individual must be able to:

1. receive stimuli presented in sequential order;
2. maintain a sequential impression of the message so that its components can be integrated into a pattern;
3. scan the pattern from within, from which to categorise the data and compare with an existing store;
4. respond differentially to perceptual impressions.

This analysis neatly parallels that given above in relation to Kagan's identification of early perceptual processing. The individual selects from an array of incoming stimuli those which are linguistically meaningful. He discriminates words and compares them with his existing store, checks the meaning and responds appropriately with an utterance of his own. The capacity to select and attend to the appropriate stimulus is the ability which Zeaman and House (1963) have shown to be deficient in adult subnormal subjects, and which has been identified as a figure-ground perceptual problem in autistic children by Hermelin and O'Connor (1974). That the child is not a passive recipient of the influences which shape him was suggested by Rutter, Birch, Thomas and Chess (1964) and reinforced by Sameroff and Chandler (1975). They proposed an active transactional relationship in which the child makes a positive contribution to his own development. Individual differences in responsiveness will not only affect what a child may extract from the environment, but what may be offered him. Apparent refusal of eye contact may be interpreted as rejection by adult caretakers, who will also respond negatively to the child's lack of response to embracing or holding. Many handicapped infants with metabolic disorders have an unpleasant smell which persists despite physical care; this also interferes with the environmental transaction, as does any facial abnormality.

When adults attempt the socialisation processes whereby the child learns to perform those behaviours which are approved and avoid those which are disapproved, the uncertainty of his perceptual experience will reveal itself in delay and inconsistency, which will often be compounded by physical incompetence. At a later age than usual, the child will attempt to feed himself and to use the lavatory, but his recognition of adult approval will be incomplete and intermittent. Control will therefore be achieved with great difficulty, and the frustrations this brings to the adult caretakers may well compound the difficulties. It is easy to see how difficult it will be for the child to establish rules of behaviour based on such apparent random successes.

This process may be seen in the light of a developmentally social learning theory Rotter (1954) proposed, that the crucial learning factor is the expectation of reinforcement contingent upon any activity. The occurrence of reinforcement leads to high expectancy, and conversely, the non-occurrence of reinforcement leads to low expectancy. The level of expectation, which is governed by the general and specific experiences of failure and success for the individual, leads directly to a corresponding level of activity. The way in which the handicapped child is able to achieve goals and meet the demands of his environment therefore depends on the amount of competence he has achieved, which in turn is related to the amount of approval or disapproval he receives from others, and to the degree to which the child is able to comprehend the activities or responses of others as approving or disapproving. Whereas the 'normal' child is able to comprehend and accept these reinforcements on a variable ratio reinforcement schedule, the handicapped child cannot cope with this low level of predictability and requires, in order to establish contingency, a schedule of continuous reinforcement for any desired activity at a level of intensity which is adapted to his limited perceptual ability. In the absence of such intensive, continuous reinforcement, at least at the outset, the handicapped child habitually experiences more failures and therefore has a low experience of goal attainment. Indeed he may fail to perceive any experience in terms of goal attainment. He therefore has a correspondingly low level of activity, less practice in any such activity and more failures. The circle of failure set is therefore established. Such life experiences serve to accentuate the performance deficits attributed in the first instance to developmental delay. There is constant interaction between the social experience of the child and his social and intellectual competence.

An inability to distinguish and categorise percepts together with a physical incapacity to encompass any meaningful interaction with the environment produces the series of failures in activity and communication described by Rotter. The child enters a cycle of failure and demotivation, and his parents, ill-prepared by their experience of 'normal' children and often, unfortunately, by the expectations and comments of professionals ('he'll be a bit slow') respond to such failures with uncertainty and inconsistency. Expecting the child to develop normally, though slowly, they find, instead, inexplicable gaps in progress, unpredictable behaviour, violent expressions of emotion and absolute refusals to co-operate. The parents' reactions may be expected to be confused and inconsistent, and management haphazard. Many retreat into totally indulgent behaviour and see their major, or only, function as parents as a purely protective one; protective both from dangers outside the child and from catastrophes they see as arising within him, such as fits, or the tantrums which are often seen as inevitable precursors of fits. (Events which have once preceded a fit are likely to be regarded, superstitiously, as definite indicators.) The parents of handicapped children are therefore handicapped themselves by false expectations and inadequate understanding of their child's development, anxiety for his welfare, and their continued grief and distress at the existence of his handicap. These factors in turn lead to abnormally inconsistent management, often conducted on the basis of inaccurate interpretations of the child's behaviour. 'If he really wanted to, he'd do it. He did it yesterday.'

The child, with his limited capacity to respond, with sensory and motor systems unable to help him to understand his surroundings, therefore imposes on his world an organisation which is inadequate and often inappropriate. He may develop a dependency on certain familiar objects, events or activities, such as rocking or shaking, catastrophic reactions to unfamiliar persons or events, refusal to try new activities, and extreme dependence on one person. The eventual results are failures in the secondary fields of self-help, socialisation and communication. Occupation is at a primitive level, and objects in the environment may be used to support ritualistic comfort activities, without any regard to their real function, but with manipulative skill which appears paradoxical, such as spinning or twiddling objects. Parents, reacting to this with more anxiety, uncertainty and distress, reinforce the cycle of inappropriate functioning. Behaviour patterns become set which may take many years to disestablish, and which actively interfere with the child's learning, and with the formation of relationships.

Grand Theories are Inappropriate

The wide variety of behaviour described suggests that it may be unproductive to look at the development of personality in the child with SLD in terms of any broad theory. Such theories give us expectations of the child's behaviour which cannot be fulfilled and cause us to reject as bizarre or 'mad' any behaviour which cannot be predicted. However, as the child with SLD is attempting, like any other, to make sense of his world, there is an inner logic to his behaviour. The idea of 'fixations' at a certain stage, common to Freud, Piaget, and some linguistic and ethological theorists, clearly does not fit the confused and uneven development as described. Rather we should think of the child completing developmental 'tasks' in some areas but not necessarily matching them in others. To suggest that extreme fear and distress at separation from a caretaker are attributable to bond disruption at a sophisticated level (Bowlby 1951) is less useful than to recognise with Rutter (1972) that the bonds may be imperfectly formed in the first place, or that they may still be in the process of formation. The child may be railing, not against separation from a 'loved' one, but against the disorganisation of a still only partly formed system of expectations. 'The baby must, of necessity, develop a certain level of communicational ability in order to form the kind of attachment evidenced by stranger fear and separation' (Bower 1977: p. 59).

Upon these expectations, the child builds his social behaviour, learning to discriminate between the approved and disapproved, and generalising these behaviours to new situations. The choices he makes condition the adult response, and lead to the characterisation which we call personality. The description of this in terms of 'placidity', 'aggressiveness', 'withdrawal', 'extraversion' is merely scratching the surface. We will not begin to understand the personality of the handicapped child until we recognise that the same rules apply as to the so-called 'normal' child. All are attempting to make sense of their environment and derive from their observations and experiences the rules of behaviour by which they operate within it (Kagan 1971). In time, the rules become internalised as 'standards' and generate that pattern of responses which we call 'personality'. In describing a personality, we operate on the basis of predicting an individual's responses; the more difficult the prediction, the more we say the person is 'complex' (a term which, when applied to the 'normal' individual is often complimentary!) For the handicapped child the process of developing rules is lengthened through delay and specific deficit, and many may not fully reach the stage of organising these rules into standards and internalising them. Personality, in these cases is seen not as 'complex' but as disorganised, and we fall back on typological descriptions which are more comforting than useful. The handicapped child is not a separate species. In him we see aspects of our own development 'writ large', and we can understand him only in terms of this development.

References

Baer, D.M. (1970) 'An age-irrelevant concept of development'. *Merrill-Palmer Quarterly of Behaviour and Development, 11*, pp. 238-45.

Bower, T.R.G. (1977) *A Primer of Infant Development.* Freeman.

Bowlby, J. (1951) *Maternal Care and Mental Health.* World Health Organization.

Bryant, P. (1974) *Perception and Understanding in Young Children.* Methuen.

Chomsky, N. (1957) *Syntactic Structures.* Mouton.

Clarke, A.B.D. and Clarke, A.M. (1974) 'The changing concept of intelligence: a selective historical review', in A.M. Clarke and A.D.B. Clarke (eds.). *Mental Deficiency: the changing outlook.* Methuen.

Creak, M. (1951) 'Schizophrenic Syndrome of Childhood'. *Cerebral Palsy Bull., 3*, pp. 501-8.

Eisenson, J. (1972) *Aphasia in Children.* Harper and Row.

Eysenck, H.J. (1981) *A Model for Personality.* Springer-Verlag.

Gesell, A. (1948) *Studies in Child Development.* Harper Brothers.

Held, R. and Hein, A. (1963) 'Movement produced stimulation in the development of visually guided behaviour'. *Jnl of Comparative and Physiological Psychology. 56*, pp. 872-6.

Hermelin, B. and O'Connor, N. (1974) 'Specific Deficits and Coding Strategies', in A.M. Clarke and A.D.B. Clarke (eds.). *Mental Deficiency: the changing outlook.* Methuen.

Hess, E.H. (1964) 'Imprinting in birds'. *Science, 146*, pp. 1128-39.

Hunt, J.Mc.V. (1969) 'The giant of developmental psychology', in J.H. Flavell and D. Elland (eds.). *Studies in Cognitive Development.* Oxford University Press.

Kagan, J. (1971) *Personality Development.* Harcourt Brace Jovanovich.

Kagan, J. and Klein, R.E. (1973) 'Cross cultural perspectives in early development'. *Am. Psychologist, 28*, pp. 947-61.

Kuhn, T.S. (1961) *The Structure of Scientific Revolutions.* University of Chicago Press.

Langdon-Down, J. (1866) 'Observation on an ethnic classification of idiocy'. *London Hospital Reports, 3*, pp. 259-62.

Lenneberg, E.H. (1964) 'A biological perspective of language', in E.H. Lenneberg (ed.). *New Directions in the Study of Language.* MIT Press.

Lenneberg, E.H. (1967) *Biological Foundations of Language.* Wiley.

Rotter, J.B. (1954) *Social Learning and Clinical Psychology.* Prentice Hall.

Rutter, M. (1972) *Maternal Deprivation Reassessed.* Penguin.

Rutter, M., Birch, H.G., Thomas, A. and Chess (1964) 'Temperamental characteristics in infancy and the later development of behaviour disorders'. *Br. Jnl of Psychiatry, 110,* pp. 651-61.

Sameroff, A. (1975) 'Early influences on development: fact or fancy?' *Merrill-Palmer Quarterly of Behaviour and Development, 21,* pp. 267-94.

Sameroff, A.J. and Chandler, M.J. (1975) 'Reproductive risk and the continuum of caretaking casualty', in F.D. Horowitz, M. Hetherington, S. Scarr-Salapatek and G. Siegel (eds.). *Review of Child Development Research 4.* University of Chicago Press.

Salapatek, P. (1975) 'Pattern perception in early infancy', in L.B. Cohen and P. Salapatek (eds.). *Infant Perception: from sensation to cognition,* Vol. 1. Academic Press.

Salapatek P. and Kessen, W. (1966) 'Visual scanning of triangles by the human newborn'. *Jnl of Experimental Child Psychology, 3,* pp. 113-22.

Tredgold, R.F. and Soddy, K. (1949) *A Textbook of Mental Deficiency.* Balliere, Tindall and Cox.

Wertheimer, M. (1961) 'Psychomotion co-ordination of auditory and visual space at birth'. *Science, 134,* p. 1692.

Wing, J.K. (1966) *Early Childhood Autism.* Pergamon.

Zeaman, D. and House, B.J. (1963) 'The role of attention in retardate discrimination learning', in N.R. Ellis (ed.). *Handbook of Mental Deficiency.* McGraw Hill.

5 THE DEVELOPMENT OF COGNITION AND PERCEPTION

Nigel Carden

Introduction

The concern of this chapter is the development of the ability to
make use of our perceptions of the world so that we can behave in
a flexible and, usually, appropriate manner, adapting to a wide
variety of situations. All life forms have some capacity to respond
to features of the environment, but humans have exceptionally
powerful abilities to analyse and synthesise information, relating it
to past experience. If these abilities fail to develop normally, then a
person's repertoire of behaviours will be limited, and the chances
of behaviour being appropriate in given circumstances will be
greatly reduced. Cognition is, therefore, of central interest to any
educator of children with severe learning difficulties.

Cognition is often seen as the unobservable process intervening
between perception and action. There may be some limited value
in this simple model, but to achieve any depth of understanding of
human development we must recognise that perception, cognition
and action are linked so intimately that the development of each
one depends on the development of the others.

The greatest contribution to the understanding of cognitive
development comes from the work of Jean Piaget, his Genevan
associates and the many investigators who have chosen to work
within the Piagetian framework. No apologies are offered, therefore, for the prominence given to Piaget's approach in this chapter.
The intention is not, however, to offer a summary of Piagetian
theory. For the reader who would like such a summary there is a
very clear chapter, which introduces the theory, in Oates and
Floyd (1976). Slightly fuller accounts are easily found, e.g. Ault
(1977) and Brearley and Hitchfield (1966). Returning to the
current chapter, what is presented is a perspective on cognition,
relevant to the educational needs of children with severe learning
difficulties, which rests largely on Piagetian principles. The first
task is to establish the place of cognition in the curriculum for
children with severe learning difficulties. Next, the mechanisms of

perception will be described, emphasising the actively selective nature of the perceptual processes. The relationships between perception, cognition and action will be discussed. Special consideration will be given to the first two periods of development, which are termed, for reasons which will be made clearer, 'sensorimotor' and 'pre-operational'. While points of relevance to the understanding of severe learning difficulties will be discussed throughout the chapter, the concluding section will cover some explicit suggestions about the type of learning environment in which pupils might improve their cognitive skills.

Why is Cognition Important?

According to a recently reported survey (Carden and Robson 1985), the main aim of teachers working with mentally handicapped children is to foster independence. In other words, teachers want their pupils to be capable of doing 'real' things in the 'real' world. The mention of 'cognition' as a curriculum area might seem initially to run counter to this utilitarian goal. Images of cognitive work might centre on materials such as logic blocks, sorted first by size, then by colour, then by shape, and finally by thickness. If there was to be a useful end point it would be seen as the manipulation of numbers, translating into social competence with money.

The account of cognition in this chapter will hopefully dispel such images. In the first place our discussion will extend from the earliest developmental levels, where there is strong empirical evidence (Kahn 1975), to support Piaget's contention that a specific level of cognitive development is a minimum pre-requisite for the emergence of expressive language. Secondly, with regard to subsequent phases of development, it is possible to point to several aspects of cognition which seem to underpin a whole variety of practical self-help skills. Apart from a small study linking relational and feeding skills (Kitzinger 1980), relevant, empirical evidence for the cognitive foundations of self-help skills is limited. Meanwhile, the connections are speculative, but a little armchair research (reported in more detail in Carden 1983) shows that there is a reasonable consensus on what aspects of cognition are thought to underpin the learning of skills needed to cope with everyday life. Whelan and Speake (1979) give a list of 55 abilities needed in order to cope with moderate support.

Cohen and Gross (1979) split cognition into 31 'pre-math sub-areas'. A cognition/coping matrix was constructed using these two sets of elements. Copies of the matrix were independently marked by the author and a small group of other professionals involved in teaching and research with mentally handicapped people. Marked cells of the matrix indicated an assumed link between cognitive areas and coping skills. Summing the number of marks in each cell showed a clearly non-random distribution, so each of the cells marked by a majority of the panel was taken to indicate an agreed relationship between cognition and coping skills. It was possible to suggest a curriculum which focused on the aspects of cognition thought to be relevant to a number of self-help skills. This curriculum will be referred to again later in this chapter.

If cognitive abilities do underpin language and other skills which have to be acquired for independent living, then this should satisfy the teachers who favour a functional goal for education. But this should not be the only reason for directly encouraging the cognitive development of children with severe learning difficulties. Cognition, from the earliest levels, is synonymous with understanding the world around us, and mentally handicapped people certainly need to learn to appreciate the properties of objects and the relationships between events. One aspect of cognition concerns problem-solving: effective problem-solving often involves being able to imagine a situation from more than one viewpoint, knowing that other people have a different perception of events. The realisation that undoing or reversing an action restores the original state of affairs lies at the heart of logical, adult cognitive activity, but this is a level, according to Woodward (1961) which is not generally reached by people with mental handicap. In Piagetian terms, most mentally handicapped people function within the first two periods, sensorimotor and pre-operational. The sensorimotor period, for normally developing children, typically extends from birth to two years or a little less. The pre-operational period follows, from two to around seven years of age.

Piaget sees the stages within these broad periods of development as stepping stones on the journey towards the more sophisticated cognitive structures of adolescence and adulthood, when abstract operations or manipulations of data can be performed. Hence, the names: 'sensorimotor' signifying that the intelligent behaviour of the infant is very directly linked to perception and action, and 'pre-operational', stressing that facility with a variety of operations has yet to be achieved. Particularly in discussing the pre-operational period, a more positive attitude might be more appropriate to our purposes, given that children with severe learning difficulties are not necessarily passing through these periods on the way to something more advanced. The ways of thinking and levels of understanding typical of the early periods of cognitive development may be the intellectual tools which the child is going to have to use for some time to come.

Perceptual Mechanisms

In the oversimplified perception — cognition — action model mentioned above, the role of perception is the passive gathering of information, to be grist to the cognitive mill. A major reason for describing the model as oversimplified is that it neglects the element of selectivity inherent in the perceptual process. Perceptual mechanisms do not pick up all the information which would be needed for a full description of any situation. Firstly, perception is passively selective in that it is tuned only to certain modalities and ranges. For instance, the human visual system senses only a small part of the electromagnetic spectrum (350-750 millimicrons). Sound is another very important modality. Transmitted variations in air pressure carry important clues as to events in the world around us, and sound is the primary channel for interpersonal communication. Limitations exist compared to other species; dogs and bats, for example, can make use of much higher frequencies.

As well as limitations within modalities, there are some sources of information which we cannot perceive directly at all. We have sense organs which pick up light, sound, heat, pressure and chemical stimulation, as well as positional and movement feedback from our own bodies, but we need a compass to interpret magnetic fields. We have to translate such information into visual terms, even though it is thought that migrating birds are directly sensitive to magnetic fields and use this in navigation. There are other examples of extensions of perceptual capacities beyond normal limits: Vickie, a young blind girl, has learned to interpret sonar signals as a partial substitute for vision to guide such behaviours as stair climbing (Bower 1984). With regard to the passive selectivity of perception, unless a child with severe learning difficulties has a specific sensory deficit, then he or she suffers only the same limitations as the rest of us.

The perceptual problems commonly associated with severe learning difficulties are more likely to arise in the mechanisms for active selectivity. Active selectivity centres round a constant monitoring of perceptual input, particularly auditory and visual. This monitoring is best understood as an economical, low-level processing of a wide range of input, which can be switched almost instantly to more detailed investigation of sharply defined features of the total available input. This switching is effected whenever the monitoring process detects potentially valuable signals. The periphery of the visual field, to give one example, provides limited resolution, but a sudden movement is readily detected and the gaze can be shifted so that the image of the moving object falls on a more sensitive part of the retina, enabling more detailed information to be extracted.

In many species the scanning for potentially important features is handled by cells actually in the retina. Humans, along with cats and monkeys, are exceptional in carrying out this process of monitoring input and directing of attention in the visual cortex, i.e. within the brain itself. Michael (1972) discusses the evidence for the location and nature of the mechanisms involved, including the classic studies of Hubel and Wiesel (1963) which show that, in kittens, the development of the nerve cells involved depends on the active movement of the young animal within its environment. Animal experiments by Held and Hein (1963) also underline the importance of active exploration in stimulating perceptual development; and work on adults learning to adapt to experimental perceptual distortions (with prismatic spectacles) shows that active, rather than passive, movement is vital in learning to cope with changed perceptions.

Another example of active selection is the well known 'cocktail party' skill, whereby one conversation is followed in detail, but if a familiar name is overheard, attention is shifted to another speaker. Broadbent (1958) offers a thorough review of traditional psychological research on human information-processing skills, including studies on selective listening.

Although attention is discussed elsewhere in this book in more detail, (see Chapter 8), it has been mentioned here because it is important to conceive of perception as an active, selective and self-regulating process. Cognition is then seen as an extension of the same process, rather than a distinct mechanism which takes over where perception leaves off. In particular, the Piagetian theory, to be discussed in the next section of this chapter, sees intelligent behaviour in the youngest children as arising from the co-ordination of perception and action, hence the term 'sensori-motor'.

The realisation that the selection of perceptual input involves a complex set of mechanisms should be accompanied by a suspicion that such mechanisms could be vulnerable to trauma. This suspicion must be strengthened by the knowledge that, for vision at least, the control is centralised in the brain. If, for whatever reason, a person has damage to, or structural abnormality of the brain, then any or all of the functions of the brain may be impaired. Thus, control of perception is at risk, along with cognitive, linguistic and motor functions. The suggestion that active exploration is needed for the development of parts of the perceptual systems also has important and worrying implications for children whose capacity for self-directed movement is limited. Special educators, therefore, have a challenging task in finding ways to structure the learning environment so that the youngest and most profoundly handi-capped children are allowed to develop the capacity to acquire relevant perceptions from their surroundings.

Piaget: A Constructional Approach to Cognitive Development

According to Piaget, an infant is not born with an appreciation of the independent existence of objects, nor an understanding that an action on one object can have an effect on other objects. Piaget does not suggest that our understanding of the world simply emerges as we grow older: rather he states that each child has to construct reality for itself. This is true of the most basic structures, such as object permanence and simple causality, and equally true of more sophisticated skills such as conservation. Development at all stages depends on the exercise of existing abilities. If the child is not active in trying out its current ways of understanding the world, then that understanding will not grow.

Leaving Piaget's own views aside for the moment, if we look at the difference between the abilities of a mature adult and the abilities of an infant of a few days or weeks, then it is tempting to say that the adult has more and better abilities. This overlooks the extent to which a baby is adapted to its biological and social position as a small and inexperienced human being. Not only is the infant equipped to survive in a community which includes a majority of adults, but, returning to Piaget, it is also poised to discover, personally, how to make sense of the world.

Despite the many differences in children's early experiences within and across cultures, Piagetian theory holds that the order in which concepts and strategies are acquired is highly consistent. Piaget assumes that this consistency is found because the order of development reflects a logical hierarchy. Those whose interest in the Piagetian literature goes beyond the search for a framework to guide educational intervention will discover something called 'genetic epistemology'. Genetic epistemology, which often seems to be Piaget's ultimate concern, hinges on the relationship between empirical studies of cognitive development and the philosophical notion of the abstract structure of knowledge. The complexities of Piaget's own writings on this topic, and the counter-arguments put by others (e.g. Brainerd 1973) need not detract from the utility of Piaget's constructional theory of development. The theory is useful for two reasons. Firstly, it gives an insight into the learning process, which can guide the educator in structuring the child's environment to foster cognitive growth. Secondly, the theory offers descriptions of behaviours which are held to develop in sequence, so this can be of value in curriculum planning and assessment.

It may be helpful, before moving on to a consideration of particular periods of development, to discuss some of the key words in Piagetian theory and to give a very brief overview of the course of cognitive development from birth to adulthood.

Key Words in the Piagetian Vocabulary

A 'schema' is a pattern of behaviour which arises initially on a specific situation but is then generalised and repeated. For example, a newborn baby has a sucking schema, applied initially to mother's nipples, but quickly extended to thumbs, rattles and squeaky toys. Through this extended application without modification, a range of objects are said to be 'assimilated' to the schema. Eventually the baby might discover that in moving a rattle to its mouth to suck, the rattle makes a noise and a rudimentary shaking schema comes into being. The modification of an existing schema or the appearance of a new one more appropriate to a new object or situation is called 'accommodation'.

'Equilibriation', the alternating and balancing of assimilation and accommodation, is central to Piaget's view of development. Achievement of biological equilibrium is a given property of all living organisms, and Piaget extends this notion to say that the human organism has a similar intrinsic tendency to achieve psychological equilibrium. In other words, in any situations where existing schemas can be applied to objects or events, then the existing schemas will either assimilate or be prompted to accommodate. Equilibriation, the search for balance between assimilation and accommodation, fuels development so long as there is opportunity to apply existing schemas at a level where they sometimes assimilate and sometimes accommodate, i.e. so long as there is appropriate 'environmental' stimulation. Given this appropriate stimulation, the generalisation of existing schemas and the development of new ones will ensure that the child shows increasing sophistication and flexibility in its behaviour.

Development, therefore, consists of a series of small steps as assimilation and accommodation maintain their equilibrium. Piaget does not accept that these steps add up to make a continuous smooth curve of development. Rather, he claims that there are discrete 'stages' marked by characteristic ways of dealing with specific types of perceptual and cognitive problems. The stages cover four major 'periods' of development, each new period starting with a dramatic shift in the ability to function symbolically, that is, to mentally represent and manipulate objects and events. When a child moves into a new stage, or even into the next period of development, existing schemas are not lost. All schemas remain in the cognitive repertoire and can still be used even after layers of more advanced schemas have been added. However, it is the exercise of the most recently acquired schemas which is part of the process of equilibriation.

Throughout the earlier stages of development, the child is said to be 'egocentric'. At first the egocentricity is absolute: Piaget's view of the infant at a few weeks old is that there is little differentiation between self, surrounding objects and other people. This extreme degree of egocentricity quickly fades, but even at the age of six or seven years, a child might still be described as egocentric, even though he or she has long been recognising the independent existence of objects and attributing causality to other people. The concept of egocentrism at this stage refers to the difficulty of the child in accepting the validity of alternative perceptions of a situation, and the related tendency to assume that his or her own view is shared by everyone else. Egocentrism can, of course, be manifested at later stages, but in the last two periods (from about seven years of age in the normally developing child) it is a tendency which has little overall impact on the course of development, whereas in the earlier years it is a major constraint on learning.

Piaget, as an academic, naturally saw the process of development as taking us from naive infancy right through to formal logic and abstract philosophical speculation. Not everyone gets that far though, and mentally handicapped adults in particular still seem to be functioning at earlier stages of development. One needs to be aware of a cultural bias inherent in Piaget's theory. What we regard as the ultimate cognitive achievements are not equally relevant in all cultures, and what we might regard, falling into ethnocentricity, as less advanced schemas, may be perfectly appropriate to situations beyond our own experience.

The Sequence of Development

Given the essential vocabulary, the broad outline of cognitive development can now be sketched. Subsequent sections fill in this outline a little for the first two periods but the later periods remain largely outside the scope of this chapter. Piaget himself draws analogies between different stages of development throughout his writings. He also tends to concentrate on one particular aspect of development in any one of his books, though with much cross-referencing. The sheer volume of his output, which spans half a century, is bewildering, and his original prose is highly descriptive but extremely complex. Summarising the periods of development is, therefore, a difficult task and it is with reluctance that a table is presented, in an attempt to span all four periods in an economical manner (see Figure 5.1). A table offers only a snapshot of a very intricate, almost organic, theory. The format is adopted from Wadsworth (1984) although the content represents the present author's own interpretation of a wide variety of Piagetian writings.

Questioning and Qualifying Piaget's Theory

Piaget is not alone in contributing to our understanding of children's cognitive development. Other psychologists have produced findings which make it clear that Piagetian theory does not represent an ultimate truth. However, it is fair to say that most of what is known about children's behaviour when faced with cogni-

Figure 5 1: Summary of the Stages of Cognitive Development

STAGE (typical ages given in brackets)	ACHIEVEMENTS
Sensorimotor period (0-2 years)	The infant gradually comes to recognise that objects and other people have an existence independent of its own self. Basic ideas of causality develop, and by the end of this period objects and events can be mentally represented. There is still a very direct link between perception and action.

The Sensorimotor period is divided into six sub-stages

Stage I (0-1 month)	Reflexive schemas
Stage II (1-4 months)	'Primary circular reactions', i.e. repetition of schemas involving own body, such as thumb sucking.
Stage III (4-8 months)	'Secondary circular reactions', i.e. repetition of schemas which chance to produce interesting results; such as hitting a mobile. Particular progress in eye-hand co-ordination.
Stage IV (8-12 months)	Co-ordination of schemas and application to new situations, allowing some simple problems to be solved. Object concept emerges. Direct imitation common: Behaviour appears intentional, and some appreciation of temporal sequences can be inferred.
Stage V (12-18 months)	'Tertiary circular reactions', i.e. experimental use of schemas just to discover what happens. Problems are solved through active exploration. Object concept sufficiently developed to allow child to predict where an object will be after transfer via several containers.
Stage VI (18-24 months)	Causal relations begin to be appreciated, particularly when people are involved. Internal symbolic representation. Systematic use of language. Deferred imitation.
Pre-operational period (2-7 years)	Still tends to be tied to own immediate perceptions, but relations with peers and complex language develop rapidly. The child can reason, but not always consistently. By the end of this period the child is approaching 'conservation', i.e.

	just beginning to recognise that some important properties of materials (e.g. number, volume) stay unchanged regardless of changes in presentation.
Concrete Operational Period (7-11 years)	Capable of reasoning and logical thought, although largely tied to the here and now. Egocentricity markedly declined, so that a situation can be imagined from several viewpoints. Conservation of number, volume and weight firmly established. Appreciates transitive relations e.g. Sue is older than John, John is older than Debbie, therefore Sue is older than Debbie. Reversibility, in the understanding that undoing certain operations restores the original state exactly, is a valuable cognitive strategy.
Formal Operational Period (11 years onwards)	Abstract logical reasoning. Capacity for 'scientific thinking'.

tive and perceptual problems can be considered in Piagetian terms. Given that this is the case, and given that the purpose of this chapter is to give a framework which is helpful to educators of children with severe learning difficulties, only a few brief paragraphs will be devoted to alternative and additional explanatory concepts.

Bruner and his associates (Bruner, 1966; Bruner (ed.) 1973) give interpretations which, in general terms, sit comfortably alongside the Piagetian position, albeit using a different vocabulary. Two notions which are emphasised more strongly by Bruner are worthy of mention. The first is 'learning set', i.e. the tendency to learn more readily that which we have been primed to learn. Bruner (1973) describes how people can be helped to solve problems by being given pointers to the kind of rules they should seek to apply. Interestingly, Bruner makes it clear that learning set can be either a help or a hindrance, and those of us working with children with severe learning difficulties should take care that our pupils do not 'get stuck' on giving the same kind of responses, regardless of the teaching situations we create.

Bruner also emphasises the importance of social influences in learning. Piaget tends to concentrate more on the influences in the opposite direction, that is on the impact of cognition on socialisation and language, than on how or what other people do and say can shape cognitive growth.

Donaldson (1978) has found several situations where children can perform better than Piagetian theory would predict. She suggests that Piaget's findings often reflect, not simply the development of cognitive structures or thinking strategies, but the inability to 'disembed' thinking from the immediate perceptual content. She shows that children can acquire and apply cognitive structures in natural and meaningful situations long before the same structures can be applied in the more formal and adult-orientated situations common in the Piagetian tradition. This is certainly a point we should take very seriously as educators of children with severe learning difficulties; and we should remember to keep our teaching contexts relevant to our pupils' interests.

The ingenious studies of Bower (1977a; 1977b) raise some more serious questions for the Piagetian approach, although Bower and Paterson (1972) openly acknowledge that Piaget has been 'amplified and extended, but not materially changed'. The implication of Bower's work is that Piaget has under-estimated the sophistication of the ways in which very young babies understand the world. This calls into question the extent to which reality has to be constructed by the child in the sense that Piaget assumes. It could be that a large measure of understanding is built in, but even if this is the case, the normally developing child still has to learn the practical application of this understanding. The mentally handicapped infant may, however, have a greater task in that he or she may be very poorly equipped to set out on the developmental journey. Intervention would be needed to teach even the skills which other children are born with. The next section should provide a basis for intervention at the earliest stages.

The Sensorimotor Period

This phase of infant development is of particular interest to those who are working with the most profoundly handicapped people, often to be found in 'special needs' or 'special care' units. Teachers of younger children with less severe difficulties will also find that many of their pupils have not yet developed the understanding of the world through their own perceptions and actions in the way that non-handicapped two-year-old children have mastered such an understanding. In either case, the educator needs to appreciate the complexities of the normal developmental sequence and to have a theoretical base for programme planning. Uzgiris and Hunt (1975) describe six areas of development within the sensorimotor period, giving situations in which critical actions can be elicited to determine a child's current level. Kahn (1976) has demonstrated the utility of the Uzgiris and Hunt scales for work with mentally handicapped children.

While Uzgiris and Hunt offer an assessment procedure, they go much further by describing in detail the Piagetian theory which was the starting point for the construction of the scales. The six scales produced by Uzgiris and Hunt will be outlined below, but first some comment will be made on three other assessments appropriate to children at the earliest stages of development. Foxen (1975) adapted Uzgiris and Hunt's 'object schemes' scale to make a quick and simple routine for probing the range of behaviours shown with a variety of common objects. Coupe and Levy (1985) have developed a more detailed and slightly more flexible procedure for the same purpose. In both cases a score sheet is completed through an informal play-based assessment, and the educational implications of a completed score sheet are usually self-evident: the educator is in a clearer position to find new objects which will prompt the child to react with a slightly changed pattern of behaviour, that is, to prompt accommodation and the appearance of a new schema.

Aspects of cognitive and perceptual functioning at a developmentally young level can also be assessed via the Behaviour Assessment Battery (BAB) constructed by Kiernan and Jones (1982). The foundations of the BAB are more eclectic than the other procedures discussed and it covers similar areas including tracking, search strategies and cause and effect learning.

Uzgiris and Hunt: Six Scales for Assessment in Infancy

Uzgiris and Hunt (1975) describe the revision of their assessment instrument, provide a concise Piagetian account of development and begin to translate this account into descriptions of observable behaviours. Uzgiris and Hunt give age norms for these behaviours with some reluctance. Ages are given here as pegs on which to hang a description of the developmental sequences.

Scale I: The Development of Visual Pursuit and the Permanence of Objects. A baby at one month is beginning to construct momentarily, through perception, an object by following it visually. At two months central processes can briefly construct an object when it is perceptually absent, so that the glance lingers at the point where a moving object passes out of sight. Not until four to five months does the infant search for a partially covered object, indicating mental construction of a whole based on perception of a part. Between five and eight months the organisation of actions becomes rather more differentiated from the perceptual construction of objects, evidenced by the tendency to return the gaze to the start of an object's trajectory if the object disappears. Around seven months the construction of the object is becoming separated from the actions previously associated with that object, sufficiently separated for the object to be found when completely covered. The object can be found even when other potential hiding places are in view, for example, if the infant watches the object being hidden behind one of two or three screens.

At nine or ten months greater persistence in searching, e.g. removal of a number of super-imposed screens, shows the object construction to be well established. Between eleven and 17 months increasing persistence and differentiation of the central processes pertaining to the object concept is implied by the child's ability to find an object in more difficult circumstances. At this stage, the child can follow a series of invisible displacements, i.e. transfers from one place to another inside a container. By 22 months a perfectly rational search strategy is shown by the infant who starts his or her search in the last place the object might have been left, then, if unsuccessful here, retraces the path of the container until the object is located.

Scale II: The Development of Means for Obtaining Desired Environmental Events.   At two months handwatching shows the schemas[1] involving hand and eye are co-ordinated in a very rudimentary differentiation of means and ends. A month later, clearer differentiation is shown by repetition of behaviour which produces interesting results, e.g. kicking at a toy. Between three and four months grasping a toy emerges as a 'scheme as a means for multiple ends': at first the hand and toy must both be in view, but at four months only the toy needs to be visible. At eight months an important step forward is made in anticipating the need to complete one scheme before executing another, e.g. dropping one object before reaching for another. Anticipation represents some beginning of a concept of time and is also shown at this age by the exploitation of perceived relationships between objects as a way to achieve desired ends. An example of this type of response is pulling at a support to obtain an object positioned on the support. By nine months the infant makes general use of common behaviour patterns to achieve a variety of ends, in particular by moving to retrieve objects in play.

At ten months increased discrimination is shown as the exploitation of relationships between objects, so that if an object does not rest directly on a support, the infant does not expect to obtain the object by pulling the support.

Between twelve and 18 months progress in anticipatory construction of means for given ends occurs. At twelve months this is shown by pulling a string tied to an object to obtain the object, when it is in view on a horizontal surface. At 13 months the child will pull vertically on a string to obtain a hidden object, and by 18 months uses a stick as an extension of the body to obtain a toy out of reach. By 20 months foresight is shown in problem solving, for example, by anticipating that a narrow tall container is likely to fall during the act of putting a long necklace in it, and consequently the infant holds the container with one hand before starting to insert the necklace. At 22 months some internal representation of both means and end is implied by anticipation of the likelihood of success or failure; as a specific example, the child does not attempt to stack a specially prepared solid ring onto a peg, but leaves the trick ring aside and stacks only the genuine rings.

Scale III: The Development of Imitation (Vocal and Gestural).
1. Vocal imitation: at one month the differentiation of the vocalising schema is implied, with the observation of 'cooing' as well as cries of distress. The baby seems to recognise its own sounds and smiles or increases mouth movements on hearing itself. At three months the baby recognises familiar speech sounds, similar to those heard in its own vocalisations, and attempts to repeat those sounds on hearing an adult make them. By nine months this facility for recognition develops to the extent of reproducing patterns of sound modelled by an adult, given that these sound patterns are ones which are commonly spontaneously produced by the infant. At twelve months there is still no accommodation to novel sound patterns, and familiar vocalisations are produced in response to novel sounds spoken by an adult. By 14 months the plasticity of the vocalising schema allows the imitation

of novel sound patterns, and by 17 months most simple new words are copied directly.

2. Gestural imitation: at four months a familiar body movement is recognised and a gestural response is made, but not until seven months is the same gesture made in response. Between eight and ten months accommodation to novel body movements increases, so that an action such as hitting two blocks together is imitated, initially inaccurately, then accurately after some experimentation, then at ten months such an action is imitated directly. At eleven months the infant can imitate several arbitrary gestures, provided it can see the part of its own body which is involved, e.g. bending a finger.

At 14 months the infant is unable to accommodate to novel body movements requiring mental representation of its own body parts and cannot, therefore, accurately reproduce a facial expression, despite attempting to make some movement in response to the adult's change in expression. Between 14 and 17 months the ability to represent body parts develops, and at least one facial gesture can be imitated. By 20 months the child's facility in both accommodating to novel gestures and representing its own body parts has increased and a variety of facial gestures can be imitated.

Scale IV: The Development of Operational Causality. At two months perceptual input can be briefly controlled by co-ordination of two schemas, as in handwatching. At three months control is more definite, with immediate attempts to repeat actions which produce interesting results. A month later such actions are generalised so that they are used in an effort to maintain interesting spectacles regardless of any real causal link. Characteristic 'procedures', e.g. hand waving or kicking can be observed whenever an interesting event stops. At five months some appreciation of causal factors outside the baby's own body is shown, with attempts to prolong spectacles by touching the objects or people involved. Not until 12-15 months has this appreciation of 'centres of causality' developed to the extent where toys are consistently handed to an adult as a request to make them work.

At 18 months the child shows objective recognition of causal links, and attempts to activate toys directly, given a demonstration. By 21 months the ability to construct behaviourally ways to activate objects has developed further so that no demonstration is needed before the child attempts to activate a mechanical toy.

Scale V: The Construction of Object Relations in Space. An infant of two months accommodates to two visual targets with a slowly shifting glance. By three months some anticipation is shown in this situation, with a rapidly alternating glance. By five months sounds are localised correctly, showing further sophistication in the construction of positions in space, and accommodation to distance is shown by accurate grasping of nearby objects. At six months movement in space is constructed, with the trajectory of a falling object being followed and the gaze shifting to its likely resting place. A month later this construction of movement in space is developed enough to allow the infant to lean forward to search for a fallen object when part of its trajectory was out of view.

At nine months, more complex construction of objects in space is achieved, and no surprise is shown when an object is rotated so that its perceptual appearance is quite different. At the same age the spatial relationships between objects are used spontaneously in container play. By 15 months the appreciation of natural forces, specifically gravity, has developed and these forces are anticipated in the way objects are related behaviourally. The infant can now build a tower of several blocks, placing each block carefully in equilibrium over another. Further construction of space, forces and objects is implied by the infant taking hold of a vertically extended string and using it to lift an object. At 18 months, familiar space is mentally represented so that the infant knows where to look for familiar objects or persons and recognises if they are absent.

Scale VI: The Development of Schemas for Relating to Objects. Initially (two months) objects are assimilated incidentally into schemas such as mouthing. At three months an object is briefly attended to in visual inspection, then at four months objects are systematically assimilated into schemas like hitting. By five or six months schemas such as shaking are becoming differentiated through accommodation to different objects. At six months the infant is not simply exercising basic schemas but is actively examining objects to discover their properties. At seven months it is the properties of the objects which influence the kind of differentiated schemas to be used, and by nine months new schemas, dropping and throwing, have emerged as a result of further accommodation to the properties of objects. The eleven-month-old infant is beginning to appreciate the everyday social uses of objects, so he or she will cuddle a doll or give an adult a cup to drink from. Further signs of the mental representation of objects are implied when the 14-month-old shows an object to an adult and uses it as the focus of an interaction. Representation in a symbolic system is demonstrated at 18 months by naming objects spontaneously.

The Sensorimotor Period: A Postscript

Reference has already been made to Bower's work on the cognitive/perceptual skills of babies. Bower's experiments allow babies to demonstrate what are, in Piagetian terms, startlingly sophisticated behaviours. While this leads us to suspect that the explanations provided within the Piagetian framework may eventually be improved on, it does not necessarily mean that approaches following Piaget's theory are invalid. On the contrary, Uzgiris and Hunt can give practical evidence that development occurs in the sequence which they describe, when tested by the situations they suggest. The value of their observational framework, for our present purposes, lies in its utility as a guide to assessment and intervention.

The Pre-operational Period

The developing child, typically around the age of two years, completes the sensorimotor phase by acquiring the ability to represent mentally in a symbolic manner its own actions and perceptions. This is a crucial step forward though the child who is going to learn the arbitrary conventions of representation in spoken and written language still has a long way to go. The end of the sensorimotor period sees the child with a practical, basic understanding of objects and their properties as these impinge on the daily life of a two-year-old. At the normal rate of development it takes another four or five years before the child can begin mental manipulations according to adult conventions. Piaget terms the strategies for such mental manipulations 'operations'.

These include the familiar mathematical functions (e.g. addition) and also logical concepts such as negation (making something be *not* what it was) and the appreciation of invariance (unless something specifically changes a property of an object, then that property stays the same). As the name suggests, the pre-operational period ends with the beginnings of operations. From our point of view there is something rather negative in any title which begins with 'pre-'. Are we always justified in assuming that the next stage will be reached? In some ways it is tempting to re-name the pre-operational period so that more emphasis is placed on its positive achievements. 'The period of the further develop-ment of symbolic function' might be appropriate, but as long as we take the point that in mentally handicapped people this period may not necessarily be 'pre-operational' in the literal sense, then it may be as well to stay with the Piagetian terminology.

The child makes a great deal of progress in the period which typically extends from two to seven years, and it is particularly relevant for teachers of older pupils who are still at this stage to understand the scope of their pupils' cognitive abilities. We will, therefore, examine briefly some of the areas of development in the pre-operational period.

Symbolic Function

Towards the end of the sensorimotor period it is inferred that the child makes mental constructions of objects which allow judge-ments to be made about where to find an object or how it will behave. Evidence is shown of schemas which involve making one object represent another. At this stage the resemblance must be close, so that a toy dog is stroked like the real thing, a toy car is 'brrmmed' on the floor, or a doll is 'fed' with a spoon. The next period of development sees a great expansion of this symbolism, both of the mental kind inferred from the child's problem-solving behaviour and also of the kind more overtly demonstrated in imaginative play. Symbolism also begins to be evidenced in repre-sentational art, but of greatest significance in the pre-operational period is the application of symbolism of the most arbitrary kind to the business of communication.

Linguistic Development

Piagetian thinking sees symbolic function as the key factor in the rapid expansion of language learning which occurs in the sensori-motor period. Language development quite rightly has its own chapter in this volume, but one point should be clarified here. Language, according to Piaget, starts to develop as a representa-tional system almost independently of communicative intent. It is usual to hear young children talking to themselves in play. Even in a conversation, despite the turn-taking routine, careful analysis can

show that the content of one child's utterance may be only tenu-
ously related to what the other has been saying. Eventually, Piaget
admits, language comes to have some bearing on cognitive
development, becoming another medium for operating on and
receiving information about the world. Many other theorists,
Bruner for example, give much greater emphasis to the role of
social influences on development with language as the vehicle for
such influences.

Egocentrism

The pre-operational child develops a good understanding of the
world from his own viewpoint, but does not, according to traditional Piagetian experiments, de-centre and appreciate how things
must appear to others. This obviously has implications for moral
and social development. The inability to see one's own perspective
and someone else's simultaneously seems to typify the tendency of
the child at this stage to concentrate on only one aspect of a given
situation at a time. This tendency can help to explain some of the
specific limitations of the pre-operational child in conservation,
cross-classification and inclusion tasks.

Reasoning

The reasoning of the pre-operational child is not the kind of consistent and logical process which is generally expected from adults.
Chunks of the child's experience and present perceptions are
related and somehow made to connect, even if the logic involved is
not shared with adults. The sort of explanations of natural
phenomena which are favoured by the child often focus on what is,
to an adult mind, the outcome of the phenomenon rather than its
true cause. Questions such as, 'When all the seas are full up, will it
stop raining?' are therefore common. We may well feel an obliga-
tion to explain rain, or whatever phenomenon is up for discussion,
in our own terms, but Piaget's theory, borne out by personal
experience, suggests that such an explanation will have little impact
on the child: only experiences which are slightly discordant with
existing schemas prompt accommodation. Ault (1977) uses an old
joke to make this point very clearly. She reminds us of the child
who asked his parents 'Where do I come from?' The reply was an
embarrassed explanation about human reproduction to which the
child responded, 'But Johnny comes from Ohio: where do I come
from?'

Classification

Simple classification is one area in which the pre-operational child comes to function according to the rules of adult logic. The youngest children (around three to four years), given a potentially sortable set of objects, respond purposefully to a request to sort, but do not apply one criterion consistently. They could make the objects into a picture, or may make a chain where each object has some similarity to its neighbour, but there is no overall shared property to the group which is formed. However, during the next two or three years most children come to be able to apply specified criteria to classify objects and can re-sort without difficulty if asked to change the criteria. Work by this author (Carden 1983), suggests that the sequence of development proposed in the Piagetian literature is equally applicable with children with severe learning difficulties, and that accurate sorting by the criteria of colour, shape and size is achieved by some children in schools for pupils with severe learning difficulties.

Class inclusion is a much more difficult task, and the pre-operational child is unlikely to grasp what is behind the classic questions such as 'Are there more blue beads or are there more wooden beads?' when he or she is shown a mixture of blue and yellow wooden beads.

Some Limitations of the Pre-operational Child

Children at this phase of development have their own ways of reasoning and may come into conflict with adults who do not appreciate the constraints imposed by the ways children understand the world.

Piaget found a lack of conservation of number (and other attributes), and other research bears out this finding in most situations, so a stable concept of number cannot be taken for granted. However, there is good evidence (see e.g. Donaldson 1978) that the pre-operational child has some conservation skills, but does not fully appreciate when and how to apply the skills. The problem seems to be most serious in highly verbal, contrived situations, and seems least acute in naturalistic settings which have some relevance to the child.

Seriation, or ordering, is another important skill which is not refined until the stage of concrete operations. Younger children can put a few (three or four) objects in order of length, but the majority of children cannot accurately order 10 objects until the age of seven or eight. Transitivity, knowing that if $A < B$ and $B < C$, then $A < C$, is an operation needed for this task.

Given these limitations, what could be covered in a cognitive curriculum for the child with severe learning difficulties who may remain at the pre-operational level for several years? An attempt to refine the curriculum through a consideration of relevance to independence skills was mentioned earlier in this chapter. Many of the areas of cognitive development highlighted by this process are areas in which competence is gained during the pre-operational period. A curriculum framework based on both developmental and utilitarian principles is presented in Figure 5.2.

A consideration of Piagetian theory suggests that in some cases our curriculum content may have been over-ambitious in the past. The framework above should provide scope for a varied pro-gramme for most children with severe learning difficulties, and offer a good chance of successful learning. There is also the hope that all the content listed should have some bearing on the learning of skills for coping independently.

Going Further

We may not wish to accept that our pupils will remain 'pre-operational' all their lives. If the curriculum above is outgrown it

Figure 5.2: A 'Pre-Operational' Cognitive Curriculum for Children with Severe Learning Difficulties

Heading	Content
One-to-one correspondence	Establishing one-to-one correspondence.
Sorting	First experiences in logical classification; early shape-size discrimination.
Relationships	Comparison of set size; Basic size/shape relations.
Ordering	Seriation of objects by length (up to 4)
Recognition of numbers	Numeral identification skills; rote counting skills; subitising.*
Time	Basic time concepts.

* Subitising is the skill of knowing how many objects there are in a small group without counting. Children at this level may subitise up to about 4 objects.

can be extended with additional content which has also been judged to have probable links with independence skills. This content takes the child well into the concrete operational period, which typically covers the age range seven-twelve years in normally developing children (see Figure 5.3).

In a chapter such as this, there is little scope to explain the curriculum in greater detail. The intention is that teachers should bear in mind the above frameworks when selecting from the materials published for use with normally developing children. The Nuffield Mathematics Project materials (1967) may be among the easiest to adapt as they are based directly on Piagetian principles.

Creating the Right Conditions

A great deal of further research is needed before we can say with certainty that there are ways of speeding cognitive and perceptual growth in children with severe learning difficulties. As educators we cannot afford to wait for such research. Our task is to develop practical approaches compatible with contemporary theory. This chapter has presented a theoretical perspective which emphasises active processes. It has been suggested that these processes are at

Figure 5.3: Extending the Cognitive Curriculum

Heading	Content
Ordering	Seriation of objects (more than four); ordination[1] concepts.
Conservation	Identity and equivalence.
Recognition of numbers	Rational counting; ordinal/cardinal relationships.
Computation of numbers	Adding and subtracting.
Time	Concepts related to the clock; time telling.
Money	Knowledge of money use; identifying notes and coins; values and relative values of notes and coins.

Note: [1] Ordination is essentially about giving a numerical value to a place in a series, i.e. first, second, etc.

their most efficient when fuelled by experiences which are relevant to the world in which the child lives. In this respect it is also helpful to recall that in the long term teachers want their pupils to learn how to do 'real' things in the 'real' world; more specifically we aim for children with severe learning difficulties to develop skills allowing the maximum degree of independence. Yet we know that there are massive difficulties in achieving generalised learning of such skills. The assumption in this chapter is that, until our pupils are equipped with a broader range of flexible cognitive strategies, these difficulties will persist. We therefore need to have cognition at the core of the curriculum, and the framework for content in this area needs to be based on both developmental sequences and on an educated guess at links with the acquisition of independence skills. In the longer term, there is a need for empirical research to test the assumptions underlying the frameworks presented in this chapter, but it is felt that for the present they will provide guidance to special educators.

Returning to implications for the structure of the learning environment, the essential principle is that the child needs to be active. This is vital because it is the consequences of the child's own actions on the environment, and then towards other people, which stimulates development. We must be aware of the way he or she sees and understands the world at any given time, so that the situations we offer can be structured to reinforce and extend the child's ability to take in information and to use it to guide behaviour.

For the most profoundly handicapped people, often with additional motor, sensory and perceptual problems, it is hard to imagine how progress could be made without detailed knowledge of what the child can already do. Uzgiris and Hunt, the BAB and more specialised assessments of schemas have already been discussed. Given such detailed knowledge the educator can intervene with clearer purpose, for example, providing objects and situations which will prompt the child to behave in new ways, and can ensure that a variety of schemas and strategies are reinforced by the overall environment. Without such intervention, many multiply handicapped people can produce only a limited range of behaviours which have consequences they can perceive; stereotyped inappropriate behaviour is the natural result. This can be avoided by the ingenuity of the educator in tapping into more positive responses and structuring the consequences to create more attractive ways for the child to spend his or her time. This will probably involve specially designed toys, electronic aids and possibly some use of microcomputers.

Microcomputer technology also has its place in cognitive work with those whose learning difficulties, though severe, are less profound. But in this case, the main consideration is to use tasks which are not arbitrary and have some relevance for the child. Real life situations and everyday objects must, therefore, be exploited to the full. Fetching the milk and serving the dinner will be the sort of situation where the child's counting abilities are shown at their best. If we are asking the child to sort objects, then it makes sense to start by letting him or her select some favourite items (e.g. sweets) from a pile of other objects; we would move on from this task to sorting objects into two sets which, in some real sense, belong in two different places, such as cars in a garage and animals on a farm.

Examples of this kind should not be hard to produce if the principles outlined in this chapter are followed. Activities must be meaningful: they must also be challenging but not daunting. This obviously implies that a great deal of individual-structured programming is necessary in helping the child to develop new structures at this level, in exactly the same way that assessment and detailed planning are vital for children at the very earliest levels of sensorimotor development.

Note

[1] Piaget wrote in French so, in translation different versions of some words have been created. Uzgiris and Hunt use 'schemes', but 'schemas' has been preferred throughout this chapter.

References

(Publications marked * are the primary Piagetian sources on which much of this chapter is based.)

Ault, R.L. (1977) *Children's Cognitive Development: Piaget's theory and the process approach.* Oxford University Press.
Bower, T.G.R. (1977a) *The Perceptual World of the Child.* Fontana Books.
Bower, T.G.R. (1977b) *A Primer of Infant Development.* Freeman.
Bower, T.G.R. (1984) 'Imagined Worlds 1: the way an infant looks at the world'. *The Listener*, 19 July, Vol. 112, no 2867, pp. 13-14.

126 *Development of Cognition and Perception*

Bower, T.G.R. and Paterson, J.G. (1972) 'Stages in the development of the object concept'. *Cognition*, 1, pp. 47-57.
Brainerd, C.J. (1973) 'Order of acquisition of transitivity, conservation and class inclusion of length and weight'. *Developmental Psychology*, 8, pp. 105-16.
Brearley, M. and Hitchfield, E. (1966) *A Teacher's Guide to Reading Piaget.* Routledge and Kegan Paul.
Broadbent, D.E. (1958) *Perception and Communication.* Pergamon.
Bruner, J.S. (ed.) (1973) *Beyond the Information Given.* George Allen and Unwin.
Bruner, J.S. (1973) 'Going beyond the information given', in J.S. Bruner (ed.), *Beyond the Information Given.* George Allen and Unwin.
Bruner, J.S., Olver, R.R., Greenfield, P.M., *et al.* (1966) *Studies in Cognitive Growth.* Wiley.
Carden, N. (1983) *An Assessment Procedure for Use in Planning Programmes to Develop Cognitive Skills in ESN(S) Children.* Unpublished M.Phil. thesis, Huddersfield Polytechnic.
Carden, N., and Robson, C. (1985) 'Teachers' views on the curriculum for severe learning difficulties'. *Br. Jnl of Special Education*, 12, pp. 31-3.
Cohen, M.A. and Gross, P.J. (1979) *The Developmental Resource: Behaviour Sequences for Assessment and Programme Planning* (2 vols.). Grune and Stratton.
Coupe, J., and Levy, D. (1985) 'The object related scheme assessment procedure'. *BIMH Jnl*, 13, no. 1, pp. 22-4.
Donaldson, M. (1978) *Children's Minds.* Fontana.
Foxen, T. (1975) *Object Schemes Assessment.* Unpublished document, Hester Adrian Research Centre, Manchester.
Held, R. and Hein, A. (1963) 'Movement-produced stimulation in the development of visually guided behaviour'. *Jnl of Comparative and Physiological Psychology*, 56, pp. 872-6.
Hubel, D.H. and Wiesel, N. (1963) 'Receptive fields of cells in striate cortex of very young, visually inexperienced kittens'. *Jnl of Neurophysiology*, 26, pp. 994-1002.
*Inhelder, B. and Piaget, J. (1964) *The Early Growth of Logic in the Child.* Routledge and Kegan Paul.
Kahn, J.V. (1975) 'Relationship of Piaget's sensorimotor period to language acquisition of profoundly retarded children'. *Am. Jnl of Mental Deficiency*, 79, pp. 640-3.
Kahn, J.V. (1976) 'Utility of the Uzgiris and Hunt Scales of sensorimotor development with severely and profoundly retarded children'. *Am. Jnl of Mental Deficiency*, 80, pp. 663-5.
Kiernan, C.C. and Jones, M. (1982) *Behaviour Assessment Battery*, 2nd edn. NFER.
Kitzinger, M. (1980) 'Planning management of feeding in the visually handicapped Child'. *Child: Care, Health and Development*, 6, pp. 291-9.
Michael, C.R. (1972) 'Retinal processing of visual images', in *Perception: Mechanism and Models: readings from Scientific American.* Freeman.
Nuffield Mathematics Project (1967) *I Do and I Understand.* Chambers and Murray.
Oates, J. and Floyd, A. (1976) *The Course of Development.* Open University Press.
*Piaget, J. (1929) *The Child's Conception of the World.* Routledge and Kegan Paul.
*Piaget, J. (1952) *The Child's Conception of Number.* Routledge and Kegan Paul.
*Piaget, J. (1953) *The Origin of Intelligence in the Child.* Routledge and Kegan Paul.

*Piaget, J. (1955) *The Construction of Reality in the Child.* Routledge and Kegan Paul.
*Piaget, J. (1969) *The Child's Conception of Time.* Routledge and Kegan Paul.
*Piaget, J. and Inhelder, B. (1969) *The Psychology of the Child.* Routledge and Kegan Paul.
*Piaget, J. and Inhelder, B. (1974) *The Child's Construction of Quantities.* Routledge and Kegan Paul.
Uzgiris, I.C. and Hunt, J.McV. (1975) *Assessment in Infancy: ordinal scales of psychological development.* University of Illinois Press.
Wadsworth, B.J. (1984) *Piaget's Theory of Cognitive and Affective Development,* 3rd edn. Longman.
Whelan, E. and Speake, B. (1979) *Learning to Cope.* Souvenir Press.
Woodward, M. (1961) 'Concepts of number of mentally subnormal studied by Piaget's method'. *Jnl of Child Psychology and Psychiatry,* 2, pp. 249-59.

6 MOTOR COMPETENCE IN CHILDREN WITH MENTAL HANDICAP

James Hogg

Introduction

It may have been that from the outset I set my sights too high. It was, admittedly, unlikely that my own attempt at juggling would ever match those of Kara ('The Greatest Juggler in the World') or Chinko ('The First Man to Juggle with Eight Balls!') or even Tom Hearns, billed as the 'lazy juggler'. Even less was I likely to be able to compete with Meunier Marcel — the Boy Champion Diabolist of the World — 6000 consecutive throws in the air on one occasion and 131 throws in a minute on another. On the contrary, to get three balls in the air at the same time was a major target rarely achieved.

These failures were not a matter of concern to my parents or teachers. Certainly no one rushed to write an individual educational programme or pored over 'fine motor skill' checklists. In that particular area the most interest that was shown was in whether my knife was held the correct way up or not. And why not? Not coming from a circus family it mattered little and no one had aspirations for me as 'Son of Chinko'. Adult concern in as far as it manifested itself was with the basic competencies of everyday life as I grew older.

It sometimes seems that our view of mentally handicapped children is less realistic. While teaching them to juggle might be the furthest thing from our minds, we seem to have adopted the view that 'motor skill' is a matter of special worry within the overall framework of their slow development. We are inclined to develop special curriculum areas concerned with motor behaviour often isolated from the actual reasons that have led us into contact with these children and their special learning difficulties. And what are these reasons? Primarily they relate to *wide ranging difficulties in the development of the academic and social competencies that permit age-appropriate adaptation to the various environments which they encounter.* The title of this article reflects this view; we do not start with an attempt to isolate motor behaviour from the

128

context in which it is employed to realise these adaptive demands. Terms such as 'motor skill' have their part to play in understanding and encouraging such adaptation, but at a lower, or finer, level of analysis of competence than is usually acknowledged. In brief, this chapter sets out to suggest the various levels that we need to consider when looking at motor competence.

There are many reasons why those of us working with mentally handicapped children have tried to isolate the motor component of competence. Conceptually the move from a global view of mental handicap as one huge deficit in intellectual functioning has led us to try to distinguish differing areas of psychological difficulty and their enhancement. This view has been reinforced with respect to motor abilities by a body of research work pointing to specific deficits in the processes underlying motor behaviour in severely and profoundly mentally handicapped children generally (for a brief review, see Hogg 1982) and Down's syndrome children in particular (for a review, see Henderson 1985). This position has been further reinforced by neurological studies pointing to abnormalities in this respect (Kirman 1975). It is then a natural step to teach activities with a high motoric component and in their own right. If anticipation, timing, suitability of grasp and sequence of movements = motor skill, then why not teach juggling, or some similar developmentally appropriate activity?

A different picture emerges if, instead of beginning at the bottom with a view of discrete motor processes, we start at the top with an overall view of motor competence — the term in our title. What do we mean by this term? At one level it conveys something more everyday than the more familiar term 'motor skill'. The medieval woodcarver, professional tennis player or Kara 'The Greatest Juggler in the World' would all be acknowledged as possessing and demonstrating motor behaviour out of the ordinary. However, after the initial acquisition of a self-help activity we do not regard performance of the activity as skilled behaviour. I am not regarded as a skilled putter-on of my socks or a skilled nose-blower, though I am competent in both spheres. We can be more explicit about use of the term motor-competence by a brief excursion into what is referred to as 'goal-directed action theory' or GDA.

Goal-Directed Actions

A goal-directed action refers to a person's goal-directed, planned, and intended behaviour in a given social setting (Von Cranach 1982). It is useful to take these terms one by one. Goal-directed suggests that the action will accomplish a specific outcome producing some change in the world. It is to be assumed that this action has adaptive consequences for the actor. The way in which this is achieved is not through random exploration but through some explicit plan of action conceived, consciously or not, before its execution. Mental representation of both goal and means to it imply that the outcome is intended by the actor. The concept of intention is one with which psychologists and philosophers have much greater difficulty than does the average person. Nor is intention a term that would be used by those who have developed behavioural techniques for use with people with mental handicap. However, we assume intention even in the most impaired of children, and our assumption invariably bears upon their attempt to realise a goal. The addition of social setting is important and should be taken in a broader sense than just 'interpersonal'. For example, the action of opening a door is part of a longer sequence of actions in an individual's life in which he or she is realising a social goal, e.g. entering the room to meet someone or leaving a building to go home. In any such action much besides motor behaviour will be involved, and we will comment on this later. For the present, however, the term motor competence is used to describe the effective realisation through the motor system of goal-directed actions leading to successful adaptation to the situation.

It should now be clearer why this is a more appropriate starting point for our discussion than a narrower focus on motor skill in itself. We only become interested in motor skill when motor considerations enter into incompetent goal-directed behaviour, i.e. when the child cannot grip a toothbrush or knife and fork, or cannot sequence movements to realise a goal. We are not interested because psychologists have shown that reaction times are on average slower by a few milliseconds in mentally handicapped children than their non-handicapped peers, or are unable to stack 29 blocks in 30 seconds, or cannot dribble a ball round skittles. It is only when effective social adaptation demands it that we find ourselves open to a judgement of motor incompetence, and we become concerned. Hence the lack of interest in my total inability to juggle.

Our view of competence as goal-directed action in a social context leads directly to a consideration of the many everyday activities in which such competence has to be displayed. These are familiar to us in curricula for mentally handicapped children across a wide ability range. They include self-feeding, dressing and toileting, as well as activities directed to care of the immediate environment such as cleaning and wider self-supporting tasks such as cooking. For most of us these are highly routinised tasks. The sequence of sub-actions that permit us to make a cup of instant coffee are repeated literally hundreds of times in the course of a year. Take kettle — turn on tap — fill kettle — plug it in ... take coffee jar and spoon — unscrew lid — take spoonful of coffee — take cup — put coffee in cup — and water — and so on. In fact so routinised does such an activity become that, unlike the early stages of acquiring this ability, we hardly think about what we are doing. In the psychologist's terms, we withdraw our attention from performance of the task.

Every one of us is more than familiar with the kinds of errors that can be made as the result of this withdrawal of attention. In making coffee in the above sequences, we have at some time failed to turn on the kettle, or turned it on without adding water, or put the water in the cup without putting the coffee in first, and so on. We see such errors as either causes for irritation or amusement in those who have achieved competence. In those acquiring the ability they signal problem points in its acquisition.

In considering goal-directed behaviour, analysis of errors in routine self-help activities has proved illuminating in understanding the nature of competent action. Reason (1984) invited people to keep diaries of errors in everyday tasks of the kind just described. His interest was in using these errors to understand the nature of the psychological control processes that permit everyday routinised tasks to be carried out. Put another way, his intention was to use this information to more fully understand the nature of goal-directed behaviour as we have defined it here. From our point of view, then, his analysis is a useful starting point from which to consider competence and incompetence in the actions of mentally handicapped children.

As many other people studying action and motor behaviour have done, Reason starts with an analogy from the vocabulary and functioning of computers to describe this system. He suggests, first, that there is an overall executive program or plan which specifies what sequence of actions has to be carried out and the order in which they have to be executed. This super-ordinate program is made up of sub-programs or sub-routines. We can imagine a situation where this super-ordinate program is 'run-off' without reference to the actual outcome in the environment. In reality, the execution of the program will be monitored by its consequences. This process of monitoring entails feedback from both the environment and from internal sources such as the muscles and organs of balance. This information is fed back, collated and passed on to the super-ordinate program in order to modify or adjust the program in the light of its failure to accomplish the intended goal. This collating activity is undertaken by a central processor.

Knowledge of Results

The role of feedback is of special significance. Feedback — or, in psychological terms, knowledge of results — is a basic characteristic of the structure of behaviour. Annett writes that: 'Rather than being simply run off as a result of prior stimulation, behaviour, both simple and complex, can be seen as governed by results *at all levels*. In a general way the feedback concept seems to be able to account for some of the complexities of behaviour and especially with flexible and adaptive behaviour' (Annett 1969). Extrinsic feedback is readily manipulable by teacher or trainer and can be verbal ('Yes that is it' or 'Turn it more') or can be signalled in the outcome of the action itself, e.g. where the end of the shoelace buckles on the eye of the shoe instead of going through it. Intrinsic feedback arises from signals from the muscles, tendons and vestibular system, i.e. organs of balance. While this is less manipulable than is extrinsic feedback, we will suggest that techniques dependent on physical prompting and manipulation do lead to the enhancement of intrinsic feedback. Clearly, too, our reinforcement of success or an approximation to it will have a feedback function as well as motivating the child. Feedback itself, however, may not be motivating, knowledge of results not necessarily encouraging continuation of the task. Be that as it may, feedback information is a critical input to the central processor.

When we are engaged on a task which demands high attention, the central processor will be kept busy relating what is happening in the environment to the action programme which in turn will continually have to be adjusted or changed. Before they finally fell to the ground, my juggling balls were watched with acute concern as their intended (programmed) trajectory deviated in height and laterality from their course and in relation to each other — unsuccessful hand and postural adjustments were implemented as the central processor told the programme that feedback indicated yet another failure was on the way. However, such attention is not required by the competent performer. Increasingly, the programme can be executed with less and less attention. In the extreme, this can be withdrawn altogether. But this is where our coffee-making types of error come into their own.

Reason analysed the everyday errors in carrying out routine actions reported in the diaries. Through appropriate analysis he was able to produce a classification of failures of action and to describe the behaviour associated with these (Reason 1984: p. 531):

1. *Repetition*: Some *actions* in the intended sequence are repeated unnecessarily.
2. *Wrong object(s)*: The intended actions were made, but in relation to the wrong object(s).
3. *Intrusion*: Unintended actions other than those associated with repetitions or wrong object(s) become incorporated into a sequence at some point.
4. *Omission*: Intended actions (other than those arising from repetitions, wrong objects, or intrusions) were left out of the sequence.

A little thought will enable you to illustrate these slips from your own experience, both in relation to your own actions in well-rehearsed tasks, and also in the kind of difficulties that mentally handicapped children have in acquiring and sustaining various everyday activities. For example, a repetition might occur in the person's cooking such as salting the potato water twice, while failure to do so would constitute an omission. It should also be added that Reason himself goes beyond this behavioural classification to consider errors in relation to the computer model described above to which he adds mechanisms concerned with intention and action as well as memory and need. For our present purpose, however, we need go no further. We have a framework in which goal-directed action can be considered in relation to competence in mentally handicapped children.

Action And Mental Handicap

With respect to the teacher and the growth of competence in the various self-help areas we have listed, Reason's analysis points towards the identification and diagnosis of failures arising from repetition, wrong object, intrusion and omission in the acquisition of a competent action sequence, and to failures in its execution when criterion on a training task has already been achieved. As Reason's analysis clearly shows, mentally handicapped people certainly do not have a monopoly on making errors! Thus, in a sequence we can begin to identify repetitions, wrong objects, intrusions and omissions. This sequence, it should be added, will almost certainly be described in the teacher's task analysis in which the various sub-actions are stated, and we will return to this point later.

The computer program analogy that he follows also takes us down vertically into increasingly narrow factors related to motor processes and their control. Thus, failure may reflect:

1. inability to sequence actions in accordance with the super-ordinate programme that has, in effect, been defined by the teacher's task analysis;
2. an inability to execute a sub-programme because of specific manipulative difficulties, e.g. the appropriate grip on the object;
3. failure to utilise external feedback when the action has not accomplished the objective — either through overt inattention to the task or because of failure to discriminate what is happening as a result of the action.

These three suggestions are not exhaustive, though we will concentrate on them later in this chapter. Omitted from them, and central to this view of competence, are need and intention. Here we identify need with motivation and in turn with the way in which motivation is dealt with in behavioural approaches to teaching, i.e. through the use of reinforcement. Intention is viewed as the development of means-end behaviour, a term derived from developmental psychology, and with a similar meaning to that of goal-directed action.

Development, Action and Competence

In considering the development of means-end behaviour we are putting the notion of competence in a developmental framework that reflects both our concern with the development time of mentally handicapped children and the fact that many severely and certainly profoundly mentally handicapped children will move only slowly to the point at which means-end behaviour is manifest.

Drawing on Piagetian theory (Piaget 1953), Hogg and Sebba (1986) have described in some detail Piaget's theory of cognitive development, its application to the assessment of mentally handicapped children and the development of programmes devised to enhance early cognitive development including means-end behaviour. Here we must be brief in dealing with these three aspects of the development of intentionality. Means-end behaviour refers to the child's ability to achieve a particular goal by separating the means of attainment from the end itself. The most familiar example of such separation is when, towards the end of the first year of life, the child removes some obstacle to reach and grasp an object behind it. In addition, such intentional behaviour will be adaptive, i.e. will show systematic changes in response to alterations in the nature of the means-end behaviour. Two important stages of this area of development occur in the second year of life. In the first half of this year the child is able to discover the means to achieve intended goals through active experimentation. Piaget (1953) describes in detail such experimentation with special reference to the use of supports, sticks and strings to retrieve an otherwise unobtainable object. This does not occur, as sometimes happens in the latter part of the first year, by accident, but involves the intentional use of schemes that even then were available, i.e. more discrete actions that generalise in an adaptive way to different objects in the environment — such as a particular grasp. In the second half of the second year, however, the child moves from the use of existing schemes in an experimental fashion to the invention of means to an end through mental combination of schemes that can involve quite new, invented ways of achieving an end. Having (1) learned to join rods in a construction kit, and (2) learned to retrieve a ball from under a chair with a short stick, the child will, when the ball is too far from the stick, join rods from the kit to an appropriate length and retrieve it that way.

The parallels to goal-directed action theory should be clear, but here of course the emphasis is on development. This development continues throughout the subsequent years from 2 years onwards, with increasingly complex strategies being evolved. These action strategies become more complex reflecting the level of understanding displayed by the child. Thus, classification of objects (e.g. by common attributes), seriation (the ordering of a set of objections by length) or block structures (e.g. the ability to build a bridge of two two-block supports and a span) all reflect the cognitive ability to organise action sequences, initially mentally, then through appropriate motor behaviour. Increasingly these mental advances will be applied to sequence behaviours necessary for adaptive competence in self-help activities, such as dressing. The important point to note is that goal-directed action is dependent upon mental growth, and it is against this background that we must consider the structure of the actions observable in behaviour. The organising framework that we must now turn to takes us back to the computer model of action. Before doing so, though, the importance of physical development should also be noted.

Early infancy, particularly, and childhood in general is marked by progressive developments in the neuromuscular system which permit an increasing range of postural adjustments, control of upper limbs, and mobility. Many books document the course of these developments. Readers may find Touwen's 'Neurological Development in Infancy' (Touwen 1976) and Holle's *Motor Development in Children: Normal and Retarded* (1976) particularly helpful as both offer readily usable assessment scales. Specific failures in development or slow maturation will undoubtedly influence motor behaviour and hence the realisation of goals in profound ways. In illustration, a study by Molnar (1978) with severely mentally handicapped children can be cited. Here the automatical postural adjustment mechanisms that enable the child to maintain postural control, e.g. sitting stably, were monitored. It was only when the specific mechanisms became functional, that a milestone such as this was achieved. Clearly an approach to motor behaviour from this perspective is complementary to the psychological viewpoint adopted in this article. Where children show abnormal or slow neurological development, direct physiotherapy or a programme of gross motor activity will therefore form part of the curriculum.

Programmes and Sequences

The computer analogy we have described has also been applied to the development of motor actions in children by Bruner (1970) and by Connolly (1973). Their proposal has been referred to as a 'modular model of skill acquisition'. Again, an overall programme specifies the complete action sequence intended. This programme is made up of sub-programmes which, at the level of behaviour, can be seen as a sequence and organisation of sub-programmes. These sub-programmes underlie the behavioural sub-components and involve a series of movements and manual grips. The overall or super-ordinate programme also specifies the sequence and organisation of the action. In line with Reason's account of the routine nature of many everyday tasks, these programmes would be 'run off' in an increasingly invariant fashion. However, where for some reason the demands of the task are altered so that the usual routine would not be effective, then the ability to use sub-programmes from other sources would be highly adaptive. For example, while a child may have learned to unscrew a jar using a palmar grasp, i.e. with the flat of the palm against the lid and all fingers employed, introduction of a smaller vessel and lid would necessitate use of a digital grip, i.e. no palmar contact and use of only finger and thumb. Moss and Hogg (1983) have shown that the most competent children (ages 12-36 months and not mentally handicapped) do show an ability to vary the way in which they accomplish a given goal in simple nursery tasks such as placing a rod in a hole.

The ability to display variance or invariance in such actions, however, is dependent upon the emergence of means-end behaviour as described above, and we would not begin training on tasks of this sort until cognitive development was emerging in this respect. In order to teach specific sequences reflecting means-end behaviour, our starting point will be a task analysis into which the needed components of generalisation are built. This approach will be described below. The development of flexible performance of a skill, however, requires further consideration and can best be approached from looking at how the individual components, or sub-programmes, of an action sequence are acquired.

Acquiring Components of a Sequence

Attractive though the analogy between motor action and computer control processes is (and it is certainly a helpful analogy in studying motor action), there is a limit to how far we should extend it. It has been suggested that there are two major weaknesses in viewing the processes underlying the components of motor behaviour as identical to computer program sub-routines. First, it would require an enormous number of such programmes in order to permit us to carry out all the actions that we are actually equipped to execute — i.e. the brain simply could not store them all. Second, as noted above, while actions do become routinised, behaviour must also adjust to changing environmental demands, although such adjustment does not necessarily occur consciously. If the juggler were never to adjust to slightly changing positions of the balls as they fall downwards, then success would be on a par with my own efforts. Thus, the programme must be able to cope with novelty.

This problem has been approached by Schmidt (1975; 1976) who has developed the concept of the motor schema. This theory has two components: (1) that the action concerned has in some way been established. For example, if a component of self-feeding, e.g. using a fork that entails pushing it into the food to impale it, is under consideration, then by observation we can see this has been learned however inadequately — the person is seen to attempt the action. This is seen as a generalised motor programme and is stored as a memory structure concerned with all possible forks and types and sizes of food; (2) there are then two schemas that govern this generalised programme. The recall schema is concerned with the relation between initial conditions (the fork and the hand poised to descend), what is intended (impaling the food), and the actual outcome (pressure insufficient, meat drops off). The recognition schema relates initial conditions to past experience of executing the action. This distinction is not important for our present purpose, but two significant consequences follow. First, the more experience gained of executing the action the stronger both schemas become; second, the greater the variability of the experience the stronger will be the schema and hence the more competent will the person become.

The first of these predictions will not surprise us and will confirm us in our belief that only through giving mentally handicapped children repeated opportunities to become competent in their actions will they meet the adaptive requirements of society. The second, however, is less obvious. It leads to the prediction that, if conditions of training are variable rather than constant, then the schema will be strengthened and competence increased. For example, let us take a simple throwing task. If the child stands in position A and throws a ball into a container at B until the ability is acquired to some preset level then this would constitute constant training. If, however, the position of the bin was moved about in training and located at B and C then we would have variable training. Schmidt's theory would then be tested by locating the bin at an intermediate position D, and beyond both B and C at E. Remember, both conditions will have entailed the same number of training trials, and neither child will have thrown to D or E. Under such conditions children undergoing variable training in tasks of this sort do perform with greater accuracy on D and E than those who have received constant training on throwing and other tasks (see Shapiro and Schmidt 1982). In a study with the author, Quigley (1982) also showed that young Down's syndrome children did indeed perform with greater accuracy following variable rather than constant condition training. With respect to the conditions which we establish in a learning situation, findings of this sort clearly point to the need to ensure variety at this stage of learning — not after a simple, invariate action has been achieved.

In its strict form, motor schema theory is applied to movements of short duration, e.g. the throw of a ball in the above example. Such movements do bear comparison to the sub-behaviours that have been seen to make up longer sequences, and the motor schema may be thought to represent a highly flexible sub-outline. How flexible remains an open question at present. If we teach a child to throw a ball at a variable target along the ground, then will this produce better performance in throwing vertically to a target high on a wall? Experimental studies suggest that this is the case and that generalisation can occur across different movements within the same general class.

The Analysis of Action and its Training

Some Curriculum Considerations

In this article we have argued that motor behaviour should be viewed as the means to realise goal-directed sequences rather than as a separate area of ability abstracted from the academic and everyday contexts in which adaptive behaviour needs to be displayed. We have also emphasised that this realisation has an important developmental dimension with advances in cognition and information processing permitting more complex sequences of action to be formulated and executed as the child gets older.

The first consequence of this position is that we should

consider motor demands in the context of wider everyday and academic areas of the curriculum. With respect to the former, the self-help area invariably entails complex sequences of actions involving high-order planning as well as the realisation of highly specific components. In virtually all such activities a strong manual element is involved in conjunction with appropriate postural control and movement. Thus, the appropriate use of manual grips finds plenty of outlet in any such activity. Dressing requires the application of adult digital grips in buttoning and a ventral digital grip if a lace needs threading (see Figure 6.1). Taking off a pullover will almost certainly require co-ordination of both hands and the use of a variety of grips including palmar grasp. Appropriate head control and maintenance of trunk posture will also be critical in all phases of dressing or undressing. Again, the way in which a child's grip changes is critical to successful manipulation. Holle (1976: pp. 34-43) describes how, in holding a spoon or crayon, this changes from the 'reverse transverse palmar' grip shown in Figure 6.1 to an 'adult digital grip'.

In the course of a day, ample opportunity is therefore offered without recourse to abstracting these functions and introducing them into what we might now call the 'jugglers curriculum', i.e. the teaching of motor behaviour in tasks outside the adaptive context in which we ultimately wish the child to function. Thus, if we aim to teach an advanced grip relevant to spoon-use, then that is where we teach it — during snack time.

At this point, however, we must introduce the developmental dimension. Are we, in the light of this argument, to throw out all the equipment and learning situations that characterise much of early education in the field of nursery and primary education generally, and special education in particular? Are the stacking beakers and blocks, the simple construction kits, even the Activity Centre to be consigned to the store room? To answer this question it should first be borne in mind that the rationale for using much of this material is initially cognitive and not motoric. It is to encourage the understanding of the relation between thought, behaviour and the world. Any curriculum which is worth its salt will make these links explicit and, just as important, will relate the cognitive ability they encourage to everyday situations that require that ability. Thus, the developing ability to relate objects during the first 18 months of life is critical to using a spoon to pick up food (Woodward and Stern 1963), while classification of objects will permit appropriate sorting of eating utensils after a meal. Lavatelli (1970a; 1970b) has produced a carefully constructed curriculum that not only utilises traditional material to teach specific cognitive skills but relates all such skills to wider everyday activities and their parallels in emerging language.

It is not, however, my intention to go too far into early child-hood cognitive curricula. These examples are chosen to show that, as with self-help activities, early cognitive activities in the curriculum have priority in their own right, embodying motor activity in their realisation. Both provide ample opportunity for enhancing motor ability.

Figure 6.1: Grips Referred to in the Text

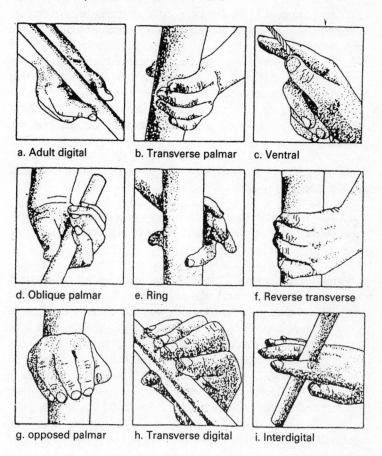

a. Adult digital   b. Transverse palmar   c. Ventral

d. Oblique palmar   e. Ring   f. Reverse transverse

g. opposed palmar   h. Transverse digital   i. Interdigital

The Analysis of Goal-directed Actions

We have discussed the concept of goal-directed action as a planned programme of intended sub-components. In selecting a curriculum objective the teacher has just such an overall plan in mind, and the aim is to provide a teaching programme that will enable the child to realise it. A crucial step in formulating the teaching programme is what has come to be known as task analysis, and a direct parallel exists between the overall or super-ordinate programme that we hope the child will acquire and the teacher's programme. This parallel includes between, on the one hand, the development of a goal-directed action by the child, and on the other the teacher's conception of the teaching programme:

1. intended goal = teaching objective or target behaviour, e.g. complete sequence of actions that characterises appropriate spoon use;
2. action sequence = teaching sequenced sub-targets, the temporal and spatial organisation of the various movements that make up the sequence;
3. sub-programme = component behaviour, e.g. the small movement of the spoon across the bowl to get food on the spoon.

If, as we should, we introduce the issue of generalisation of training then we can add:

4. wide applicability of action plan = generalisation of taught behaviour, e.g. using different spoons with bowls/plates and varying types of food.

Within the framework of behavioural teaching techniques, task analysis occupies a central place, but one which receives little detailed discussion in many training programmes. As this is crucial to our present argument, we will pursue the technique a little further. For clarity's sake we will illustrate the procedure, not through the teaching of how to juggle eight balls at once, but with two tasks selected from a recent study of manipulative skills in young children (Hogg 1981). Anyone turning to this study will see that many of the ideas being offered now reflect a response to its findings, in that there the focus was on direct teaching of specific manipulative and constructional activities. The value of looking again at the study, however, is that great care was taken in both task analysis and analysis of the sub-behaviours and their general-isation, and the procedure illustrates well the parallels drawn above.

A formal approach to task analysis developed by Shepherd (1976) was employed and applied to two tasks, threading a flexible wire through a disc (effectively a large bead) and building a bridge out of blocks with two two-block sides and a single spar. Figures 6.2 and 6.3 show the task analyses for threading and bridge building respectively. In the left hand column the super-ordinate operation to be redescribed is given, the operation itself being described in the second column in italics. This is given the same number as the super-ordinate but prefixed with a capital letter, P. The plan is described, followed by the subordinate opera-tions numbered consecutively. A line is then ruled across the page and various subordinate operations treated as super-ordinate opera-tions, which are futher redefined. In column 3, reasons for stopping analysis are given, while training notes appear in column 4.

The structure is clearly shown for the two tasks in Figures 6.4 and 6.5. In terms 1, 2 and 3 the intended goal (1) in Figure 6.2 is super-ordinate 1, i.e. 'Wire is threaded through "disc" and allowed to drop to knotted end of thread'. There is then a hierarchy of sub-targets (2), made up at the first level of super-ordinates 2-5, i.e. 'Pick up and position wire' (2); 'Pick up and position disc' (3); 'Thread wire through disc' (4); 'Change hands used to hold disc and wire in order to pull wire through disc'. These components are further broken into 6-16. Any given sub-task component can be viewed as (3) — a sub-programme. The generalisation tasks described in the original paper constitute (4). Though based on observation of the child's performance, this task analysis may have to be revised for the individual child. However, pre-testing will allow us to locate where defects exist in the child's programme of action aimed at realising this goal.

Further flexibility may have to be introduced if the child succeeds in a component using a different motor behaviour, e.g. varying grip from that described, or using different actions across trials. Further flexibility could be introduced deliberately into the structure of the training in order to develop a more adaptive action programme in the child. In this sense, adaptive means that the child will be able to apply his or her general programme to a variety of different types of material in differing situations. Thus,

Figure 6.2: Task Analysis of Disc Threading

Super-ordinate	Task component, operation or plan	Reason for stopping analysis	Notes on performance recommendations and further analysis
1	*Wire is threaded through 'disc' and allowed to drop to knotted end of thread* p1, 2 and 3 can be executed sequentially (2-3 or 3-2) or simultaneously, 4 and 5 must follow 2 and 3 in that order		
	2. Pick up and position wire		
	3. Pick up and position disc		
	4. Thread wire through disc		
	5. Change hands used to hold disc and wire in order to pull wire through to knot		5. Is optional as the child can simply release the disc while retaining the thread and allow it to fall down to the knot
2	*Pick up and position wire* p2, 6 and 7 occur in sequence		
	6. Pick up wire at a point on it that will allow sufficient rigidity but adequate length	Task solution	6. It is always possible the child will pick up the wire at an inappropriate point and subsequently adjust the position of the grip. This would require fuller task analysis if the child encountered special difficulties here
	7. Bring wire to disc hole	Task solution	
3	*Pick up and position disc* p3, 8 and 9 occur in sequence		
	8. Pick up disc to permit location of wire in hole	Task solution	8. Again the child may need to make subsequent adjustments to achieve the appropriate orientation of the disc. Here further task analysis would be called for
	9. Bring to wire end	Task solution	
4	*Thread wire through disc* p4, 10 and 11 occur in sequence		
	10. Locate wire in hole	Task solution	
	11. Move wire through hole till it emerges at other end	Task solution	

5	*Change hands used to hold disc and wire in order to pull wire through disc* p5, 12-16 occur in sequence		As indicated above p5 may not need to be taught as the child may achieve the desired objective without employing this form of hand co-ordination
	12. Release grip on wire	Task solution	
	13. Grip disc with free hand	Task solution	
	14. Release original grip on disc	Task solution	
	15. Grip wire with hand freed from disc	Task solution	
	16. Pull wire through disc till it reaches the knot	Task solution	

the programme would not be a rigid one which would be useless in the real world with its ever altering demands. Among the many approaches to this problem that have been discussed in the context of generalisation training (see Stokes and Baer 1977) is 'training on sufficient exemplars'. These authors suggest that the aim of such an approach is to enable the trainee to form an induction that will effect generalisation sufficiently to satisfy the problem posed. Thus, in contrast to my example above, the training sequence determined by the task analysis would be applied, not to one set of material, but to a variety of different discs and threads or blocks, in which appearance, size and other relevant characteristics would be varied.

This approach to teaching goal-directed action finds its fullest expression in general case programming. Colvin and Horner (1983) describe this procedure in the following way: 'General case instruction refers to those behaviours performed by a teacher or trainer which increase the probability that behaviours will be successfully performed with different target stimuli, and in different settings, from those used during training.' These authors describe the six stages in developing such a programme and these are summarised in Chapter 2 of this book.

Within task analyses of the sort illustrated, and in general case programming, there is the possibility of planning and of specific motor difficulties emerging, the task analysis allowing us to identify at which particular sub-component the difficulty is occurring.

Figure 6.3: Task Analysis of Bridge Building

Super-ordinate	Task component, operation or plan	Reason for stopping analysis	Notes on performance recommendations and further analysis
1	*Build five block bridge with model visible* p1. Operations 2, 3 and 4 are carried out in sequence		1. The analysis describes the task of replicating a bridge consisting of two sub-assemblies (supports) and an arch linking them that responds to a model already built by the teacher.
	2. Place block either side of wooden strip adjacent to visual cue		
	3. Place 3rd and 4th blocks on 1st and 2nd blocks already placed		Depending on whether forward or backward chaining is employed the sequence can be 2-3-4 or 4-3-2
	4. Place arch on stretching block assemblies		
2	*Place block either side of wooden strip* p2. Do 5 then 6 then 7 then 8		The visual cue referred to is a white band on the red wooden strip the width of the block. If the first block is placed partly outside this strip, then within a tolerance of 2 cm this is accepted as correct placement. However, the 2nd block must be placed, with the same tolerance and with the further pre-requisite that any non-overlap is on the same side as the first block
	5. Select 1st block	Task solution	
	6. Place block within 1 cm wooden strip and overlapping visual cue	Task solution	
	7. Select 2nd block	Task solution	
	8. Place it on opposite side of wooden strip to 1st block within 1 cm and overlapping visual cue	Task solution	
3	*Place 3rd and 4th blocks on 1st and 2nd blocks already placed* p3. Do 9 then 10 then 11 then 12		
	9. Select 3rd block	Task solution	
	10. Place it on either 1st or 2nd blocks	Task solution	
	11. Select 4th block	Task solution	
	12. Place it on 1st or 2nd block depending on location of 3rd block	Task solution	

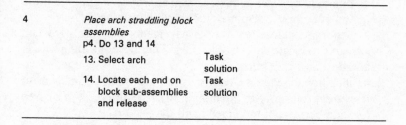

4	*Place arch straddling block assemblies*	
	p4. Do 13 and 14	
	13. Select arch	Task solution
	14. Locate each end on block sub-assemblies and release	Task solution

Figure 6.4: Disc Threading. Diagram illustrating hierarchial organisation of task

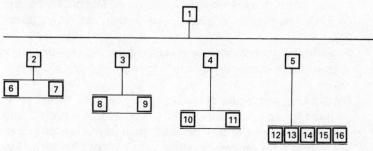

Figure 6.5: Bridge Building. Diagram illustrating hierarchial organisation of task

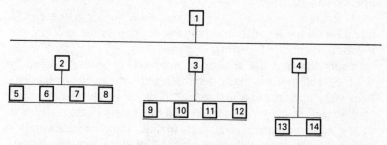

There is no formal prescription to 'diagnose' what is going wrong but the following suggestions can be made:

1. sub-component not realised in behaviour. For example, the child may not be exhibiting the sub-behaviour in a way that would permit realisation of the sub-goal, e.g. failure to adopt a digital grip on a button in order to push it through the button hole;

2. omission of a sub-behaviour, e.g. appropriate grip on button but no attempt to grasp material round button hole;

3. apparent failure to use visual feedback, e.g. persistent attempts to locate wire in hole in bead but never locating wire in aperture despite it buckling;

4. inability to exercise control over movement, e.g. lack of consistent trajectory in attempting to place an object in a given location because of too much hand shake;

5. lack of timing in co-ordination of movements, e.g. not bringing hands together at the same time to grasp object or having them in the right place at the right time if the object is moving;

6. insertion of inappropriate sub-behaviour into sequence, e.g. correctly grasping door knob but rotating in the wrong direction;

7. insertion of sub-behaviour in correct form but at wrong place in sequence, e.g. adding water to teapot then adding tea leaves.

Behavioural techniques involving prompting and verbal guidance (both to be eventually faded), augmented feedback and temporary adjustment of task demands (e.g. increasing the size of a button hole then progressively decreasing it) can be applied to enhance performance. Prompting itself may be viewed as a technique in which feedback from internal senses is provided through appropriate guidance.

A technique such as this last one aims to focus the child's attention on the essential discriminable features of the task that are involved in criterial performance and has been referred to as 'stimulus shaping'. Its application to teaching severely mentally retarded children has been demonstrated with nursery and self-help tasks and in some instances will prove more effective than traditional shaping techniques. It might be borne in mind that it is at the sub-component level that, in line with Schmidt's motor schema theory, variability of training will produce greatest generalisation when environmental demands related to that subcomponent change.

A Complementary Approach

We have emphasised in this article an essentially psychological approach to the question of goal-directed action and its motor component. With increasing severity of mental handicap specific physical problems will manifest themselves demanding specialist attention in the form of physiotheraphy (see Chapter 12 of the present volume). Visual and auditory problems will also occur in combination in rubella-damaged children. Here the starting point for intervention will differ markedly from the behavioural approach to action sequences noted above, though when success-ful will open the way for use of behavioural techniques.

Co-active intervention techniques were initially developed for use with rubella virus-damaged deaf-blind children primarily by Van Dijk (1977), though the approach has subsequently been used with physically and with mentally impaired children. It is based partly on the assumption that the basis for all learning is initially motoric, and also on the fact that many deaf-blind children do have residual vision and hearing that they can employ with appro-priate intervention. It is also claimed that other sense modalities, notably touch and smell, can be brought into play in a complemen-tary fashion.

As with behavioural techniques, stress is laid on the initial development of clear programme objectives. Complete curricula have been produced, notably by McInnes and Treffry (1982). In contrast to behavioural approaches, great emphasis is laid on emotional bonding between teacher or parent and the child in the early stages of intervention. McInnes and Treffry write: 'Regard-less of which type your multiply sensorily deprived child is, the first step is to make contact with him and to begin to establish an emotional bond. You will provide the motivation which will encourage the child to reach outside himself and to initiate inter-action between himself and the environment' (McInnes and Treffry 1982).

Intervention begins with close physical contact between teacher and child, e.g. with both on the floor and the latter supine between the teacher's legs. Chosen actions are guided by the teacher and the following sequences of reactions by the child described: resists; tolerates; co-operates passively; enjoys; responds co-operatively; leads; imitates; initiates. This sequence parallels the development of imitation from co-active responding, through to co-operative responding, and finally reactive responding.

Imitation is regarded as an important psychological develop-ment in ensuring that the child is learning to react to the environment. Similarly, co-active intervention will encourage anticipation also bringing the child more fully into contact with reality. Activities involving rhythm and repetition encourage awareness of temporal order. Again, an emphasis in co-active therapy on temporal order will enhance short-term memory (Van Dyke 1977), STM being poor in deaf-blind children. Development of an understanding of temporal order is also seen as critical to the development of communication which constitutes a major curriculum target area for co-active therapy.

Hogg and Sebba (1986) describe the use of co-active therapy with deaf-blind, profoundly retarded, multiply handicapped people in early cognitive development, communication, motor competence, and self-help competence on the basis of McInnes and Treffry's (1982) curriculum. It should be borne in mind that the effectiveness of the approach with this group has yet to be evaluated and that these authors themselves are concerned that '... proven extreme brain damage ...' may limit its effectiveness (Hogg and Sebba 1986; p. 6). However, given the special problems of multiply impaired, profoundly retarded people, the techniques of co-active intervention do offer an approach to their education which can lead into the voluntary production of goal-directed strategies and, in several respects, is compatible with specific behavioural techniques, such as prompting, shaping and imitation.

Conclusion

I have tried in this chapter to begin putting back together again the mentally handicapped child who, seen in the perspective of recent curriculum developments, has looked increasingly fragmented. The argument presented, however, should not be taken as one against the development of a carefully structured curriculum or the analysis of behaviour and training conditions. However, in the real world, cognition, language, social experience and motor behaviour are usually intimately bound up in almost every interaction in which we engage. The more we can retain these links the better, and there is no more appropriate place to start than with the re-integration of motor behaviour into the activities they serve. To achieve this re-integration we are certainly going to have to keep many balls in the air at the same time and leave behind the comfort of checklists and individual educational programmes as they have evolved in many schools. In this sense, learning to juggle still presents itself as a highly desirable skill.

References

Annett, J. (1969) *Feedback and Human Behaviour.* Penguin Books.

Bruner, J.S. (1970) 'The growth and structure of skill', in K. Connolly (ed.). *Mechanisms of Motor Skill Development.* Academic Press.

Connolly, K. (1973) 'Factors influencing the learning of manual skills by young children', in R.A Hinde and J. Stevenson-Hinde (eds.). *Constraints on Learning.* Academic Press, pp. 337-65.

Colvin, G.T. and Horner, R.H. (1983) 'Experimental analysis of generalisation: an evaluation of a general case program for teaching motor skills to severely handicapped learners', in J. Hogg and P.J. Mittler (eds.). *Aspects of Competence in Mentally Handicapped People:* Vol. 2 of *Advances in Mental Handicap Research.* Wiley, pp. 309-43.

Henderson, S.E. (1985) 'Motor skill development in Down's syndrome', in D. Lane and B. Stratford (eds.). *Current Approaches to Down's Syndrome.* Holt, Reinhart and Winston.

Hogg, J. (1981) 'Learning, using and generalising manipulative skills in a pre-school classroom by non-handicapped and Down's syndrome Children'. *Educational Psychology, 1,* pp. 319-40.

Hogg, J. (1982) 'Motor development and performance of severely mentally handicapped people'. *Developmental Medicine and Child Neurology, 24,* pp. 188-93.

Hogg, J. and Sebba, J. (1986) *Profound Retardation and Multiple Impairment.* Croom Helm.

Holle, B. (1976) *Motor Development in Children: normal and retarded.* Blackwell.

Kirman, B. (1975) 'Genetic errors: chromosome anomalies', in B. Kirman and J. Bicknell (eds.). *Mental Handicap.* Churchill Livingstone, pp. 121-65.

Lavatelli, C.S. (1970a) *Early Childhood Curriculum — a Piaget Program.* American Science and Engineering Company.

Lavatelli, C.S. (1970b) *Teacher's Guide to Accompany Early Childhood Curriculum.* American Science and Engineering Company.

Molnar, G.E. (1978) 'Analysis of motor disorder in retarded infants and young children'. *Am. Jnl of Mental Deficiency, 83,* pp. 213-22.

Moss, S.C. and Hogg, J. (1983) 'The development and integration of fine motor sequences in 12- to 18-month-old children: a test of the modular theory of motor skill development'. *Genetic Psychology Monograph, 107,* pp. 145-87.

McInnes, J.M. and Treffry, J.A. (1982) *Deaf-Blind Infants and Children: a developmental guide.* Open University and University of Toronto Press.

Piaget, J. (1953) *The Origin of Intelligence in the Child.* Routledge and Kegan Paul.

Quigley, N. (1982) 'An experiment to investigate motor schemas in Down's syndrome children'. Third year psychology dissertation, University of Manchester.

Reason, J. (1984) 'Lapses of attention in everyday life', in R. Parasuraman and D.R. Davis (eds.). *Varieties of Attention.* Academic Press, pp. 515-49.

Schmidt, R.A. (1975) 'A schema theory of discrete motor skill learning'. *Psychological Review, 82,* pp. 225-60.

Schmidt, R.A. (1976) 'The schema as a solution to some persistant problems in motor learning theory', in G.E. Stelmach (ed.). *Motor Control: issues and trends.* Academic Press, pp.41-65.

Shapiro, D.C. and Schmidt, R.A. (1982) 'The schema theory: recent evidence and developmental implications', in J.A.S. Kelso and J.E. Clark (eds.). *The Development of Movement Control and Co-ordination.* Wiley, pp. 113-50.

Shepherd, A. (1976) 'An improved tabular format for task analysis'. *Jnl of*

Occupational Psychology, 49, pp. 93-104.

Stokes, T.J. and Baer, D.M. (1977) 'An implicit technology of generalization'. *Jnl of Applied Behaviour Analysis, 10,* pp. 349-67.

Touwen, B.C.L. (1976) 'Neurological development in infancy'. *Clinics in Medicine, 58,* SIMP with Heinemann, pp. 99-110.

Van Dijk, J. (1977) 'What we have learnt in 12½ years: principles of deaf-blind education', in M.R. Jurgens (ed.). *Confrontation Between the Young Deaf-Blind Child and the Outer World: how to make the world surveyable by organised structure.* Swets and Zeitlinger B.V., pp. 1-10.

Von Cranach, M. (1982) 'The psychological study of goal-directed action: basic issues', in M. von Cranach and R. Harre (eds.). *The Analysis of Action.* Cambridge University Press, pp. 35-73.

Woodward, W.M. and Stern, D.J. (1963) 'Developmental patterns of severely subnormal children'. *Br. Jnl of Educational Psychology, 33,* pp. 10-21.

7 THE DEVELOPMENT OF LANGUAGE AND COMMUNICATION

Juliet Goldbart

Introduction

The last ten years have seen some dramatic changes in conceptualisations of child language which have implications for teaching language or communication skills to children with severe learning difficulties. In particular, there has been a shift of attention away from the structure of language towards the use of language, and hence towards the view adopted in this volume by Roulstone (Chapter 12) of the child as communicator. Unfortunately, the transfer of these ideas from academic theories of normal child language to classroom activities for teaching impaired or ineffective communicators has been slow. However, there is now a wide range of ideas for developing a language and communication curriculum based on contemporary views of the acquisition of language and communication skills.

The impetus for these changes has come from two related findings. First, a dissatisfaction with traditional, syntax-based, formal intervention programmes described by Roulstone as utilising asymmetrical interactions where the child is allowed only to take the respondant role (e.g. Bricker and Bricker 1974; Guess and Baer 1973). While success can be achieved in the programme, there is little evidence that the learned behaviours were generalised and used, communicatively, outside the teaching setting. The second issue relates to findings that children tend to stick at the single word stage (Leeming, Swann, Coupe and Mittler 1979). Mittler and Berry (1977) consider that this is partly due to the adults' reinforcement of labelling. These two problems, lack of generalisation and the possible teaching of maladaptive behaviours, have led teachers, speech therapists and researchers to look for a broader perspective on language and communication, and hence a sounder basis for intervention programmes.

In this chapter I will briefly review theories of language acquisition, explore the language of mentally handicapped children and adults and, finally, suggest a range of approaches to a language

153

and communication curriculum. Although words like 'language' and 'communication' are freely used, the precise meanings of these terms need to be understood. The following definitions will apply in this chapter.

Language is a set of rules by which meaning is conveyed. It can be made overt in many forms, e.g. English, Cantonese or Swahili, and many written and pictographic forms. Language has four rule systems:

1. phonology, concerning the rules governing the speech sounds used in a particular language, and in what positions and combinations, e.g. sv does not occur at the start of words in the English language, but does in Italian (similar rules hold in written language, but are harder to extract in signed or symbolic languages);
2. morphology, concerning the rules for changes in meaning which come about by the addition or prefixes and suffixes, or other changes within the word, e.g. view, review, preview; view, viewing, viewed;
3. syntax, concerning the rules for sequencing and organising words within sentences;
4. semantics, concerning the rules for the meaning or content of words.

Speech is one of the overt forms of language. It is an observable, recognisable behaviour. We make this conversion from language to speech using three main factors:

1. articulation, the process of producing speech sounds by movements of the speech organs, e.g. lips, tongue, palate and teeth;
2. voicing, the vibration at the level of the larynx which occurs when some sounds are made, e.g. v, d, z and not when others are made, e.g. f, t, s;
3. stress and rhythm, referring to the use of intonation patterns and emphasis in speech e.g. we can make the sentence, 'He's called John' a comment or a question.

Communication is a system of interpersonal interaction, the transmission of some message between two or more people. It has one further rule system: pragmatics which concerns the rules for the use of language in a communicative context, e.g. conversational turntaking, topic maintenance, making indirect requests.

As we will see later in this chapter, the child with severe learning difficulties often has little or no recognisable speech. These children may have very limited language skills or they may make their language overt by means of some sign or symbol system. Either way most of them will be making more or less successful attempts at communicating their opinions, needs and wishes. It is important, therefore, to focus attention on the mentally handicapped person as a communicator; hence the orientation of this chapter will be towards the development of communication as well as of language.

If we look back at how researchers have accounted for language acquisition in normally developing children, we may be able to draw implications for teaching children with severe learning difficulties.

Theories of Language Acquisition

Until the end of the 1960s, there were two main theories of language, each giving rise to its own account of language acquisition. These theories have become known by various titles including those referring to their key protagonists. On the one hand, the 'Chomskyan' or 'Grammarian' approach (Chomsky 1957, 1965), on the other, the 'Skinnerian' or 'Behaviourist' approach (Skinner 1957). Chomsky proposed a 'transformational grammar', a reductionist system allowing description of the structure of all possible utterances in a fully developed (mature user's) language system (see de Villiers and de Villiers 1978 for greater detail). The language of immature users (usually children) is described in relation to the mature system, and children are assumed to have an innate 'language acquisition device'. This enables them to extract data from language they hear, analyse it according to linguistic rules and produce novel sentences. In contrast, Skinner's account of language acquisition depends on the adult's selective reinforcement of the child's imitations of adult utterances.

While neither account was entirely satisfactory on its own in explaining how children acquire language (for a further discussion of this see Crystal 1976), both had something to offer to people trying to improve the language skills of people with severe learning difficulties. According to a 'grammarian' account, mentally handicapped people would be viewed as having immature or damaged brains and hence impaired, delayed or even non-existent language acquisition devices. Intervention here would have to involve presenting the child with clear and explicit examples of grammatical rules to make it easy for the rules to be extracted. The behaviourist approach to remediation would emphasise the need for reinforcement of attempts to communicate, together with clear models that the learner can imitate.

Most of the published attempts at language intervention with mentally handicapped people in the 1960s and at least the early 1970s follow these two strands. Usually the methods for teaching are behaviourist, but the selection of target behaviours was often influenced by the grammarian approach (Baer and Guess 1973; Garcia, Guess and Byrnes 1973; Guess, Sailor, Rutherford and Baer 1968), expecially where the learners had already acquired some spoken language. Some researchers in the mid-1960s felt that neither the behaviourist approach, nor the grammarian approach as it then stood, had taken sufficient account of how children's language actually grows and develops. These researchers (e.g. Brown 1973; McNeill 1970) studied the language actually used by young children.

Although influenced by Chomsky and the grammarian approach, both Brown and McNeill emphasised the need to look at meanings encoded in young children's language, that is in semantic development. From the work of Brown and McNeill, and those who followed their approach (e.g. Bloom 1970; Bowerman 1973) it became apparent that early language could equally be categorised and analysed using a semantic framework. Researchers like Brown and Bloom, and others (Snow 1972; Nelson 1973) drew on both Chomsky's and Skinner's ideas. However, their emphasis on semantics, cognitive development and the role of adult input has led them to be considered as a new approach: the psycholinguistic approach. Despite the fertile nature of research, its influence on the education of children with severe learning difficulties has been slow.

The final section of this chapter will examine the part that semantics and pragmatics can play in this work.

The Importance of Semantics

The shift in interest from syntax to semantics in the early 1970s arose in part from a realisation that the child's level of thinking and understanding about the world heavily influenced what he or she was communicating, and also from the limitations of looking at syntax in children just learning to talk. Trying to assign syntactical labels to single words did not work too well; it was more helpful to look at content or meaning than structure.

Leonard defines semantic notions (or semantic roles) as 'those aspects of cognitive structure that the child may attempt to communicate' (Leonard 1984; p. 153). Thus, the meanings which children attempt to express are reflections of their understanding of objects and events. It is not surprising then that the first meanings children attempt to communicate relate to objects to people and things that happen to objects or people. The most commonly cited examples are 'existence', 'non-existence', 'disappearance' and 'recurrence' (Bloom 1973; Bloom and Lahey 1978).

Existence.   The child comments verbally or non-verbally on the existence of an entity. This may include requesting the name of the entity, e.g. 'that!' or 'what's that?'

Non-existence. The child comments on the absence of an expected entity, e.g. 'No ' 'Shoe?'

Disappearance. The child comments on, or requests the disappearance of an entity, e.g. 'gone', 'bye-bye'.

Recurrence.   The child comments on, or requests the re-appearance of an entity, e.g. 'more', 'again'.

Other writers have described the fuller range of meanings that children go on to express as they progress from sensorimotor to pre-operational level in their cognitive development and which may require more than a single word or symbol or sign. The precise content of these lists vary from writer to writer. The following list is from Leonard (1984).

Semantic Notion	*What is being expressed*
Nomination	naming
Recurrence	awareness of potential for re-appearance or re-enactment

Denial	the rejection of a proposition
Non-existence	recognition of the absence of an object formerly present
Rejection	prevention or cessation of an activity or appearance of an object
Action + Object	an animate receives the force of an action
Agent + Action	an animate initiates an activity
Location	spatial relationship between two objects
Possession	object is associated with someone or something
Attribution	properties not inherently part of the class to which the object belongs
Experience + Experiencer	animate affected by event
Action + Instrument	inanimate causally affected in an activity

Obviously we can communicate these meanings in more or less complex ways, from frantic arm flapping, to requests that an event be repeated, to a lengthy memorandum with the same purpose. In fact, we could think of language development, at least in part, as being the increasing complexity of syntax and morphology used to transmit a particular meaning.

Later in this chapter we will examine approaches to intervention which draw on a semantic framework for the selection of target behaviours, and where teaching methods are based on children understanding and communicating about cognitive notions, that is about objects and events in the environment.

Pragmatics: The Social Functional Approach

Linguists had known for some time that the same sentence could mean different things depending on the context in which it was said and the way it was said, and in the 1970s this realisation that the function of an utterance was important began to affect the study of language acquisition. Bruner (1975) and Bates, Camaioni and Volterra (1975) demonstrated that the sounds and gestures children made before they used recognisable words often had purposes which could be interpreted by a receptive observer.

Many researchers have shown that the child's communicative competence begins well inside the first year. Bates *et al.* (1975) identify stage 5, or possibly stage 4 of Piaget's sensorimotor period as the point from which clear functional communicative behaviours can be identified. However, even before this, the baby's main care givers have paved the way for this development in their early interactions. Bruner (1983) has identified four stages leading towards the beginnings of spoken language. The first, phase 1, lasting from birth to six months, involves the establishment of joint attention, that is the infant and the adult attend to the same object, person or event in the same way. The primary care giver brings this about by attention-getting strategies like shaking the object, by talking and by using the infant's name or phrases like 'Look!' During the second phase, intentional communication is established. The infant is increasingly interested in objects and starts reaching for them. By about eight months (Bruner 1978) the baby incorporates looking at the adult in the act of reaching. The infant at this stage has two reaches, a 'reach-for-real' and a 'reach-for-signal'. The adult reinforces this by giving the infant the object being reached for or giving encouragement for additional effort.

During phase 3, vocalisation is incorporated into the act, and the reach, at least in some circumstances, becomes a point. The adult responds by incorporating the object or event in question into what he or she is saying to the child. Joint reference has clearly been established by this point. In the final phase, the child starts to use words, naming and commenting on objects and events. Adults facilitate this by labelling the objects of joint reference and then, using questions, encouraging the child to verbalise about the object. Joint attention and joint reference are seen by Bruner and others as being very important for language learning.

In phase 2 we can see two clear functions emerging. Bates *et al.* (1975) describe one as a 'protoimperative' where the child uses the adult to achieve a desired end; for example, an open-handed reach towards the biscuit tin, accompanied by alternately looking to the adult and the biscuit tin. During phase 3 a vocalisation, perhaps 'Uh uh uh!' would be added to the communicative act. The other function Bates *et al.* describe is the 'protodeclarative'. The intention here is to establish joint attention to the object or to obtain attention from the adult. By phase 3 the reaching gesture has become a point and will be accompanied by a vocalisation e.g., 'dah!' which seems to serve as a comment.

From these early, simple functions others develop. As with semantic notions many different writers have categorised the range of functions we need to be able to communicate fully. Halliday's list is arranged developmentally, the first four functions being acquired before the latter three (Halliday 1975). (The first two will be recognisable from Bates *et al.* above).

Halliday's Functions

Function	Its purpose
Instrumental	: satisfying one's needs.
Regulatory	: controlling the behaviour of others.
Interactional	: establishing and defining social relationships.
Personal	: expressing awareness of self, of opinions and feelings.
Heuristic	: seeking information.
Imaginative	: pretending, expressing fantasy.
Informative	: giving information.

Ways of using semantic and pragmatic functions in teaching communication skills will be discussed in the final section of the chapter. Syntactical, semantic and pragmatic accounts should not be thought of as mutually exclusive, but rather, complementary approaches to the analysis of communication. At different stages of development, however, one approach may be more useful than another.

Speech and Language Abilities of Mentally Handicapped Children and Adults

What then is known about the current status of speech and language abilities of the mentally handicapped? The findings of two recent surveys provide us with some useful guidelines, although they focus only on children of school age, are cross-sectional rather than longitudinal and have only sampled a limited number of schools.

The first study, Leeming *et al.* (1979) found that 26.5 per cent of children in ESN(S) schools could not use or imitate single words and a further 7 per cent were only at the stage of using single words. Kiernan, Reid and Jones (1981), in the second survey, support this with their finding that 31 per cent of children in ESN(S) schools and 65 per cent of children in hospital schools had, at the most, three single words to express their needs. Many of these children will, of course, be much more limited in their expressive abilities. Leeming *et al.* found that about 33 per cent of 10 year olds use phrases or sentences over two words in length, about 26 per cent use two-word utterances, leaving about 41 per cent functioning below this level. At the 16+ age range the percentage using grammatical phrases over two words in length goes up to about 55 per cent although 18 per cent have not even acquired single words.

Some would argue that mentally handicapped people's language and communication difficulties simply reflect their delayed development, therefore intervention is unlikely to be effective. However, it seems (Snyder and McLean 1976) that, for many mentally handicapped people, language is more delayed than other areas of development. Certainly, Leeming *et al.*'s data would suggest that very slow progress is made during middle childhood. For all these reasons intervention on language and communication skills, at all levels from pre-verbal to complex sentences, is likely to be needed across the age range.

There are two other ways that researchers have studied language development. One, which we will consider in some detail, is the type of language input that mentally handicapped people receive from other people. The other involves fine-grained studies of how mentally handicapped children compare to normally developing children in very specific areas of language, for example, morphology. The aim of these detailed studies has generally been to find out whether the language of mentally handicapped people is simply delayed, or reflects a more complex deviance from normal development. This has implications for the extent to which we can adopt a developmental model (selecting target behaviours and teaching methods from normal development) and to what extent we need to find alternative rationales for selecting target behaviours and methods.

In a fuller review, Kiernan (1985) concludes that 'the delay or similar sequence hypothesis gains more support from published data than the deviance or difference hypothesis'. However, as Kiernan concedes, different aspects of language (phonology, morphology, etc.) may be differentially delayed. Unfortunately, most of this research has been carried out with more able mentally handicapped subjects. More severely mentally handicapped people are likely to have additional sensory and structural handicaps which may have severe effects on their language learning ability. Hence, in a school for pupils with severe learning difficulties, a developmental model may not be appropriate for all language intervention work.

Another area of interest is the extent to which language teaching and intervention might be responsible for differences between normally developing children and those with severe learning difficulties. For example, some researchers have found (discussed in Hedge 1980; 1981) that mentally handicapped children's early language contains a higher ratio of nominals to other parts of speech, perhaps because our teaching has focused on teaching object names. This brings us onto a very important issue: the language input received by mentally handicapped people.

Talking to Mentally Handicapped Children and Adults

If we accept the idea that children learn language from what they hear and, furthermore, that much of the language heard by young children is carefully tailored to help them in this learning, then it is important to discover whether or not people talking to mentally handicapped language learners also make appropriate adjustments. The findings of many studies of mothers talking to their mentally handicapped children have been of little use since the children were matched with normally developing children on the basis of chronological or mental age. This ignores the greater delays that often exist in language as compared with other aspects of the child's development.

Studies like those of Rondal (1978) and Buckholt, Rutherford and Goldberg (1978) where the children are matched on measures of linguistic development find the language of mothers of Down's syndrome children to be very similar to that of mothers of normally developing children. This suggests that mothers of Down's syndrome children are sensitive to the levels of understanding and language use of their children and are, hence, providing them with appropriate language input. However, it should be noted that these are studies of young children; it may be more difficult for parents as their children get older, and cues, such as age, size, expressive language abilities and comprehension become more and more dissonant. Some studies of mentally handicapped children have found qualitative differences in the way mentally handicapped and normally developing children converse with their mothers. Jones (1977) finds them initiating less and Terdal, Jackson and Garner (1976) find them less responsive. These findings have led to suggestions that it is harder to maintain an interaction with a handicapped child, so parents and others adopt slightly different styles of interaction in order to try and keep conversation going. This is, of course, a contentious area and needs further research.

There are a small number of studies which have looked at interactions between mentally handicapped children and adults, and teachers and residential staff. Beveridge and Hurrell (1980) recorded teachers' responses to 2000 initiations made by four children in each of ten classes in ESN(S) schools. The most common responses were brief verbal acknowledgements — then moves away or redirects attention (33.4 per cent), ignoring (23.3 per cent) and simple, immediate responses — e.g. 'yes', 'good' — (20.3 per cent). Responses which maintain the interaction make up a much smaller percentage: verbalisation expanding content or idea (15.6 per cent) and verbalisation changing content or idea (1.5 per cent). It looks, from these data, as though teachers (at least in this study) may be missing opportunities for engaging in interactions with their pupils aimed at encouraging language development.

Similar findings occur in studies of staff in residential establishments. Prior, Minnes, Coyne, Golding, Hendy and McGillivary (1979) found staff using 'instruction' most frequently and 'conversation' least frequently. They also found a very high frequency of staff ignoring initiations by residents. Pratt, Bumstead and Raynes

(1976) reported that talk had the function of controlling rather than informing. This is important because Tizard, Cooperman, Joseph and Tizard (1972), in a study of residential nurseries, found that talk defined as 'informative' was better for residents' language development than that defined as 'controlling'. Furthermore, they found that the frequency of informative utterances was a good predictor of the comprehension abilities of the children. All these studies seem to suggest that adult language is, potentially, an important factor in the language development of children with severe learning difficulties.

All the levels of analysis discussed so far, syntax and morphology, semantics and pragmatics, have something to offer in terms of the teaching of language and communication. But their importance changes with the current level of communicative skills of the person we are trying to teach. We will be discussing some speculative ideas for individuals at a pre-intentional level and lead on through early intentional communication to ideas for enabling those using simple sentences to communicate more effectively in real-life settings. Thus, a framework of a communication curriculum is to be outlined — but is not intended as definitive.

General Guidelines for Promoting Communication

If we adopt the view that we learn language in order to communicate, it follows that the person who has nothing to communicate has little incentive for language learning. It could then be argued that the classroom where everyone is toiletted regularly, where food and drink are distributed at set times, where toys and activities are provided and changed at regular intervals and where anyone having difficulties with a task is noticed and helped swiftly, may be a classroom where there is little to communicate and the environment may not be beneficial for language and communicative development.

Kiernan and Reid (1983) argue that the individual needs four things in order to communicate:

1. the 'idea of communication', that is the realisation that he or she can affect the behaviour of others by vocalisations or actions;
2. 'something to say', in other words the person must have wishes, needs or preferences that they want others to know about;

3. 'reasons for communication', the person must believe that, by communication, he or she can get other people to satisfy his or her wishes, needs or preferences;

4. 'a means of communication', whether through words, natural gestures, signs, symbols, facial expressions, or any combination of these, the individual must have a way of expressing him or herself.

In the next section we will be describing some ideas for working with individuals who have not yet acquired the first of these four requirements, and the subsequent sections consider ways of facilitating increasingly sophisticated means of communication. Thereafter, it is the responsibility of staff to set up situations in the classroom or training centre whereby individuals have some need to communicate. We will propose four broad areas for setting up situations which promote communication.

1. Giving children the opportunity to indicate real choices, needs and preferences, for example, 'Do you want milk or orange?' 'Which apple do you want?'

2. Giving the child the opportunity to request and refuse events and objects, for example, 'Do you want to go to the toilet?'

3. Setting up the occurrence of unpredictable events, or the non-occurrence of normally reliable events, for example, breaking the tips off pencils or taking the refill out of biros, taking the middle pin out of classroom scissors or handing round an empty biscuit tin.

4. Setting up opportunities for problem-solving by individuals and groups, for example, three children to bring a large or heavy object from one side of a crowded classroom to another, a child to obtain a desired toy which is within sight but out of reach. (I am indebted to many class teachers for these devious ideas!)

Deciding on appropriate methods and contexts for this kind of work is likely to involve sensitising ourselves to the way in which pupils are currently attempting to communicate, using assessments like the Affective Communication Assessment (Coupe, Barton, Barber, Collins, Levy and Murphy 1985) and the Pre-verbal Communication Schedule (Kiernan and Reid 1985) which will be described in the next two sections. Thus, we can become aware of systematic ways in which particular individuals may attempt to affect their environment. By responding to these albeit unsophisticated attempts we are, at the very least, reinforcing attempts at communication.

For an individual to make progress it is essential that all the important people in his or her environment are familiar with, and understand, the means of communication he or she uses. This has wide implications when we consider the range of non-verbal communications systems that may be used within a school. It is also a reminder that parents and/or residential care staff need to be involved in the teaching of language and communication skills, at least to the extent that they, too, understand the means of communication and the range of functions the person in their care may be trying to express.

With pupils or trainees on any kind of intervention programme we should be ensuring that classroom situations provide the opportunity for appropriate use of the target behaviours they are learning in the programme. This is essential if we are to avoid the problem of lack of generalisation experienced in earlier attempts to teach language behaviours. It will also provide a check on the functional nature of our target behaviours, for, if we cannot find a context for learners to use what they have learned, we are not selecting useful behaviours!

Finally, for some pupils, a language and communication programme may simply involve selective reinforcement for using already established communicative behaviours in the classroom or elsewhere. The range of pragmatic functions used may be extended by this method, whereby a small range of words or signs are used for an increasing number of purposes, or the number of partners a child will communicate with can be extended with the help of, for example, co-operative dinner-ladies. Again, this is important if the child or adult is going to be able to exert control over his or her environment outside the classroom.

Intervention at the Pre-intentional Level

This concerns those profoundly mentally handicapped people who appear not to demonstrate any attempts at communication. These children would score on very few sections of the Pre-verbal Communication Schedule (P.V.C.) (Kiernan and Reid 1986), perhaps only those described by Kiernan and Reid as 'Pre-Communicative Behaviours'. It may be, however, that these individuals have behaviours or responses which do communicate to the receptive observer though they may not even be intentional. Coupe *et al.* (1985) have devised an 'Affective Communicative Assessment' which is intended to help parents, classroom staff and others to identify reliable responses to events, people or other stimuli. Although these responses are not intentional communication they may be interpretable as indicating likes or dislikes. In the next stage in Coupe *et al.*'s work, guidance is given to identify ways of facilitating the individual's development from this pre-intentional stage to intentional communication.

In her studies of normally developing babies of six to eleven months, Gibb Harding (1983) describes how the mother, already responding to a wide range of her infant's behaviours, comes to infer intentional communication when the infant gestures or vocalises or regards her or an object as part of some goal-directed behaviour. She responds consistently to these behaviours; she interprets them as intentional, giving important feedback. We could see this as the mother shaping communicative behaviour; and it certainly suggests that, having identified some consistent behaviours emitted by a child, we need to respond to those in a reliable way. This is aimed at giving feedback which should help the transition to intentional communication. However, many children or adults at this level have cognitive delays and motor and sensory difficulties which limit their progress towards goal-directed behaviour. While there is, as yet, no clear proof that training of cognitive skills at this stage promotes communicative development, the close connection between intentional communication and goal-directed behaviour suggests that intervention in this area of the curriculum might be profitable. (See Roberts and Schaefer 1984 for a particularly good chapter on this topic.)

Early Intervention Based on Pragmatic Functions

Early in this chapter we presented Halliday's list of pragmatic functions (Halliday 1975). This, or a similar list by Williams (1980), could serve as a guide to a curriculum for intervention at the pragmatic level. Having observed what functions the child expresses, and in what contexts, we can intervene by teaching later functions, e.g. by giving the child information which needs to be passed to someone else, or by methods discussed under the section in this chapter on 'General guidelines for promoting communication', and by extending the contexts in which these functions are expressed.

An assessment scheme for pre-linguistic and pre-verbal individuals who may, nevertheless, have some functional communication, is Kiernan and Reid's Pre-Verbal Communication Schedule (PVC) (Kiernan and Reid 1985). It provides a framework for parents, classroom staff, etc. to assess and evaluate the types of things a pre-verbal individual is trying to communicate and what means he or she is using in these attempts. The individual's responses to other people's attempts at interaction are also evaluated. From the information gleaned in the assessment, the child or adult can be taught more sophisticated or more readily understandable methods of expressing things they have shown a wish to communicate, and also be introduced to situations where they may have other pragmatic functions to express. By basing targets for teaching on what we know the child or adult wants or needs to communicate, we are teaching skills which are more likely to generalise to use outside the teaching context. We are also avoiding the authoritarianism which Muma (1978) sees as pervading most attempts at language intervention, where the individual learner's needs are not given sufficient consideration.

An example of work at this level would be the shaping of a clear gesture, perhaps one drawn from a recognised sign system, to enable the learner to request items on view, or another gesture for rejecting something that is being offered. Thus, a repertoire of gestures, signs, symbols or differentiated vocalisations (or combinations of these) can be built up so that the learner can express a wide range of functions.

Intervention at the Semantic Level

As described earlier, many writers see a semantic framework as the best way of classifying or describing very early language development. Leonard (1984) clearly distinguishes semantic notions and cognitive notions, describing semantic notions as those aspects of cognitive structure that the child may attempt to communicate. Interpreting this distinction strictly leads to direct teaching of semantic roles, whereas a rather looser distinction allows the teaching of cognitive pre-requisites as part of a programme to teach semantic roles. Thus, we have two methods for intervening at the semantic level.

The first method is Leonard's own. He recommends assessing children to identify the roles or notions they are expressing. Then, by modelling, the range of use of roles already established is expanded by using them with different exemplars. Then, again by modelling, new roles are taught using familiar words and contexts.

The second intervention method was proposed and researched by Brinker (1978) and has been extended by Kiernan and Reid. This involves selecting a play context in which the learner can observe and act out a specific range of cognitive roles, and hence a variety of semantic roles can be expressed to describe or request these various cognitive acts. The two contexts chosen by Brinker were a tea-party and putting a doll to bed. The child is encouraged to play with the toys, for example a doll, doll's dress and shoes, a bed and a blanket and a hairbrush. The teacher, using short utterances at a level appropriate to the child's level of understanding, describes the child's play, thus modelling a defined set of semantic roles. The child's understanding can be assessed by the teacher requesting certain items or actions from the child. When the child can be seen to understand a range of semantic roles these can be extended to expressive use by means of role reversal (Kiernan and Reid 1983).

It can be seen that this approach builds on the establishment of joint attention and joint reference described earlier in this chapter, whereby shared interest in objects provides a teaching context. The emphasis is on the linking of cognitive development, early symbolic play and early language development. (For further discussion of this area see McConkey 1984.)

Barton and Coupe (1985) demonstrate how children were taught to express a wide range of semantic roles, with gestures, single words or vocalisation plus gesture. The methods involved performing or observing very simple events or objects, like disappearance, existence and recurrence, and being prompted through and having modelled expression of the appropriate semantic role. This work is particularly useful since it provides a bridge for children who are intentionally communicating a range of pragmatic functions, but are not yet ready for the two methods described earlier in this section which assume a certain level of play with objects.

If the learner participates successfully in a semantic-based programme like that of Leonard (1984) or Brinker (1978) described above, it is probably appropriate to start thinking about

extending the structures they are using, that is to consider intervention at a syntactical level.

Intervention at the Syntactical and Morphological Level

This is the most extensively researched level of language intervention with children with severe learning difficulties. The aim has
usually been to use behavioural methods of modelling and reinforcement to increase specific aspects of the structural complexity
of our subjects' utterances. Limitations of intervention approaches
have occurred due to pupils' difficulties in generalising to spontaneous use (Harris 1984). The major problem seems to be that
the context for this type of intervention programme is far removed
from the situation in which we normally use language, that is a
communicative situation (Muma 1978). This is supported by
Roulstone (see below Chapter 12) in her appeal that we emphasise
the notion of the 'child as communicator'.

Earlier in this chapter we defined communication as the transmission of some message between two or more people. A teaching
situation which involves mainly imitation or picture description
does not, therefore, involve much communication and is far
removed from the contexts (also described earlier in this chapter)
in which children normally acquire language and communications
skills.

An additional problem, certainly until the mid 1970s, has been
the dearth of syntactical and morphological assessment material. If
we wish to follow a developmental model and select targets for
teaching on the basis of normal developmental data (as recommended by e.g. Bloom and Lahey 1978; Miller and Yoder 1974;
Ruder and Smith 1984), we need a way of identifying what structures a particular individual has at any given level, and which are
missing. This task was greatly facilitated by the publication in 1976
of the LARSP (The Language Assessment, Remediation and
Screening Profile) (Crystal, Fletcher and Garman 1976) which
enables a spontaneous language sample to be analysed to produce
a profile of the speaker's use of different morphological and syntactical structures.

This analysis requires a good knowledge of linguistics. Hence
this type of assessment is best done by a speech therapist or a
teacher and therapist working together. It is useful from the stage
where the child is using two words (signs or symbols) such as 'big
car', 'mummy ball'. We can then set up play/teaching situations in

which the as-yet-unused target structure can be used. The target in this context is a grammatical structure, e.g. subject verb (SV). The range of possible SV utterances is, of course, very large, and a wide range of exemplars can be used, the choice of materials determining which exemplars are appropriate.

This method described and evaluated by Martin, McConkey and Martin (1984) involves an adult and a child attending to the play situation, the adult either modelling utterances which relate to the actions the child is performing in the play situation or expanding very simple comments the child makes such that they encode one more piece of information about the action or event. For example, if the child pouring tea, says 'tea!' the adult might say 'yes, pour tea!', or 'mm, tea in cup!'

By extending this approach using 'loose-training', defined by Ruder and Smith as 'a method of training wherein the acquisition of a particular linguistic form is designed to occur across more than a single stimulus condition or linguistic context' (Ruder and Smith 1984: p. 6), it is anticipated that generalisation will be promoted. So, for the structure SV, suitable play settings might be a small group of children performing actions like jumping, walking, clapping and singing, or a teacher and a child playing with small dolls and some dolls' house furniture acting out actions like cooking, riding, washing and so on. The play contexts should be chosen so that the names of the objects and actions are within the child's single word (or sign or symbol) vocabulary, and so that the contexts themselves are interesting and enjoyable for the child. Thereafter, the child must have opportunities to use these newly acquired structures outside the teaching situation.

The more specific knowledge teachers now possess about the child's current level of language development and the type of input that is appropriate to this level helps them to respond appropriately to different children's initiations during the classroom day (cf. above comments on research by Beveridge and Hurrell 1980).

Later Intervention Using Pragmatics

The functional use of language, having been proposed as a framework for intervention with learners still at a pre-verbal stage, has influenced intervention at what might almost be considered the opposite end of the spectrum: work with severely learning disabled school leavers and adults who do have some spoken language. The aim here is to enable these students to use the language skills they have acquired more effectively in everday situations. One aspect of this curriculum is similar to contemporary approaches to foreign language teaching, for example Wilkins' 'Minimum Adequate Grammar' (Wilkins 1974). This involves using role play and other functional situations to give students practice in using expressions of time, space and quantity; giving them formats for requesting, stating, agreeing, preferring; practising asking for and giving instructions and directions etc.

In parallel with this we need to draw on social skills training, in working on non-verbal communications e.g. appropriate eye contact, proximity and touching in a variety of communicative situations, using different registers for different social partners and developing skills for coping with conflict situations. This work appears effective but is in need of formal evaluation.

Intervention on Speech Sounds

At certain points in the child or adult's acquisition of language it may be thought that specific intervention on the production of speech sounds would aid intelligibility. Such decisions are best made in discussion with a speech therapist. It is important to remember that intelligibility is affected by the correctness of the structure of an utterance as well as the correctness of the sounds, so improving speech sound production will not necessarily be a priority for mentally handicapped people.

Language Kits and Programmes

A number of widely used kits and programmes are available for use with children with severe learning difficulties. But how does a teacher or speech therapist select a good programme which is appropriate to a particular individual's or class's needs? In developing a curriculum it is important for staff to be aware of available programmes, to evaluate their appropriateness and usefulness as a basis for curriculum content. Over the past 15 to 20 years a wide diversity of kits and programmes has been published, many designed specifically for use with moderately and severely mentally handicapped children. They vary enormously in such ways as the aspects of language and communication they cover, the age and abilities of learners they are designed for, the knowledge and skills they require of teachers, their flexibility and the extent to which they have been evaluated.

Two very good articles save the teacher or therapist the background research needed to evaluate a range of programmes. In the first of these articles Harris (1984) submits 23 published programmes to a very rigorous evaluation mainly centred on the approach to language that the programme takes and the extent to which the programme has been evaluated. Some of the well-known programmes which are subjected to Harris's scrutiny are 'The Derbyshire Language Programme' (Masidlover and Knowles 1982), 'The First Words Language Programme' (Gillham 1979) and 'Two Sentences Together' (Gillham 1983), 'Language Development Through Structured Teaching' (Robson 1982) and 'Putting Two Words Together' (McConkey and O'Connor 1981), the latter two being the most favourably reviewed.

In the other article, Kiernan (1984) considers only four programmes but the article clearly demonstrates how to evaluate a programme, and I have drawn on his criteria, as well as those of Harris to provide a flowchart to aid the decision-making process for teachers and speech therapists.

Figure 7.1: A Flowchart for Selecting Language Programmes

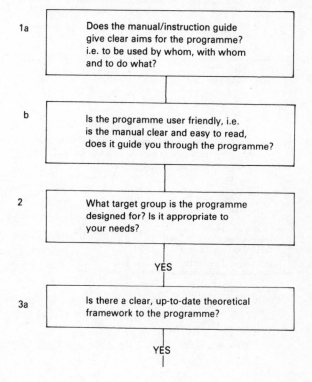

Figure 7.1 continued

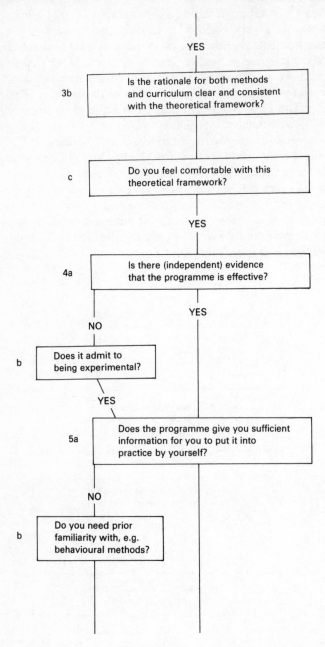

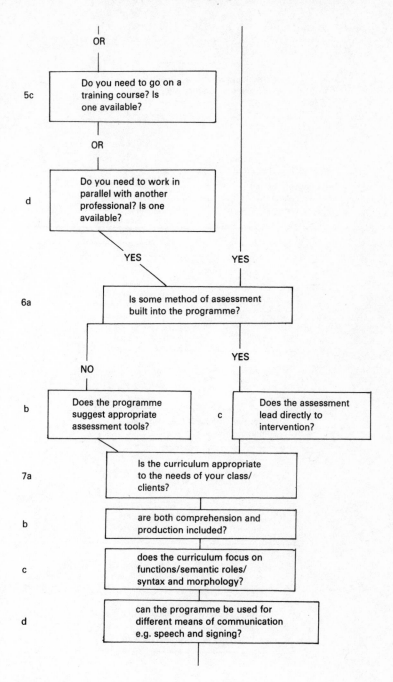

5c — Do you need to go on a training course? Is one available?

OR

d — Do you need to work in parallel with another professional? Is one available?

YES   YES

6a — Is some method of assessment built into the programme?

NO   YES

b — Does the programme suggest appropriate assessment tools?

c — Does the assessment lead directly to intervention?

7a — Is the curriculum appropriate to the needs of your class/ clients?

b — are both comprehension and production included?

c — does the curriculum focus on functions/semantic roles/ syntax and morphology?

d — can the programme be used for different means of communication e.g. speech and signing?

Figure 7.1 continued

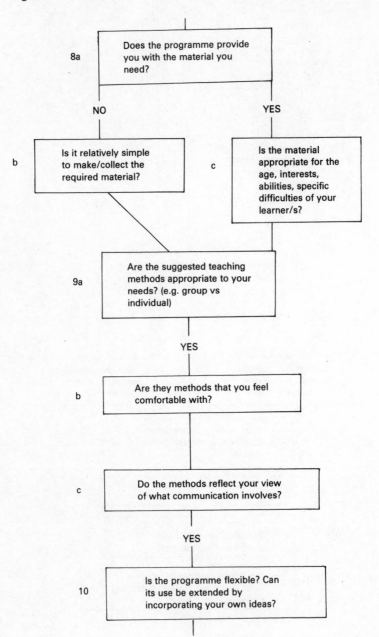

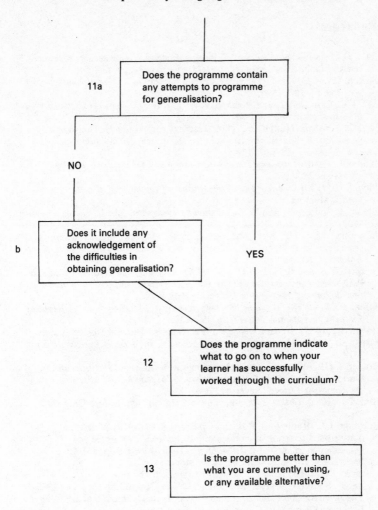

Conclusions

Any chapter on communication and mental handicap must, necessarily, be selective. I am conscious of a number of important issues which have so far been omitted; for this reason, the chapter finishes with an annotated bibliography to provide the reader with a range of good references and give greater detail on topics discussed as well as, at least background reading on topics not covered.

References

Baer, D.M. and Guess, D. (1973) 'Teaching productive noun suffixes to severely retarded children'. *Am. Jnl of Mental Deficiency, 77*, pp. 498-505.
Barton, L. and Coupe, J. (1985) 'Teaching first meanings'. *Mental Handicap, 13,* no 2, pp. 67-70. BIMH.
Bates, E., Camaioni, L. and Volterra, V. (1975) 'The acquisition of performatives prior to speech', *Merrill-Palmer Quarterly, 21*, pp. 205-16.
Beveridge, M. and Hurrell, P. (1980) 'Teachers' responses to severely mentally handicapped children's initiations in the classroom'. *Jnl of Child Psychology and Psychiatry, 21*, pp. 175-81.
Bloom, L. (1970) *Language Development: form and function in emerging grammars.* MIT Press.
Bloom, L. (1973) *One Word at a Time: the use of single-word utterances before syntax.* Mouton.
Bloom, L. and Lahey, M. (1978) *Language Development and Language Disorders.* Wiley.
Bowerman, M. (1973) 'Structural relationships in children's utterances: syntactic or semantic?', in T. Moore (ed.). *Cognitive Development and the Acquisition of Language.* Academic Press.
Bricker, W.A. and Bricker, D.D. (1974) 'An early language training strategy', in R.L. Schiefelbush and L.L. Lloyd (eds.). *Language Perspectives: acquisition, retardation and intervention.* University Park Press.
Brinker, R.P. (1978) 'Teaching language in context, a feasibility study'. *Revue de Phonetique Appliquée, 46-47*, pp. 195-203.
Brown, R. (1973) *A First Language: the early stages.* Harvard University Press.
Bruner, J. (1975) 'The ontogenesis of speech acts'. *Jnl of Child Language, 2*, pp. 1-19.
Bruner, J. (1978) 'Learning how to do things with words', in J. Bruner and A. Gurton (eds.). *Wolfson College Lectures 1976: Human Growth and Development.* Oxford University Press.
Bruner J. (1983) *Child's Talk: Learning to Use Language.* Oxford University Press.
Buckholt, J.A., Rutherford, R.B. and Goldberg, K.E. (1978) 'Verbal and non-verbal interaction of mothers with their Down's syndrome and non-retarded infants'. *Am. Jnl of Mental Deficiency, 82*, pp. 337-43.
Chomsky, N. (1957) *Syntactic Structures.* Mouton.
Chomsky, N. (1965) *Aspects of Theory of Syntax.* MIT Press.
Coupe, J., Barton, L., Barber, M., Collins, L., Levy, D. and Murphy, D. (1985) *The Affective Communication Assessment.* Available through Manchester Education Committee, Crown Square, Manchester.
Crystal, D. (1976) *Child Language, Learning and Linguistics.* Edward Arnold.
Crystal, D., Fletcher, P. and Garman, M. (1976) *The Grammatical Analysis of Language Disability.* Edward Arnold.
Garcia, E., Guess, D. and Byrnes, J. (1973) 'Development of syntax in a retarded girl using procedures of imitation, reinforcement and modelling'. *Jnl of Applied Behaviour Analysis, 6*, pp. 299-310.
Gibb Harding, C. (1983) 'Setting the stage for language acquisition: communication development in the first year', in R.M. Golinkoff (ed.). *The Transition from Prelinguistic to Linguistic Communication.* Lawrence Erlbaum.
Gillham, W. (1979) *The First Words Language Programme.* George Allen and Unwin.
Gillham, W. (1983) *Two Words Together: a first sentences language programme.* George Allen and Unwin.

Guess, D. and Baer, D.M. (1973) 'An analysis of individual differences in generalization between receptive and productive language in retarded children'. *Jnl of Applied Behaviour Analysis, 6,* pp. 311-29.

Guess, D., Sailor, W., Rutherford, G. and Baer, D.M. (1968) 'An experimental analysis of linguistic development: the productive use of the plural morpheme'. *Jnl of Applied Behaviour Analysis, 1,* pp. 297-306.

Halliday, M. (1975) *Learning How to Mean: explorations in the development of language.* Edward Arnold.

Harris, J. (1984) 'Early language intervention programmes'. *Assoc. for Child Pscyhology and Psychiatry Newsletter, 6,* pp. 2-20.

Hedge, M. (1980) 'Issues in the study and explanation of language behaviour'. *Jnl of Psycholinguistic Research, 9,* pp. 1-22.

Hedge, M. (1981) 'An experimental-clinical analysis of grammatical and behavioural distinctions'. *Jnl of Speech and Hearing Research, 23,* pp. 864-76.

Jones, O.H.M. (1977) 'Mother-child communication with pre-linguistic Down's syndrome and normal infants', in H.R. Schaffer (ed.). *Studies in Mother-Infant Interaction.* Academic Press.

Kiernan, C.C. (1984) 'Language remediation programmes: a review', in D.J. Müller (ed.). *Remediating Children's Language.* Croom Helm.

Kiernan, C.C. (1985) 'Communication', in A.D.B. Clarke and A.M. Clarke (eds.). *Mental Deficiency: the changing outlook (remediation).* Methuen.

Kiernan, C.C. and Reid, B.D. (1985) *Preverbal Communication Schedule.* NFER. in press.

Kiernan, C.C. and Reid, B.D. (1983) *Foundations of Communication and Language: Course Materials,* 2nd edn. Thomas Corum Research Unit.

Kiernan, C.C., Reid, B.D. and Jones, L.M. (1982) 'Signs and Symbols: A Review of Literature and Survey of Use of Non-verbal Communication systems'. University Institute of Education, *Studies in Education, no. 11.*

Leeming, K., Swann, W., Coupe, J. and Mittler, P. (1979) *Teaching Language and Communication to the Mentally Handicapped.* Evans/Methuen Educational.

Leonard, L.B. (1984) 'Semantic considerations in early language training', in K.F. Ruder and M.D. Smith (eds.). *Developmental Language Intervention.* University Park Press.

Martin, H., McConkey, R. and Martin, S. (1984) 'From acquisition theories to intervention strategies'. *Br. Jnl of Disorders of Communication, 19,* pp. 3-14.

Masidlover, M. and Knowles, W. (1977). *The Derbyshire Language Scheme.* Unpublished, available from Psychological Service, Education Office, Grosvenor Road, Ripley, Derbyshire.

McConkey, R. (1984) 'The assessment of representational play: a springboard for language remediation', in D.J. Müller (ed.). *Remediating Children's Language.* Croom Helm.

McConkey, R. and O'Connor, M. (1981) 'Putting two words together'. Available from St Michael's House Research, Upper Kilmacud Road, Stillorgan, Co. Dublin.

McNeill, D. (1970) *The Acquisition of Language: the study of developmental psycholinguistics.* Harper and Row.

Miller, J.F. and Yoder, D. (1974) 'An ontogenic language teaching strategy for retarded children', in R.L. Schiefelbusch and L.L. Lloyd (eds.). *Language Perspectives: Acquisition, Retardation and Intervention.* University Park Press.

Mittler, P. and Berry, P. (1977) 'Demanding language', in P. Mittler (ed.). *Research to Practice in Mental Retardation, Vol. II: Education and Training.* IASSMD.

Muma, J. (1978) *Language Handbook.* Prentice-Hall.

Nelson, K. (1973) 'Structure and Strategy in Learning to Talk'. *Monographs of the*

Society for Research in Child Development, 38.

Pratt, M.W., Bumstead, D.C. and Raynes, N.V. (1970) 'Attendant staff speech to the institutionalized retarded: language use as a measure of the quality of care'. *Jnl of Child Psychology and Psychiatry, 17,* pp. 133-43.

Prior, M., Minnes, P., Coyne, T., Golding, B., Hendy, J. and McGillivary, J. (1979) 'Verbal interactions between staff and residents in an institution for the young mentally retarded'. *Mental Retardation, 17,* pp. 65-9.

Roberts, K. and Schaefer, R. (1984) 'Cognitive abilities and infant language intervention', in K.F. Ruder and M.D. Smith (eds.). *Developmental Language Intervention.* University Park Press.

Robson, C. (1982) *Language Development through Structured Teaching.* Drake Educational.

Rondal, J.A. (1978) 'Maternal speech to normal and Down's syndrome children matched for mean length of utterance', in C.E. Myers (ed.).*Behaviour in the Profoundly and Severely Retarded: research foundations for enhancing the quality of life.* AAMD.

Ruder, K.F. and Smith M.D. (1984) *Developmental Language Intervention.* University Park Press.

Skinner, B.F. (1957) *Verbal Behaviour.* Appleton-Century-Crofts.

Snow, C.E. (1972) 'Mother's speech to children learning language'. *Child Development, 43,* pp. 549-65.

Snyder, L.K. and McLean, J.E. (1976) 'Deficient acquisition strategies: a proposed conceptual framework for analysing severe language deficiency'. *Am. Jnl of Mental Deficiency, 80,* pp. 338-49.

Terdal, L.E., Jackson, R.H. and Garner, A.M. (1976) 'Mother-child interactions: a comparison between normal and developmentally delayed groups', in E.J. Marsh, L.A. Hammerlynck and L.C. Hardy (eds.). *Behaviour Modification and Families.* Brunner Mazel.

Tizard, B., Cooperman, O., Joseph, A. and Tizard, J. (1972) 'Environmental effects on language development: a study of young children in long stay residential nurseries'. *Child Development, 43,* pp. 337-58.

de Villiers, J. and de Villiers, P. (1978) *Language Acquisition.* Harvard University Press.

Wilkins, D.A. (1974) 'Notional syllabuses and the concept of a minimum adequate grammer', in S.P. Corder and E. Roulet (eds.). *Linguistic Insights in Applied Linguistics.* AIMAV; Didier.

Williams, C. (1980) *Towards Teaching Communication Skills,* revised edn. BIMH.

Annotated Bibliography

1. General Books on Language Development

A good introductory text, either for the reader who wants to fill in some background details, or to recommend to parents: Crystal, D. (1976) *Child Language, Learning and Linguistics.* Edward Arnold. More detailed, and more complex accounts of language acuisition in normally developing children: Cruttenden, A. (1979) *Language in Infancy and Childhood.* Manchester University Press; Lock, A. and Fisher, E. (1984) *Language Development.* Croom Helm, in association with the Open University. This book is included because it is designed to accompany the Open University course on 'Language and cognitive development' which may be of interest to readers. Owens, R.E.

(1984) *Language Development: an introduction.* Charles Merrill; de Villiers, J. and de Villiers P. (1978) *Language Acquisition.* Harvard University Press.

2. General Books on Language and Mental Handicap

A very thorough review article examining key issues is Kiernan, C.C. (1985) 'Communication', in A.D.B. Clarke and A.M. Clarke (eds.). *Mental Deficiency: The Changing Outlook (Remediation).* Methuen. A useful study of language and language teaching in ESN(S) schools is Leeming, K., Swann, W., Coupe, J. and Mittler, P. (1979) *Teaching Language and Communication to the Mentally Handicapped.* Evans/Methuen Educational.

3. Contemporary Approaches to Language Intervention

The following all explore the issues relating to teaching language to children whose language and communication skills are delayed or disordered, either as a result of severe learning difficulties, or a wide range of causes. Bloom, L. and Lahey, M. (1978) *Language Development and Language Disorders.* Wiley; McLean, J. and Snyder-McLean, L. (1978) *A Transactional Approach to Early Language Training.* Charles Merrill; Müller, D. (ed.). (1984) *Remediating Children's Language.* Croom Helm; Ruder, K. and Smith M. (1984) *Developmental Language Intervention.* University Park Press. Additionally, all volumes in the Language Intervention series edited by R.L. Schiefelbusch, published by University Park Pres and, more directly related to work in schools, a series of articles by I.P. Bell in *Mental Handicap*, Volumes *10, 12* and *13*, 1982, 1984 and 1985.

4. Cognitive Development and the Relationship Between Cognition and Early Language Development

Assessment of cognitive development during the sensorimotor period: Uzgiris, I. and Hunt, J. (1975) *Assessment in Infancy.* University of Illinois Press. Follow-up work on the above can be found in Dunst, C.J. (1980) *A Clinical and Educational Manual for use with the Uzgiris and Hunt Scales for Infant Psychological Development.* University Park Press; and Coupe, J. and Levy, D. (1985) 'The object related scheme assessment procedure'. *Mental Handicap, 13,* pp. 22-4. Complex, but very thorough accounts of early cognitive development and its relation to language development can be found in Bates, E. (1979) *The Emergence of Symbols: cognition and communication in infancy.* Academic Press; Golinkoff, R.M. (1983) *The Transition from Prelinguistic to Linguistic Communication.* Lawrence Erlbaum, especially the chapter in this volume by C. Gibb Harding. A chapter along similar lines, but specifically related to infants with severe learning difficulties is by Roberts and Schaefer in the book by Ruder and Smith in section 3. above. A slightly simpler account of cognition and language development which would serve as a very useful introduction can be found in Chapter 4 of R.E. Owens, section 1. above.

5. Syntax and Morphology

For more detailed accounts of syntax and morphology, including assessment and intervention strategies, see Crystal, D., Fletcher, P. and Garman, M. (1976) *The Grammatical Analysis of Language Disability.* Edward Arnold; Crystal, D. (1979) *Working with LARSP.* Edward Arnold; and Robson, C. (1982) *Language Development through Structured Teaching.* Drake Educational.

6. Phonology

The following are both good contemporary studies of phonology, but are difficult
without background knowledge. Ingram, D. (1976) *Phonology Disability in
Children.* Edward Arnold; Grunwell, P. (1982) *Clinical Phonology.* Croom
Helm.

7. Bilingualism and Mental Handicap

There are an increasing number of mentally handicapped children and adults who
need to be able to communicate in two (or sometimes more) languages.
Examples in the UK are English/Welsh, English/Punjabi/Urdu and
English/Gujerati and, in North America, English/French and English/Spanish.
There are now some good books on bilingualism in otherwise normally
developing children, e.g. Hatch, E. (1979) *Second Language Acquisition.*
Newbury House; and McLaughlin, B. (1978) *Second Language Acquisition in
Children.* Lawrence Erlbaum. We have no references specifically aimed at
teachers and therapists working with mentally handicapped people. The best
available reference is likely to be Miller, N. (1984) *Bilingualism and Language
Disability.* Croom Helm. Additional help *may* be available from the College of
Speech Therapists' special advisors on bilingualism. They are: Mr S.
Abudarham, Dept of Health Sciences, City of Birmingham Polytechnic,
Franchise Street, Birmingham B42 2SU; and Ms S. Munro, School of Speech
Therapy, South Glamorgan Institute of Higher Education, Llandaff, Cardiff
CF5 2YB.

8. Augmentative Means of Communication

The increasing interest in signing and symbol systems means that many volumes
have been addressed specifically to these topics. As we have tried to indicate in
this chapter, it is the selection of target behaviours and teaching methods which
is crucial, rather than the means of communication (signs, symbols, speech, etc.)
However, it is important to consider individual needs when selecting a system
for a particular child. Useful references here are: Jones, P. and Cregan, A.
(1986) *Signs and Symbols: communication for mentally handicapped people.*
Croom Helm; Peter, M. and Barnes, R. (1982) *Signs, Symbols and Schools.*
NCSE (a general introduction to different types of AMC); Musselwhite, C. and
St Louis, K. (1982) *Communication Programming for the Severely
Handicapped.* College Hill Press.

9. Kits and Programmes including Computer Software

As indicated earlier there are two good articles evaluating kits and programmes;
Harris, J. (1984) 'Early language intervention programmes'. *Assoc. for Child
Psychology and Psychiatry Newsletter,* 6, pp. 2-20; and Kiernan, C.C. (1984)
'Language remediation programmes, a review', in D.J. Müller (ed.).
Remediating Children's Language. Croom Helm. The best source of
information on software packages for language teaching will be your local
Special Education Micro-Electronics Resources Centre (SEMERC), S.E.
England: Grange Remedial Centre, Ilford, Essex; S.W. England and S. Wales:
Bristol Polytechnic; N.W. England, N. Wales and N. Ireland: Manchester
Polytechnic; N.E. England plus Cumbria: Newcastle Polytechnic. Similar
services have been available for Scotland from the Call Centre, University of
Edinburgh, but this centre may have to close due to financial constraints.

8 THE LEARNING PROCESS

Peter Evans

Introduction

Mentally handicapped children are fairly readily identified by the experienced clinical eye, and even a very brief encounter indicates that these children have learning difficulties of a very generalised sort. Indeed this has now become so widely accepted that the concept of learning difficulty has become the kernel of the definition of special educational needs in the 1981 Education Act. But an important qualification must be made, since a learning difficulty is not viewed as a deficit that is something which is 'within the child' but is seen as a problem that is at least partly related to the provision that is made. Thus some children, who might be described as experiencing learning difficulties — but would almost certainly not be severely mentally handicapped — may be helped to overcome, perhaps completely, their learning difficulties if the curriculum with which they are presented is structured appropriately, both in terms of content and method of presentation, in order to meet their individual needs.

The Education Act is thus very much in line with current educational thinking which recognises that mentally handicapped children in particular have individual needs relating to learning difficulty which can only be met by presenting these children with the appropriate experiences in school. Furthermore this view which relates to the child's learning and his demonstrated skills and competences very much plays down the importance of concepts like mental age (MA) or intelligence quotient (IQ): these measures, while being of some value in terms of giving general guidance to curriculum content, are by the same token too global to have much value in the specification of individualised teaching programmes.

The discussion above has used the terms 'learning difficulty' loosely; in the context of this chapter it is necessary to look more closely at what this term has come to mean. In order achieve this, it is necessary to consider what the term 'learning' implies.

For the learner, learning is an active, dynamic process which

183

necessitates that three functional requirements are met. First, whatever it is that is to be learned must be attended to or registered by the learning system. If a listener cannot attend to a speaker and remember a sentence from the beginning to its end then it is not possible to extract the full meaning of that sentence. Second, that particular material must be retained in memory either for immediate or later recall as appropriate. Third, the material must be retrievable from memory in the right conditions, e.g. in answer to questions or as part of a dialogue with another person.

Serious empirical work relating learning theory to mental retardation did not really begin until the late 1940s and early 1950s. At that time, understandably, the general question was: how do these children differ from non-handicapped groups? This question itself requires a certain sort of experimental design and is really demanding answers of the sort that would lead to ideas of deficits being developed. For instance, if it is shown that the SLD child can attend less well than a non-handicapped peer in some experiment which compares SLD children with non-SLD children, then we can call this an 'attention deficit'.

This kind of approach held sway for some 20 or so years and is still important. However, in the mid 1960s workers became dissatisfied with this approach because it seemed to offer little help or guidance to practitioners. Thus workers of a more practical persuasion turned to theories and methods such as applied behaviour analysis (operant psychology) which seemed to offer ways of organising teaching that could be shown to lead to progress. This view asked for a different sort of understanding of the child. Instead of asking where is he now? and, how is he different from other children? the question of interest became how can we get him from where he is now to some appropriate level at some point in the future? This represented a switch from a classificatory approach to an educational or developmental view. Researchers working in this latter conceptualisation began to speak in terms of delays rather than deficits in learning.

In the late 1960s and early 1970s the developments referred to above were paralleled by radical changes in thinking in psychology about human learning. Behaviourism was seriously challenged as a theoretical account of learning by cognitive psychologists who argued that learning took place through an active analysis of experience. Interest switched to this view, since it appeared to offer a more productive way forward in the understanding of human cognitive processes such as thinking and reasoning, and language. Psychologists and teachers working with the mentally handicapped now found themselves with an uncomfortable paradox. On the one hand behaviour modification techniques derived from the behavioural stance of operant psychology appeared to work extremely effectively with mentally handicapped children, but on the other hand the theory they presented was seriously flawed. Furthermore, and what is almost worse, behavioural approaches were and still are heavily censored by educationalists as being demeaning to children and almost non-educational.

This chapter takes the view that, to understand properly the learning processes of children with handicaps requires that we give serious considerations to the cognitive view. We need to understand how the learning system of the non-handicapped person operates at a functional level (how does this person set about learning this task so that he can use it effectively in the future?) and how this relates to the non-handicapped person's learning processes. This will be recognised as essentially a developmental or even a normative model which is quite in keeping with the concept of special educational needs.

The task for the teacher, then, becomes one of turning this knowledge into a programme which works for the child, and it is proposed that behaviour modification techniques represent sound ways of achieving this goal. The teacher must understand how to present the work to the child systematically so that the child can operate on it in a way which is commensurate with his current cognitive structures and preferred mode of learning. This is an incredibly difficult task for the teacher: this chapter attempts to present some of the fundamental ideas and knowledge that are required and which are based largely on an information-processing approach to learning. Accordingly the chapter begins with a discussion on learning from a cognitive standpoint. It begins with a discussion of attention in learning and then goes on to look at ways in which memories may be encoded and stored. This is followed by a short discussion about the major models of memory. The associative models of classical conditioning and operant learning are dealt with towards the end of the chapter, and it concludes with an example of how the whole approach may work in planning an educational programme concerned with teaching the value of money.

In conclusion, learning must be seen as an active, dynamic

process in which the learner is involved in transactions with teaching. In so doing he is attempting to extract meaning from his experiences or to put some organisation or systematic structure onto these experiences. If the teacher presents tasks which connect with his past learning, thus providing for success, she rewards that success, thus providing the encouragement and motivation to continue. It is likely that the to-be-learned material will be attended to and registered, and the first requirement of learning will be fulfilled. A consideration of attention in learning is given in the next section.

Attention in the Learning Process

The concept of attention has been developed in a large number of ways in psychology. From the point of view of the teacher perhaps the most common problem relates to children who are distractable or inattentive, preventing both themselves and others from attending to the task in hand. Evans and Hogg (1984) have produced a rating scale which is completed by class teachers and which attempts to measure such behaviours in children with severe learning difficulties. They found that there were wide individual variations with respect to the extent to which teachers rated the children in their classrooms as having good attentional skills or being inclined to be distractable and that the scores related to verbal ages as assessed by the English Picture Vocabulary test (Brimer and Dunn 1972); children with higher verbal ages were rated as less distractable than children with lower verbal ages.

There can be little doubt that teachers perceive this as a problem. There is a large literature which discusses ways of dealing with attentional problems that uses behaviour modification principles and which has been reviewed recently by Barkley (1983). These methods are concerned, for example, with increasing the child's on-task behaviour but will not be discussed further here. However, there is another context in which attentional skills may develop which relates very importantly to the educational context and which helps to link the child's memory system to the outside world. For many children, it is an over-simplification to say that they show difficulties with attention since, in some contexts they may and in others they may not. This distinction (as for all of us) relates to our own level of interest in the topic and whether we find the work easy or difficult.

Attention in the learning process may then be seen as a means by which relevant aspects of the environment come to be perceived. This view has been studied extensively, over a number of years by Zeaman and House (1963; 1979) in experiments on discrimination learning in which they have argued convincingly that not only is attention a key component in the learning process but also that children with learning difficulties have their greatest problem in this area. In their work they present children with different coloured stimuli between which they have to learn to discriminate. Estes (1982) has presented the experimental design neatly as an attribute-by-value table. In such an experiment the learner is presented with pairs of stimuli which vary in two dimensions, colour and shape, e.g.

	Circle	Triangle
Red	+	+
Green	–	–

The child has to learn to make a positive response to red and to ignore green. In the table above a plus sign indicates a rewarded stimulus. It should be clear that, in order to learn the problem successfully, the dimension of shape must be ignored since it is inconsistently associated with rewards. Zeaman and House (1963) have argued that the problem that mentally handicapped children have is one of attending to the correct dimension. In the problem presented above there are at least two dimensions present namely colour (red–green) and shape (circle–triangle) and the problem requires the child to ignore shape and attend to colour in order to be able to perform appropriately. They argue that it is the learning to select the correct dimension from all of the other competing dimensions which presents the problem for the mentally handicapped child. Once this has been decided there is no difference between handicapped and non-handicapped children in their rate of learning of the instrumental response or which one of the two stimuli (red and green) on the colour dimension is the one which actually predicts reward.

Discrimination-learning techniques are of course used extensively in schools for children with SLD, e.g. in learning about colours, shapes etc. The work described above reminds us that tasks must be presented in a way that will require children to attend to the underlying dimensions of the problem since it is argued that attention to the relevant dimensions of the task is a necessary pre-requisite to accurate performance with the specific stimuli. The fact that the manner in which stimuli are presented is important to effective attentional learning and its transfer has been demonstrated in other discrimination-learning paradigms which emphasise memory (Hogg and Evans 1975) and stimulus complexity (Richards and Evans 1981). Very briefly, these studies demonstrate the importance of engaging the child analytically with the task in order to encourage attentional learning.

Attentional processes have also been investigated from another important perspective derived from information-processing theory. It has long been argued that we are unable to attend to all the stimuli in the outside world that are competing for our attention since our capacity for attending to separate tasks is limited. Some selection therefore needs to be made. It is likely that we will attend to things that we know something about already, and it has been suggested that the more a process has been practised, the less voluntary attention it requires. If a process is extremely highly practised it requires little or no attention and becomes automatic. Cognitive processes have thus been divided into two types, automatic processes which need little attention and deliberate processes which need close attention (Shiffrin and Schneider 1977).

An example of this process at work is often given in terms of learning to drive a car. At first there seems to be a multitude of things to do at once. Suppose you are getting into the driving seat of a car. What do you do? If you are a driver you might find it difficult at first to describe the exact sequence of events. At some point you must sit in the seat, close the door, put on the seat belt, put the keys into the ignition switch, check that the gear box is in neutral, adjust the choke, start the engine, etc. All of these things need to be carried out but the sequence is not necessarily of importance. When it comes to changing gear in a manual transmission, however, the sequence of events is important. A skilled driver can carry these events out automatically, without thinking about them. Yet for the novice they require deliberate thought.

These skills, however, also appear to interact with other cognitive processes (e.g. Kahneman 1973). If you imagine that you are driving and taking part in a conversation you will find it relatively easy to have a discussion with a passenger on a trivial topic but relatively difficult if the conversation is more complex. Further if the complexity of the driving skill required is increased, due to an emergency on the road for example, you will probably disengage from the conversation entirely. Thus it is proposed that attention is divided according to the level of learned skill and the immediate demands of the situation. (For a more extended account of this process the reader is referred to Wessells 1982, pp. 95 ff.).

This distinction between automatic and deliberate attention may also provide a useful alternative account of the work of Zeaman and House (1979) described above. For example, it may be argued that, in contrast to the non-handicapped child, the child with learning difficulties is less able to handle multi-attribute problems such as the one presented above because his overall skills in dealing with such problems are less automatised. Thus he has relatively less available processing capacity with which to deal with the dimensions of the problem, and his selection of the correct dimension is slower. While research with this type of explanation of attentional problems in children with learning difficulties is at an early stage, it is actively being pursued by Brookes and McCauley (1984). In the view of the author it represents an important way of looking at attentional processes from a dynamic stand point and has the advantage of providing an explanation of the attentional deficit (the term used by Zeaman and House) in terms that allow for potential remediation.

It is important from the point of view of considering mentally handicapped children to appreciate that, if the analysis presented above is correct, then it is not only cognitive learning which will be competing for limited attentional resources but motor skills also. If the child has physical handicaps, it may require a considerable amount of his attentional resources in order, for example, to sequence a set of limb movements, thus reducing the amount left free for attending to the external environment. In a child in which there may be an overall inefficiency in processing information in contrast to his chronological age peers, his resources may be allocated necessarily across a much wider range of skills, reducing his general ability to attend to communicating efforts on the part of the teacher. In a practical context physiotherapists may suggest that children must be in a comfortable position in order to be able to learn. As far as I know there is no evidence for this, but the suggestion is certainly in line with the proposal made above.

The discussion on attention in learning given above suggests that attentional skills themselves are highly related to the extent and efficiency of the learning process itself. In terms of automatic processes we are obviously referring to well-rehearsed mechanisms — which itself implies the intimate involvement of long-term memory. Clearly, if learning that is represented in long-term memory is to be of much functional use in aiding the attentional processes, thus opening the way for further learning, it must in some way allow the child to organise his experiences in order to facilitate their use.

Indeed it has been proposed that the child does this by structuring the learning experiences through the grouping together of similar items, facts or objects, or whatever it is that is being learned. Referring again to the work of Zeaman and House (1979) this may be seen as an example of a way of systematically presenting material to the learner in order to encourage such grouping of the stimuli to occur. As has already been mentioned, such methods are used widely in schools for children with SLD with regard to tasks that require children to sort objects systematically such as coins, colours and so on.

Organisation and Memory

Since one of the points of learning is for the child to develop a semblance of order from the potentially chaotic events that he experiences, it is perhaps not surprising that it has been proposed that learning is represented in memory in an organised way. Much of the work that has been carried out is on verbal memory, although it has been argued that all permanent representations in long-term memory, including visual and auditory memories, are of the same kind, (e.g. see Anderson 1980). Nonetheless there is general agreement that the information must be organised.

In fact it has been argued that it is almost impossible to prevent human beings from functioning in this way. If someone were to ask you to go to the shops and buy a range of different items, you would almost certainly sort them according to the type of item, e.g. vegetables and fruit or soap and toothpaste, and this would probably correspond quite closely to the sort of shop which stocked these items. This phenonemon has been demonstrated in an experimental context by Bousfield (1953) who presented a list of nouns to his subjects. The nouns were presented in a random order, but comprised examples of different categories, animals, furniture and so on. On recall the adults involved in the study did not recall the items in the order in which they were presented but in categories: the animals were recalled in one cluster, the furniture in another. This example of clustering in free recall has been demonstrated on many occasions and has also been studied in the mentally handicapped. Again, there are many studies which show that the handicapped do organise the material but to a much lesser extent than do non-handicapped people (Herriot, Green and McConkey 1973; Spitz, 1979). This suggests that the method of processing is the same but the extent is different.

This idea which is fundamental to learning has been shown to operate within certain constraints. Miller, in a classic paper (Miller 1956) argued that items that were to be remembered could be seen as 'chunks' of information. Chunks could be represented by a wide range of material. They could, for example, be individual numbers 7, 2, 3 and so on, or they could be parts of sentences or even whole sentences. The human being could only hold a certain number, namely 7 ± 2 chunks, in his mind at any one time, and this constraint imposed limits on what could be attended to or kept directly in mind at any particular moment. This general idea has been central in the development of thinking in this approach to learning and to suggestions that have been made concerning how knowledge is represented in memory.

The Representation of Knowledge in Memory

In response to the issues raised above Collins and Quillian (1969) have proposed that information may be represented and stored in a hierarchical form in which some information is super-ordinate to other. For example there may be a general category of birds which would include examples in subordinate categories. Canaries and budgerigars are both examples of birds: because of their similarity they might be stored metaphorically closely together since they may be seen to be subjectively highly related. This example may be contrasted with, say owls and eagles which are also birds but which have very different behaviours and habitats from canaries and budgerigars. Moreover the child's experiences of those types of bird might be very different in terms of where they might or might have not been seen and so on. Other categories could be stored in their own hierarchical networks which may also be attached to the bird hierarchy if relevant. For example, fishes are an identifiable sub-group of animals, and both categories may come together under a higher order category heading such as animals. The network may be represented as shown in Figure 8.1.

This is not intended to imply that these relationships inevitably represent actual zoological classifications, although in the context of curriculum planning that might be what could be worked towards. Moreover, if the child's networks, or representations of the world, do reflect highly idiosyncratic structures in which there is little shared commonality with other people's structures (which may often be the case in children with severe learning difficulties), this could prove a considerable handicap to further systematic learning since there may be little shared common ground.

We thus have a conception of knowledge as being represented in a permanent form in some type of organised hierarchical system. Anderson (1980) has extended the thinking to include a more sophisticated view of language and logic and has proposed that these ideas may be stored in the form of propositions in associative networks. In this view a proposition is the smallest unit of knowledge that can stand as a separate statement or the smallest unit about which it is possible to make the statement 'true' or 'false'. For example, the sentence — The teacher gave Susan a small jig-saw — may be seen to comprise two simpler sentences or ideas: 1. The teacher gave Susan a jig-saw; 2. The jig-saw was small. Each represents a single unit of meaning or a proposition. Using the procedure suggested by Kintsch (1974) this may be further

Figure 8.1

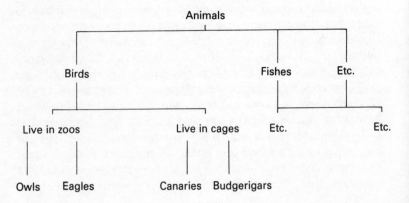

analysed into a list containing relations or verbs followed by a sequence of arguments. In this example the relations would be the verb 'give' and the adjective 'small'. The arguments correspond to the nouns namely 'teacher', 'Susan' and 'jig-saw'. The relations state connections between the nouns, and the sentences above may be written — 3. (*Give*, Teacher, Jig-saw, Susan, *Past*); 4. (*Small*, Jig-saw). This representation would be the same for the following sentence which has the same meaning but is of a different grammatical form: 5. Susan was given the small jig-saw by the teacher. It proposed that the meaning of information may be stored in networks made up of propositions of the sort described above which illustrates very briefly how linguistic representation may become involved.

However, the implications of the views expressed are profound. For they suggest that weaknesses in the ability to organise or structure information in a systematic way and so develop communicable meaning will have a downwardly spiralling effect on the child's future cognitions and potential development. This is because material that could connect with the existing network may fail so to do and thus be treated as 'new' and correspondingly 'meaningless' to the child. In this way incoming information is not simplified through the extraction of commonalities or made sensible. The world that the child experiences remains complex and intransigent.

Sensory Memory

It must be made clear immediately that meaning does not exist solely in the verbal modality. If you were asked to conjure up in your mind a picture of a close relative or good friend, or the leaning tower of Pisa or a dandelion or any other object that you might have experienced previously in the visual modality you will probably be able to see the image clearly in your mind's eye. Similarly, examples could be given for auditory or olfactory memory. Given that this is the case there can be little doubt that, as human beings, we possess the ability to reproduce and experience sensory images under voluntary control. In these examples we are, of course, reproducing an image from memory, and it is remarkable how detailed these images can be even with relatively little experience of the object. A study by Standing, Conezio and Haber (1970), for example, investigated some aspects of this skill in the visual modality by presenting subjects with a series of 2,560 slides of scenes such as panoramic vistas, for 10 seconds each. Scores on a later recognition test showed an average of 85 to 93 per cent correct: remarkable results given the usual poor memories that most of us experience! Evidence such as that presented above provides a convincing argument that visual memory in some picture-like form not only exists but does so in a very effective form. Furthermore the fact that these experiences exist also in other sensory memories raises the question of whether or not sensorially-based and visually-based information are stored in a single codified form before being reconstructed in the modality in which they were experienced, or whether they are stored as separate codes. This former view has been called single code theory (e.g. Anderson 1980), and the latter, dual code theory (e.g. Paivio 1971). Whichever of these arguments eventually wins the day is perhaps not of great concern to us here, but it does raise the important question of the visual-verbal distinction within the developmental context.

Sensory, Episodic and Semantic Memory

In the preceding section it has been suggested that memories exist in different forms, and a major distinction has been made between a sensory type of memory (vision was the main example used) and more verbally-based memory. But a further distinction must be made — between memory for contextually related events or episodic memory and that for more abstracted experiences or semantic memory.

Episodic memory refers to memories in which the contexts of the experiences which are memorised are important. Episodic memory is involved when information relating to such questions as, Did it rain yesterday? are required. Such information lacks the capability of generalisation since the events described are essentially independent. Episodic memory may thus be contrasted with verbally-based memory which does permit generalisations and inferences to be drawn. This type of memory is therefore context-free and tends to involve information concerning rules, facts and meanings which may exist in an abstracted form. Semantic knowledge is required in the answering of questions which require an understanding of a rule, for instance, adding numbers that involve carrying digits requires a rule which, once learned, can be generalised from very simple examples to more complex cases.

In the next section some of the implications of this view are discussed with regard to the mentally handicapped person.

Coding, Information — Evidence Pertaining to the Mentally Handicapped

The theoretical and experimental work developed with non-retarded populations which has made up the bulk of research discussed up to now has been considerably more extensive than studies carried out with retarded populations. The studies however suggest that in the visual modality memory may be relatively unimpaired in SLD children.

Visual Memory. One aspect of visual memory which is of particular interest is that of the so-called photographic memory or, more formally, eidetic imagery. This type of visual imagery, which appears to have photographic qualities to the extent that the images appear in a very visual form and in exact detail, is not commonly found but does appear more frequently in children than adults. Allport (1924) for example reported an experiment in which he presented English children with a series of pictures for them to memorise. They were detailed pictures, and each was presented for 35 seconds and then removed from view. One of the pictures showed a village street with the German word *Garten-wirtschaft* on a sign over a shop. Many of the children reported being able to 'see' the sign in memory; a few of them were able to spell out the 16 letters of the word correctly, and more of them made only a few errors. Furthermore they could do this from left to right or right to left with equal ease and of course none of the children spoke German.

Eidetic imagery has also been investigated in mentally retarded children. Siipola and Hayden (1965) explored eidetic imagery in both brain-injured and familial mentally retarded children aged between four and twelve with average IQs of 67 (range 47-88). They found that, as with non-retarded groups, children who displayed eidetic imagery were infrequent but of those that did nearly all were found in the brain-inured group.

Apart from the remarkable results of studies on eidetic imagery there has been other work which has also focused on visual memory. Brown (1972) for example used a recognition memory task with moderately retarded children: 120 items were presented in a continuous sequence whereby the children had to recognise whether or not the pictures had occurred before. These children were very efficient at this task with a mean of 96 per cent correct responses indicating that their visual memory in a recognition task was extremely good. Furthermore these memories were retained over two days, and the children were able to discriminate pictures presented on the first day from those presented on the second. Other studies (e.g. Lamberts 1981) have also demonstrated that visual memory is relatively unimpaired in children with severe learning difficulties.

Work developed within a different experimental context by O'Connor and Hermelin (1963; 1978) also suggests that children with low verbal abilities tend to use modality-specific coding strategies. That is to say, they have demonstrated that children classified as having severe learning difficulties tend to use visual coding in preference to an auditory-verbal coding which was preferred by children with higher verbal ages. However, it should be pointed out that this effect was only seen in mentally handicapped children who did not show obvious sensory deficits. For those multiply handicapped children with difficulties in hearing and/or seeing it is probably safest to assume that the coding will be strongest in the modality which the child can use best (O'Connor and Hermelin 1978).

Results from studies such as those described above offer some explanation as to why the use of signing and the visual modality in general appear to be good ways of gaining access to children with learning difficulties in order to help them learn. For, if such children have relatively intact visual memories, clearly this process should be utilised by teachers. A study by Reid and Kiernan (1979) supporting this view also may be interpreted as supporting the dual code theory. They presented mentally retarded children (IQ range 27-68) with spoken words and manual signs as encoding categories and demonstrated that these two input systems reflected different mechanisms. In this way signs which can have an instant impact on the system may be relatively easily remembered and serve to act as ways to foster relationships between objects and words. Indeed, Bricker (1972) and Van Biervliet (1977) have both shown that manual signing can indeed act to facilitate word-object associations.

However, as the evidence which exists suggests that it is young children, in contrast to adults (e.g. Hunter 1964), who tend to exhibit better eidetic memory and that it appears to decline with age (Haber and Haber 1964), the suggestion is that visual memory is transcended by verbal forms, which are preferable because of their flexibility, as literacy skills become emphasised in schools (Richardson 1969). For this reason it is important for teachers of children with severe learning difficulties to regard the usefulness of visual and/or sensory input as a starting point only in a cognition system which needs to progress to verbal forms of processing.

Retrieval. Developing a good memory implies in part that it is possible to produce correct answers to questions on demand. Given the amount of information that we all have readily available to us, and the fact that we have limited capacities, it should be immediately clear that unless the material we have learned is organised or structured in some way it will remain unavailable. Hence the more structure that can be imposed on material by the learner the more likely it is that it will be accessible when required. Following this argument therefore it should be clear that the form in which learning takes place is absolutely crucial to its effective retrieval and that these two processes are very heavily dependent upon one another. Often a lack of retrieval is due to a lack of accessibility of the information rather than its lack of availability. That is to say, it is there in the mind, but is not triggered by the question that is being asked. Sometimes a re-formation of the question and/or the addition of hints may help to make the information spring into consciousness.

The other side of the coin to effective retrieval is of course forgetting or the apparently complete failure to retrieve material. There have been two sorts of general theories that attempt to account for forgetting. One is that forgetting occurs as a function of time. That is, the memories just fade away through lack of use. This has been called the trace decay theory. The second is that memories are interfered with by other experiences, and this is known as the interference theory. There are two ways in which this can happen. In the first, old material interferes with material that is currently being learned (pro-active interference), i.e. forwards in time. In the second, items which are learned after the to-be-remembered material interfere retro-actively with it, i.e. backwards in time (retro-active interference). These views, however, are rarely discussed today since the current interest is focused much more on how to prevent forgetting by providing appropriate learning in the first instance using techniques which help children to organise and structure their learning. One of these strategies, however, is known as directed forgetting and has recently attracted some interest (Bray 1979).

One important aspect to consider in the retrieval process is that memories are not thought to be merely found and pulled out in the identical form in which they were experienced. Instead, it is thought that they are reconstructed from some basic underlying representations (e.g. Anderson 1980). Semantic memory implies that the essential meaning of the material is retained and reproduced when appropriate. However the exact form in which it is remembered will depend on a range of other factors, such as the child's past experience and his understanding of what he has learned (Bartlett 1932).

Concluding Comments

There is a need for a memory system which is structured and organised but flexible. The flexibility comes partly from being able to structure material in ways which relate it to past learning in a wide variety of ways. It stands to reason that the more sophisticated the past learning the more likely it is that the new learning can be attached to more networks and thus the more likely it is that learning can be used flexibly. Children who are lacking learning and experience are therefore likely to have less sophisticated structures and consequently less likely to develop flexible cognitive organisations.

In summary four main points emerge. The first is that the learning system sorts information in a structured way. Second, sensory memory may represent a different coding process from verbally based memory. The third is that there is a continuum that runs essentially from concrete representation to abstract representation (episodic — semantic) in the way in which information is stored and utilised, and the fourth is that memories that are retrieved are reconstructions of experience.

Models of Memory

The previous sections have discussed ways in which information may be organised through a process of attention and memorising, and we have looked at coding and have attempted to identify some of the end points of the learning process. Particularly with regard to the verbal system we have seen that verbal learning may be represented propositionally and in an organised and structured fashion. But how does the system operate in order to achieve this end and how can it be facilitated? These questions require further consideration of the memory process.

There are two general models that have been developed to account for the memory process. The first of these emphasises the structure of the system and argues that the system comprises three stages, namely a very short-term process lasting for about a second, a short-term memory operating for a short period of time, around 15 seconds, and a long-term store which has an indefinite time duration. The second model explores the functions that are involved in coding information or the levels of processing. It essentially argues that memory is best viewed as a single process in which phenomena of short- or long-term memory depend on the extent to which the learner has processed the to-be-learned information.

The Structural Model

As mentioned above, this model comprises three stores, a very short-term, almost physiological, store, a short-term and lastly a long-term memory store. From the point of view of the teacher the most important of these stores are the last two, and it is on these that we shall focus. The short-term store operates, it has been proposed, for up to 15 secs (Atkinson and Shiffrin 1968) and has a limited capacity, namely 7 ± 2 chunks of information. What is important about the notion of chunking is that information that can be effectively encoded by the learner can be more efficiently stored and can be decoded or elaborated when required for recall. In this way the limited capacity of the short-term system may not be such a limitation since it can still operate on a highly complex set of information by being able to utilise the long-term store of memories. Information which is essentially difficult to encode (perhaps because the learner has little experience of it) will lead to less of it being remembered than information with which the learner has extended experience. For example the familiar sequence THECATSAT is extremely easy to remember because of learned predictability contained within the phrase but the unfamiliar sequence TEHICTAAS which contains the same letters is less easy. Information stored in the short-term memory is forgotten either through the process of interference or through decay where the memory trace may just fade away through lack of use or rehearsal.

Long-term memory has, in contrast, an unlimited capacity and retains information over a long period of time. Forgetting occurs, not because the item is not there, but because it cannot be retrieved. An analogy might be filing papers away in such a manner that you cannot find them. They are there, somewhere, but lost — or, in memory terms, operationally forgotten.

In such a model it is clearly of importance to have a process whereby information can be shifted from the short-term store. Atkinson and Shiffrin (1968) have proposed a set of control processes that would serve this function. The two most important of these are rehearsal — either vocal or sub-vocal repetitions of the to-be-learned material — and encoding — the information is transferred in a way that will make it readily storable in long-term memory. It is these control processes which are of especial interest to us here, and an elaboration forms a central feature of the functional model which is to be described next.

The Functional Model

This model of the memory processes does not require the supposition of two or more memory stores but sees the phenomena of short-term memory and long-term memory as manifestations of different levels of processing (Craik and Lockhart 1972). Thus memories which are held only for a short time are processed at a minimal level (e.g. merely repeating a list of items over and over again) and will not last long once attention has been withdrawn. Information which is maintained for a long period of time has undergone a deeper level of processing in which the meaning of the material has been extracted from it. In this way limitations on the capacity of memory come from limitations in our ability to process actively the material or information in a way that is relevant or meaningful to the learner. Because this latter view emphasises what the learner, or the teacher in aiding the learner, must do in an attempt to encourage long-term memory, it is the model that is assumed to be of most relevance to the teacher: its implication will be developed further. Thus earlier views that mentally retarded children suffer from short-term memory deficits but seem to have relatively unaffected long-term memories even if true (and this, as a completely unqualified statement is almost certainly not true, e.g. Ellis (1978), have little place in the levels of processing model. Following Ellis (1978) it is safer to assume that mentally handicapped children have difficulties at all stages of learning. It is part of the teacher's job to understand these difficulties in a way which will prove helpful when planning teaching programmes or activities.

Strategies in Learning

One of the principle findings that comes out of recent research on the representation of knowledge is that memories which are recalled over the long term are essentially reconstructions based on stored propositions. It comes as no surprise that, in order to encourage effective long-term memory or learning, a deep level of processing (in Craik and Lockhart's terminology) is required: such an elaboration of material that is to be learned should allow it to be related to what the child already knows in an appropriate and organised fashion in order to assist in its translation to long-term storage. Thus the more the material can be elaborated, the more intricately it can fit into an associative network and the more likely it is that it will be recalled when appropriate. Furthermore, such an elaboration should allow the potential for information to be generalisable since it is stored, not as a set of separate units, but as part of a network.

In general research work which has investigated the effects of various techniques that encourage organisation of the material and also its elaboration have shown improvements in memory. Again this is an area which is actively being pursued. For example, Glidden (1979) itemised six strategies which have been investigated for improving the performance of mentally handicapped children in learning and memory tasks. They are:

1. the labelling of items and their repetition;
2. the grouping of terms to capitalise on the clustering phenomenon and the requirement to organise material in order for effective learning to take place;
3. the provision of cues pertaining to categories to be remembered given at both presentation and at recall (e.g. Herriot 1972);
4. the rehearsal of the to-be-learned material;

5. the formation of images representative of the work that is to be acquired (Taylor and Turnure 1979);
6. the verbal elaboration of the material (Taylor and Turnure 1979).

All of these areas have an extensive research background which is too detailed for exposition here: the interested reader can refer to the work referred to above, much of which is available in Ellis (1979).

Metamemory

It is not possible to introduce the topic of memory without referring to a set of studies, relatively recently developed, that research an aspect of memory known as metamemory. Metamemory refers to the child or adult having a knowledge of the memory system and how it works or an awareness of various strategies that may be useful in trying to learn. For example if you wish to telephone for a chimney-sweep or some other infrequently used tradesman you may look up a local person in the telephone directory and locate a number. In order to be able to dial the number you must remember it between averting your eyes from the directory to the telephone dial. You probably know that if you do this without engaging in some active memory plan you will immediately be unable to remember the number. Hence you know that you have to engage in a deliberate strategy such as rehearsal. Since you do not want to remember the number for long, you know that a rehearsal strategy is adequate; processing in depth is not required. If, however, the number is important you may wish to use it repeatedly, and you might select a different strategy in order to provide more elaborate processing. For example, a series of digits that many people have to remember are those used with high street cash dispensers. How did you remember your four digit sequence? I know that I had to elaborate on the numbers by abstracting a rule that allowed me to reconstruct the number at a later date. The details of the strategies that people use are probably totally idiosyncratic, but the memoriser has a knowledge of appropriate strategies that are useful for him in order to achieve effective learning.

Brown (1978) points out that there is a serious weakness in skills of this sort in very young and retarded children, although they appear to improve with age. She reviews a great deal of her own work in trying to supply these strategies. This research is currently very underdeveloped, and the results at present appear to be mixed, some suggesting that training in metamemory is helpful, (e.g. Friedman, Krupski, Dawson and Rosenberg 1977) and others indicating the complexities (e.g. Brown and Campione 1977). Nonetheless this is clearly an important area and will be developed more in the years to come. It may also be pointed out that the skills associated with metamemory form an integral feature of the curriculum for at least one school for children with severe learning difficulties (Rectory Paddock Staff 1983). The combined operation of the factors discussed above have been included in the concept of working memory. Its function appears to be to maintain in an active state, through rehearsal, elaboration etc., information that is being used in a current task.

Concluding Comments

It has been proposed that learning and memory may be facilitated by providing a situation in which active elaboration on the part of the child is required, and that he may be helped in this process through the deliberate use of strategies. The choice of strategy according to the demands of the task is a fairly sophisticated skill which appears to come later in development.

Learning Through Association

The previous sections have introduced the topic of learning from a point of view that emphasises the role of information processing in cognition. However, many authors have proposed that the goal-directed pragmatic approach based on the behaviour modification literature, which requires teachers to be quite specific about the behavioural targets they are encouraging the children to attain, is the most useful theoretical position to adopt. This approach has as its basis the work on classical conditioning developed originally by Pavlov (1927) and on operant learning, the term originally coined by Skinner (1938). Both of these procedures show that the method by which material is presented to children is of central significance to their learning. There have been many developments and elaborations of these systems over the years, and the reader who is interested in theoretical developments could not do better than to read Mackintosh (1983). The various applied points are taken up in

Chapter 2 in more detail. This chapter will, therefore, concern itself with a brief introduction to these ideas.

Classical Conditioning

As has already been noted, one of the fundamental points of learning is to produce order or system out of potential chaos. When the child first comes into the world he is armed with a number of reflexes that are mainly concerned with immediate survival (such as the sucking reflex) and which immediately begin to function to make his world more predictable and hence, more organised. These reflexes can readily be shown to be conditionable through experience, and the classical conditioning paradigm has been used. It can be demonstrated that an unconditional reflex (UR) (such as sucking) can be elicited by an unconditional stimulus (US) (a nipple in the mouth). If the US is systematically and frequently preceded by a second stimulus or conditional stimulus (CS) that in the first instance is neutral (i.e. it does not lead to sucking when presented) then following such CS-US pairings, the CS will, on presentation, eventually lead to sucking responses which are called conditional responses (CR). This model is frequently shown schematically:

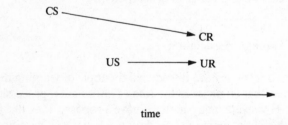

In the diagram the onset of the CS is shown as preceding the US in time. This is a crucial distinction for efficient learning. The CR is shown as being different from the UR since the two responses are often not identical in every respect, e.g. the amplitude. The sequence in which CS and US are presented is crucial since it has been established for some time that the backward conditioning sequence of US-CS does not lead to effective conditioning and must be avoided. Studies of classical conditioning in the mentally handicapped have demonstrated that the procedure can lead to learning even in the most profoundly handicapped child (e.g.

Hogg, Remington and Foxen 1979), although even in this carefully controlled study that used the eyeblink reflex as the UR to a puff of air as US and a tone as a CS they failed to obtain conditioning in some of their sample.

Since classical conditioning appears to be of especial significance in the development of behaviour involving the emotions (since these may be seen as URs, e.g. fear, anxiety, excitement etc.) it has been used therapeutically mainly with behaviours which involve such reactions (e.g. Bandura 1969). Techniques developed from classical conditioning therefore are important in a full understanding of how environmental stimuli can come to have certain effects and influence learning.

Operant Learning

Classical conditioning may be seen as a passive procedure in which the child is a mere recipient of external stimuli which have an involuntary effect. Operant learning on the other hand requires that the child emit some voluntary behaviour or operate on the environment in order to produce certain consequences. If these consequences are favourable for the child and lead to an increase in the probability of the response reinforcer occurring again, then the consequences are said to be reinforcing. If they lead to a decrease in the child's behaviour they are said to be punishing. Note that under this definition one man's meat may well be another man's poison, and whether or not a consequence is reinforcing or punishing can only be gauged by its effect on the behaviour and is not dependent on its physical properties — e.g. whether it's food such as chocolate or a smack to the leg.

Again, however, as with classical conditioning the sequence in which environmental events are experienced by the child are essential to his learning. Reinforcers that are delivered independently of responses do not lead to learning. A CS presented after a US does not lead to classical conditioning. It is useful to think of these processes as a way of organising the environment or structuring it in such a way as to expedite learning or to encourage it, or to motivate the child. In the view of the author it does not provide a very adequate account of the learning process itself, but it does show how the environment may be organised in part by the teacher in order to facilitate learning.

Thus far we have only considered single pieces of behaviour: just as one swallow does not a summer make, so one piece of behaviour hardly makes an individualised programme. This means that we need to put together pieces of behaviour into a relevant sequence. In this way a start may be made on the construction of the individualised curriculum. In operant psychology this is known as shaping or chaining, and again the method is discussed fully in Chapter 2.

Cognitive Behaviour Modification

Within the behaviour modification literature there is an approach called cognitive behaviour modification (Meichenbaum 1977) which utilises a verbal strategy and which has been shown useful in helping children to learn and to control their own behaviour. This involves, for example, the teacher presenting a task to the child and saying out loud the steps that she would take in order to solve the problem (e.g. Meichenbaum and Goodman 1971).

This method may be seen to be rather similar in concept to the metamemory procedure whereby the child learns a strategy to enable him to attack the problem, thus establishing common ground between the information-processing and associative learning approaches. However it is likely that, as with strategy-training approaches, those based on cognitive behaviour modification are likely to be of most value with children who are at a higher level of development and not functioning mainly with sensory memory.

Some Implications for Programme Development

This chapter has taken the view that, in order to plan programmes that are effective for the child with learning difficulties, the teacher has to externalise the learning process and present the teaching programme in a structured way which takes this process into account. The central requirement of the system is that, in order to learn, new material must be actively organised by the child and related to his current knowledge; the simple intention to learn is not enough. The ideas presented also appear in differing ways when described by different authors, e.g. the problem of the match (Hunt and Kirk 1974), the zone of proximal development (Vygotsky 1978), the development of schema through assimilation and accommodation (Piaget 1970). Thus it may be argued that the child with learning difficulties has problems in learning partly because he is not efficient in the process of structuring knowledge for himself, and so it behoves the teacher to bridge that gap.

Some advocates of the structured approach to teaching the handicapped imply a certain passive linearity to their teaching programmes, e.g. EDY (McBrien and Foxen 1981; Ainscow and Tweddle 1979), and to some extent this is implied by the operant model of learning. However, if the arguments put forward in this chapter are accepted, this becomes only the first step in the chain: if what has been learned is left at this point there may be a danger of creating associative networks that are not networks at all but merely unrelated strands of knowledge. If this occurs, it is likely to lead to a failure to generalise which, as Stokes and Baer (1977) have pointed out, is a problem with the operant approach.

What is needed are methods which lead to links being developed between the various strands of knowledge. It is proposed that this be advanced through the presentation of methods structured to be commensurate with the manner in which knowledge is thought to be constructed in the memory system. This process may be stimulated by and through the use of active strategies such as discrimination, rehearsal, imagery, elaboration and so on, which help to make the to-be-learned knowledge relevant to the child's own personal network, thus facilitating the attentional process. Finally, remembering that it has been proposed that retrieval from memory is essentially a reconstructive process, it is suggested that this be practised also by requiring the child to demonstrate his knowledge with respect, not only to the present work, but also to work that has been carried out which is related and in the immediate past. This may then be related to new ideas or people or situations in order to encourage the organisation of material and the interlinking connections, the development of rules and hence the generalisation of the learning. What is being advocated is an approach to learning in which the teacher organises the environment so as to require the child to make active interactions with it. This structure must be commensurate with the learning and curriculum needs of the child and should be based on an understanding, not of a static learning process, but of a dynamic system which has identifiable properties and a preferred *modus operandi.*

Let us look at a typical learning task and work through these ideas. Suppose the task is to learn to discriminate between certain coins and to use this learning effectively. First the teacher must select some relevant coins: let us use a 1p piece and a 2p piece as a starting point. First of all, we must be certain that the child can effectively discriminate between the two coins. That is to say, he recognises that the colour is irrelevant and can attend appropriately to the size dimension and can demonstrate this through some observable performance exercise. For example he can reliably sort 1p and 2p pieces to a high criterion: say, in 20 choices, no errors over several days. Elaboration could be introduced by asking him to talk about the coins (their colour and size for example), using working memory to establish a deep level of processing and encouraging long-term memory. This very simple example of learning has had the effect of developing attentional skills through the learning of a discrimination. It requires the establishment of categories (in this case big and small) which must be remembered through a demonstration that the sorting can still be carried out accurately over a number of days. The question of generalisation can now be considered from a number of viewpoints. Does the learning of this task lead to easier learning of a similar discrimination between two other coins e.g. a 5p and a 10p piece? Can he sort the 1p and 2p coins in other situations, e.g. other classrooms, or with other teachers asking him to sort the coins? Can he sort the coins in a real shop?

This is a very simple example, but if we introduce the 5p and 10p coins the problem immediately becomes quite complex. One way of approaching this problem might be as follows:

1. require accurate performance of the 1p/2p sort;
2. require accurate performance of the 5p/10p sort;
3. put the four coins together and require accurate performance of the sort — perhaps by providing four containers into which the child may place the coins.

So far we have two separate structures that may look like this:

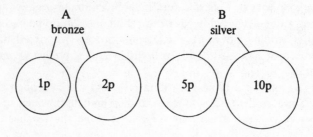

and they need to be interlinked so that value becomes the principle for the sort:

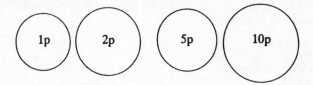

Of course the problem here is that value disturbs the size ordering.

Eventually we need a cognitive structuring that looks something like the following which brings together the pieces of learning:

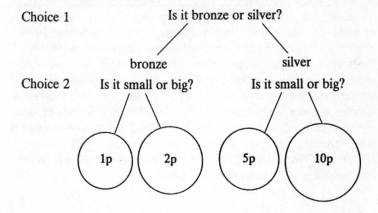

This arrangement could probably be developed by requiring the child to sort the four coins when presented in a pile with four containers in a specified order. Value might be developed by associating the coin with a range of items that the child likes that the teacher can put into the child's known order of preference. Generalisation of these skills can then be carried out as before.

This is a method of carrying out task analysis based on choices that emphasise cognitive processes but which always have behavioural concomitants, and there are probably other and perhaps better ways of achieving the same end. Perhaps as an interesting exercise you could work out what to do in order to introduce the heptagonal coins of 20p and 50p into the above network? Hopefully you can see that this approach encourages structure, clustering and sequencing as well as general attentional skills which the child can readily use in other circumstances. This encourages observation skills by making him aware that systematic differences in the environment are meaningful, must be learned and responded to differently.

Concluding Comment

This chapter has attempted to give an outline of the learning process and to relate information-processing approaches to behavioural ones at a functional level, if not a theoretical one, and to try to demonstrate how such knowledge is useful for teachers in thinking about programme planning. Readers must remember, however, that there is also a developmental component to this process, on which there has not been space to elaborate in this chapter, although it has received some discussion in terms of memory codes developing from sensory images — episodic — semantic memory. However, there are also the important views put forward by writers such as Piaget (1970) and Bruner (1964) but which are covered elsewhere in this book. The significance of some of these ideas, especially the Piagetian ones, have been discussed with regard to mental handicap by Chatelanat and Schoggen (1980) and Woodward (1979), and the interested reader is recommended these sources as starting points.

References

Ainscow, M. and Tweddle, D.A. (1979) *Preventing Classroom Failure.* Wiley.
Allport, G.W. (1924) 'Eidetic Imagery'. *Br. Jnl of Psychology, 15,* pp. 99-120.
Anderson, J.R. (1980) *Cognitive Psychology and Its Implications.* Freeman.
Atkinson, R.C. and Shiffrin, R.M. (1968) 'Human memory: a proposed system and its control processes', in K. Spence and J. Spence (eds.). *The Psychology of Learning and Motivation,* Vol. 2. Academic Press.
Bandura, A. (1969) *Principles of Behaviour Modification.* Holt, Rinehart and Winston.
Barkley, R.A. (1983) 'Hyperactivity', in R.J. Morris, and T.R. Kratochwill (eds.). *The Practice of Child Therapy.* Pergamon Press.
Bartlett, F.C. (1932) *Remembering: an experimental and social study.* Cambridge University Press.
Bousfield, W.A. (1953) 'The occurrence of clustering in the recall of randomly arranged associates'. *Jnl of General Psychology, 49,* pp. 229-40.
Bray, N.W. (1979) 'Strategy production in the retarded', in N.R. Ellis (ed.). *Handbook of Mental Deficiency, Psychological Theory and Research.* Lawrence Erlbaum.

Bricker, D.D. (1972) 'Imitative sign training as a facilitator of word-object association with low functioning children'. *Am. Jnl of Mental Deficiency, 76,* pp. 509-16.

Brimer, M.A., and Dunn L.M. (1972) *The English Picture Vocabulary Test.* Educational Evaluation Enterprises.

Brookes, P.H. and McCauley, C. (1984) 'Cognitive research in mental retardation'. *Am. Jnl of Mental Deficiency, 88,* pp. 479-86.

Brown, A.L. (1972) 'Context and recency cues in the recognition memory of retarded children and adolescents'. *Am. Jnl of Mental Deficiency, 77,* pp. 54-8.

Brown, A.L. (1978) 'Knowing when, where and how to remember: a problem of metacognition', in R. Glaser (ed.). *Advances in Instructional Psychology,* Vol. 1. Lawrence Erlbaum.

Brown, A.L. and Campione, J.C. (1977) 'Training strategic study time apportionment in educable retarded children'. *Intelligence, 1,* pp. 99-107.

Bruner, J.S. (1964) 'The course of cognitive growth'. *Am. Psychologist, 19,* pp. 1-15.

Chatelanat, G. and Schoggen M. (1980) 'Issues encountered in devising an observation system to assess spontaneous infant behaviour — environment interactions', in J. Hogg and P. Mittler (eds.). *Advances in Mental Handicap Research,* Vol 1. Wiley.

Collins, A.M. and Quillian M.R. (1969) 'Retrieval time from semantic memory'. *Jnl of Verbal Learning and Verbal Behaviour, 8,* pp. 240-7.

Craik, F.I.M. and Lockhart, R.S. (1972) 'Levels of processing: a framework for memory research'. *Jnl of Verbal Learning and Verbal Behaviour, 11,* pp. 671-84.

Education Act 1981. HMSO.

Ellis, N.R. (1978) 'Do the mentally retarded have poor memory?' *Intelligence, 2,* pp. 41-54.

Ellis, N.R. (ed.). *Handbook of Mental Deficiency, Psychological Theory and Research,* 2nd edn. Lawrence Erlbaum.

Estes, W.K. (1982) 'Learning, memory and intelligence', in R.J. Sternberg (ed.). *Handbook of Human Intelligence.* Cambridge University Press.

Evans, P.L.C. and Hogg, J. (1984) 'A classroom rating scale for use with mentally retarded children'. *Br.Jnl of Clinical Psychology, 23,* pp. 187-94.

Friedman, M., Krupski, A., Dawson, E.T., and Rosenberg, P. (1977) 'Metamemory and mental retardation: implications for research and practice', in P.M. Mittler (ed.). *Research to Practice in Mental Retardation: education and training,* Vol. 2. IASSMD.

Glidden, L.M. (1979) 'Training of learning and memory in retarded persons: strategies, techniques, and teaching tests', in N.R. Ellis (ed.). *Handbook of Mental Deficiency, Psychological Theory and Research.* Lawrence Erlbaum.

Haber, R.N. and Haber, R.B. (1964) 'Eidetic imagery 1: frequency'. *Perceptual Motor Skills, 19,* pp. 131-8.

Herriot, P. (1972) 'The effect of category cues on the free recall of retarded adults'. *Psychonomic Science, 28,* pp. 341-2.

Herriot, P., Green, J.M., and McConkey, R. (1977) *Organisation and Memory: a review and a project in subnormality.* Methuen.

Hogg, J. and Evans, P.L.C. (1975) 'Stimulus generalization following extradimensional training in educationally subnormal (severely) children'. *Br. Jnl of Psychology, 66,* pp. 211-24.

Hogg, J., Remington, R. E., and Foxen, T.H. (1979) 'Classical conditioning of profoundly retarded multiply handicapped children'. *Developmental Medicine and Child Neurology, 21,* pp. 779-86.

Hunt, J. McV., and Kirk, G.E. (1974) 'Criterion-referenced lists of school readiness: a paradigm with illustrations'. *Genetic Psychology Monographs, 90* (1st half), pp. 144-82.

Hunter, I.M.L. (1964) *Memory*. Penguin Books.

Kahneman, D. (1973) *Attention and Effort*. Prentice-Hall.

Kintsch, W. (1974) *The Representation of Meaning in Memory*. Lawrence Erlbaum.

Lamberts, F. (1981) 'Sign and symbol in childrens' processing of familiar auditory stimuli'. *Am. Jnl of Mental Deficiency, 86*, pp. 300-8.

Mackintosh, N.J. (1983) *Conditioning and Associative Learning*. Oxford University Press.

McBrien, J.A. and Foxen, T.H. (1981) *Training Staff in Behavioural Methods*. Manchester University Press.

Meichenbaum, D. (1977) *Cognitive Behaviour Modification*. Plenum Press.

Meichenbaum, D., and Goodman, J. (1971) 'Training impulsive children to talk to themselves: a means of developing self-control'. *Jnl of Abnormal Psychology, 77*, pp. 115-26.

Miller, G.A. (1956) 'The magical number seven, plus or minus two: some limits on our capacity for processing information'. *Psychological Review, 63*, pp. 81-97.

O'Connor, N. and Hermelin, B. (1963) *Speech and Thought in Severe Subnormality*. Pergamon Press.

O'Connor, N., and Hermelin, B. (1978) *Seeing and Hearing and Space and Time*. Academic Press.

Paivio, A. (1971) *Imagery and Verbal Processes*. Holt, Rinehart and Winston.

Pavlov, I.P. (1927) *Conditioned Reflexes*. Oxford University Press.

Piaget, J. (1970) 'Piaget's theory', in P.H. Mussen (ed.), *Carmichael's Manual of child Psychology*, 3rd edn. Wiley.

Rectory Paddock Staff. (1983) *In Search of a Curriculum*, 2nd edn. Robin Wren Publications.

Reid, B., and Kiernan, C. (1979) 'Spoken words and manual signs as encoding categories in short-term memory for mentally retarded children'. *Am Jnl of Mental Deficiency, 84*, pp. 200-3.

Richards, S.J. and Evans, P.L.C. (1981) 'Effects of complexity of learning on relational responding in transposition in young ESN(M) children'. *Educational Psychology, 1*, pp. 141-51.

Richardson, A. (1969) *Mental Imagery*. Springer-Verlag.

Shiffrin, R.M. and Schneider, W. (1977) 'Controlled and automatic human information processing: II perceptual leaarning, automatic attending, and a general theory'. *Psychological Review, 84*, p. 127-90.

Siipola, E.M. and Hayden, S.D. (1965) 'Exploring eidetic imagery among the retarded'. *Perceptual and Motor Skills, 21*, pp. 275-86.

Skinner, B.F. (1938) *The Behaviour of Organisms*. Appleton-Century-Crofts, 1938.

Spitz, H.H. (1979) 'Beyond field theory in the study of mental deficiency', in N.R. Ellis (ed.). *Handbook of Mental Deficiency, Psychological Theory and Research*, 2nd edn. Lawrence Erlbaum.

Standing, L., Conezio, J. and Haber, R.N. (1970) 'Perception and memory for pictures: single-trial learning of 2560 visual stimuli'. *Psychonomic Science, 19*, pp. 73-4.

Stokes, T.F. and Baer, D.M. (1977) 'An implicit technology of generalization'. *Jnl of Applied Behaviour Analysis, 10*, pp. 349-67.

Taylor, A.M. and Turnure J.E. (1979) 'Imagery and verbal elaboration with retarded children: effects on learning and memory', in N.R. Ellis (ed.). *Handbook of Mental Deficiency, Psychological Theory and Research*, 2nd edn. Lawrence Erlbaum.

Van Biervliet, A. (1979) 'Establishing words and objects as functionally equivalent through manual sign language'. *Am. Jnl of Mental Deficiency, 82*, pp. 178-86.

Vygotsky, L.S. (1978) *Mind in Society: the development of higher psychological processes.* M. Cole, V. John-Steiner, S. Scribner, and E. Souberman (eds. and trans.). Harvard University Press.

Wessells, M.G. (1982) *Cognitive Psychology.* Harper and Row.

Woodward, W.M. (1979) 'Piaget's theory and mental retardation' in N.R. Ellis (ed.). *Handbook of Mental Deficiency, Psychological Theory and Research,* 2nd edn. Lawrence Erlbaum.

Zeaman, D. and House, B.J. (1963) 'The role of attention in retardate discrimination learning' in N.R. Ellis (ed.). *Handbook of Mental Deficiency.* McGraw-Hill.

Zeaman, D. and House, B.J. (1979) 'A review of attentional theory', in N.R. Ellis (ed.). *Handbook of Mental Deficiency, Psychological Theory and Research.* Lawrence Erlbaum.

9 SENSORY HANDICAP

Hearing Impairment

Chris Williams

Deafness is a hidden disability. Deficits in socialisation and communication are the only overt clues to the level of handicap. Where little is expected of the hearing-impaired child the disability disappears to the casual observer. For the child the handicap remains. In this way hearing impairment differs significantly from many other forms of disability which can be signalled by physical signs. The only signal for a deaf child might be a hearing aid. And even then, such an aid will be designed to be as unobtrusive as possible. Contrast this with the process of enhancement used in marketing seeing aids as items of personal jewellery. This indicates something of the differential value system we use to judge visual as opposed to auditory loss. The hearing-impaired child is born into such a value-laden community. His or her handicap is thereby compounded. It is impossible for a hearing person to experience the effect of total hearing loss, although it is true that virtually all hearing persons will at some time experience partial loss. The critical difference is the absence or virtual absence of language competence.

When such a hearing impairment occurs in conjunction with an intellectual impairment, as it does in at least 10 per cent of individuals with an intellectual impairment (Kropka and Williams 1979), a compounded handicap results. The effects are not simply additive, they are multiplied. Not only does the intellectual impairment lead to a chronic learning disability but the hearing impairment also adds its contribution to a profound disability, particularly in handicapping the development of language and communicative skills. To add further to this special group of individuals with greater difficulties than most hearing-impaired people are those whose intellectual impairment arises from the condition Down's syndrome. Here, it is now known, at least 80-90 per cent have some degree of hearing loss (Cunningham and McArthur 1982). It is critically important when working with children having both intellectual and hearing impairments not to over-estimate their disabilities. It is tragically common that a slow-learning, hearing-impaired child will be ascertained at a lower level of intellectual ability than might his non-hearing-impaired peers (Bond 1981). This will not only have direct effects on the expectations of his or her parents and teachers, but also on placement and ultimately his or her whole life-time experiences throughout adulthood (Williams 1982).

Classification of Hearing Impairment

One of the first problems encountered when trying to establish a taxonomy for hearing impairment is that there is no universally agreed system. Descriptions of types of deafness vary according to age of onset, site of pathology and degree of hearing loss. A funda-mental difference exists between hearing loss that occurs before, during or shortly following birth and that which occurs much later. The distinguishing feature is the onset of language. Where deafness precedes language development a condition known as pre-lingual deafness exists. Such children will find it difficult, if not impossible, to acquire a functional competence in spoken language (Conrad 1979). This is not to say that they will not become competent communicators. Where deafness occurs following the onset of language development, the term post-lingual deafness is used. Such children are likely to use spoken language as their main channel of communication, although many will need specialised help in order to maintain their competence. The second variable in defining deafness is the site of the impairment responsible for the hearing loss. This can be anywhere along the auditory pathway from the outer ear to the projection area on the cortex which interprets sound into meaning.

Causes of Deafness

Loss of hearing is a natural process that will invariably affect virtually everybody as they age. This process of presbyacusis can occur at different rates, and some elderly people may never be significantly impaired. It is due to the gradual atrophy of the sensitive hair-cells and the auditory nerve fibres of the cochlea in the inner ear. It may be accelerated by infection or exposure to loud noises. All other causes of loss of hearing depend upon an imposed condition creating an impairment where, otherwise, none would exist. Of the two main types, conductive and sensori-neural, conductive deafness can result from traumatic, pathological, or mechanical events that produce damage or obstruction to the sound-conducting apparatus of the outer ear. Children may particularly suffer from blockage by wax or foreign objects, or they may have damage to the ear drum from injury or infection.

The second major type of hearing impairment involves the neurological apparatus of sound reception — transmission-transduction-interpretation — each component of which can be damaged. Such damage can occur before, during or following birth and is often the cause of pre-lingual deafness. Pre-natal damage can result from inherited or acquired causes. There may be a family history of deafness indicating genetic predisposition, or there may have been a maternal viral infection such as rubella or cytomegalovirus. The hearing of a child may be damaged during the birth process as a result of trauma or anoxia. The hearing may also be impaired during the first few months of life by infection or, in some cases, the anti-bacterial treatment for those infections.

With such variability in aetiology it is difficult to establish effective preventive measures although the incidence of rubella-induced deafness is rapidly reducing following the campaign for vaccination of all girls aged between 11 and 13 years.

The importance of aural hygiene as a preventive measure can be overlooked, particularly where children or adults are grouped together such as in long-stay hospitals. A regular wax inspection and removal can reduce a considerable amount of hearing impairment in such circumstances.

It is possible to establish a descriptive definition of deafness that considers the degree of loss in physical terms related to the loudness or intensity of sound that can be heard at different frequencies. A numerical label can be attached to such a loss and a classification system developed giving a range of hearing loss in decibel terms. A normally hearing person would have a 'threshold' hearing level of 0 dBs; they would hear a sound of 30 dBs intensity as a whisper; of 60 dBs as conversational speech and a sound of 90 dBs as a shout. A sound level of 120 dBs approaches the point of discomfort and damage if prolonged. A pure-tone audiogram provides a measure of hearing level intensity across a range of frequencies from 250 Hz to 8,000 Hz.

Hearing loss is generally not evenly distributed across these frequencies. It is usually the higher frequencies that are differentially lost leading to inability to discriminate consonant sounds, and often the ability to hear female and child voices is also

Figure 9 1: Summary of Classification and Definition

CHARACTERISTIC	VARIABLE	
Age of onset	Pre-lingual	
	Post-lingual	
Degree of severity	Mild	30-50 dB
	Moderate	50-70 dB
	Severe	70-90 dB
	Profound	+90 dB
Site of impairment	Conductive	
	Sensory-neural	
	Mixed	
Origin of deafness	Congenital	
	Acquired	traumatic
		environmental
		pathological
		senility

differentially distorted. A broad classification based on physical loss has normal threshold hearing within the range 0-30 dBs, a severe loss at 60-90 dBs and a profound loss beyond 90 dBs.

A more functional definition of hearing impairment considers the effect of the loss on communication. Deafness is then defined as a 'loss of hearing sufficiently severe to render an understanding of conversational speech impossible in most situations with or without a hearing aid' (Mindel and Vernon 1971). The partially hearing have been defined as 'those who (with or without a hearing aid) have some useful hearing and whose method of communication is by speech and lip-reading' (Lysons 1984).

Inner/Outer Language

While the normally hearing child of three years of age will have acquired a 1,000 word vocabulary, the deaf child will barely have realised the use of a limited range of gestures and expressions. He will not yet know that objects have labels and that mouth movements convey information and, more importantly, can influence the actions of others. But most critically he will not have 'internalised' his language to become the mechanism whereby he can think for himself. The tools of problem-solving for the hearing child are denied to his deaf companion. As Conrad (1979) asserts '... we may be sure that a child entering school with no external language because of deafness will have no internal language either'. The learning efficiency of the normally hearing child is phenomenal and will never again reach such a pitch as when first taught. The deaf child is, in many respects, ill-prepared for such a rapid expansion of knowledge. The foundation course in language is missing or faulty and has deliberately to be constructed, using valuable time that might otherwise be used in adding to knowledge. The critical issue is the nature of this language. Whether it is to be the natural language of the hearing or that of the deaf – this forms the basis of the oral-manual conflict. If speech is so important to thought then how does a born-deaf child develop his thought processes unless through speech? Speech then becomes the main thrust of early education – but at what cost? For over 100 years, effectively since the Congress of Milan in 1880, the accepted wisdom on educating deaf children has been to use an oral-visual approach with speech and lip-reading as the means of communication. Conrad (1979) has reported extensively on the effect of oralism as an educational strategy for deaf children, and in many respects has found it wanting.

Developing Speech

Speech acquisition by normally-hearing children occurs over a period of several years beginning from babbling sounds within the first few months of life culminating in an extensive, expressive and receptive vocabulary and vocal repertoire by the age of five years. Schooling does not influence this process significantly. The learning of such a complex set of skills proceeds generally without effort and trauma and arises through a constant interaction with speaking adults and siblings who prompt, correct and reinforce production. All of this depends heavily on hearing. For the child who is born deaf or who goes deaf in infancy this natural interaction is severely restricted: the child cannot hear his or her own attempts at speech or the speech of others. The natural process of language-learning is absent. To compensate for this, an unnatural and instructional approach has been developed where communication is established using other modalities, mainly visual and tactile.

The post-lingually deafened child is not so handicapped. His or her speech and language skills have been established. The effect of their hearing impairment is a gradual decrement in quality of voice production as self-monitoring deteriorates. The rate of loss can be diminished by skilled teaching and speech therapy and, more recently, by the use of feed-back from computer-generated visual displays of sounds produced by teacher and pupil.

Developing Sign. The natural language of born-deaf people is a visual language. It is expressed by whole-body, hand or finger movements using a conventional system of both iconic and symbolic signs. It is received visually and in some cases tactually. It has a vocabulary and a syntax, which, although differing from that of vocal language, is nevertheless systematic, lawful and legitimate. Competent signers have no problem conveying all of the nuances and abstractions previously thought the exclusive property of spoken English (Kyle and Woll 1983). The myth of signing as a second-class language has hindered its acceptability among traditional teachers of the deaf. The myth has been exposed, and a greater recognition of the value of gesture and sign, as well as speech, for communication between deaf-deaf dyads, deaf-hearing dyads and also hearing-hearing dyads, has been recognised. The inclusion of body language in social-skills training exemplifies this acknowledgement of value (Spence 1980). Combining both spoken and non-spoken language into a system of 'total communication' is now recognised as one of the primary tasks of the social education of hearing impaired children (Schaeffer 1980). The inclusion of the family of the deaf child in this teaching must be a pre-requisite for success. Most deaf children have hearing parents who have no experience of deafness or of communicating with deaf people. They must also be involved in developing total communication competence, if only to dispel the belief that if only the child could be taught to speak and lip-read he or she would become as if hearing. The child born of deaf parents, paradoxically, can be in a better position, having been brought up in a setting where gestured language was the norm. The danger to be avoided is the underestimating of the cognitive ability of a born-deaf child because of a communication difficulty. The presence of primarily deaf persons in a setting designed for helping mentally handicapped people may not be to their benefit unless special provision be made in those settings for their unique needs (Kropka and Williams 1979).

The Impact of Technology

Developments in the technology of micro-electronics are increasingly becoming relevant to the needs of disabled people. This is especially important in hearing impairment where one of the distance sensory receptors is damaged. Technological aids can have at least three major areas of impact. The first, and probably most important, is in prevention, early detection and amelioration of the disability. Prevention through vaccination against rubella infection is having a dramatic impact on the incidence of virus-induced deafness. Computer-based registers and record keeping can increase significantly the efficiency of this preventive procedure. Early detection of hearing loss can now be effected by using an audiological crib for the new-born whereby whole body movements of the baby can be detected under varying conditions of sound input. This is essentially a much-refined startle-response detection and can be carried out without requiring the active co-operation of the subject or the attachment of equipment. Early detection can lead to treatment or remediation. The developing use of implanted electronic cochlear substitutes offers some promise to establish at least a degree of sound perception even if, at present, the discrimination of sound may be limited. It may be that direct auditory cortex stimulation by implanted electrodes will become a viable intervention for some cases of sensori-neural deafness.

The greatest potential growth in the use of micro-electronics is probably to be in the development of communication aids. For some children it is possible to overcome much of the disability of a hearing impairment by the skilful use of an auditory amplifier. The simple use of a hearing aid, following training, for both receiver and transmitter, can offer a significant level of extra help that is needed to overcome the initial inability to hear sufficient sound to enable adequate discrimination to be developed. The crucial variable is the training in its proper use rather than its intrinsic design. The aid does not restore normal hearing: it merely amplifies sound – all sound. The listener has to learn to distinguish the signal from the background noise, although this task can be made easier by classroom design and closer proximity of the teacher. Developments in aid design have virtually eliminated the body-worn aid in preference for the post-aurally worn amplifier, both for functional and aesthetic reasons. A device which attempts to overcome some of the disadvantages of the hearing aid, but which can only be used in a teaching setting, is the speech trainer. This is an amplifier to which is attached a microphone and headphone set. The amplification of sound can be restricted to the input and can be variably adjusted on output to suit the hearing characteristics of the child. Several children can use such an aid simultaneously.

A further refinement of this system is the induction loop system where signals are converted into radio frequencies transmitted by the speaker's microphone and received by the listener's hearing aid. Again the benefits of the system are counter-balanced by the disadvantages of interference and reduced opportunity to monitor speech production when tuned to the loop transmission. The most sophisticated developments use radio transmission with combined microphones and transmitters worn by the teacher and a receiver-amplifier worn by the pupil.

Assessment

There are two strings to the assessment bow. One string attempts to provide comparative data in order to indicate whether a particular facet of intellect, personality or cognitive functioning is within the range of normality, above it, or below it. Such a strategy permits the rank-ordering of an individual along a variety of dimensions; but often, little else. This approach is typified by the assessment of intelligence where a comparison between the performance of the individual being assessed is made with that of a standardisation group selected to be representative of the population as a whole. By manipulating the difficulty of the various problem-solving items, a model of the distribution of intelligence can be generated which has known statistical properties. Such a procedure did have value when selective education required a cut-off point for special educational provision. This need is gradually diminishing, and an assessment of cognitive ability is becoming more of a descriptive statistic than an administrative classification. There is a wide variety of tests of intellectual competence, both verbal and non-verbal, although few are directly applicable to the hearing-impaired child. Nevertheless a well-designed test of performance skills in the hands of an experienced assessor can provide an accurate estimate of intellectual ability (Reed 1973).

Possibly the most widely-used formal assessments of cognitive ability are those developed by Wechsler (1944; 1949) and currently available in updated and revised versions for both children and adults. The non-verbal sub-items of these tests can be presented conveniently using sign or gesture and can provide reasonably valid estimates of levels of cognitive functioning. It may be that the recent British Ability Scales (1983) will support the

Wechsler tests and enable comparisons to be made with a more relevant standardisation group than previously has been possible.

The second string to the bow consists of assessments that are essentially individualistic; they document personal characteristics using a criterion-based assessment format. The testing of hearing levels fits into this category of idiographic assessment. In this case, a purely physical set of parameters, amplitude and frequency, are used as descriptors of a level of individual functioning.

The assessment of hearing impairment can vary from the informal 'screening' assessment of new borns to the technologically sophisticated electro-physiological procedures available in specialist centres. There should no longer be any instances of a hearing-impaired child being overlooked and wrongly ascertained as mentally handicapped when loss of hearing is the main, and sometimes, the only, disability.

Apart from intellectual and auditory function testing, the teacher also needs to be able to carry out a descriptive assessment of social competence and of any behaviour problems that may be presenting. The first stage of any individual plan of teaching must be that of describing the current behavioural repertoire of the individual. Skills in observing and recording behaviour, either by direct testing or unobtrusive observation, are vital tools in individualising the curriculum. Observing and recording behaviour can be extremely time-consuming if all behaviour is included. It can be extremely unreliable if only subjective impressions of overall behaviour are recorded. Between these two extremes lie a considerable number of observational strategies that permit acceptably reliable and valid conclusions to be drawn from samples of behaviour observed periodically. Time-sample recording at specified intervals using objective criteria for coding units of behaviour over a sufficient period of time, depending upon the frequency of the behaviour, will allow a stable base-line to be generated, against which changes in behaviour can be compared.

An alternative strategy is to use, or create, a criterion-referenced check list based either upon a developmental schedule or a task analysis of specified skills. Numerous such scales exist, but probably the best known include the Vineland Social Maturity Scale, The Bristol Adjustment Guides and the Progress Assessment Charts. Each of these assessment forms can provide an initial statement of the present behavioural repertoire of the child or adult. The advantage over informal or locally developed assessments is that using a standard format allows comparisons to be made both within and between groups. By using the same form at regular intervals over a period of time, a picture of progress can be built up.

Assessment, however, is more important than this. It is the preliminary step in setting up an individual programme plan (IPP). Such an IPP must contain objectives both for the student and the teacher based upon the assessment. Individuals are named who take responsibility for parts or all of the programme, and dates are set for review and revision. This strategy produces a continuously updated and therefore current individual curriculum and teaching plan. For children with special learning needs this is a crucial component of their education. Without this focus on their individual needs children with learning disabilities, especially if due to learning impairment, may well not maintain or develop their skills in socialisation and communication. It is the privilege of professional teachers to play their part in ensuring that impairments do not inevitably develop into handicaps.

Conclusion

Without the means to communicate, the child with severe learning disabilities is at a significant disadvantage in his or her quest for independence. It matters little that the source of disability is social, physiological, biochemical or structural, the effect is the same, and it is the responsibility of the professional teacher, together with the carers of that child, to develop strategies to overcome the disabilities so that they do not become unnecessarily handicapping.

Communication, as the primary social skill, requires not only a fully functioning biological system, but also a social context within which the symbology of communication is functional. Hearing impairment provides the double disability of a damaged individual and a devalued symbol system. It would be a tragedy if deaf children could only communicate with other deaf children. The tragedy would not be confined to the hearing-impaired child. The idealistic goal of oralism neglected the possibility of the 'hearing world' making steps on its part towards a communication with deaf people. The integration of children with special educational needs in mainstream schooling may, in a generation, explode the myth of segregation for special schooling. The rapid growth of sign and symbol systems in the education of non-communicating and hearing-impaired children (Kiernan, Reid and Jones 1982) indicates a recognition of such alternative methods. These methods are available to all, whether disabled or not. And the inclusion of non-verbal communication in ordinary education could go a long way to enabling integration and acceptance to become the norm rather than the exception for hearing impaired children (Dale 1984). Early detection and the identification of the specific impairments must become the regular practice of all local services for children. It should not happen again that the developmental disabilities of a hearing-impaired child could be confused with those whose disability arises from an intellectual impairment. The distinction can sometimes be difficult to make as the causes of deafness and of mental handicap can be common, but the needs of the child are different and must be met differently.

It is with an increasing awareness of these special needs of hearing-impaired children that we all may benefit from a learning of new skills in communication and a greater tolerance of disability. The deaf person need then no longer be asked to play the role of a 'child of a lesser god'.

Visual Impairment

David Ellis

Type of Visual Impairment

The two most common terms for visual impairment, 'blindness' and 'partial sight' concern the more severe degrees of visual loss. Their definition in the UK has become largely an occupational one, in line with the requirements for registration with a local authority as blind or partially sighted. Blindness, for this purpose is 'so blind as to be unable to do any work for which eye-sight is essential', while 'partial sight' is applied to those who are not blind but substantially and permanently handicapped by visual loss. This accords well with the educational definition given by the Vernon Report (DES, 1972). Doctors, social workers, or others (e.g. parents or teachers) can initiate the registration process, but the essential role is that of the ophthalmologist who must assess the patient and certify the extent of visual loss.

Ophthalmologists make their judgement on the basis of two

main aspects of visual function, acuity and visual field. Acuity concerns the sharpness or clarity of vision, as determined by the eye's shape and its ability to focus light. Defects in this function can be corrected with appropriate lenses (spectacles). Visual field concerns the ability of the retina (a layer of light-sensitive cells at the back of the eye) to detect light and transmit its effects to the brain. Damage to parts of the retina can mean loss of parts of the 'picture' which the eye perceives. Tunnel vision, for example, involves the loss of peripheral vision which allows us to detect moving objects nearby, but which is less sharply focused than central vision, which we use to look at fine details such as a person's face, or writing.

The acuity is expressed as a 'Snellen' fraction. An acuity of 6/60 Snellen indicates that the person can see, at a distance of 6 metres, what a person with normal vision can see at 60 metres. Registration is usually available when acuity is 3/60 or less, or 6/60 if the visual field is also restricted. The commonly accepted standard for partial sight is 6/18. Various estimates suggest that severe visual impairment (blindness and partial sight) is very much more common among the mentally handicapped population. Ellis (1982) found visual handicap was about ten times more common in residents of mental handicap institutions in England and Wales, than among the normal population, while Warburg, Frederiksen and Rattlefft (1979) found that blindness was about 200 times more common in mentally handicapped children below the age of 20. Visual acuity defects do not always produce blindness as many of us who wear spectacles will know. Unfortunately, it is now well documented that mentally handicapped people are more likely to show hyperopia (long sight) while there is evidence that people with Down's syndrome are more likely to show myopia (short sight) than the normal population.

Another acuity defect, astigmatism, arises from variations in the shape of the lens with the result that while an image may be in focus in for example the horizontal plane, it is unfocused in the vertical plane and vice versa. Astigmatism is also more common in mentally handicapped people (Woodruff 1977). Most acuity defects can be corrected with appropriate spectacles, and a number of studies have shown that the majority of mentally handicapped people who need spectacles will use them correctly if the lenses prescribed are correct for them. Teachers and nurses who work with mentally handicapped children will be well aware of the risks of loss or damage to spectacles. This may result, in part, from inadequate preparation for their use. New glasses always produce a strange effect on the user's perception. Introduction to them for short periods at first, plus structured training in tolerating the frames, will often produce good results. But continuing rejection of them may be due simply to wrongly prescribed lenses. Mentally handicapped people are not always easy to assess optically, and cultivating a good relationship with the optician may prove time well spent. It is important to note that an uncorrected acuity defect can render the subject blind, while if the defect remains uncorrected there may be an irreversible loss of vision (amblyopia).

Strabismus and nystagmus are both due to movement disorders of the eyes and both occur more commonly in the presence of cerebral palsy. Strabismus (squint) involves the eyes looking in slightly different directions. One eye usually becomes dominant to avoid the confusion of two superimposed visual images. Squint can be corrected surgically and, if done early enough, is believed to restore normal visual function. If uncorrected, however, the non-dominant eye may become amblyopic. Nystagmus is rapid, jerky movements of the eyes. It occurs sometimes as part of a wider neurological syndrome and is not thought to be very responsive to treatment.

Mental and Visual Handicaps

As noted above, visual handicaps are much more common in the mentally handicapped population and this seems most likely to be due to similar types of cause at the genetic and prenatal (or congenital) stages of development. The most common genetic cause of mental handicap, Down's syndrome, carries a greater risk of cataracts from birth, and of later deterioration in visual acuity, while cerebral palsy, a congenitally produced impairment is also commonly associated with both mental and visual handicaps. Low birthweight and pre-term deliveries are more likely to result in both mental handicap and visual handicap, and it is not surprising therefore if some of these children are born with both types of handicap.

There are many conditions in which mental and visual handicaps co-exist, which cannot be discussed here in detail. The interested reader is referred to Jan, Freeman and Scott (1977) for an excellent discussion of the problems and needs of visually handicapped children and adolescents, and to Ellis (1986) for a collection of studies and reviews on various aspects of sensory and mental handicap.

Developmental Delay

Several discussions have appeared in print of the delays in early development which are thought to arise in children with severe visual handicaps. The best documented recent evidence for such delay is that of Reynell (1978), who compared rates of development of blind and partially sighted children with that of sighted children up to age five years. Five developmental areas were assessed (social adaptation, sensorimotor understanding, exploration of the environment, verbal comprehension and expressive language) and delays of between one year and 18 months were found by age five. Delay in social adaptation depended initially on poor co-operation in, for example, dressing and feeding routines, and may have been due to the over-protection of visually handicapped children by their parents.

Of perhaps greater significance are the delays in 'sensorimotor understanding' and 'exploration of the environment' because they reflect the importance of vision for the child's understanding of space and movement. Many teachers will recall the importance attached by Piaget to the role of vision in early learning. Hand-eye co-ordination for example, allows an infant to act on the environment by touch and by manipulating objects. Piaget stressed that actions are the foundations of understanding for the child about the nature of the world. The child constructs reality by observing how his activities affect the world. He also learns to understand himself as part of the world but separate from objects. These basic understandings are foundations upon which abstract ideas and symbolic thinking (including language) are built. Loss of vision means that there is a need to organise experience and thought deliberately around an alternative sensory channel, usually hearing. But hearing will be less effective than vision in co-ordinating and encouraging motor movements like crawling, reaching and exploring until about one year old. Consequently it is important to initiate the infant's use of other senses including taste and touch, to increase motivation and stimulate learning opportunities which the blind infant will not use spontaneously.

Part of this early learning about the world also involves the use of words to label objects and experiences. Reynell found that delays in verbal comprehension became apparent between blind and partially sighted children at the stage when 'jargon' words begin to give way to use of words as object labels. Blind children can learn to use words without knowing what they mean if they have not experienced the physical referents for the words, through other senses.

It is important to return, briefly, to the area of social adaptation because our understanding has grown in the last decade or so, of the importance of early parent—child interactions for later language and social development. The basic skills of social communication begin to develop long before the child's first words emerge. In their moving or babbling, young babies are often active in fairly repetitive rest—activity cycles. Mothers usually use the 'rests' or pauses to respond with a verbal commentary on the baby's activities. These exchanges are the building blocks for later communications skills, helping to introduce the baby to the turn-taking conventions of conversation and to the facial and bodily movement cues which give emphasis to the spoken message and indicate 'starts' and 'stops'. Much of these exchanges depend on visual features such as smiles, facial movements, like raised eyebrows or widening eyes, hand waves, nods, mouth movements during speech and on visual observation of eye-pointing to indicate objects being discussed or mimes and demonstrations of what to do. Eye contact is also used to indicate that speaking will start or stop. For the mother, visual following by her child indicates interest in the shared activity, and smiles given or received can be a powerful motivator to keep on working (see Schaffer 1977). Most of these features are lost where a severely visually handicapped child is involved. A blind child may 'still' (sit very quietly) when a new noise occurs, in order to learn its significance, but the mother may misinterpret this as disinterest or lack of awareness by her child.

Parental Support.   It will be obvious from these summary comments that the quality of the early interaction between parent and blind infant is critical to the child's development. But parents recently delivered of a multiply handicapped baby are not equipped automatically with the skills and understanding which their child will need. Most evidence shows that parents welcome early, truthful and constructive information about how to cope with the needs and demands of their handicapped infant. 'Doing the right thing' in this context is valuable for the child and is also likely to be therapeutic for the parents. Early support from skilled teachers of the blind or other specialised professionals such as social workers for the blind will be most desirable. Ideally the parents should be encouraged to develop their own special skills, particularly as access to professionals is often difficult to obtain. Apart from specialists employed by local authorities, help during the school years can be obtained from a number of peripatetic educational advisors for the blind, employed by the Royal National Institute for the Blind.

Delay due to Mental Handicap.   Delays which arise due to visual impairment could be due equally to mental handicap. The greatest risk is that mental handicap may be assumed incorrectly to be the cause, and that care givers will conclude that extra efforts to stimulate the child are pointless. It is vital that encouragement in the areas of motor/mobility skills, language/communication and social interaction is maintained in order to minimise the risk of developmental delay in the early years. Nevertheless it is known that about 70 per cent of children born with severe visual handicaps also suffer one or more additional handicaps, including mental retardation.

Where retardation is suspected, the appropriate strategy is to follow the same general curriculum as would be used with a visually handicapped child of normal intelligence, but to break down the skills to be learned into smaller chunks or steps. This should not be taken to mean that a retarded child should be pushed to reach the same ultimate levels of performance which we may come to expect of a normal child. Consider communication skills by way of example: these are vitally important in the development of a blind child; if retardation is also present it will be unrealistic to thrust the child into learning braille directly. Instead, communication based on for example some Makaton signs can be substituted in order to establish the idea of a system of signs carrying meanings. Whether braille skills are considered later should depend on progress made with the more basic communications system and the likely importance of braille skills for the child's future.

If the decision is made to teach braille to a retarded, blind child this can be approached by breaking the skill down into a series of component skills which can be learned individually and then re-combined into the major skill. Progress will be slower, but it will still be made. Profoundly retarded and/or physically handicapped children will require more time, attention to detail and ingenuity from the teacher. Teachers will also benefit from learning more specialised behavioural teaching techniques. It is generally true (if somewhat provocative) that if behavioural training is correctly designed and carried out, then any failure to learn is due to the error of the teacher who designed and applied the programme rather than of the pupil. Anything learnable can be taught by such techniques so long as the goals aimed for are within the pupil's range of ability, and the latter can only be determined by trying the former. Regular assessments and evaluations of the child's progress are also desirable to give teachers and parents an indication of improvements and of areas of greatest need.

Assessment Methods

Sensory handicap makes most formal psychometric (IQ) tests difficult to use properly. A common strategy used by psychologists is to use 'verbal' parts of standard tests and to ignore those parts which depend on the use of vision (Ellis 1978). This allows the visually handicapped child's functional level to be compared with that of visually intact children (as indicated by the test norms). The disadvantages are that the skills which are not assessed concern aspects of intelligence (usually performance IQ) which consequently cannot be measured; also, early developmental delays may have influenced the child's achievement on mental functions, such as language, which are assessed, and the results may underestimate the child's true capabilities.

Developmental assessments, usually in the 0-5 year age range, depend less on a single IQ result. Recently the Reynell–Zinkin Scale has been devised specifically for visually handicapped children. A related approach employs prescriptive assessment methods where a check-list of skills in an 'easy-to-hard' sequence, relating to various self-care and social activities, is filled in to determine a pupil's current level of performance in these areas. The items not passed indicate the skills to be taught next as part of a regular and systematic training approach. The Maxfield–Buchholz Scale is broadly of this form, being a 'blind' version of the Vineland Social Maturity Scale. Recently check-lists like the Peabody Mobility Scale (PMS) have been devised, which incorporate both assessment and teaching approaches. The PMS is designed specifically for retarded people and is described by

Harley and Hill in Ellis (1986). This book also includes Langley's excellent and detailed description of assessment techniques for visually and mentally handicapped people.

Prescriptive assessment methods are intended as a beginning to the teaching approach rather than as an end to a classification process. An adequate curriculum for mentally and visually handicapped people is difficult to summarise in a few sentences. The above discussion has focused on the needs of congenitally blind infants, but much of this material may need to be taken into account when working with older children. Many will be developmentally delayed by school age because of failures by parents to understand and meet their needs adequately or because of real limitations in learning ability. Many visually and mentally handicapped children may require extensive, individualised training in order to build up an understanding of space, communication and social interaction. Teachers should encourage language learning based on practical experiences through the remaining senses. Vibration cushions can be used operantly to reinforce a child for performing a new skill correctly. (The following are recommended for more detailed descriptions of teaching approaches: Mori and Olive 1978; Sykanda and Levitt 1982; Tretakoff 1977; Uslan 1979; Rogow 1982; and Sonksen 1982.)

Every teacher should learn how to use sighted-guide techniques correctly with visually handicapped pupils. The pupil holds the guide's elbow from behind with the nearest hand. The guide announces to the pupil what will happen next at each change, e.g. 'I'm moving forward now', or 'there's a step up, just here'. Walking in this way allows the pupil to walk safely just one step behind the guide, while conversation can be carried on naturally. The guide must take care to ensure that the pupil is not led into doorposts or other obstacles. It is important to announce your approach verbally, some way from a blind person, to avoid unexpected surprise arrivals. Keeping the furniture and fittings in the same place will help to make the learning of mobility skills more worthwhile. Ensure that for example wheelchairs are not parked in a regular mobility route until the blind pupil can learn how to feel for unexpected objects. Doors left open which stick out into a walkway are lethal for a moving, blind person. The visually handicapped person should be encouraged to walk with one arm held diagonally across the chest as a 'buffer' against unexpected objects.

Acquired Handicaps and Residual Vision

People who develop visual impairments after birth have a lesser problem to cope with in some ways, as they have gained a visual idea of the organisation of the world and possibly some concept of the objects to which words refer. They still require help in developing mobility and occupational skills, and initially they may become depressed by the loss of vision. As several visual impairments show a gradual onset and may not result in total blindness, it is important to maximise the use of residual vision. This can be achieved by better illumination, magnification and similar coping strategies. These considerations can be adapted to some mentally handicapped people with appropriate modifications.

Behaviour Disorders in Visually and Mentally Handicapped People

The mentally handicapped population is known to include a substantial proportion who engage in problem behaviour, including aggression, self-injury, stereotyped (repetitive) behaviour or social withdrawal. Blind, retarded people seem to be particularly at risk for stereotyped or self-injurious behaviours (Ellis 1985), both of which involve repetitive movements. While such problems are still not fully explainable, there are two popular types of explanation. Firstly, they appear to have some stimulation value for the person, usually helping to maintain an optimum level of arousal for the brain. The implication is that people who engage in stereotypy may be under-estimated, and there is some evidence that blind-retarded institutional residents are less frequently occupied than others (Ellis 1985). Secondly, it is probable that self-injury also has some communication value, by helping to manipulate the behaviour of staff or parents. If this proves to be so, there is some value in giving priority to teaching children better communication skills, and opportunities to use them to gain the attention of others more appropriately.

Eye-pressing is a common form of behaviour which is both stereotyped and possibly self-injurious. It seems to result from attempts to generate some stimulation of the visual reception areas in the brain as patients with no direct neurological link between eyes and brain do not press their eyes in this way (Jan, Freeman, McCormick, Scott, Robertson and Newman 1985). Finally, sleep disorders are also fairly well known among blind children, presumably because of a lack of visual evidence about the time of day.

This problem may be distressing for parents or night care staff, but can be overcome using appropriate training methods which encourage the child to learn a predictable bed-time pattern ending in sleep, or in going to sleep again if early waking occurs.

Specialised Resources

Visual and mental handicaps in the same person do not produce an additive influence, but one in which the negative effects of both handicaps multiply one another and increase the extent of disability suffered. Thus poor language development may arise from one of these handicaps and limit the mental skills available to make sense of living experiences in the absence of visual evidence. This lack of experience may limit further learning and, sometimes more importantly, encourage onlookers to assume a lower level of ability, which in turn affects their expectations of the child's ability to function effectively and therefore possibly the opportunities they provide for the child. As the sequence progresses, the child comes to behave at the functional level expected of him, regardless of his real potential.

It seems to follow from this supposed cycle of degradation that staff teaching these pupils should be doubly trained in handling the needs of both visual and mental handicap. The costs implied by such specialisation may be justified by grouping the children into one unit, but 'special' schools are becoming unfashionable at present on grounds of segregation. The problem of course, is that failure to respond to a multi-handicapped person's particular needs may also result in a form of segregation! Specialised staff skills seem to be the core of the solution, and contact with similar specialists may help to limit any feeling of isolation for a specialist teacher working in an 'integrated' school. We must be aware of sacrificing the needs of multiply impaired people in order to meet a social ideal.

One consequence of the reluctance to make specialised residential provision for post-school age visually and mentally handicapped adolescents is that they have often been consigned to the back wards of long-stay institutions where the segregation could be more real and unending. There is much emphasis now, however, on reducing dependency on institutional care and increasing the use of community-based alternatives for mentally handicapped people. It should be stressed that the proportion of retarded people with severe visual impairments is unlikely to decrease in the forseeable future, so investment in developing specialist staff skills will not be wasted. The wider deployment of such skills should serve to improve the independence of visually and mentally handicapped pupils and thus help them to meet the demands of a more community-oriented way of life. Seen from this perspective it is easy to justify the mandatory provision of specialist training for teachers in schools for children with severe learning difficulties. There is no good reason why retarded and visually impaired children should be less well provided for than are their contemporaries within a normal range of ability.

References

Bond, D.E. (1981) 'Hearing loss, language, cognition, personality and social development', in *Ways and Means no. 3. Hearing Impairment.* Globe Education.

British Ability Scales (1983) NFER-Nelson.

Bristol Adjustment Guides (1984) NFER-Nelson.

Conrad, R. (1979) *The Deaf Schoolchild: language and cognitive function.* Harper and Row.

Cunningham, C.C. and McArthur, K. (1982) 'Hearing loss and treatment in young Down's syndrome children'. *Child: Care, Health and Development, 7*, pp. 357-74.

Dale, D.M.C. (1984) *Individualised Integration.* Hodder and Stoughton.

DES (1972) *The Education of the Visually Handicapped.* HMSO.

Ellis, D. (1978) 'Methods of assessment for use with the visually and mentally handicapped; a selective review'. *Child: Care, Health and Development, 4*, pp. 397-410.

Ellis, D. (1982) 'Visually and mentally handicapped people in institutions. Part I: their numbers and needs'. *Mental Handicap, 10* (4), pp. 135-7.

Ellis, D. (ed.) (1986). *Sensory Impairments in Mentally Impaired People.* Croom Helm.

Jan, J.E., Freeman, R.D., McCormick, A.Q., Scott, E.P., Robertson, W.D. and Newman, D.E. (1985) 'Eye-pressing by visually impaired children'. *Developmental Medicine and Child Neurology, 25*, pp. 755-62.

Jan, J., Freeman, R. and Scott, E. (1977) *Visual Impairment in Children and Adolescents.* Grune and Stratton.

Kiernan, C., Reid, B. and Jones, L. (1982) *Signs and Symbols: use of non-vocal communication systems.* Heinemann Educational Books.

Kropka, B.I., Bamford, J. and Williams, C. (1983) 'From "Cabbages" to "Kings" in one month: or, with the deaf–blind, you never know till you try'. *Mental Handicap, 11*, pp. 10-13.

Kyle, J. and Woll, B. (eds.) (1983) *Language in Sign.* Croom Helm.

Lysons, C.K. (1984) *Hearing Impairment.* Woodhead–Faulkener.

Mindel, E.D. and Vernon M. (1971) *They Grow in Silence: the deaf child and his family.* National Association of the Deaf.

Mori, A. and Olive, J. (1978) 'The blind and visually handicapped mentally retarded; suggestions for intervention in infancy'. *Jnl of Visual Impairment and Blindness, 72*, pp. 273-9.

Progress Assessment Charts (1969) SEFA Publications.

Reed, M. (1973) 'Deaf and partially hearing children', in P. Mittler (ed.). *The Psychological Assessment of Mental and Physical Handicaps.* Tavistock.

Reynell, J. (1978) 'Developmental patterns of visually handicapped children'. *Child: Care, Health and Development, 4,* pp. 291-303.

Reynell, J. (1979) *Developmental Scales for Young Visually Handicapped Children.* NFER.

Rogow, S.M. (1982) 'Rhythms and rhymes; developing communication in very young blind and multihandicapped children'. *Child: Care, Health and Development, 8,* pp. 249-60.

Schaeffer, B. (1980) 'Spontaneous language through signed speech', in R.L. Schiefelbusch (ed.). *Non-speech Language and Communication.* University Park Press.

Schaffer, H.R. (ed.). (1977) *Studies in Mother—Infant Interaction.* Academic Press.

Sonksen, P.M. (1982) 'Care of the visually handicapped baby'. *Maternal and Child Health.* July, pp. 282-7.

Spence, S. (1980) *Social Skills Training with Children and Adolescents.* NFER-Nelson.

Sykanda, A.M. and Levitt, S. (1982) 'The physiotherapist in the developmental management of the visually impaired child'. *Child: Care, Health and Development, 8,* pp. 261-70.

Tretakoff, M.I. (1977) 'The evolution of programs for blind mentally retarded children in residential facilities'. *Jnl of Visual Impairment and Blindness, 71,* pp. 29-33.

Uslan, M. (1979) 'Orientation and mobility for severely and profoundly retarded blind persons'. *Jnl of Visual Impairment and Blindness, 73,* pp. 54-8.

Vineland Adaptive Behaviour Scales (1984) American Guidance Service.

Warburg, M., Frederiksen, P. and Rattlefft, J. (1979) 'Blindness among 7700 mentally retarded children', in V. Smith and J. Keen (eds.). *Visual Handicap in Children. Clinics in Developmental Medicine, 73,* pp. 56-69. Spastics International Medical Publishers and Heinemann Medical.

Wechsler, D. (1944) *The Measurement of Adult Intelligence.* Williams and Wilkins.

Wechsler, D. (1949) *Intelligence Scale for Children.* Psychological Corporation.

Williams, C. (1982) 'Deaf not daft'. *Special Education: Forward Trends, 9,* pp. 26-8.

Woll, B., Kyle, J. and Deuchar, M. (1981) *Perspectives on British Sign Language and Deafness.* Croom Helm.

Woodruff, M.E. (1977) 'Prevalence of visual and ocular anomalies in 168 non-institutionalized mentally retarded children'. *Can. Jnl of Public Health, 68,* pp. 225-32.

PART THREE: THE PEOPLE INVOLVED

Part 3 sets out to discuss the roles of some of the many people who may be involved in the education of children with severe learning difficulties and, in so doing, outlines many of the factors that determine their roles. In the first part of Chapter 10, Philippa Russell sets the background to parental involvement by looking at the difficulties many parents face in the day-to-day coping of life with a handicapped child. She is providing a context far wider than the school in discussing parental reaction to professionals and services and shows the need to understand the permeations of parental response in order to gain partnership. The second section draws together research findings on parental involvement. Helen McConachie outlines the different kinds of involvement, from workshops to home-teaching to involvement in the school curriculum. She discusses the turnabout from seeing parents as part of the cause to recognising them as part of the solution and questions the assumption that equal partnership implies equal roles.

In Chapter 11, Mike Johnson stresses the accountability of the school, and the fine balance between over-detachment and over-protective care. He points to the need for critique, a realistic appraisal by each individual of what other individuals are able to contribute and the reliance on co-operation for effective deployment of staff.

Chapter 12 has an input from a variety of professionals whom the child with severe learning difficulties may well encounter, both during the school years and beyond. Certain key aspects arise in this chapter — the foremost consideration being the need to be flexible and responsive to changes in demand. In the majority of areas demand far outstrips supply so that many professionals see their role as primarily a resource, concerning themselves with assessment, advice, support, designing programmes, monitoring progress, adapting materials and passing on specialised research material. Without a doubt the team approach, whether multidisciplinary, transdisciplinary, or interdisciplinary, relies heavily on the skills of inter-professional dialogue, for only through this can each individual's input be seen within the context of the development of the whole child.

10 PARENTS AS PARTNERS

The development of close working relationships between teachers and parents of children with severe learning difficulties has been one of the most striking developments in special education in the 1970's and 80's. However, there are no prescriptive answers as to how to achieve those relationships most successfully. A true partnership requires respect for the equal value of the contribution of each partner to the child's total education. In the following two chapters, words such as 'dialogue' and 'balance' are used in expressing the nature of the process of developing a co-operative relationship, a process which requires creativity and understanding from both teachers and families.

Philippa Russell describes, from the family's point of view, the complexity and variety of reactions to handicap, changing feelings over time, family needs, family interaction and so forth. She also refers to the ordinary difficulties of parenting in elucidating the background of which teachers need to be aware in establishing communication with parents.

Helen McConachie then describes a variety of practical ways in which parents and teachers can work together as partners in the education of children with severe learning difficulties. For teachers, parents are an irreplaceable resource in moving towards the educational aims of the school. Joint action may extend to assessment, curriculum design, programming, teaching and monitoring of children's progress. However, in 'bridging the gap', teachers need also to understand individual families' needs and their aims for their children and for themselves. The key to partnership lies in developing flexible and individually appropriate strategies and goals for co-operation.

The Changing Scene

Philippa Russell

Parental Attitudes to Handicap and Special Educational Needs
There can be few more distressing situations for a family than the

239

discovery that their child has special educational needs. Traditionally, parents of handicapped children were themselves regarded as emotionally aberrant. As Hewett (1970) noted, 'The general tendency to characterise parents of handicapped children as guilt-ridden, anxiety laden, over-protective and rejecting beings is unfortunate.' She went on to comment that 'while it is true that such cases exist, the majority of coping parents are unduly stigmatised by this generalisation. Their common characteristics appear much more to be the need for money, services and information, and that counselling without these latter is of little value.' Parents, therefore, wish to know that they are normal people reacting to excessive stress rather than abnormal people unable to cope.

In learning to cope with any disability (of whatever severity), parents need to develop a positive relationship with the professionals who can help their child. If educational decision-making, clinical problems, resources, options and general prognosis are shared, parents can learn a great deal. They may also educate the professionals. But above all, parent participation will ensure that the parents themselves become stronger. They can cope with an apparently insoluble problem because they have learned that there are goals which can be achieved and that their handicapped child is a member of the family as well as a disability. There are problems in parent participation. As Morris (1976) noted, 'The exact pattern of relationship between support services and therapeutic and educational facilities and the mechanisms by which a proper mix is achieved between family burden and service provision needs yet to be developed'. The balance of services at the right time and the parental involvement may pose difficulties. But there are rich rewards if 'shared care' becomes a reality. As the Warnock Report also commented:

Although we tend to dwell upon the dependence of many parents on professional support, we are well aware that professional help cannot be wholly effective – if at all – unless it builds upon the parents' capacity to be involved. Thus we see the relationship as a dialogue between parents and helpers working in partnership ... Professionals have their own distinctive knowledge and skills to contribute to parents' understanding of how best to help their handicapped child, but these form a part, not the whole that is needed. Parents can be effective partners only if professionals take notice of what they say and of how they express their needs and treat their contribution as intrinsically important. (para 9.6 p. 151).

Like all dialogues, partnership between professionals and parents of handicapped children requires enthusiasm, commitment – and a willingness to recognise the varied factors in family life which may affect directly a parent's ability to be a 'partner' at a particular time. Most parents of handicapped children experience some negative feelings, a sense of failure and a feeling of pressure at some point in their child's life. Recognising and overcoming these usually transient feelings must be a part of partnership – which must also recognise other parts of a family's life: their culture; past and present parenting skills and the quality of the relationship which a caring professional can offer.

Parents and Professionals – Barriers to Acceptance of Services

Attitudes to the Birth of a Handicapped Child.   There are certain motives and needs common to all births. Firstly, it is not accidental that pregnant women are said to be 'expectant'. They are expectant of a healthy, normal child who will fulfil at least some of their hopes for future family life. In cases where the child is handicapped, there may be a great gulf between the image and the reality. Many parents cannot handle the initial stress and go through a period of shock and irrational or aggressive behaviour. R.D. Laing is reported to have said that the 'official date of public events could be out of phase with the structure of experience'. Unfortunately, the date of the 'public event' for the family — the unequivocal medical diagnosis — may not be accepted until weeks or months later. By then the family may not even have regular contact with caring professionals. They may also conceal distress and ambivalence beneath a superficial shell of competence.

Professional understanding of the impact of the birth of a handicapped child on family dynamics is vital if subsequent educational treatment is to be effective. The birth or diagnosis of a handicapped child appears in some cases to precipitate a breakdown in the normal, mutual support systems between parents. In extreme cases, Brian Tew (1976) (quoted in Stephen Kew 1976) suggested in his survey for the Welsh National School of Medicine that the divorce rate among parents of severely handicapped spina bifida children was 10 times greater than the national average if the child lived and three times greater if the child died. Bradshaw and Lawton (1985), looking at 75,000 severely disabled children known to the Family Fund found, conversely, that 10.3 per cent of spina bifida children in their survey were living in single parent families (of whatever origin) as compared with 11.3 per cent of the UK child population. However, they note that the general proportion of single parents was higher in the overall Family Fund sample (13.9 per cent) than in the UK population. Bradshaw and Lawton point out the difficulties of interpreting such data which could mean that: more marriages broke up, *or* that more severely disabled children were born to single parents, *or* that single parents with a disabled child were less likely to marry or remarry because of their difficulties. In view of the general increase in the divorce rate in the United Kingdom and in the number of step-families, it would be interesting to speculate whether the existence of a disabled child affected subsequent marriage for the caring parent. The Family Fund research also indicated that more single parent families existed within certain disabilities (which included mental handicap; rubella; epilepsy and severe burns). While it is not possible to pinpoint precise cause and effect between these conditions and family stability, all pose problems which may excite feelings of guilt or stigma, and the figures at least argue for further investigation and more family support.

If the data available on family break-up is unclear, a number of studies indicate that a handicapped child may cause structural changes in family relationships which, in turn, may lead to depression and feelings of isolation. Gath's work on families with Down's syndrome children (Gath 1978) did not find that a milder degree of handicap precipitated divorce or separation in the families in her study. But 33 per cent of the mothers suffered from clinical depression in the first 18 months, and sexual and emotional problems were common among mothers and fathers.

Interestingly, she found that young fathers had particular difficulties. One father's observation that he had always believed that fathering a normal child was something any man could do is worth considering. Fathers, feeling subtly excluded from the care of a handicapped child, may lack a network of friends or relatives to confide in. Cunningham (1984) found that fathers appeared to have different aspirations for a first son and take longer to accept the handicap than the mother. Similar observations have been made about difficulties in acceptance by Leiderman (1974) and others with regard to increase in marital difficulties after the birth of a baby who had been nursed in a special care unit – even if the child had no significant difficulties in later life. Clearly – as the Honeylands Therapy Programmes (1979) also found – family relationships are at risk when a potentially handicapped child is born. This risk may be exacerbated when the child is a first child – and if fathers' needs are neglected.

Again, while it has been established (Cunningham 1984) that most families go through predictable stages in adapting to handicap, proceeding through shock, denial and hostility to adaptation and orientation, Gath (1978) and others have found that families are more likely to be unhappy a year after birth. Cunningham (1984) had also noticed that intensive professional input in the early months tended to level off at about the first birthday, when parents might indeed feel depressed at recognising the permanence of the handicapping condition. Clearly family relationships must be taken into account in planning the future for a handicapped child. Brazleton (1976) suggested that the success of intervention programmes should be measured, not only by the child's development, but by 'increased family comfort, decrease in the divorce rate, lower incidence in behaviour problems in siblings ... perhaps by pretty soft signs but they may be a lot more important as measures of effectiveness of intervention than is a rise in IQ or increased motor capacity on the part of the child'. Brazleton described working with the family as the 'softwork of paediatrics' and queried how many paediatricians (or indeed professionals in other disciplines) were ready and willing to do this. Yet many assessment centres, district handicap teams and family support centres are already embodying the concept of family support as an integral part of treating the child.

Special Parent, Special Child? Successful parenting of a handicapped child will not only depend on recognition of the child's special needs because of the handicap, but on the parents' ability to be competent, caring and confident parents to any child. Research by Wolkind and others at the London Hospital (1981) has shown clearly that many mothers suffer from depression when caring for young children. Whether the cause of this depression is isolation because of break-down in the nuclear family; the problems of inner-city living (where current research studies have focused); greater expectations of parenthood or the general cumulation of tasks involved in being a parent to a young child, it clearly impairs the mother/child relationship. Working with families of handicapped children must, therefore, take into account the needs of all families of young children and endeavour to ensure that both parents are able to enjoy their roles and feel effective – whatever the particular needs or problems of their child.

Research by Robin and Josse at Clanart in France (Robin and Josse 1984) makes the hypothesis that all mothers develop a process of anticipation in interacting with their babies. 'Each mother has a plan for her child. It is a changeable plan, which is at the same time an interpretation of his behaviour and a projection into the future.' Robin and Josse argue that the child, as he matures, develops new characteristics which, in turn, restructure his image in the eyes of his mother. The mother learns from this restructuring how to help the child on to the next stage of development. The concept of 'anticipation' is particularly relevant when a family has a 'special child'. Cunningham (1984) noticed that parents began to feel at ease with the diagnosis of a handicapped child at different stages. But most accomplished this stage within the period weeks 8-16. This acceptance in turn often coincided with the baby showing such normal infant behaviours as making eye contact, smiling, making developmental progress. The child became an individual to the parents. During these early months many families began to claim that their child was no different to other children in the family. But, from the ninth month onwards, when developmental gains became slower, doubts and concerns began to re-emerge. The children in effect, were not meeting the goals on the 'life plan' envisaged by their parents.

The 'life plan' concept of parents' perceptions of their child is important to recognise, since disappointments in the early life of a child with special needs may cloud and distort expectations of that child's future development. Trout (1983) comments on a 'cyclical pattern that exacerbates both the attachment conflict and the handicap itself'. He referred to the 'false messages' given by the baby with a cleft palate whose feeds are protracted and difficult for the mother; the child with a sensory handicap who fails to respond; even the hypersensitive premature baby whose fragility seems increased by frequent crying and jerky movements. Research suggests that hospitalisation can produce damaging effects on mother/child relationships even when the child's development and social attachments are developing normally. Many sick and handicapped children have frequent periods of hospitalisation. They are more likely to have had early experiences of neonatal and special care baby facilities. Leiderman (1974) and others have emphasised the problems subsequently experienced by parents in terms of bonding and positive expectations. Supporting parents of children who have had, or may expect to have, special needs must be an integral part of helping the child and encouraging realistic expectations for the future.

Caring for the Carers. The concept of 'parents as partners' cannot be implemented effectively without giving due consideration to parents as 'carers'. All children are demanding, but as Oakley (1974) noted, 'Motherhood has a single long-term goal, which can be described as the mother's own eventual unemployment. A 'successful' mother brings up her children to do without her.' Unfortunately the pathway to independence may not be so clear where a child has special needs. Severe disability may delay seriously developmental milestones and provide fewer tangible rewards for hard work and effort. Some parents may become trapped in routine care needs. A study by Glendenning (1983) found that 50.1 per cent of severely disabled children over five (361 children) could not be left alone for even ten minutes in a day. In these circumstances practical support and help must precede parental involvement in educational goals.

Wilkin's study of families with mentally handicapped children found that there was no evidence that relatives, friends and neighbours contributed significantly to the day-to-day problems of caring for a disabled child (Wilkin 1979). Carey (1982) similarly described the support received by another sample of families with mentally handicapped children as 'negligible, in terms of support from the informal social network'. Both studies, together with Baldwin (1985) and Glendenning (1983) emphasise the burden of care laid upon mothers. Indeed Wilson (1982) considered that 'family care' should be seen as a euphemism for 'care by mothers'. No study has suggested that fathers would be unwilling to care more – and formal evidence suggests that patterns of unemployment are involving more men generally in child care, nursery school and playgroup settings. However, as McConachie (1982) noted, more attention needs to be given to how and when fathers can and should be involved and to developing a positive role. Parental participation in any educational programme must depend not only upon the parents' willingness to share in educational activities, but also upon other demands made on the family's time and energies. The practical and physical isolation of many families with a disabled child (highlighted in recent studies from the Equal Opportunities Commission 1983) indicates the need to consider care as a factor in education and, in particular, to find ways of involving both parents in all the child's activities.

Voluntary organisations, popularly regarded as major sources of practical help, seem to be valued more for the emotional, personal and social help offered, as well as for their information resource, than for direct aid. Bradshaw (1980), looking at membership of voluntary organisations by Family Fund users, found no more than 50 per cent in membership of appropriate organisations. Parents of spina bifida children however, were high joiners (71 per cent) and informal evidence suggests that the majority of parents of mentally handicapped children will join MENCAP at some point in their child's life. The surprisingly low take-up of help from the voluntary sector may reflect the fact that the majority of children with special needs do not fit neatly into the single disability category, and parents may not know which organisation to join. There are still few multi-handicap groups (such as Contact a Family) which can cater for a wide range of special needs on a local basis. Additionally, some parents may prefer to drop in and out of voluntary organisations according to their particular needs. In rural areas distance and transport may pose major problems.

Both the Wolfenden (1978) and Warnock (DES 1978) reports stressed the potential of the voluntary sector in meeting the needs of disabled people and their families. Warnock indeed attached 'very great importance to the work of parents' groups in providing support and in making shared arrangements for their children's care and education'. The 1981 Education Act for the first time lays duties on DHAs to notify parents of any voluntary organisation which might be able to help them, and it seems probable that parents' support groups in the field of special educational needs will play an important future role – as have the Parent Coalitions of the USA. Perhaps the responsibility for a healthy and supportive voluntary sector must to some extent be assumed by professionals. Referral from schools, child health services or social services will encourage membership. Similarly recognition of the supportive and educative role of the voluntary sector will produce more productive partnership in the future. Many voluntary agencies see one of their primary roles as being that of 'honest broker'. As they move to the two (though not necessarily linked) roles of 'named person' and 'advocate', partnership becomes a necessary objective for both sides.

A Sense of Failure.   Guilt and rejection are also common reactions which may impair parent/professional relationships. Guilt is perhaps one of the reactions most commonly ascribed to parents of handicapped children. It may be linked to shock and to the search for a diagnosis. More often, however, guilt results from the parents' failures (in their eyes) to help their child develop. Precisely because many children with even relatively minor disabilities need to be taught skills elaborately which other children acquire spontaneously, parents are bound to feel inadequate. Without proper help and support in acquiring the necessary skills, and in accepting slow progress and potentially low achievements, it is easy for parents to feel dissatisfied not only with themselves but with the parenting role. Such parents may appear to reject the child, demanding residential care. In reality the demand is for assistance in recognising their role and, as Key, Hooper and Ballard (1979) noted, 'There is a great need for confirmation of the parents' ability to cope with the situation ... they need sympathetic support and reassurance to build this self-confidence'.

It is perhaps worth saying that very few parents reject the 'special needs' child simply because he is handicapped or seen as failing. Rejection is rather a strong reaction to their inability to cope. Feelings of parental failure are self-critical reactions often expressed in parents' groups. This feeling of failure to produce a normal child or of not being able to handle the child later in life may also be linked to some 'scapegoating' of other problems onto the child. A recent American study of parents of handicapped children entering family therapy (Tymchuck 1979) found that a high number of mothers equated their failure to produce and rear a 'normal child' with other personal failures such as overweight, difficulties in school, poor self-image or marital problems.

Such parents may be demanding of professional time. They will almost certainly benefit from counselling and parents' groups. But the demonstration of skills by which they can control and help their child will also produce improvements in other areas. This, however, also imposes problems on professionals. The Honeylands Home Therapy Scheme found that some parents could not work with their child until they themselves had been helped. In such circumstances, successful demonstration by home therapists or teachers might actually reinforce parental feelings of incompetence. Tymchuck's study (1979) found that parents' groups could be invaluable at this juncture in restoring the parent's damaged self-image. Parents could learn to see themselves as people with difficulties, not failures. Most importantly, groups could demonstrate that they liked parents and child and found them worthwhile. As the Southend Scheme for parents of mentally handicapped children (Pugh and Russell 1977) also found, groups could not only legitimise hostile or aggressive feelings which parents themselves might have feared, they could also be powerful agents for acceptance of local professional services.

Denial of Special Needs.   Denial of disability is probably more common in children with mild or moderate handicaps, where parents' inappropriate expectations may not become apparent until the child enters school. But parents of children who have acquired disabilities (through road accidents, birth injuries or other causes of brain damage) may actively deny the existence of permanent disability in the absence of any congenital defect. By pursuing a vigorous (albeit despairing) 'shopping expedition' in search of new treatment or therapy programme, parents may be reinforced in their beliefs that cure is round the corner. If, in addition, 'new' treatments provide sympathetic attention to parents, they are likely to be pursued avidly. The possibility of regeneration of brain cells, for example, following brain damage, must be attractive to parents who are still convinced that rehabilitation will be possible. Such pursuit of 'fringe' treatment may also be part of the denial process, since acceptance of existing services may be felt as 'labelling' the child as handicapped. Similar feelings are sometimes expressed by parents who are reluctant to claim DHSS allowances or to join voluntary organisations. They are denying reality and will need careful help. Writing of services at Honeylands, Rubissow, Jones and Brimblecomb (1979) noted that 'beginning work when developmental problems are not acknowledged by the parents but have been noted by the doctor means that appropriate activities suggested by a therapist from her own knowledge might be meaningless to the parents'. Similar problems arise in a teaching situation when parents have not acknowledged that their child has a significant problem. The prevalence of denial of even major degrees of handicap – in particular mental retarda-

tion, which may carry considerable stigma – is born out by
Wolfensberger and Kurtz (1974), who found that only 42 per cent
of a sample of parents of mentally handicapped children actually
admitted to the mental handicap, referring to 'language delay' and
more acceptable problems. If parental acceptance of reality is
delayed until after treatment has begun, dissatisfaction and poor
professional relationships are inevitable.

'Shopping' for New Treatment Programmes.   Professionals may
find themselves in a difficult and ambiguous position if a family
opts for controversial treatment programmes for their child. Initial
hostility or criticism are likely to ensure that contact with that
family is broken. However, the professional has a duty to the child
– and many families desperately need the advice they reject.
Unfortunately, many of the more controversial approaches to
handicap or learning difficulties are expensive in time, labour and
finance. If money is raised by local Rotary clubs, pubs or social
clubs to provide such treatment, the family may, for the first time,
feel important. Not only are they the object of local solidarity and
good will, but their 'handicapped' child appears an asset and not a
deficit. The mother, in particular, may feel excited about local
press interest and perhaps by active participation from volunteers.
Since many parents of handicapped children greatly fear rejection
of their child by friends and neighbours, such optimistic treatment
may well initially produce new self-confidence and acceptance for
the child. As three parents (Key, Hooper and Ballard 1979) noted,
'In the early days parents may have hopes and expectations which
the professionals consider unrealistic. For example, many parents
express the wish for a cure or the longing to wake up one morning
to find their experiences were a bad nightmare'.

Unfortunately, some treatment programmes which promise cure
(and hence can demand tremendous involvement from friends and
neighbours as well as parents) do not necessarily justify their
claims. Local interest and volunteer participation in labour-
intensive therapy programmes are dependent upon improvement
being maintained. Local schools which supply large numbers of
volunteers for a few months (perhaps as part of a time-limited
community service programme) cannot guarantee such support in
the holidays. Volunteers, equally, may become bored if there is no
emotional feedback for them. Long-term programmes of rigid
patterning or exercises are unlikely to offer the interaction and

satisfaction they need. Equally parents may become embarrassed because neighbours and friends, having given time and money, look for results for their investment.

In such a situation, the family is trapped. If they do not proceed with a programme – which may totally disrupt normal family life for negligible rewards – they have, in effect, wasted money and time. On the other hand, proceeding with a programme which is non-productive and unrewarding is also stressful. In the end the family itself may break under the stress, the child may be admitted to residential care. A background cause of such a spiral of crisis is undoubtedly the time which some parents take to accept a child has a handicap and that they themselves need help. If acknowledgement of the reality comes slowly, parents may actually have slipped out of routine contact with caring professionals. Unless assistance and support is offered persistently, such parents may present an efficient front while concealing many difficulties. Parents may feel a real dilemma in accepting help and, as noted in the Honeylands Progress Report (1979), 'we have to confront the truth that most professionals in the field of child care and education are not comfortable about permitting parents to define their needs and use a service "on demand"'.

Family Problems.   While some families will resort to 'fright and flight' and refuse to acknowledge initially that their child has a problem, others may become over-anxious, over-dependent and endeavour to implement rigidly any advice given in order to help their child. An immediate danger is that parents may misunderstand principles for 'recipes' for successful intervention. One of the early dangers of the Portage model was that its 'little blue box' led to it being seen as a universal cookbook for improving family performance and development in a handicapped or disadvantaged child. In recent years the application of behaviour modification principles to childhood disorders has stimulated wide interest in training parents to share in effective modification of their child's behaviour problems and to maximise development. The application of behaviour modification to parent training continues to grow – although there is increasing concern about the lack of controls and evaluation in some instances. As early as 1974 O'Dell wrote, in a critique of early intervention that, 'like many applied areas of behaviour modification, parent training is quickly expanded by the vacuum of need' (O'Dell 1974).

The principles of behaviour modification may imply dangers to some parents without adequate professional support and guidance. Desperation may lead parents to exaggerate and increase treatment programmes, or to set unrealistic goals. Disappointment will inevitably follow. Anxious parents may not understand the need to ration one-to-one work with a child to short time spans and may use private tutors – or indeed purchase additional teaching material from the wide range of books and other aids now available in high street bookshops. In an unpublished paper about parents of severely handicapped children (Ricks 1982), Ricks noted that some of the most caring and competent parents easily became over-dependent on professional advice. These parents lost any sense of self-judgement in dealing with their child and would turn to the hospital for advice on trivial issues like treatment for the common cold or even the number of hours television viewing appropriate to their own family. Thus significant parental concern and willingness to share in a treatment programme became distorted into a maladaptive response to the child's difficulties and over-dependence on outside judgements.

Unfortunately, maladaptive responses, where the parent is over-coping and working hard to help the child, may provoke hostile or critical reactions in professionals. Indeed, parents may feel despair at what they perceive as professional rejection of their efforts. In this situation, counselling, advice and ongoing support are critical in order to help parents feel competent – and to demonstrate that professionals themselves are vulnerable. Mutual respect must form the basis of any treatment programme.

Some parents may also 'over-cope' because the child's learning problems are related to some other chronic and possibly life-threatening condition which colours home life and limits expectations. Children with cystic fibrosis may present little problem in the classroom, if their condition is well managed. But parents who are faced with the unpopular postural drainage each day, who must fear every winter cough and cold and who will often see other children die from the condition may be reluctant to take part in any programme which places additional stress on them and their child. Many parents are reluctant to acknowledge that their child has a 'hidden handicap' such as diabetes, and it is not uncommon for a child's asthma or diabetes to be revealed suddenly and dramatically on a school outing or games field before the school health services have been able to detect the condition. Some conditions, such as epilepsy, carry considerable stigma although the child in the ordinary school is likely to be well controlled and – superficially – little affected by the condition. Many parents endeavour to conceal such conditions (occasionally to the extent of denying them – or deliberately misunderstanding questions – on forms for school medical records). Their very real anxieties are suffered alone because of a belief that the child will be less valued if his difficulty is identified. Yet certain highly effective treatments (such as anti-convulsant drugs) may cause special educational needs if the child is poorly maintained on the dosage prescribed. Teachers need to encourage parents to be honest about any problem relating to a child (since parents may be quite unaware of its direct relevance to education) and also to share information. Inappropriate medication for epilepsy is more likely to become apparent in the classroom than in the home. Similarly, the asthmatic child may have more 'trigger' attacks at school because of the variety in the school environment than he does at home. In such circumstances the school health service may be a good bridge between classroom and home – but will itself be limited if relevant information is withheld and not fed back.

Accepting the wide and individual responses of parents to the knowledge that they have a child with a handicap or other special educational needs is particularly important when a child enters the education system. Traditionally schools have not formed a major part of the welfare net. Education has been perceived as being primarily for the child rather than a participative interaction with the whole family. But helping children with special educational needs, within the wider terms of the 1981 Act, must require a recognition of the full implications of partnership with parents. Such partnership does not require parents to be treated as professionals. Their responsibilities and rights are of equivalent status, but they are special because of the special and continuous relationship of parent and child.

Parents may have wider social, emotional and family needs into which partnership must be fitted. The balance of needs and expectations – by parents and professionals – may be finely drawn. But effective partnership within the education system will depend on honesty, respect and realistic expectations which recognise both the potential and limitations of parental involvement. Many parents need time and counselling in order to become agents rather than clients. Partnership is thus a continuous process which can adapt – and be adapted – for the mutual benefit of parents, children and professionals.

Parents' Contribution to the Education of their Child

Helen McConachie

The importance of parents' collaboration in their children's education has been recognised now for many years, from the Plowden Report (1966) 'Children and their Primary Schools' to the Warnock Report (1978) 'Special Educational Needs'. Many books and papers have been published summarising current developments in the partnership of professionals with parents of handicapped children (e.g. Paul 1981; Pugh 1981; Mittler and Mittler 1982; Mittler and McConachie 1983; Russell 1983). The aim of the present chapter is to outline briefly some examples of collaboration with parents of children with learning difficulties, and to review factors which need consideration in their further implementation. The chapter will conclude with the presentation of a rationale for involvement of parents in their children's education. The intention of the chapter is to provide a basis for discussion by school staff of their developing policy as regards collaboration with parents.

Pre-school

In the past decade, the major focus of activity in working with parents has been in the education of young handicapped children, even before they enter school. Home-visiting programmes have become an established part of the educational scene, and are particularly appropriate for rural communities (e.g. Brynelsen 1983). However, they are by no means nationally available. Generally, the service involves a home-teacher visiting an individual family at regular intervals, assessing the child periodically and deciding with the parent on developmentally appropriate activities for the parent to carry out with the child. In the Portage system (which originated in Wisconsin, USA, but which has been adopted internationally) the home-teacher has a resource of activity cards linked to a developmental checklist. The teacher uses the cards to devise up to three or four instruction and recording sheets for the parent to follow and fill in during the week before the next visit (Shearer and Shearer 1976). As the aim is for each activity target to be achieved by the child within the week, the home-teacher needs to rewrite some targets into small steps as well as using checklist items. Home-visiting programmes usually operate a close back-up system, with supervision meetings for all home-teachers every week or so. The initial training is short and health visitors, social workers, psychologists, nursery teachers, other parents, etc. have all become successful home-teachers (e.g. Rayner 1978).

Some home-visiting programmes visit less frequently (e.g. Sandow and Clarke, 1978; Cunningham 1983) and suggest that frequent prolonged visiting may set up a dependency of the parents on the home-teacher which is ultimately undermining of the parents' confidence (Berry and Wood 1981). Achievement of a good balance, so that appropriate support is given where it is needed, and so that parents' own ideas on child-rearing are not overruled, relies on the development of a sensitive relationship between home-teacher and parent. Thus, the home-teacher needs to have skills in listening and counselling as well as in giving developmental advice. Otherwise, for example, in prescribing new and time-consuming activities, the home-teacher may overburden an already hard-pressed parent, or seem to imply that parents can never 'do enough'. On the other hand, it is certainly reported by many parents that they gain great satisfaction and relief through being able to do 'something to help the baby' (Cunningham 1983). Research results have suggested an increased rate of development of children over baseline rate (e.g. Barna, Bidder, Gray, Clements and Gardner 1980; Glossop and Castillo 1982) or in comparison with a control group (e.g. Sandow, Clarke, Cox and Stewart 1981; Cunningham 1982).

One variation in use of the Portage materials has been to group parents together, for example, with the nursery teacher of the local special school, in order to create a group for mutual support, as well as to give parents ideas on structured activities for the children (e.g. Cook 1982). Self-help groups of parents of handicapped children of all ages have been a vital source of strength for many families. Some were started initially by professionals; others employ professionals to run activities which they have planned jointly, for example, the Two-to-One weeks of intensive teaching organised by the Kith and Kids group (Collins and Collins 1976; Pugh 1981). Toy libraries have often evidenced the same sharing between parents and professionals on an equal footing of focused activity with children (Riddick, 1982).

One effect of these and other programmes may be that parents come to have higher expectations and skills for collaboration with school staff than may have been the case in the past. Cunningham has noted the reaction of several professionals to meeting 'experienced' parents of young children: 'They have obviously been well trained at coping with us' (Cunningham 1983: p. 98). It is often the case that one aim of pre-school programmes in particular is to promote gradually parents' knowledge of the network of services available, and their skills in communicating successfully with key individuals in those services (e.g. Beveridge, Flanagan, McConachie and Sebba 1982). There is also, however, an important role for a 'named person' in reducing this burden, by liaising with services on behalf of parents.

Partnership in the School Years

The implementation of the 1981 Education Act (in 1983) has meant that handicapped children are now the responsibility of the Education service from the age of two years or even younger. Thus, children with severe learning difficulties and their parents are coming into contact with school staff at a time when the nature of the child's handicap may still be unclear, and parents are still trying to come to terms with the handicap. The negotiation of a collaborative relationship is therefore by no means simple and demands again the achievement of balance so that parents, for example, recognise their own needs and do not push their child and themselves too hard in educational activities.

During the child's school years, many kinds of collaboration between parents and teachers may be envisaged, from 'ordinary' activities such as sports days and fund-raising, to 'special' measures such as home–school diaries and case conferences (see Smith 1983). The Warnock Committee recommended that parents be 'seen as equal partners in the educational process' (Warnock Committee 1978: p. 150): at its ultimate, this may be taken to mean giving parents the opportunity of full involvement in the processes of curriculum design, assessment, programme planning, teaching and recording of children's progress. The 1981 Education Act enshrined the right of all parents to be involved in assessment during their child's school career, and in a yearly review of programme planning and evaluation.

However, this is only one interpretation of the Warnock Committee's recommendation, and the word 'opportunity' above should be stressed. Firstly, parents of handicapped children have often been viewed as part of the problem, or not considered at all; the sudden shift to seeing them as part of the solution may take some parents by surprise (Turnbull and Turnbull 1982). Parents do not all have the same time, capability, energy or interest in being educationalists. Some may see their primary role as providing 'the best possible environment in a socially intact family, in which the handicapped child can best use his or her new abilities' (McConachie 1983: p. 213). Many want to be able to rely on teachers' expertise and to take a break from full-time, all-round responsibility for the child, perhaps finding time to live their own lives.

Secondly, an 'equal partnership' does not have to imply that parents have to become educationalists. A partnership can be equal even when the contributions made by the two sides are very different in nature. Teachers need to draw on parents' extensive knowledge of the child, particularly in the early years, and particularly if the child behaves rather differently at home from how he or she behaves in school (cf. findings regarding the richness of language interactions of non-handicapped young children at home in comparison with school: Tizard, Hughes, Carmichael and Pinkerton 1983a; 1983b). Parents create a variety of emotional and social experiences for their children, which may allow planned generalisation and use of skills learned at school, even if curriculum design, assessment and teaching remain largely the province of the child's teachers. Collaboration can thus be feasible without diluting either partner's unique contribution.

Some surveys of parental involvement in ordinary schools have developed a taxonomy of levels of involvement (e.g. Smith 1980), from general support of school activities, to helping in the classroom, to becoming a parent governor. Offering parents a clear range of possibilities may be one way of improving home–school communication. Another is simply asking the parents about their preferences for collaboration. A recent survey of Manchester special schools found that teachers seemed more confident in telling parents about arrangements or about their children's activities, than in asking parents about relevant family matters or for suggestions for the child's programme (Burman, Farrell, Feiler, Heffernan, Mittler and Reason 1982). The survey stimulated several schools to canvass parents' opinions, either through questionnaires or through interviews with all parents at home (e.g. Boucher 1981). Where meetings are arranged for staff and parents, it has been found important, in facilitating high attendance, to consult parents about arrangements which will suit them (e.g. transport, baby-sitting), but most especially about the content of the meetings, so that parents find it personally relevant. Structuring the meetings so that less assertive parents have a chance to have their views listened to has also been shown to be appreciated (Hailstone 1984).

Increasing Parents' Skills.   One way of increasing parents' involvement in their children's education, which has been adopted by many schools for children with severe learning difficulties, is a parents' workshop. This differs from a support group in being oriented toward increasing parents' skills in helping their children progress. It may thus form a useful adjunct to annual reviews in facilitating greater communication between parents and teachers about assessment and programme-planning in the school. Workshops have generally taken the form of a six- to 12-week course, often held in the evenings, to which parents come without their children. The session will often be structured in two halves, with some form of presentation, for example, about how to observe a child's current abilities, and then an opportunity for small group discussion, with parents focusing on how they can work with their own child (Cunningham and Jeffree 1975; Attwood 1979; Capie, Taylor and Perkins 1980; Hattersley and Tennant 1981; Firth 1982; Gardner 1983). Evaluation has generally been restricted to reports of attendance levels, parents' expressions of satisfaction and the number of programmes carried out successfully with children. Studies which have measured parents' teaching skills following a short course have shown that parents can successfully acquire skills (e.g. Sandler, Coren and Thurman 1983; Baker, Prieto-Bayard and McCurry 1984). However, on more searching evaluation, it may be found that parents do not actually carry out teaching at home as intended (Gardner 1983; Baker *et al.* 1984), and that parents of older children have difficulty in successfully implementing programmes with only this degree of support (e.g. Firth 1982).

As a result, a mixture of workshop sessions and home visits may be advocated, or workshops extended so that they become a less frequent but more on-going part of the school programme. Other measures have been suggested to encourage participation by less confident parents, e.g. those who do not speak English as a first language, and by parents who are under greater economic and social stress, e.g. single parents. Baker *et al.* (1984) suggest, from the experience of numerous group workshop formats, that arrangements should be made for interpreters, transport and child care, that parents should be given incentives (e.g. a certificate) for taking part, that didactic presentations should be minimised, and active involvement of parents as observers and teachers be maximised, and that progress through the workshop from one aspect of the content to the next should be based on demonstrated skill, i.e. parents going at their own pace. In the long term, it has been found that parents often do not carry on with structured programmes or recording of child performance. However, a good proportion give evidence of using consistent teaching principles in day-to-day activities with their children, promoting the child's independence (Clark, Baker and Heifetz, 1982). This kind of opportunistic teaching, or acting spontaneously in line with a model of good practice in handling the child, seems ultimately the most important product of collaboration aimed at passing on teaching skills to parents. Workshops held in the evening give more opportunity for both parents to be involved, than do day-time meetings (or the home-visiting programmes mentioned above). What is the effect of involving one parent only? It has been found that mothers experience difficulty in conveying to fathers the content of workshops where the latter have not attended (Hattersley and Tennant 1981; Firth 1982). Also, as children progress, it can be found that mothers express more positive attitudes, but fathers become more negative (Sandler *et al.* 1983). It may be that the intervention is not taking account of the whole family as a system. Siblings may resist greater concentration on the handicapped child, and fathers may undermine the mother's efforts, e.g. not wanting to push the child too much (Corney 1981). Increased confidence and consistency in handling the handicapped child by all family members is a desirable goal, given the child's need for structure in order to learn.

One way of passing on ideas and skills to parents who have not attended workshops, and of maintaining the skills of those who have, is the use of manuals of teaching methods and ideas written especially for parents. Very many have now been published, some specifically for parents of children with severe learning difficulties. Evaluation of their usefulness is, however, overdue; one early survey noted that many behavioural teaching manuals demanded a high level of reading skill (Bernal and North 1978). A selected list of recent British publications is given below:

D.M. Millard *Daily Living With a Handicapped Child.* London: Croom Helm, 1984.
E. Newson and T. Hipgrave *Getting Through to Your Handicapped Child.* Cambridge: Cambridge University Press, 1982.
J. Warner *Helping the Handicapped Child with Early Feeding.* Winslow, Buckingham: PTM, 1981.
C. Cunningham and P. Sloper *Helping Your Handicapped Baby.* London: Souvenir Press, 1978.
J. Carr *Helping Your Handicapped Child.* Harmondsworth: Penguin, 1980.
V. Shennan *Help Your Child to Learn at Home.* London: MENCAP, 1978.
E. Whelan and B. Speake *Learning to Cope.* London: Souvenir Press, 1979 (about the handicapped young adult).
D. Jeffree, R. McConkey and S. Hewson *Let Me Play.* London: Souvenir Press, 1977.
D. Jeffree and R. McConkey *Let Me Speak.* London: Souvenir Press, 1976.
D. Jeffree and S. Cheseldine *Let's Join In.* London: Souvenir Press, 1984.
R. Lear *Play Helps.* London: Heinemann, 1977.
C. Kiernan, R. Jordan and C. Saunders *Starting Off.* London: Souvenir Press, 1978.
D. Jeffree, R. McConkey and S. Hewson *Teaching the Handicapped Child.* London: Souvenir Press, 1977.
B. Riddick *Toys and Play for the Handicapped Child.* London: Croom Helm, 1982.

The above description of workshops and manuals has been fairly extensive in order to lead to presentation of two main conclusions: 1. parents can be skilled contributors to the education of their handicapped child; and 2. schools have a responsibility for making flexible arrangements for collaboration with parents in such a way as to promote easy and individually appropriate involvement. These conclusions are elaborated further below.

Parent–teacher Collaboration.   Education authorities are now evolving various ways of implementing the expectation enshrined in the 1981 Education Act that parents will contribute to initial and continuing assessment of their children's special educational needs. For example, parents may make their contribution individually, or they may collaborate in joint assessment with professional staff. The responsibility for facilitating parents' full involvement lies with the professionals. However, Kerfoot and Gray have warned that 'although parents are laudably encouraged to contribute to the assessment process, the nature of their involvement is threatened by a system which remains inaccessible because of bureaucratic and professional jargon' (Kerfoot and Gray 1984: p. 20).

Parents and teachers may jointly assess the children through use of the PIP Developmental Charts (Jeffree and McConkey 1976), or the Pathways to Independence Checklists (Jeffree and Cheseldine 1982), etc. However, perhaps the most effective course is to link assessment directly with teaching goals by utilising the school curriculum in assessment. The curriculum needs to have been designed with this purpose in mind. Ideally, this might imply an objectives-based curriculum, with a clear strategy prescribed for using a proportion of the items in assessment (cf. Ainscow and Tweddle 1984). Benefits of joint assessment include establishing a shared positive vocabulary for discussing the child, and acknowledging from the start the parents' expertise in regard to their child. It then leads on naturally to discussion of parents' and teachers' priorities and goals for teaching. The Manchester survey of special schools found that many headteachers commented on parents' unrealistic expectations for their child, and a lack of understanding of teaching methods (Burman *et al.* 1982). If a shared dialogue has not been created from the time of the child's entry into school, then such miscommunication is only to be expected. Sharing of information is also vital when pupils are in their final years before leaving school, when parents will have the responsibility of deciding on future plans. A survey of school-leavers with severe learning difficulties showed that many skills learned in school were not practised at home; parents lacked information about the school programme and about future possibilities (Cheseldine and Jeffree 1982). The '13 plus' assessment, and annual reviews up to 19 years of age, should address themselves to tackling this type of problem. Of course, the added dimension here is the young adult's own plans and wishes. For example, he or she may want to retain some aspects of privacy, and not have parents fully conversant with all aspects of school activity (Johnson and Ransom, 1980). A three-way process of sharing information and priorities will require even more deliberate organisation.

From the literature, it now seems that many schools for children with severe learning difficulties are attempting programmes of joint teaching between home and school. Parent and teacher may work on the same skill (e.g. a self-help skill such as hand-washing) concurrently, sharing methods and information on progress by telephone or by a home–school diary. On the other hand, the teaching may proceed consecutively, with agreed areas of work for parent and teacher (McCall and Thacker 1977). For example, a parent might start toilet-training at home and then ask the school to follow the same procedures; or a child might learn to use the self-service canteen at school, by a careful step-by-step programme, with the parents maintaining new skills and generalising them to other settings in the local area. However, in practice such joint programming can be difficult to implement (Saunders, Jordan and Kiernan 1975). Some local authorities have a policy of employing 'carers' whose role is precisely to liaise between home and school in the implementation of programmes and handling strategies. Self-help skills, communication skills and behaviour problems are likely to be the areas of greatest success, perhaps because they are of immediate functional relevance for parents.

Parents can also contribute to the planning of the overall curriculum for the school, by suggesting priorities and by evaluating its appropriateness. For example, one school found parents' reactions and advice invaluable in redesigning its school leavers' curriculum to include a section on sex education (Leacroft School 1983).

In annual reviews, a structured curriculum can enhance specific and positive communication between parents and teachers about progress and future planning. The system in Britain is not as structured as that in the United States, where each child has to have an agreed, written Individual Education Plan (IEP). However, research into IEP meetings may have some lessons for the conduct of review meetings in Britain. For example, in a survey of over 2,000 parents, about half reported that their child's IEP had been decided on before the meeting between parents and teachers – parents were not able to participate in decision-making about the plan. Other studies have indicated that teachers tend to monopo-

lise the conversation and that parents' contributions are largely
confined to personal and family issues, and they are not encouraged to comment on educational matters (Turnbull and Turnbull
1982). Measures to improve on this state of affairs include preparing parents effectively for the meeting by, for example, giving them
a list of questions to consider beforehand and having one member
of staff act as a 'parent advocate', drawing parents into the
discussion. Turnbull and Strickland (1981) present several suggestions and a challenging list of twelve competencies required of
professionals who are associated with parental involvement in
programme-planning meetings.

One major obstacle to parent–teacher collaboration is teachers'
relative lack of preparation for this role in their pre-service
training. Teachers are expected to pick up skills incidentally, and
few will have attended skills-based, in-service training for working
with parents. Teachers have been trained to make the best use of
their direct contact time with children, and spending time with
parents may not at first seem a comparable priority. Also, they
may be reluctant to put extra pressure on parents, even though this
reluctance may inadvertently reinforce parents' feelings that they
have nothing to contribute. It may be difficult for teachers to
change from a didactic to a facilitative role in working with
parents, individually or in groups (Cunningham and Jeffree 1975).
In-service training for teachers may thus be a priority, and a recent
book, *Working with Parents: A Practical Guide for Teachers and
Therapists* (McConkey 1985), will prove a useful resource.

However, individual teachers cannot effect much change alone
– the school as a system will need to facilitate parent–teacher
collaboration. For example, it may need to be incorporated in
teachers' job descriptions and contract time allocated for home
visits and evening workshops. Children who have severe learning
difficulties require teachers and parents to work in partnership,
fully appreciating together how the environment restricts or
facilitates children's development, not only within the school or
within the home, but in the wider society (Barton and Moody
1981).

Rationale

The reasons why partnership with parents is, in theory, essential to
good educational practice include:

1. parents are already the primary influence on their children, and are already 'teachers'. This teaching is not planned or systematised. All parents respond to their children's initiations, and 'scaffold' their activities (Bruner 1975), elaborating on the child's cues and making links with the larger world. The style of interaction between parent and child is well established by the time the child enters school. Interventions can proceed best by respecting and enhancing this 'natural' interaction (Beveridge *et al.* 1982). Otherwise parents may be encouraged to feel they automatically have to do something 'special', which may disrupt the flow of turn-taking with the child (Mogford 1979). Enhancing parent–child interaction involves helping parents to plan ahead, to be consistent and clear, and to appreciate how finely-graded may need to be the steps in acquisition of new skills;

2. parents do want information and help on practical activities to do with their children. Professionals are often concerned about whether parents 'accept' that their child is handicapped. Many parents do continue to have recurring feelings of grief ('chronic sorrow', Wikler, Wasow and Hatfield 1981) and may feel defeated by lack of progress or newly revealed complications in the disability. However, professionals must be wary of protecting themselves by 'sparing' the parents. Surveys have shown repeatedly that parents lack and want full information about their child and about available services and benefits. And even fairly soon after the child's diagnosis of handicap is confirmed, parents are likely to resolve their conflicting feelings with the question 'What can we do to help?' (Cunningham 1983). A vital role of the teacher may be to foster parents' confidence that they are competent people capable of improving their own situation, and caring well for their child;

3. to a greater degree than in regular schools, the curriculum for children with severe learning difficulties will include goals which are also immediate priorities for parents. Examples are social skills, domestic skills and leisure skills. Thus, collaboration between parents and teachers in drawing up and implementing the curriculum makes obvious sense. Involving parents also gives a broader base of assessment of each individual child's functional needs, interests and current skills. Clear agreement will be needed between parents and teachers, for example, on the degree of independence which is being aimed at for the child;

4. the nature of severe learning difficulties is such that children need enhanced structure in order to learn. They thus need consistency of handling, so that it is obviously of benefit if parents and teachers have evolved a shared practice in terms of teaching methods. Also important are maintenance and generalisation of learning, which all too often are left to chance once the child has demonstrated initial acquisition of a skill. As parents spend more time with their children than teachers do, they are well placed to carry over skills from school to home and to foster their expression in a variety of situations. However, these stages in learning require proper planning in advance and good information-exchange between parents and teachers. It might be argued that parents do not have the time to collaborate with teachers; however, it may be far more time-consuming to carry on doing things for a child, or to cope with disruptive behaviour, when some support from a teacher in promoting consistency of handling or maintenance of learning would have made all the difference, and might prevent some problems from arising in the future.

Parents are an integral part of the multi-disciplinary team whose aim is to promote the quality of life of the handicapped child. It is clear that approaches to collaboration of teachers with parents must be flexible in order to take into account differing family situations and philosophies. This chapter attempts to suggest some ways in which schools may enhance parents' contribution to the education of their child. Unfortunately, the state of the art does not yet allow the laying-out of simple guidelines; however, the goal of partnership has proved and will continue to prove a spur to teachers' creativity.

References

Ainscow, M., and Tweddle, D. (1984) *Early Learning Skills Analysis.* Wiley.

Attwood, T. (1979) 'The Croydon workshop for the parents of severely handicapped school age children'. *Child: Care, Health and Development,* 5, pp. 177-88.

Ayer, S. (1984) 'Community care: failure of professionals to meet family needs'. *Child: Care, Health and Development,* 3.

Baker, B.L., Prieto-Bayard, M. and McCurry, M. (1984) 'Lower socio-economic status families and programs for training parents of retarded children', in J.M. Berg (ed.). *Perspectives and Progress in Mental Retardation,* Vol. 1. University

Park Press, pp. 459-68.

Baldwin, S. (1985) *The Costs of Caring: Families with Disabled Children.* Routledge and Kegan Paul.

Barna, S., Bidder, R.T., Gray, O.P., Clements, J. and Gardner, S. (1980) 'The progress of developmentally delayed pre-school children in home teaching schemes'. *Child: Care, Health and Development, 6,* pp. 157-64.

Barton, L. and Moody, S, (1981) 'The value of parents to the ESN(S) school? an examination', in L. Barton and S. Tomlinson (eds.). *Special Education: Policy, Practices and Social Issues.* Harper and Row.

Bernal, M.E. and North, J.A. (1978) 'A survey of parent training manuals'. *Jnl of Applied Behavior Analysis, 11,* pp. 533-44.

Berry, I. and Wood, J. (1981) 'The evaluation of parent intervention with young handicapped children'. *Behavioural Psychotherapy, 9,* pp. 358-68.

Beveridge, S., Flanagan, R., McConachie, H. and Sebba, J. (1982) *Parental Involvement in Anson House.* Anson House Pre-school Project Paper 3. Dr Barnardo's.

Boucher, J. (1981) *Parents as Partners.* Talk given to extra mural department course, University of Manchester, in Burman *et al.* (1982).

Bradshaw, J. (1980) *The Family Fund: An Initiative in Social Policy.* Routledge and Kegan Paul.

Bradshaw, J. and Lawton, D. (1985) '75,000 severely disabled children'. *Developmental Medicine and Child Neurology, 27,* (1), pp. 25-33.

Brazleton, T. (1976) 'Case finding, screening, diagnosis and tracking – discussant's comments', in T.D. Tjossem (ed.). *Intervention Strategies for High Risk Infants and the Young Child.* University Park Press.

Bruner, J. (1975) 'The ontogenesis of speech acts'. *Jnl of Child Language, 2,* pp. 1-19.

Brynelsen, D. (1983) 'Infant development programmes in British Columbia', in P. Mittler and H. McConachie (eds.). *Parents, Professionals and Mentally Handicapped People.* Croom Helm.

Burman, L., Farrell, P., Feiler, A., Heffernan, M., Mittler, H. and Reason, R. (1982) *Parental Involvement in Special Education: report of questionnaire.* Manchester School Psychological and Child Guidance Service.

Capie, A.C.M., Taylor, P.D and Perkins, E.A. (1980) *Teaching Basic Behavioural Principles.* BIMH.

Carey, G.E. (1982) 'Community care – care by whom? Mentally handicapped children living at home'. *Public Health, 96,* pp. 269-78.

Cheseldine, S.E. and Jeffree, D.M. (1982) 'Mentally handicapped adolescents: a survey of abilities'. *Special Education: Forward Trends* (Research Supplement), *9,* pp. 19-23.

Clark, D.B., Baker, B.L. and Heifetz, L.J. (1982) 'Behavioural training for parents of mentally retarded children: prediction of outcome'. *American Journal of Mental Deficiency, 87,* no. 1, pp. 14-19.

Collins, M. and Collins, D. (1976) *Kith and Kids.* Souvenir Press.

Cook, E. (1982) 'Portage parent support scheme', in R.J. Cameron (ed.). *Working Together: Portage in the UK.* NFER-Nelson.

Cooke, K. and Lawton, D. (1984) 'Informal support for the carers of disabled children'. *Child: Care Health and Development, 10,* 2, pp. 67-81.

Corney, M. (1981) 'A lost child lives on'. *New Forum, 7,* pp. 54-6.

Cunningham, C.C. (1982) *Down's Syndrome: an introduction for parents.* Souvenir Press.

Cunningham, C.C. (1983) 'Early support and intervention: the HARC infant programme', in P. Mittler and H. McConachie (eds.). *Parents, Professionals and Mentally Handicapped People.* Croom Helm.

Cunningham, C.C. (1984) *Early Parent Counselling.* HARC.

Cunningham, C.C. and Jeffree, D. (1975) 'The organisation and structure of workshops for parents of mentally handicapped children'. *Bull. of the Br. Psychological Society, 28,* pp. 405-11.

Cunningham, C.C. and Sloper, P. (1977) 'Parents of Down's syndrome babies: their early needs'. *Child: Care, Health and Development, 3,* p. 325.

Cunningham, C.C. and Sloper, P. (1977) 'Down's syndrome: a positive approach to parent and professional collaboration'. *Health Visitor, 50,* no. 2.

DES (1967) Central Advisory Council for Ed. *Children and their primary schools,* (Plowden Report). HMSO.

DES (1978) *Special Educational Needs.* Report of the Committee of Enquiry into the Education of Handicapped Children and Young People. (Warnock Report). HMSO.

Equal Opportunities Commission (1983) *The Experience of Caring for Elderly and Handicapped Dependents.* Manchester EOC.

Firth, H. (1982) 'The effectiveness of parent workshops in a mental handicap service'. *Child: Care, Health and Development, 8,* pp. 77-91.

Gardner, J. (1983) 'School-based parent involvement: a psychologist's view', in P. Mittler and H. McConachie (eds.). *Parents, Professionals and Mentally Handicapped People.* Croom Helm, pp. 166-75.

Gath, A. (1978), *Down's Syndrome and the Family: the Early Years.* Academic Press.

Glendenning, C. (1983) *Unshared Care.* Routledge and Kegan Paul.

Glendenning, C. (1976) *Voluntary Organisations for Handicapped Children and their Families.* University of York Social Policy Research Unit.

Glossop, C. and Castillo, M. (1982) 'Summary of present and future research into the Portage model', in R.J. Cameron (ed.). *Working together: Portage in the UK.* NFER-Nelson.

Hailstone, E. (1984) *Stay-Away Parents: how to draw them in.* Home and School Publications.

Hattersley, J. and Tennant, L. (1981) 'Parent workshops in Worcestershire', in G. Pugh (ed.). *Parents as Partners.* National Children's Bureau.

Hewett, S. (1970) *The Family and the Handicapped Child.* George Allen and Unwin.

Honeylands Progress Report (1979) *A Resource Centre for Handicapped Children and Their Families.* Paediatric Research, Royal Devon and Exeter Hospital, Exeter.

Jeffree, D. and Cheseldine, S. (1982) *Pathways to Independence: checklists of self-help, personal and social skills.* Hodder and Stoughton.

Jeffree, D. and McConkey, R. (1976) *PIP Development Charts.* Hodder and Stoughton.

Johnson, D. and Ransom, E. (1980) 'Parents' perceptions of secondary schools', in M. Craft, J. Raynor, and L. Cohen (eds.). *Linking Home and School,* 3rd edn. Harper and Row.

Kerfoot, S. and Gray, P. (1984) 'Humanizing the 1981 Education Act'. *Division of Educational and Child Psychology Newsletter,* No. 16, pp. 20-2.

Kew, S. (1976) *Handicap and Family Crisis.* Pitman Publishing.

Key, J., Hooper, J. and Ballard, M. (1979) 'Perspective on the home visiting project provided by three parent observers'. *Child: Care, Health and Development, 5,* pp. 103-9.

Klaus, M. and Kennell, J. (1970) 'Mothers separated from their newborn infants'. *Paediatric Clinics of North America, 17.*

Leacroft School (1983) *Core Curriculum: school leavers' programme mark 2, for school and home.* Manchester Education Committee.

Leiderman, P.H. (1974) 'Mothers at risk: potential consequences of hospital care of a premature infant', in E. Anthony (ed.). *The Child and His Family.* Wiley.

McCall, C. and Thacker, J. (1977) 'A parent workshop in the school'. *Special Education, 4*, pp. 20-1.

McConachie, H. (1982) 'Father of handicapped children', in N. Beail and J. McGuire (eds.). *Psychological Aspects of Fatherhood.* Junction Books.

McConachie, H. (1983) 'Fathers, mothers, siblings and the family: how do they see themselves?' in P. Mittler and H. McConachie (eds.). *Parents, Professionals and Mentally Handicapped People.* Croom Helm.

McConachie, H. (1983) 'Examples of partnership in Europe', in P. Mittler and H. McConachie (eds.). *Parents, Professionals and Mentally Handicapped People.* Croom Helm, pp. 205-20.

McConkey, R. (1985) *Working with Parents: a practical guide for teachers and therapists.* Croom Helm.

Miller, N. (1984) *Setting up for Self-Help.* Contact a Family/Mental Health Foundation.

Mittler, P. and McConachie, H. (1983) *Parents, Professionals and Mentally Handicapped People: approaches to partnership.* Croom Helm.

Mittler, P. and Mittler, H. (1982) *Partnership with Parents.* National Council for Special Education.

Mogford, K. (1979) 'A study of interaction and communication in remedial play', in E. Newson, J. Newson, J. Head and K. Mogford. *Play in the Remediation of Handicap: report on an action research project, 1971 to 1976.* Nottingham University Toy Library, pp. 72-9.

Oakley, A. (1974) *The Sociology of Housework.* Martin Robertson.

O'Dell, S. (1974) 'Training parents in behaviour modification: a review'. *Psychological Bulletin, 81*, pp. 418-33.

Paul, J.L. (1981) *Understanding and Working with Parents of Children with Special Needs.* Holt, Rinehart and Winston.

Philip, M. and Duckworth, D. (1982) *Children with Disabilities and their Families: a review of research.* NFER-Nelson.

Pugh, G. (1981) *Parents as Partners.* National Children's Bureau.

Pugh, G. and Russell, P. (1977) *Shared Care: support services for families with handicapped children.* National Children's Bureau.

Rayner, H. (1978) 'The Exeter home-visiting project; the psychologist as one of several therapists'. *Child: Care, Health and Development, 4*, pp. 1-7.

Ricks, D. (1982) Unpublished paper. Harperbury and University College Hospitals.

Robin, M. and Josse, D. (1984) 'Maternal language and the development of successive infant identities'. *Early Child Development and Care, 17* (2/3), pp. 167-77.

Rubissow, J., Jones, J. and Brimblecombe, F. (1979) 'Handicapped children and their families: their use of available services and their unmet needs', in *Mixed Communications: problems and progress in medical care,* No. 12. Nuffield Provincial Hospitals Trust, Oxford University Press.

Russell, P. (1983) 'The parents' perspective of family needs and how to meet them', in P. Mittler and H. McConachie (eds.). *Parents, Professionals and Mentally Handicapped People.* Croom Helm, pp. 47-61.

Sandler, A., Coren, A. and Thurman, S.K. (1983) 'A training program for parents of handicapped pre-school children: effects upon mother, father and child'. *Exceptional Children, 49*, pp. 355-8.

Sandow, S., and Clarke, A.D.B. (1978) 'Home intervention with parents of severely sub-normal pre-school children: an interim report'. *Child: Care, Health and Development, 4*, pp. 29-39.

Sandow, S., Clarke, A.D.B., Cox, M.V. and Stewart, F.L. (1981) 'Home intervention with parents of severely subnormal, pre-school children: a final report'. *Child: Care, Health and Development,* 7, pp. 135-44.

Saunders, C.A., Jordan, R.R. and Kiernan, C.C. (1975) 'Parent–school collaboration', in C.C. Kiernan and F.P. Woodford (eds.). *Behaviour Modification with the Severely Retarded.* Study Group 8, IRMMH. Associated Scientific Publishers, pp. 195-210.

Shearer, D.E. and Shearer, M.S. (1976) 'The Portage Project; a model for early childhood intervention', in T.D. Tjossem (ed.). *Intervention Strategies for High Risk Infants and Young Children.* University Park Press, pp. 335-50.

Smith, B. (1983) 'Collaboration between parents and teachers of school-age children', in P. Mittler and H. McConachie (eds.). *Parents, Professionals and Mentally Handicapped People.* Croom Helm, pp. 141-52.

Smith, T. (1980) *Parents and Pre-school.* Grant McIntyre.

Tizard, B., Hughes, M., Carmichael, H. and Pinkerton, G. (1983a) 'Children's questions and adults' answers'. *Jnl of Child Psychology and Psychiatry,* 24, pp. 269-81.

Tizard, B., Hughes, M., Carmichael, H. and Pinkerton, G. (1983b) 'Language and social class: is verbal deprivation a myth?' *Jnl of Child Psychology and Psychiatry,* 24, pp. 533-42.

Trout, D. (1983) 'Birth of a sick or handicapped infant: impact on the family'. *Child Welfare,* Vol. LXII (4), Child Welfare League of America.

Turnbull, A.P. and Turnbull, H.R. (1982) 'Parent involvement in the education of handicapped children: a critique'. *Mental Retardation,* 20, pp. 115-22.

Turnbull, A.P. and Strickland, B. (1981) 'Parents and the educational system', in J.L. Paul (ed.). *Understanding and Working with Parents of Children with Special Needs.* Holt, Rinehart and Winston, pp. 231-63.

Tymchuck, A. (1979) *Parent and Family Therapy: an integrative approach to family interventions.* S.P. Medical and Scientific Books.

Wikler, L., Wasow, M. and Hatfield, E. (1981) 'Chronic sorrow revisited: parents vs. professional depiction of the adjustment of parents of mentally handicapped children'. *Am. Jnl of Orthopsychiatry,* 51, pp. 63-70.

Wilkin, D. (1979) *Caring for the Mentally Handicapped Child.* Croom Helm.

Wilson, E. (1982) 'Women, the "community" and "the family"', in A. Walker, B. Blackwell and M. Robertson (eds.). *Community Care.* Oxford.

Wishart, M., Bidder, R. and Gray, O.P. (1980) 'Parental responses to their developmentally delayed children and the South Glamorgan Home Advisory Service'. *Child: Care, Health and Development,* 6, pp. 361-76.

Wolfenden (1978) Report of the Wolfenden Committee. *The Future of the Voluntary Organisations.* Croom Helm.

Wolfensberger, W. and Kurtz, R. (1974) 'Use of retardation-related diagnostic and descriptive labels by parents of retarded children'. *Jnl of Special Education,* 8, pp. 131-42.

Wolkind, S. (1981) 'Depression in Mothers of Young Children'. *Archives of Disease in Childhood,* 56, no. 1, pp. 1-3.

11 THE ROLE OF THE SCHOOL STAFF

Mike Johnson

Introduction

One of the features that distinguishes special schools from those in mainstream education is the much clearer accountability that can be demanded from them. Mainstream schools must meet the criterion that their practices result in greater learning and development in children than would have obtained had the children just been left in the environment. Special schools must meet the criterion that learning and development are greater than would have obtained for the child in a mainstream school. At a time when the Children's Legal Centre, among others, is claiming that any form of separate education amounts to discrimination and as such is ethically unacceptable, special schools must meet this criterion in full.

This implies that a school staff must be very clear about their aims for the children in their care. These aims should be open to scrutiny, not only by other professionals, but also by the child's parents. They should stem wherever possible from a clear, theoretical basis and lead to predictions about expected progress in both short and medium term, the accuracy of which would form a powerful source of accountability. All this suggests that a major function of the role of the staff must be to maximise the amount and quality of the information that can be made available whenever a decision is to be made.

Part of this information is bound to come from nothing more tangible than their own feelings. So long as staff are clear about this, it is a source of strength. We make many vital decisions in our lives on the basis of feelings. There are children, even in mainstream, who make it difficult for us to take to them. To feel this way is natural — to act upon it to the child's detriment is unacceptable. Staff can be on their guard to monitor their feelings about children. If these feelings are negative — why? If behaviours or responses on the part of the child can be noted, action is possible. A recent BPS Conference dealt with this point in a behavioural context. Any long-term interaction between two people must involve good and bad qualities and aim to maximise the effects of the former while mitigating the latter. Mutual staff support is an important mechanism for achieving this.

In a special school staff there is a very complex role and professional structure. This is often exacerbated by the fact that the person who acts to fulfil a role is not always the person who has the role professionally. A classroom assistant may give all the appearances of teaching a child and recording the results. A teacher may be giving physio- or speech therapy or, equally, may be washing or toileting a child. Teachers, assistants and parents may be sitting together just holding the children on their knees and doing mother/child-type activities with them. The professional side of the role comes in taking responsibility for what is done, planning its development and evaluating the results in the medium term. This process is hampered by salary differentials based on qualifications and status and taken from the structure in mainstream schools where classroom assistants or auxiliaries have a much more clearly defined role to do with routine tasks or preparation of materials rather than direct contact with children. It is also hampered by people who look to other professionals to validate their competence rather than to the effects they have upon the children. A further problem is caused by those who 'hoard' their expertise as though it were a non-renewable source.

The pace in special schools is usually a slow one. It may well be that any particular classroom may at one time be highly organised and even frenetic. However, developments and changes are not usually dramatic and need careful recording techniques to reveal them. The day itself is constrained by the distances some children have to travel and therefore the times at which they arrive and must leave. There are interruptions for the many 'caretaking' functions to be performed — toileting, breaks, lunch, exercise, medication, etc. For some children the amount of time that their sensory functions seem to be operating efficiently and/or their energy level is high enough for efficient responding may be limited.

The awareness and enrichment parts of the curriculum, of vital importance and contained in such activities as music, dance, storytime, assemblies, etc. may well demand disproportionate amounts of time for marshalling, moving, changing the children. This in turn may lessen the impetus that would be present in a mainstream school. Events such as Harvest, Easter and, most dramatic of all,

Christmas, while potentially providing exciting foci for the children's work, can readily become ends in themselves, thereby applying yet another retarding force. All these events can be sources of normalisation. What makes a national group, a club, a family cohesive and recognisable is, in large measure, the 'rituals' they observe together. The saying, 'The family that prays together stays together', is one sidelight on this fact. Our children must take part in a life together. Festivals are also rich sources of curriculum implementation. They have always generated art, music, writing, discussion. The key is to remember the curriculum basis and make sure that the balance between what the teacher does and what the children do is struck sensibly. In terms of time, simple rules like 'We don't start Christmas before December 1st!' are extremely helpful.

In special schools, expectations of the children are generated directly by the staff who are also to articulate and evaluate them. A very clear responsibility lies upon them to ensure that the pace of learning is optimised. There must be mutual staff support so that each staff member feels that there is someone who knows and cares about how well their pupils are developing and to ensure that that progress is observed from an informed understanding.

The main difficulty here is the balance between a clinical over-detachment and over-emotional pity. The key to that balance is respect — respect for the pupils and their right to an individual human life and respect for themselves as compassionate competent professionals. Finally there is a curriculum itself. History has left a great residue of outside influences in the special school. The traditions of medicine and charity compounded with philosophical theory die hard. In mainstream schools the curriculum still has as its ultimate reference point the lives of the children outside school, both in the present and the future. The one is usually related to the other. With children with severe learning difficulties the reference point is far less clear. Yet the Warnock Report (DES 1978) claimed that the aims of education were the same for all; but the curriculum content leading to those aims differs considerably. Unfortunately there may be a temptation to make the child fit into the curriculum and not see that, however elegant or theoretically logical the curriculum structure, both management and content revolve round the developing needs of individual pupils. Many special schools have gone well beyond this point in their curriculum development. It is still worth remembering, however, that children as a group are continually changing as society changes, and occasionally 'checking back' is no bad discipline.

The curriculum is a structure and a process which allows the children to develop. A good example is the use or misuse of techniques based, sometimes loosely, on the theory of behaviourism. It is important to draw a distinction here. Because in many key areas of curriculum articulation it is useful to work with objectives that are behavioural does not mean that we must embrace behaviourism to the exclusion of all else. It is perfectly possible to be concerned with what children actually do and take any one of a number of theories — Piagetian, personal construct, Rogerian for example — to explain why they do it. Teaching to behavioural objectives, if used well and appropriately, is a valuable means of getting to the individual. The key here is to consider of what value it will be to the child to have a behaviour in his repertoire and what opportunities we are going to give him to use it once he has it. If this criterion is omitted then the method becomes self-sufficient and must then be part of the other methods that have taken parasitic root in some schools: sense training, ITPA, Frostig Psychomotor training and most insidious of all Dolman-Delacato patterning. A school staff must be strong enough as a team to look at their own collective expertise for methods that suit their children and are possible within the personal and material 'tools' at their disposal.

Thus, when one considers the role of the school staff one looks for a structure that will facilitate multi-directional information flow and objective emotional responses within a caring, respectful environment. A structure that is versatile enough to cope with the inherent complexity of the situation it must serve, effective in ensuring that there is a clear impetus towards medium-term goals meaningful in social and philosophical terms so that the work may take place in a context that respects all those that are involved in it — pupils, staff and parents. The staff of any school does not only consist of those individuals who meet there each day. Even without considering the very informal and personal forces that act upon them from their families, situations and personal aspirations, there are some very clear influences from outside the school. Most common among these are HMI, LEA Advisors, Governors and parents.

HM Inspectors

HMI are a particularly interesting group at present. Following the Rayner Commission (DES 1983a), there has been a major increase in their numbers. They have become involved in the surveying and inspection of teacher training courses and it is envisaged that they are soon to be able to insist on receiving 'invitations' to visit university departments. Their reports are now published; and, far from becoming a potential source of embarrassment to the schools concerned, it seems to be having the greater effect on LEA and government because of their lack of reluctance to indicate when shortcomings may be seen as caused by LEA funding. This causes some irritation, particularly in those town halls where such funding has been predicated on what has been perceived as goverment policy (TES 44, 27 July and 14 September 1984.)

As far as an individual school is concerned, therefore, the HMI who has responsibility for them may be seen as a source of help as much as interrogation and evaluation. They will be able to suggest comparisons with other schools, make contacts within which experience can be widened and support in-service and other initiatives in the interests of staff and curriculum development. They can bring to the staff a wide and rounded knowledge of the contemporary scene and indicate where the particular school fits into it. Through their courses organised at national level they can provide a very real impetus in a particular direction and offer dissemination of the results of experimental initiatives. As yet the number of reports on severe learning difficulties schools is very limited, but will doubtless grow as the new teams become established.

Local Authority Advisor

Similar in function, but with a much more clearly defined and parochial role, is the LEA Advisor. In a survey of LEA arrangements for the curriculum (DES 1979) over 70 per cent of LEAs cited the advisor as their source of information about curriculum in schools, well over 50 per cent referred to the importance of the advisor in disseminating curriculum policy, and over 25 per cent referred to their role as initiators of such policy. Frequent references were made to the contributions of advisors in the provision of in-service training, stimulation of curriculum development and the disbursement of special funds. Eighty per cent saw them as a source of help to schools in deciding on the relative emphasis they should give to particular aspects of the curriculum. They are clearly sources of knowledge and expertise, facilitators of individual careers as well as providers of feedback and guidance. They are, in many ways the first line of validation for the sometimes internally autonomous structures that make up a special school. Role conflict may arise from their sometimes conflated advisory and inspectorial roles. In a period of rate-capping and recession this conflict may be sharpened, and heads of schools need to mobilise pressure groups from parents, handicap support groups, such as the Spastics Society, MENCAP etc. Contacts with the advisor should be frequent enough for policy trends and changes to come as no great surprise to the school, but not so frequent that the role of the head is compromised.

The Advisor together with senior administrators has to ensure that the LEA responsibilities under the 1981 Act are being discharged. They must also ensure that the school has an up-to-date curriculum statement (Circulars 8/81 and 1/83, DES 1981; 1983b). These are all part of the mechanism by which the accountability of the school is ensured. It is likely that about three to four times a term informal contact with the head and once or twice a year direct contact with the staff on in-service days or in-house courses would seem appropriate. Naturally, if some project, either of organisational change or curriculum innovation or development, is envisaged then this may well lead to a more intensive, if short-term, input.

The School Governors

School governors also have a supportive role. Following the Taylor Report (DES 1977), the 1981 Education Act and the activities of pressure groups such as ACE, their future, which at one time looked rather bleak, is now entering a phase of renewed vigour.

They have a less direct, yet potentially very important, evaluative–consultative role. The very preparation of reports-to-governors can form a most useful discipline for a headteacher. Governing bodies often contain considerable expertise and usually have as members well-read, interested and influential people. Not only can they mount a searching and valuable discussion of such reports, but they can also be a valuable source of support, material and influence. They can actively support the head in consultations with the LEA, promote the school to the community and provide a valuable independent but knowledgeable source of opinion in the matter of promotions and appointments. Since the Taylor Report, teachers and parents from the school have had the right to representation, and a large number of LEAs now consult with governors about local policies affecting schools and other general educational matters. A majority said that governors were now much more involved in the discussion of curriculum issues within the school (DES 1977).

The Head Teacher

The head teacher's role is to bridge the gap between these external forces (we will return to parents later) and the internal structure of the school. Richardson (1975) talks about the 'boundary function' of the head. Coulson (1980) talked about the head as a 'filter'. Watts (1980) extended these somewhat defensive notions to a more dynamic two-way transmitter of pressures. Packwood (1983) uses the analogy of an hour-glass with the head taking a crucial position in the centre. However, this underestimates the broad base on which headship stands. This base is one of authority or legitimised power.

One can characterise this, following Weber (1947), in certain 'types' of heads, eg: The first head has an immaculate brochure on the school and can produce checklists and curricular plans at the drop of a hat. A steady flow of communications goes out to parents but change tends to be seen as something that will disrupt the smooth flow of the 'system'. An alternative to this is ritual authority. Here, clear traditions and forms of behaviour are practised in the school. School assemblies will be formal affairs, and the various roles in the school are symbolised by notices, rooms, colours, etc. Communication is formal and stratified. Outside professionals see the head and few others, tea is on a tray, possibly with the deputy. Thirdly there is charismatic authority where the head's own personal qualities cause others to strive for her goals. Here the head is as likely to emerge from a classroom group as from her room. Where the other heads wear suits she dresses well, but casually. Everyone knows and loves her. This latter is the important point. The charismatic head seeks emotional approval from staff, parents and pupils — 'They'd do anything for her'.

There are excellent qualities in each of the three types, and we can recognise elements of all of them in heads we have known. Headship is a lonely position. Just as for an author or a child the sight of a blank, virginal sheet of paper can be most inhibiting, so for a head a school can be a forbidding place, like a house of cards where to touch the wrong one, or any ineptly, can bring the whole lot crashing down. Small wonder that defences of paper or notices or emotional blackmail are created.

However, hopefully, these can be relegated to props and professional authority can be substituted. Here Hughes (1977) introduced the concept of 'leading professional'. He saw the head as a very well qualified and experienced teacher taking headship as a professional role. This would mean that it would be the expertise of the head, her ability to determine the way forward on the basis of current thinking, her skill in getting her staff to develop the necessary techniques and structures, her support of them via interest and careful critique, that gave her authority and control. These heads know what is going on in their schools. The staff know that she knows, but trust that it is concern and interest, not a desire to 'check-up', that motivates her. From this base of common theoretical stance and personal trustworthiness comes an ability to increase the democracy within the school.

The head and staff have a common language which means that communication can be simple and direct. The head will ensure that all staff know what is going on — the good news and the bad. Visitors are accessible to all and introduced to anyone who is met. Decision-making rarely has to be formalised because the necessary discussion is taking place constantly. The head may well lead, but the direction is predictable to all. A good test of this structure is its flexibility. Problems arise when theory takes over. A good theory is a tool. It enables its user to conceptualise complexities efficiently, but any theory only has a given range of convenience. Human behaviour is too large to be encompassed by any one theory. Those who are true professionals are also humble enough to perceive that range and recognise that larger concepts such as concern and respect and charity are of greater importance. The singleminded pursuit of one theoretical stance can only lead to sterility and to the emergence of one of the three styles under the cloak of professionalism. The bureaucrat would develop checklists of ever-increasing complexity and fineness of gradation, the ritualist better systems of job-description and room management structures, the charismatic, staff meetings that develop all the characteristics of a revivalist service. The professional must always have a strong sense of the pragmatic.

In-service training of staff is an essential element. This can develop, as well as capitalise on, the skills of staff. Added to this there should be a regular input from outside the school. It may be through a teacher who regularly reads and digests relevant journals for her colleagues, a teacher on a course who reports back regularly, the use of Advisors or the local training organisation. The welcoming of students and a willingness to encourage, accept and consider their often naive and ill-formed questions and even criticisms can also be a useful stimulus to a continual search for stretching experiences. Thus the professional head serves almost as a focal point.

As training for teachers in special schools becomes increasingly an in-service activity, polytechnic, college and university tutors will become partners with the schools who co-operate with them. The life of the school is thus enriched by access to new literature, techniques, questioning etc. NAHT (1985) makes this staff development point very firmly in an excellent overview of the conditions conducive to effective staff development and the strategies and tactics to be employed.

The Deputy Head

Coulson and Cox (1975) suggested that 'teachers regard the deputy as one of themselves without the right to prescribe behaviour for them'. The head usually does not see the deputy as in any way standing between her and the teachers. Ironically, although special schools tend to be quite small places, the head often resolves this anomalous situation by taking on a concept from secondary school management and gives the deputy control over a structure rather than over people. The deputy may well take as her area of concern the curriculum, the organisation of resources, in-service training. Certainly, it is likely that she will have a dual role — combined with that of a 'teacher'. Important decisions to be made about the deputy will be the proportion of time spent teaching, and whether this should be as a teacher with responsibility for a class or selective teaching. A 75 per cent teaching committment seems a good rule of thumb, and experience suggests that caution should be exercised before this is assigned to one class as the class-teacher. The demands on the deputy's time are often unpredictable in their incidence, and a more flexible structure is indicated than would be possible if she were also in charge of a class. Indeed time to facilitate in-service training is essential.

While the style adopted by the deputy will of necessity be individualised, it must, nevertheless, be imposed to some extent by the head. It may be a reflection of the head's style or complementary to it. Paradoxically, many writers have seen the deputy as less free to shape her own role than a class teacher. Any power she has stems from willingness and an ability on the part of the head to delegate. In an all-age school there may be scope for delegation of responsibility for the lower end of the school, more so in split-site working. However, there are clear, practical limits to the degree of autonomy available. The head always retains responsibility — that cannot be delegated — and a coherent policy throughout the school is essential. There are too many examples of mainstream infant and junior schools where the two heads cannot agree on methods for teaching reading and numbers, to the clear detriment of the children, for us to be happy for deputy heads to 'do-their-own-thing'.

The deputy must have a real, objective function not, as Martin (1979) put it, 'the somewhat bizarre ragbag of tasks associated with the role of deputy head'. Fulfilling that role will be an essential pre-requisite for the efficient functioning of the school, but can be discharged in the person's own style. Thus the curriculum can be kept under constant scrutiny in relation to current published thinking and all staff drawn in and encouraged to take their part in curriculum development. Resources can be husbanded and deployed in such a way that the time lag between ordering and need is eliminated. Fund-raising bodies are never in doubt as to what the school can make good use of and are also in no doubt that the children are getting full value from the latest act of largesse. In this way the deputy has a constructive, complementary role to that of the head. She can enable the head teacher the better to see the staff's point of view (be it emotional or pragmatic), she can help the staff better to understand the head's intentions, she can negotiate between regulations and requirements and their effects in practice. As the head mediates between outside and the school, so the deputy bridges the gap between head and staff. Coulson and Cox (1975) summed up the staff's expectations of the deputy as encouraging and supporting the staff, functioning as a go-between in respect of the head and the teachers, acting as a good practitioner, a competent administrator and a subordinate who expects the head teacher to make the final decision on all important school matters but nevertheless questions and challenges those decisions. All contemporary writers seem to agree that Burnham's concept of the head as instrumental leader, the deputy as socio-emotional leader (Burnham 1968), lacks validity. Indeed, with the advent of scale 2 and 3 teachers with responsibility for particular age ranges or degrees of handicap, the role of the deputy becomes slowly eroded. It may well be that, in the future, a structure that consists solely of these roles, dispenses with the deputy and designates a 'senior teacher' to stand in for the head in her absence, would be one that has the merit of being nearer to reality.

Scale Post Holders

If the role and function of the deputy head ranges from ambiguous to diffuse the discussion of 'scale posts' is somewhat esoteric. Hoyle (1969) looks at them as examples of differentiation and stratification. Differentiation is the division of labour into different roles, stratification the ranking of these roles in a hierarchy of status, power and remuneration. They are very much the creatures of Burnham salary negotiations rather than a product of educational or even social needs. The process began with posts of special responsibility in 1945, reached its full flower in 1956 when there were no less than 39 different status levels in schools and consolidated to five levels of scale posts in 1971. The current restructuring negotiations can be seen as a way of getting back to a more flexible version of this earlier system, with merit-rating in some form substituted for clearly spurious 'posts' for looking after the first aid box or organising the PE store.

Schools, even special schools, are not immune to the problems of stratification. One can argue that teachers need to increase their skills and knowledge constantly so as to be of greatest value to their pupils. This process is costly in terms of time and effort. To encourage them to do this, incentives in the form of increased salary, status and power must be offered. Such efforts can be seen as enlightened self-interest. However, it could also be assumed that stratification encourages self-interest at the expense of pupil-interest. The knowledge and skills that are acquired in furthering a career are not necessarily those of most value to pupils. There is a distressing tendency for professionals to take their evaluation and validation from other professionals rather than their clients — in this case the children. It is clearly unrealistic to think that a teacher's self-motivation is provided totally by the children's responses. However, as we indicated when examining the role of the head it is important to ensure that any legitimate sources of satisfaction such as those gained from being in a team, having the regard of prestigious people such as doctors, advisors, HMI, etc. should relate back to the children and their parents and not be at the expense of them.

This naturally comes into sharp focus when promotion is considered. If promotion goes to those who fulfil professional but not client-related criteria, then resentment and rejection of leadership can only follow from those who are unpromoted but good with children. Falling rolls have manifestly affected the stances of both teacher unions and LEA. Research would suggest that satisfaction is not a simple function of promotion opportunities, but that commitment to teaching as a career may be affected for the worse and LEAs may well have to be imaginative in devising opportunities other than those related to promotion.

Thus, if a special school has an allotment of scale posts derived from statement-of-points value, it is probably better to see these as related to a meaningful support structure rather than some sort of 'responsibility'. It is illogical to claim that the allowances are for extra work. This is to walk straight into the problem of comparing a class teacher's work for and on behalf of the children with another scale teacher's administrative, pastoral or curricular duties. Teaching as a profession is a full-time commitment: comparisons are always invidious. It may be useful to group classes by chronological age. The 1984 Scottish Curriculum Publication 'Learning Together' puts a powerful case for this. To have a scale post holder responsible for co-ordination of the three main age-related areas may well be functional. There will always be someone to monitor and oversee in the most positive way. A sense of team may well be fostered. It may also be useful to have a designated post for special care or profoundly retarded, multiply handicapped children. The only caveat is that these teams always relate constantly and organically to the whole. All the children must remain the responsibility of all the staff.

What is argued for is payment for having management responsibilities; for ensuring that communication takes place; for collecting in, thinking about and forming proposals on the basis of information; for being responsible for the delegation of responsibility and monitoring the results of that delegation. Thus, becoming a scale post holder makes a teacher more accountable and implies a greater part for the overall process of accountability. Thus, she would always be responsible, for not only the work of others, but for the progress of groups of children. This all goes to enhance the position of the class teacher. In a special school more than in any other, the children are clearly extremely dependent upon the skill, expertise and interest of their classroom teacher.

The Classroom Teacher

So to the classroom teacher. All the foregoing relates to structures set up with the intention of facilitating the interactions of a classroom teacher with her children. The LEA, Governors, senior staff, etc. can have a profound effect in limiting or extending what is possible in a classroom — they cannot determine it. Children with severe learning difficulties are very susceptible to their environment. Much has been made of their supposed inability to make use of incidental learning. There have been suggestions that their problems are caused mainly by the input side of their cognitive system. However this may be, it is certainly a gross exaggeration to say that they will not learn anything they are not taught directly. Even the most casual contact with children in severe learning difficulties schools will reveal that they have learned a great deal that it is most unlikely they were taught. Even young, or developmentally young, children can be seen to have made a start on producing an internalised model of reality. It may well be that this model is fragile, in some cases even fragmentary, but to deny them a model is to deny them humanity. One must not assume that incidental learning will not occur. Therefore the teacher must structure her work as if it will and constantly probe. Some children seem only to learn incidentally the wrong things!

The start of this process is the ability to communicate with the multitude of professionals who can potentially be involved in the child's life. The more her own assessment, programme-planning, recording and evaluating are on a sound basis the more sure she can feel that her contribution has comparable validity. The more, also, she can professionally question and even challenge their ideas and offer constructive criticism. A useful in-service training activity is actually to spend a day with each of the relevant professionals while they do their jobs. On the other side of the coin is the ability to work with a classroom assistant/parent volunteer, etc. Here the roles are reversed, and clarity of aims and methods must be communicated while, at the same time, accepting and building on their legitimate comments, expertise and criticism.

The teacher must, with all this, remain aware of the whole child as an individual. He is not just a collection of attributes. He has strengths to be capitalised on, weaknesses to be compensated for and his own views about how best to do this. In this he is no different from us. There is the story of the two boys outside the dentist. One clutches the side of his face. 'I'd have that tooth out if I were you', says his friend. Between clenched teeth, 'So would I, if I were you!' replies the first. He has a personality, a predisposition to compensate or avoid. While in no way definitive these factors are worthy at least of consideration. The class also has its own 'personality' as does the school. The teacher must be conscious of the 'environmental design' within which her work takes place and herself as part of it. The teacher is a model for learning. She may well be the most accessible model the child has. Her classroom displays, her care with his things as well as hers, her handling of others, both adults and children are vital classroom management elements that affect children — often with unpredictable power.

One of the major determinants is the degree to which she and her assistants can create a caring environment. This refers to the sheer quality of the relationship offered to the children. Wilson (1980) writes of this in terms of care, concern, respect, kindness, consideration and love. The essential feature is the desire and ability to convey to the pupil the feeling that he matters and that he can affect the world.

Clearly one important determinant of the likelihood of this happening is the teacher's capacity for such feelings towards others and the allied ability to express them. It is difficult to give when you feel deprived. The staff team have a clear supportive role here, and the greater the degree of emotional openness between them the greater the possibility of their being able to offer help. However, another major determinant is time. It is also difficult to offer what Rogers (1967) calls 'positive regard' in a pressed and stressful situation. This is where management skills come in. These provide an organisation and action structure so that there is always time to think about and respond positively to any child. The analogy of driving a car is a useful one. When you are learning, everything seems to be happening at once and very quickly. As you progress you build up whole patterns of responses that you can emit in a co-ordinated fashion in response to what you now recognise as patterns or sequences in the behaviour of others. Games and sports are similar in the way they are performed by novices and experts.

Thus with the skill of teaching, the main weapon in the teacher's armoury is her skill at observation. What are the most useful behaviours each child can emit and under what set of circumstances? What things doesn't he do that we feel we must try to get him to do? Do we have any reason to believe that he can't as opposed to the simpler explanation that he doesn't? Observations should be made over as wide a range of situations as possible with a firm intention of looking for the most positive account of each child's potential to discover the situations within which he can give his best and what good functions can be mobilised to compensate for poor functions. Related to this must be a willingness to make this knowledge available to colleagues — preferably in a way that does not challenge or threaten their own sense of expertise.

Next the class teacher should have a clear grasp of available assessment instruments, what information they give and particularly what task the children seem to believe they are being set by them. Taken by and large these are of most use in testing hypotheses rather than generating curriculum ideas. As a result of her observation the teacher may decide that, if the task is set in this way, the child will be able to learn it, if in another he will not. A test can often be used as a convenient 'mini-situation' to check out such an hypothesis. Tests can also be useful as a way of monitoring the progress of children over time — so long as they then do not begin to dictate the content of the curriculum.

The next step is choosing the appropriate curriculum goals. It is the teacher's responsibility to maintain a whole set of balances. There must be a balance between different parts of the curriculum. There are, for example, those things the child must know, those we want to ensure he has experienced, and those that we just want to enjoy being part of in our own way. Each child has a right to a balance of these each day. Again there is a balance of progress and feedback of that progress. Having stated the goals and objections to be considered, the next step is observation. We must evaluate those observations and decide where modifications need to be made. Sometimes these will be to aspirations, sometimes to methods or contexts of teaching, sometimes to auxiliary matters like sight and vision aids, sometimes to assessment methods that are not sensitive enough. Modifications may be made to aspirations — gladly to enlarge them, very reluctantly to reduce them.

Internalisation of this process of observation, assessment, teaching, recording, evaluation will produce the sense of relaxation and availability of time that is essential for empathy to grow. The process will be helped, not hindered by close association with parents. On an ethical level the child is their responsibility. They have the care of him for far longer than we do. He is part of their lives. The teacher should take care to find out what sort of an individual they want to have as their son or daughter. This is not the place to join the current debate about how far parents 'own' children, certainly up to age 16, but even at a simple level it is clearly not a good idea to encourage children to do things we know their parents do not agree with or behave in ways their parents will not understand or approve of.

This also extends to other teachers. Teachers are all part of the school community. They must reach a common understanding on agreed behaviours. In this they are no different from their mainstream colleagues. Rutter (1979) in 15,000 hours and more recently HMI (1984) and Hargreaves (1984) have pointed to the importance of agreed and consistent approaches to children across a whole staff. In a special school, because of the closed nature of the institution, it is the responsibility of each teacher to ensure that that is the highest common factor not the lowest common multiple! Staff should never collude at bad practice or lack of professionalism in a colleague. The dangers of this are clear in Oswin's description of 'Ward 7' (Booth and Statham 1982). If we refrain from saying anything so as not to upset good relationships we either have no real confidence in those relationships or else we value them more than our responsibility to the children.

This is particularly so where general social behaviour is concerned. We make great use in special schools of developmental models. We think often in terms of developmental age either overall or in a given area of functioning. We must ensure that the implications of this are known to all those who come into contact with the child. We ourselves must also remember it when we see the child outside the strict learning context. It will affect the way they eat, react to others, understand interactions, conceive of time, can delay gratification, respond to frustration, etc. Just going back and watching babies and nursery school children is a very valuable in-service activity. Having in mind what is reasonable to expect from a child in sheer human terms can be most profitable. It results in not expecting table-manners, 'waiting behaviour', or being 'grown-up' when such features are not yet within the child's grasp. Work towards them, of course, but to be censorious and punitive when the child does not manifest them is clearly unreasonable. This may seem obvious, but I have regularly observed scenes in dining halls, particularly, where demands made on children were, by any standards, completely inappropriate. Again I reflect this back to personal experience. An upsetting lunchtime can mar the rest of the day. Feeling that important people don't understand us can make even going to work a very stressful experience. So it is also for the children.

If all this sounds complicated — it is. These are the special skills for which we justify removal of children from mainstream schools. To remove them and then not to offer these skills is inexcusable. However, most do enjoy the work. Many would work nowhere else. They are stretched, but acknowledged and fulfilled. To be conscious of a danger is 90 per cent of the way towards avoiding it.

Thus we see the teacher as a skilled professional — but more than just skilled. It is no use just producing better and better checklists, finer and finer gradations. Massive strides have been made by action research projects at such establishments as the Hester Adrian Research Centre, Thomas Coram Unit and the like. However there was life before EDY, and there is life beyond EDY. What schools need to develop on the foundation given by these methodologies is change management. Assessment based on observation means that the teacher must be able to observe her children at all times. She needs to develop an ability to see the essentials of what a child is doing, to spot the time scale within which variation takes place, to observe which of his sensory functions are operational, at what percentage level, which motor systems are showing greatest co-ordination, what effort the child seems capable of. Sylva, Roy and Painter (1980), in the Oxford project, have produced a clear exposition of the techniques involved.

She must also be able to make more formal assessments from time to time — preferably to validate hypotheses generated from the observations rather than to produce answers — and this means knowing what demands the assessment will make of this child and how he will see the interpersonal situation created. All this must be recorded. Recording child behaviour is one of the most vital activities carried out by classroom personnel. In addition there should be some sort of informal, ongoing record system that any adult can add to whenever something significant occurs. There should also be a readily available indication of the current place in the curriculum held by each child and what behaviours and reactions can and should be demanded of him. With this will be a direct statement of his priority teaching targets and objectives. It is the teacher's job to see that this information is communicated to others. The scale post holder responsible for the team she is in will monitor not only that it is being done but what facilities and materials are necessary to make sure that it can be done efficiently.

Effecting plans then becomes a natural interaction composed of a variety of methods, modulated according to the situation available. Monitoring and evaluation are wider skills — best thought of as in relation to some goal. The curriculum philosophy should indicate what that goal might be. The life chances of the child in relation to his background, environment and predispositions must be a powerful source of direction. 'Learning Together' suggests three major points of evaluation, the 1981 Act demands a yearly review. Understanding the implications of what is decided at these assessment points and then articulating the new sense of direction are major classroom tasks. All this gives a very clear answer to the question, 'What are the child's special educational needs and how are they to be met?' An indication of the likely answer was given in the child's statement. The school has a duty to clarify it annually at the review. Assessment-based teaching means that an up-to-date answer is always available.

The Classroom Assistant

The role of the classroom assistant stems from the role of the teacher in a continuum. The relationship is often a complex one. The term nursery nurse used to be used, and, indeed, many classroom assistants have NNEB training. The term is unfortunate. Most of the pupils are not in a nursery, nor do they need a great deal of nursing as they are not ill. However, the salary scale, union membership and often quite extensive personal experience of some classroom assistants makes for difficulties that should not exist. There is no rational excuse for having 'nursery nurse' as the designation of an adult in a unit for 16–19-year-olds, who quite happily attend a youth club and goes to the local college of further education. The role of the classroom assistant is to help to put into effect what the teacher decides is right for the children.

Naturally there will be consultation between them but the teacher has the professional responsibility, so ultimately she must be accountable for any judgement that is made. This is captured in the best room management systems where focus and limits of any role are clearly defined and delineated. It is lost in situations where, while the teacher is teaching, the classroom assistant 'has the rest'. It is also lost if particular roles are permanently performed by one individual. To perform a role with a child gives a much clearer picture of the child's response to it than just hearing about it from others. Status comes from responsibility for decisions, not from carrying them out. A difficulty with rotating roles, however, is their appearance to the children. If, however, the caring principle enunciated earlier is followed, then each role can be seen by the children as another manifestation of care.

Care staff in general, whether qualified or unqualified, must be an integral part of the school's in-house, in-service training. They need to know why teachers want to do things a particular way, they need to know where their observations of the children can be of value. The teacher must show her respect, both for them and for their expertise. Their position must not be undermined by contradiction or criticism in front of the children. For the care staff themselves, caring must never become a routinised, starched nursing duty. It is one human being helping another less able human being have a more enjoyable life. The main impact of this statement comes at times that are crucial for all of us — meal times, toileting and bedtime. It is not easy to help a profoundly retarded, multiply handicapped child with bad teeth and a poor lip closure to feed day after day and not want to 'get it over with' or relieve the boredom and possible distaste by talking to the nearest adult. However, if we know it is not easy, it is poor management that has the same person doing it all the time. It is very noticeable to an outside observer how the behaviour of even very damaged children changes in relation to the attention levels of the adults around them. A mother is guided in her interactions with her young child by the child — professional carers must use their professionalism, and their work must be organised in a way that allows them to do so.

In large measure the child-care staff condition the emotional dimension in the class. Their interactions with each other and the teacher provide a powerful model for the children: the way they do their work is as important as what they do. For them, more than any others in the school the quality of their work is of paramount importance.

Conclusion

What has been described is a very complex system of interactions between individuals. The formal structure of this system has developed by analogy and accretion and is only one of a range of possible systems. It is, to a very large extent, an internally autonomous system. Quite clearly the quality of co-operation within that system is of vital importance. Laslett (1977) has suggested that the effectiveness of intra-staff or interdisciplinary co-operation depends on a realistic appraisal by each individual of what other individuals are able to contribute. Both giving and asking advice should be seen as positive attributes, as should the more difficult behaviour of taking advice! The word 'critique' should enter the staff's vocabulary to replace the word 'criticism'. The forming of relationships is one of the most important activities that children have to learn and develop.

Effective and sustained work with children with severe learning difficulties can be emotionally demanding, and for those staff who make major contributions the need for counsel and support can be very real. Such support may come from the head, but it can equally well be a mutual thing where the staff seek to develop co-operative and supportive attitudes to each other for the right issues. All involved are responsible for ensuring that schools do not become insular in their autonomy.

They can use one particular outside reference group — the

parents. As 'Learning Together' and the 1981 Act (DES 1981) suggest, parents should have a much more detailed control over their child's curriculum. As they are brought structurally into planning, evaluating and observing their child's progress, we will see the need to consult them in detailed terms of how we handle their child and how that compares with the way they handle him and with what results. We will also see our role as facilitating that child to become the adult that they would have him be and with whom they may have to spend the rest of their lives. We can but approach the task with a very healthy humility.

Our society will not pay the price for a fully integrated cradle-to-grave provision for people with major impairments. It expects parents to cope from birth to two-three years, for nearly half of each year until 16 or 19 years (holidays and weekends) and then to whatever. We have the child for, on average five to seven years out of his life. The resources at our disposal during this time are legion compared with what is offered to parents. If, during that time, we do not focus on the child and his good to the exclusion of all else, then we cannot in any sense be said to be 'bridging the gap'.

References

Booth, T. and Statham, J. (eds.). (1982) *The Nature of Special Education.* Croom Helm.

Burnham, P.S. (1968) B. Allen (ed.). *Headship in the 70s.* Blackwell.

Coulson, A. and Cox, M. (1975) 'What do deputies do?' *Education, 3-13*, 3, pp. 100-3.

Coulson, A.A. (1980) 'The role of the primary head', in T. Bush, R. Slatley, J. Goodey and C.C. Riches (eds.). *Approaches to School Management.* Harper and Row.

DES (1977) 'A new partnership for our schools' (the Taylor Report). HMSO.

DES (1978) *Special Educational Needs.* Report of the Committee of Enquiry into the Education of Handicapped Children and Young People (The Warnock Report). HMSO.

DES (1979) 'Local Authority Arrangements for the School Curriculum: a report on the Circular 14/77 Review'. HMSO.

DES (1981) *Education Act 1981*: Circular 8/81. DES.

DES (1983a) *HM Inspectors Today: standards in education.* (Report of the Rayner Committee). HMSO.

DES (1983b) *Assessments and Statements of Special Educational Needs.* Circular 1/83. DES.

Hargreaves, D. (1984) *Improving Secondary Schools.* ILEA.

HMI (1984) *Slow learning and less successful pupils in secondary schools.* DES.

Hoyle, E. (1969) *The Role of the Teacher.* Routledge and Kegan Paul.

Hughes, M.G. (1977) 'Consensus and conflict about the role of the secondary school head'. *Jnl of Educational Studies*, 25.

Laslett, R. (1977) 'Disruptive and violent pupils: the facts and the fallacies'. *Educational Review, 29*, June 1977, pp. 152-62.

Martin, P.J. (1979) 'Decision making in primary schools'. *Research in Education, 21*, May 1979, pp. 79-92.

NAHT (1985) *Staff Development and Appraisal*, NAHT.

Packwood (1983) 'Helping the Amateurs in a Professional World'. *Education, 162*, no. 5, 28 July 1983, pp. 86-87.

Richardson, E. (1975) *Authority and Organization in the Secondary School.* Macmillan.

Rogers, C. (1967) *On Becoming a Person.* Constable.

Rutter, M.C. (1979) *Fifteen Thousand Hours.* Open Books.

Sylva, K., Roy, C. and Painter, M. (1980) *Childwatching at Playgroup and Nursery School.* Grant McIntyre.

Rutter, M., Maughan, B., Mortimore, P. and Ouston, J. (1979) *Fifteen Thousand Hours.* Open Books.

TES (1984) Various letters and articles and replies e.g. 27 July p. 40, 14 September p. 5.

Watts, J.W. (1980) *Towards an Open School.* Longman.

Weber, M. (1947) *The Theory of Social and Economic Organization.* Oxford University Press.

Wilson, M. (1980) *The Education of Disturbed Pupils.* Methuen.

THE ROLE OF LINKED AGENCIES

THE EDUCATIONAL PSYCHOLOGIST

Peter Farrell

In writing about the role of educational psychologists and their work with children with severe learning difficulties, it is necessary to set it in the context of psychologists' wider roles in Local Education Authorities, their training and the numbers currently working in the United Kingdom.

The last 14 years have seen a considerable growth in the number of educational psychologists, in the variety of roles they are expected to perform and in the range of skills they have to possess. This growth was sparked off by the publication of the Summerfield Report in 1968 (DES 1968) which recognised the need for psychologists to emerge from child guidance settings and develop a more effective service to schools. A ratio of one educational psychologist to every 10,000 school children was recommended. The early 1970s saw the incorporation of the junior training centres into education, a change in the role of the school health service in relation to special education, the development of a variety of new facilities in social service settings, the reorganisation of local government and, in 1975, the introduction of new procedures for assessment and placement of children in special schools. All these changes increased the demands on psychologists' expertise and time and resulted in a considerable growth in the number of educational psychologists from about 300 in England and Wales in 1968 to around 900 in 1978. The Warnock Report (DES 1978) recognised these developments and recommended that there should be a ratio of one educational psychologist to 5,000 children aged 0-19. Since then, financial cutbacks in LEAs have restricted the growth in the number of educational psychologists to around 1,100 in 1984, so that only a tiny minority of LEAs have reached the ratio recommended by Warnock.

In order to become qualified, an educational psychologist needs to possess an honours degree in psychology, or its equivalent, teacher training, at least two years' teaching experience and a one-year professional training course in educational psychology, which is usually at a masters degree level. An educational psychologist is trained to assess children aged 0-19 years who may display learning and/or behaviour problems and to give advice on their management. This assessment may be conducted in schools, homes, clinics, hospitals or social services settings. The range of advice offered can vary from recommendations for a change of school to the drawing-up of a detailed programme to overcome learning or behaviour problems. Psychologists may also undertake direct treatment of children themselves, usually adopting some form of counselling procedure depending on the needs of the case. Frequently psychologists will consult with colleagues from social service departments, and consequently they need to become experts in the way these services operate as well as the organisation of LEAs. In addition to working with individual children, educational psychologists run courses and workshops for teachers, social workers, parents and other professionals. They may also help schools to plan organisational changes and they may advise local authorities on how the needs of children with problems are being met. In order to keep abreast of developments in a rapidly changing field, they need to keep up to date with and inform others of current research and new techniques in assessment, treatment and programme-planning.

An LEA psychological service is headed by a principal educational psychologist who, in addition to having overall responsibility for running the service, is also involved with senior officers in policy and planning for children with special educational needs. Large authorities generally have a few senior psychologists who are each responsible for a different geographical area. Basic grade educational psychologists may therefore be responsible to a senior educational psychologist and through him or her to a principal. In their day-to-day work they generally cover an area of a county or a city, thus ensuring that ordinary and special schools relate to one psychologist only, and therefore a co-ordinated and consistent service can be provided. A few LEAs have appointed educational psychologists, sometimes at a senior level, to work with particular client groups, including children with severe learning difficulties; however, such appointments are the exception rather than the norm. There is no standard and prescribed format as to how educational psychology services should be run, and it is left to each service to make its own decisions as to how to divide educational psychologists' time between the many client groups for whom the service is responsible.

Psychological services in LEAs offer many things to many people. The work that a given educational psychologist may provide for children with severe learning difficulties has to be viewed in the context of his or her generic role and training and in relation to the number of educational psychologists working in the local authority. In a few LEAs an educational psychologist may be able to visit a school for children with severe learning difficulties for one session per week, while in other, less well-staffed LEAs he or she may only be able to visit when requested to do so, or to carry out the statutory reviews under the 1981 Education Act.

Role of Educational Psychologists With Children With Severe Learning Difficulties

Assessment

Ever since mentally handicapped children came under the umbrella of the education services, educational psychologists have had a key role in their assessment and placement. The 1981 Education Act has formalised the educational psychologists' role in this process, although in certain cases clinical psychologists undertake the assessment of pre-school children who are referred to hospital settings. However, it is the educational psychologist who has to co-ordinate the psychological 'advice' on such children and make the appropriate recommendations to the LEA (DES 1981). Having a detailed knowledge of the resources in the local authority, they are well placed to recommend the most suitable facility to meet the needs of children with severe learning difficulties. In addition to assessing children for placement, educational psychologists are also involved in the statutory review of children during the year in which they become $13\frac{1}{2}$. Furthermore, they may be asked to assess and review children at other stages in their education, particularly if alternative schools are being considered.

The techniques that an educational psychologist might use when assessing a child with severe learning difficulties will partly depend on the questions being asked and on the amount and quality of the available background information. If the child is of pre-school age and little is known about him or her, and the question of the child's schooling is being considered, it is likely that the psychologist will ask the parents and the staff who know the child well to complete a development chart. In addition, the child's play might be assessed through carefully observing him or her 'playing' with a variety of different materials. If the child is able to respond to conventional testing, it is possible that the psychologist will ask him or her to attempt language, copying and perceptual motor items from a variety of psychometric instruments. All the assessment findings taken together will provide basic information concerning the child's development in a number of important areas: language — expressive and receptive; motor skills — gross and fine; and self-help and independence skills. The assessment will not be sufficient to plan a detailed teaching programme, but it should give pointers as to the appropriate school for the child.

A psychologist may use different techniques when reviewing a child who is already in a school for children with severe learning difficulties, but who is presenting particular learning problems. In this case the psychologist is usually being asked to help to unravel the learning difficulty and contribute to the planning of an alternative programme of work. In this instance, it is likely that the staff will know the child very well, and completing developmental charts is unlikely to be particularly helpful. Consequently a psychologist might use a more sophisticated assessment technique, like the Uzgiris and Hunt Scales or the Behaviour Assessment Battery, as these are more prescriptive and may answer the questions concerning the child's failure to make progress. Alternatively, the child may be re-assessed on the school's curriculum to see if the objectives chosen for him or her are appropriate; if they are not, alternative objectives might be chosen and a teaching programme drawn up. This would be closely monitored, and if the child continued to fail to make progress, then a further revision of the programme would be required — and hence assessment and teaching would go hand-in-hand.

This brief summary of assessment techniques in mental handicap illustrates how important it is for the psychologist to work closely with all staff and the parents in order for the assessment to be useful. Gone are the days when the psychologist disappeared with the child into a separate room and assessed him or her with an IQ test. The interactive nature of assessment that is prevalent today means that the psychologist becomes one of a number of specialists, including the parents, and all have something to contribute to the assessment and programme planning. Indeed, as educational psychologists are busy people, and as the majority of the assessment techniques are open to all professionals to use, the psychologist's specialist skills may not be needed in a great many cases, except when decisions about schooling are being made or when the child is presenting particular difficulties. For an up-to-date review of the range of assessment techniques that are available, their theoretical background and new approaches which are developing, readers are referred to Hogg and Raynes (1986).

As a result of a multidisciplinary assessment of a young child who has severe learning difficulties involving at least a doctor, a teacher, the parents, as well as an educational psychologist, a statement of his or her special educational needs will almost certainly be made and in the vast majority of cases this will include a recommendation for a school for children with severe learning difficulties. Other options that are available in a few LEAs are units in ordinary schools or full time placement in an ordinary class with support from specialist teachers.

However, some children may be thought to be suitable for schools for children with moderate learning difficulties. In the mid-1970s most educational psychologists considered that children with IQs less than 50 should go to the old ESN(S) schools and children with IQs between 50 and 70 should to to ESN(M) schools. However, the Warnock Report and subsequent legislation stressed the importance of looking at the special educational needs of the child and of matching these to the curriculum offered at the special schools and facilities available. Consequently, the criteria which currently determine whether a child is recommended for a school for children with moderate or severe learning difficulties is dependent upon the curriculum and teaching methods which operate in each school and on whether these can meet his or her assessed special educational needs.

It follows that a full assessment of the child which leads to appropriate recommendations being made must inevitably include an assessment of the setting in which the child will be placed. In addition, educational psychologists should assess other settings in which the child functions including the home, school or nursery and community. All of these environments play an important part in contributing to the child's future welfare.

The formal assessment of all children with special educational needs at 13+ came about as a result of the 1981 Education Act and is primarily intended to be a focus for planning for the child's final years in special education before reaching adulthood. Inevitably the educational psychologist's role in the assessment of children with severe learning difficulties at this age is much less crucial, as the teachers know the child well and hopefully progress is being made, particularly if the school's on-going assessment is based on an evaluation of the child's progress in the curriculum. Consequently the educational psychologists' role is one of co-ordinating developmental information on the child, of undertaking more detailed individual assessment if this information is not complete, of discussing the child's progress with the relevant agencies and of confirming that existing programmes of work are meeting the child's needs.

In-service Education

In the past few years educational psychologists have increased their input to INSET considerably, particularly in the area of children with severe learning difficulties. Initially, following the amalgamation of the old junior training centres into education, psychologists ran many courses on assessment and intervention in mental handicap. However, the EDY course (see Foxen and McBrien 1981; McBrien and Foxen 1981) contributed to a considerable increase in psychologists' involvement in INSET work. Following the dissemination of the EDY Workshop to educational psychologists in the United Kingdom, many have run and are still running EDY courses in various local authorities (Boucher and Feiler 1982; Cocks and Gardner 1978; Farrell 1985). In some areas the position has now been reached where staff in schools have been trained as EDY instructors, and they now organise their own training with little or no help from educational psychologists. In addition to EDY work, educational psychologists have also run goal-planning courses (Bowdler and Collier 1982) and courses on classroom management techniques, many using the model outlined by Thomas (1985). Others (e.g. Presland 1981) give accounts of courses in managing behaviour problems in schools for children with severe learning difficulties, and indeed this is still a priority area for INSET. The contribution which an educational psychologist can give to INSET varies considerably throughout the United Kingdom, depending very much on the availability of psychologists and on their particular interest and expertise.

The Curriculum for Children with Severe Learning Difficulties

The recent interest in writing objectives-based curricula, mainly instigated in the United Kingdom by Ainscow and Tweddle (1979), has meant that many schools have adopted this approach. Some educational psychologists have run curriculum-planning workshops (Gardner and Judson 1982) and many more have advised schools on this approach, often joining in working groups within schools. Burman, Farrell, Feiler, Heffernan, Mittler and Reason (1983) and Cameron (1981; 1982a) have written papers which look at the whole area of planning curricula using objectives-based approaches. The development of objectives-based curricula in schools for children with severe learning difficulties has implications for the development of individual educational programmes, for assessment and for recording children's progress. Educational psychologists have a part to play helping schools formulate realistic programmes for children, recording progress simply but clearly and reporting to parents in an accurate and constructive way.

Children Who Present Management Problems

Frequently educational psychologists are asked to advise staff on the management of individual children who are presenting a behaviour problem. This may involve counselling the staff or the parents or planning a detailed behavioural programme and monitoring its progress. In addition some schools for children with severe learning difficulties have developed units for behaviourally disturbed children. Educational psychologists can be of help in planning for these units, in clarifying their objectives, in ensuring that the criteria for children's admission and discharge are fully discussed, in advising on staffing levels, on management strategies, on taking baselines and on evaluating progress. Some guidelines on the use of 'time out' rooms have recently been published (Farrell 1984).

General Advisory Work

An educational psychologist who visits a school for children with severe learning difficulties on a regular basis hopefully gets to know the staff well and can offer general support and encouragement to all who work there. In addition there will always be new developments and innovations, such as the development of microtechnology — where psychologists are in a position to advise on the appropriate use of computers in schools — and the advent of the 1981 Education Act — where educational psychologists can interpret and explain procedures and help facilitate their smooth operation.

Work With Parents

Like all professionals who work with handicapped children, educational psychologists realise the importance of involving parents to the full in their children's education. A working party of psychologists and social workers in Manchester has recently published a booklet which summarises good practice in involving parents of children with special educational needs in their education (Burman *et al.*, 1984). Many professionals have run parent workshops (e.g. Moore, Nikolski and Presland 1981; Bevington, Gardner and Cocks 1978). The literature is voluminous on this subject. In addition, many educational psychologists have been closely connected with Portage work (Cameron 1982b; Dessent 1984), and some LEAs have appointed educational psychologists to monitor and supervise Portage projects. Recent examples exist where parents are becoming actively involved in working jointly with a school to plan educational programmes for their children; hopefully this development will continue where psychologists and others can make their contribution.

Conclusion

In concluding this short section, two unrelated points should be made which are directly related to the contribution psychologists can make to work with children with severe learning difficulties. Firstly, the effect of the 1981 Act on the role of educational psychologists in general has had an inevitable influence on their role in schools for children with severe learning difficulties. The assessment procedures that are now in use are more complex and take longer to complete than they did previously. Consequently, some psychological services have reduced the time psychologists can give to special schools in order to provide extra time to complete the section five assessments of children in the mainstream sector. This means that psychologists may have less time to spend on INSET or general advisory work, particularly as the statutory 13+ reviews have to assume a high priority. Secondly, the considerable

increase in knowledge and skills in the last ten years of professionals who work with mentally handicapped children, and which may, in part, be attributable to the work of educational psychologists, has meant that several schools have reached a level of expertise where support from a psychologist as described above (other than that mandated under the 1981 Act) is hardly necessary. However, even in these schools there is a valuable role for psychologists in keeping the staff informed about recent research and helping them to develop and extend their curriculum, so as to take account of new advances in child development. Other schools, however may still require a great deal of support for some years to come. Part of an educational psychologist's skill is to assess accurately the needs and requirements of the special schools to which he or she is assigned, and to give help accordingly.

References

Ainscow, M. and Tweddle, D.A. (1979) *Preventing Classroom Failure.* Wiley.
Bevington, P., Gardner, J.M. and Cocks, R.P. (1978) 'An approach to the planning and evaluation of a parental involvement course'. *Child: Care, Health and Development. 4*, pp. 217-27.
Boucher, J. and Feiler, A. (1982) 'Training teachers of children with severe learning difficulties. *A.E.P. Jnl, 5*, (8), pp. 37-40.
Bowdler, D. and Collier, D. (1982) 'Kermit the Goal Planner'. *Newsletter of the Division of Education and Child Psychology*, No. 9, pp. 21-3.
Burman, L., Farrell, P.T., Feiler, A., Heffernan, M., Mittler, H. and Reason, R. (1983) 'Redesigning the School Curriculum'. *Special Education: Forward Trends, 10* (2), pp. 33-6.
Burman, L., Farrell, P.T., Feiler, A., Heffernan, M., Mittler, H., and Reason, R. (1984) *Parental Involvement in Special Education: report of a questionnaire 1981-82.* City of Manchester Schools Psychological and Child Guidance Service.
Cameron, R.J. (1981) 'Curriculum development I: clarifying and planning curriculum objectives'. *Remedial Education, 16*, (4), pp. 102-8.
Cameron, R.J. (1982a) 'Curriculum, development II: teaching and evaluating curriculum objectives'. *Remedial Education, 17*, (3).
Cameron, R.J. (ed.). (1982b) *Working Together. Portage in the UK.* NFER-Nelson.
Cocks, R.P., and Garner, J.M. (1978) 'The role of the educational psychologist in the education of severely subnormal children'. *A.E.P. Jnl, 4* (2), pp- 13-20.
DES (1968) *Psychologists in Educational Services* (The Summerfield Report) HMSO.
DES (1978) *Special Educational Needs.* Report of the Committee of Enquiry into the Education of Handicapped Children and Young People. (The Warnock Report) HMSO.
DES (1981) Education Act 1981. Circular 8/81. HMSO.

Dessent, T.A. (ed.). (1984) *What is Important about Portage.* NFER-Nelson.
Farrell, P.T. (1984) 'Guidelines for professionals who use time out procedures with children who have special educational needs'. *Newsletter of the Division of Education and Child Psychology*, No. 13, pp. 14-15.
Farrell, P.T. (ed.). (1985) *EDY Its Impact on Staff Training in Mental Handicap.* Manchester University Press.
Foxen, T. and McBrien, J. (1981) *Trainee Workbook.* Manchester University Press.
Gardner, J. and Judson, S. (1982) 'Curriculum planning for the handicapped', in R.J. Cameron (ed.). *Working Together, Portage in the UK.* NFER-Nelson.
Hogg, J. and Raynes, N. (eds.). (1986) *Assessment in Mental Handicap: a guide to tests, batteries and checklists.* Croom Helm.
McBrien, J. and Foxen, T. (1981) *Instructor's Handbook.* Manchester University Press.
Moore, S., Nikolski, I. and Presland, J. (1981) 'A workshop for parents of young handicapped children'. *A.E.P. Jnl, 5* (5), pp. 40-4.
Presland, J. (1981) 'Behaviour Modification in ESN(S) Schools'. *Occasional Papers of the Division of Education and Child Psychology, 5* (2), pp. 25-33.
Thomas, M. (1985) 'An Introduction to Classroom Management', in P.T. Farrell (ed.). *EDY Its Impact on Staff Training in Mental Handicap.* Manchester University Press.

THE SPEECH THERAPIST

Sue Roulstone

Speech therapy services have become an established part of the educational service for pupils with severe learning difficulties, although the extent of the contribution varies considerably from one district to another. Reporting on speech therapy services in 1972, the Quirk committee recommended that development of provision for the mentally handicapped population should be a service priority (DES 1972), and since then, the commitment to schools for children with severe learning difficulties has gradually increased. A recent survey of speech therapy provision for mentally handicapped people concluded that Quirk's recommendations had indeed been acted upon, but that provision was patchy. The number of sessions provided weekly to ESN(S) schools ranged from 0.04 to 10.0; that is, one school may be serviced by a speech therapist on a full-time basis whereas another may receive less than one visit a month (McCartney, Kellett and Warner 1984). Differences in staffing levels are undoubtedly responsible for some of this variation, but it must also be due in part to differing perceptions of speech therapy service priorities and of the role of the speech therapist in such educational settings. It is also important to point out that speech therapists are employed by the National Health Service and not by Education Authorities and that organisation of speech therapy services may differ from one district to another. For example in some districts, therapists who work with individuals with severe learning difficulties are grouped under a 'mental handicap unit'. In others, they are part of a more generic community service which has developed specialities in special education.

So how can we describe a speech therapist's role? At the most fundamental level, they are trained to deal with all manner of communication disorders. The name of the profession is somewhat misleading since it implies a much narrower field than is actually covered. The initial training, now to degree level, examines in detail the development and breakdown of communication and the management of communication disorders from linguistic, psychological, social and medical viewpoints. Difficulties with language development are often cited as a defining feature of mental handicap (Snyder and McLean 1976). However, in any one school, the heterogeneous population with its variety of medical diagnoses and experiential histories will result in a complex miscellany of communication impairments. Speech therapists are in a position to assist in the assessment and analysis of the nature and severity of those difficulties and in devising and implementing intervention programmes.

Historically there seems always to have been conflict between speech therapists and teachers over the teaching of language, both regarding it as their prerogative: speech therapists have sometimes been told by schools to confine their involvement to aspects of speech and intelligibility and to leave language to the teachers; speech therapists would argue that their brief should cover all aspects of communication handicap. Such conflicts are not conducive to the development of effective working relationships and seem to be linked as much to the vested interests of both groups and attempts to 'professionalise', as to false perceptions and lack of insight into each others' areas of skill.

This gives us a broad view of a speech therapist's work, but how this is implemented on a day-to-day basis is obviously open to interpretation. The traditional way of operating has been for the therapist to withdraw children who are referred for speech therapy, assess their speech and language skills and, if appropriate, to implement a programme. The child would be returned to the classroom and recommendations made to the teacher regarding the follow-up of therapy targets. Additional information would be gathered from parents, teachers, psychologists, etc., in order to monitor and modify programmes.

Many speech therapists and teachers feel this is to be an inappropriate way of trying to tackle communication disorders in children with severe learning difficulties for a number of reasons. Firstly, even if a speech therapist works full-time in a school, it would be impossible to provide all the input needed to all the children with speech and language difficulties. For example, Leeming, Swann, Coupe and Mittler (1979) found that approximately two-thirds of children attending ESN(S) schools in Manchester and Cheshire were not using fully grammatical sentences. One-third of the pupils were at or below the level of imitating single words. Of those children who were using some speech, nearly 28 per cent were rated by teachers as being unintelligible to strangers. Most people would agree that these children require structured intervention on a daily basis, and such numbers cannot be dealt with by a lone speech therapist. Secondly, to work with children only in the seclusion of a withdrawal room inhibits the exchange of information and skills between teacher and therapist, hence making the development of an effective working relationship difficult. This is not to say that withdrawal of children is never appropriate, but that if it is the only mode of treatment used, the speech therapist's work becomes separate and isolated, rather than being an integrated part of the whole curriculum. Furthermore, an assessment conducted in a withdrawal room is unlikely to produce a representative sample of a child's communicative behaviour. Again, this is not to say that this type of assessment is not valid, only that it is inappropriate to consider it in isolation.

Withdrawal of the child not only presents problems for assessment, it also raises questions regarding the validity and effectiveness of the intervention programme. This traditional method of intervention is child-centred and assumes that the cause of the child's communications difficulties rests entirely within the child and that intervention should focus solely on the child. It fails to take account of the child's communicative environment, the demands and expectations of the child, the range of social roles open to the child and the opportunities for communication both in and out of school. For example, Mittler and Berry (1973) suggest that an adult's tendency to reinforce one-word labelling responses may be partly responsible for delay in moving to two-word utterances. If a child only ever participates in asymmetrical interactions where they are allowed only to take a respondent role, then opportunities to develop language as a social and cognitive tool will not be available. Language occurs in context as an 'instrument for regulating joint activity and joint attention' (Bruner 1975); the social functions that language serves for the child determine the semantic options they create for themselves and how these are realised structurally (Halliday 1973). So if a child is never expected or allowed to take on the role of initiator, there is unlikely to be any social or cognitive pressure to develop a 'demand' mode or the syntactical construction for questions. Following from this, the speech therapist who operates entirely in withdrawal rooms is ignoring factors in the environment which are fundamentally related to the child's success as a communicator.

Despite these factors, some therapists continue to operate along traditional lines. To some extent this may reflect varying theoretical standpoints: if one supports a child-centred view of communication difficulties, then one is more likely to view the child's performance as being the sole focus of therapy. However, it is also likely that, because it is a traditional way of operating, expectations from other professionals — and perhaps also from some quarters within the speech therapy profession — make it difficult and threatening (both for the therapist and others) to change the system. If a speech therapist works mainly in the withdrawal room and has relatively little working contact with other staff in the school, a mystique develops around their work. Strong boundaries develop between the perceived role of the speech therapist and others in the school and it can then be difficult to break away from the practices associated with that role.

It seems that a more flexible approach is needed in order to develop a role which is appropriate to the needs of the children and the school. So for individual establishments, the exact nature of the speech therapy involvement should be negotiated in the first instance and be open to change as the relationship between the school and the therapist develops. This requires a good deal of adaptability from both parties. The speech therapist's role could therefore be seen as a resource for the school. It has been suggested elsewhere that a 'resource' model for speech therapy involvement in schools for children with severe learning difficulties has three components: consultant and skills transmitter; co-ordinator; participant in the school (Roulstone 1983) The next section will look at these three components in more detail, expanding on the possible interpretations of each and on the resources which the speech therapist can bring to each aspect.

Consultant and Skills Transmitter

Tomlinson has suggested that professionals are guilty of defining the needs of their clients for them. 'Professionals generally claim to know better than others the nature of certain matters and to know better than their clients what ails them or their affairs (Tomlinson 1981). The resource model, while still seeking to offer 'expert' advice through a consultative approach, would aim to offer a service that was more responsive to the demands of their clients. The suggestions made by the Warnock committee regarding a possible brief for resource centres can perhaps be applied to speech therapy and the area of communication disorders. These centres were to be places of specialist expertise and research, used for curriculum development, in-service education, as advisory centres for parents and other professionals and as libraries for specialised equipment (DES 1978; para 8.13).

In terms of speech therapy then, the service may be providing input to initial teacher training or be involved in workshops at individual schools on topics related to language development, speech and language problems and intervention strategies, orofacial movement and feeding mechanisms and so on. As individuals from training backgrounds that are different to those of teachers, speech therapists will inevitably have a view of language that is slightly different to a teacher's; but rather than being a cause of conflict, this can be used in the development of curriculum content, to stimulate discussion and to bring different ideas to the assessment stage and to subsequent programme planning.

Since such large numbers of these children have difficulties in the area of language and communication, it would seem reasonable to include the speech therapist right from the start. In a consultative capacity the speech therapist should be part of the team assessment of every child who enters the school. Subsequent involvement might then fall somewhere on a continuum from offering general advice, supporting the annual review system now required by the 1981 Education Act, to providing more specific information and intervention according to the individual child and the problems involved in developing appropriate individual programmes.

The initial stage in providing an appropriate programme for a child is to try to establish their current level of functioning, through a thorough assessment of their speech and language skills. For some children, this will be a relatively straightforward process where a child can be slotted into the appropriate stage in the school's curriculum or into a scheme such as the Derbyshire Language Scheme (Knowles and Masidlover 1979). For others, a more detailed description will be necessary so that strengths and needs can be identified and individual target behaviours planned. The speech therapist's resources can be tapped here to help analyse the child's difficulties and to choose appropriate methods of assessment.

Although standardised assessments such as the Reynell Developmental Language Scales (RDLS) (Reynell 1977) are still used to assess children's language, evidence from the field of psycholinguistics suggests that, used on their own, they are unlikely to produce a valid picture of the child's capabilities. It is generally argued that language, being complex, occurring in context, does not easily lend itself to standardised assessment. As Muma comments (Muma 1983), there is a certain irony in the fact that:

> Specialists in learning disability and some traditionally oriented speech-language pathologists claim to have competencies in language, yet they unwittingly violate a fundamental aspect of language by reducing it to simple irrelevant dimensions in clinical assessments.

The problem becomes acute when dealing with children with severe learning difficulties since few standardised assessments are designed for these individuals. For example, using the English Picture Vocabulary Test, Leeming *et al.* (1979) found that in the ESN(S) schools of their sample, nearly 30 per cent of the children were untestable, either because they were physically unable to point or because they lacked the skills necessary to link pictures and words or to make a choice. Assessments such as the RDLS or the Symbolic Play Test (SPT) (Lowe and Costello 1976) are designed to be more attractive to and appropriate for a lower age range although the results are less reliable at the lower (and upper) limits of a test. These assessments are used by speech therapists in other clinical contexts but most would feel them to be less appropriate for children with severe learning difficulties. As standardised tests, they provide normative data on a child's verbal comprehension and expressive language (RDLS) and on the child's play level (SPT), showing how they function relative to their peers in the standardisation population. Since, by this stage in the educational process it will already be clear that the children do not compare favourably with their peers in mainstream education, it becomes more important to describe their language and associated skills than to produce normative data in order to develop appropriate programmes. Both assessments also yield useful qualitative data of course, but it must be remembered that, as with all standardised assessments, only a small sample of behaviour and only a few aspects of the area of skill/behaviour are being assessed. Furthermore these assessments do not examine a child's communication behaviour in an interactive context.

So, rather than relying only on the standardised assessments, it is necessary to sample a child's communicative skills across a range of physical contexts and with a number of communicative partners. The speech therapist can advise on the areas which may need further investigation, on the types of samples which might yield useful information and can help with the analysis and interpretation of data. Based on their knowledge of psycholinguistics, some therapists may have developed their own methods of analysis. Most therapists however, rely on procedures developed by linguists and psychologists which are usually based on patterns of normal cognitive and communicative development.

At the bottom end of the developmental ladder, a speech therapist can assist in the assessment of those behaviours and stages of development which are precursory to language, such as attention, object permanence and the early object-related schemas such as mouthing, banging, dropping, etc. The communicative functions proposed by Halliday (1975) can be used as a framework to examine the functional range of a child's communicative attempts even before first words appear. Once a child is beginning to communicate verbally, then other linguistic analyses can be used. For example, the 'Language Assessment and Remediation Screening Procedure' (Crystal, Fletcher and Garman 1976) commonly known as 'LARSP', provides a framework for the analysis of a child's (or adult's) grammar. The procedure has provided a much needed structure to therapists' assessment of spontaneous speech and to programme planning. Unfortunately, the use of LARSP has sometimes led to an emphasis on grammatical structures to the exclusion of more functional aspects of language and communication. If, as Mahoney suggests 'the set goal of language is never a specific linguistic structure. Rather, linguistic structure is a means for achieving the set goal of efficient communication' (Mahoney 1975), then one needs to look not just at grammar, but at its relation to the meanings being expressed, and to the use of language by the child. Procedures following LARSP have made steps towards this by extending the profiling procedure to other areas such as semantics (PRISM) and phonology (PROPH and PROP) (Crystal 1982), although these are not linked to a developmental order as is LARSP.

Another procedure being used by speech therapists is that proposed by Bloom and Lahey (1978). In a similar way to the Crystal profiles, the Bloom and Lahey procedure gives a framework for the analysis of a child's language, examining this time the developing semantic-syntactical relationship in the child's utterances. Unlike standardised assessments, the profiles that result from the above procedures provide a direct link through to intervention targets. The profiles are not mutually exclusive, and a combination may be needed in order to gain a clear view of a child's communicative skills. It may be that one proves more useful than another with different types or severity of communication problems. For example, in the writer's view, the Bloom and Lahey procedure provides a particularly useful framework for the development of first meanings in a child both from expressive and receptive viewpoints.

The above discussion has focused on only a small number of procedures used by speech therapists; they would also be able to help in the assessment of orofacial structure and function, with respect to feeding skills and drooling as well as articulation, in the analysis of a child's phonology (i.e. their sound system) and those skills, such as turn-taking and topic maintenance, which could be linked under a heading of discourse analysis. Most of these assessments discussed so far centre on the child's performance, albeit some looking at naturally occurring contexts. However, by moving out of withdrawal rooms, therapists can examine and advise on ways in which everyday situations can be better utilised by members of the team to create a communicatively demanding environment. This may be in terms of modifying the language used with the children by team personnel or in terms of the social roles that the children are expected or allowed to assume.

On a day-to-day basis, speech therapists can demonstrate intervention strategies and be available for discussion and advice. They may be able to recommend useful literature, have information on communications aids, relevant resource materials etc. In a consultative capacity, the speech therapist will be concerned to extend these services to all in the school who are involved with the children and outside the school to the family and to residential placements.

Co-ordinator

As indicated earlier, the speech therapist cannot be regarded as the sole implementer of a language programme. However, Craig (1983) suggests that a speech therapist's skills in dealing with language-disordered children will promote early communicative success and that therefore they should be working closely with a child in the early stages of a programme. It is also important that speech therapists continue to work directly with the children (i.e. not becoming entirely systems oriented) in order to maintain and develop their own skills. Craig also suggests that the difficult task of planning programmes in such a complex area as language benefits from the involvement of a therapist who has a knowledge of normal and abnormal patterns of development and who has skills in analysing and modifying interactive patterns (Craig 1983). Implementing programmes and strategies within a classroom situation also needs a thorough understanding of classroom management. Many schools now have a teacher appointed as language co-ordinator, and it would seem appropriate that these two people, the speech therapist and the teacher who takes special responsibility for language, should work together to co-ordinate this very complex area of the curriculum.

Once the child's communication skills have been described and evaluated, an intervention programme can be planned jointly by the teacher and the speech therapist, in terms of the target behaviours, structured activities and the general teaching strategies. Although structured activities will be planned and implemented for individuals and for groups of children, this work will take up a relatively small part of the child's school day. In addition, various people will be interacting with the child throughout the day. If they, too, are aware of the overall targets and appropriate teaching strategies, they can use their interactions to further the teaching goals. For example, targets for a child might be the use of language in an instrumental function, to demand goods, and the use of language to cause objects or actions to recur. The structured activity within the classroom might require that a child who is building a tower or threading beads ask for 'more' bricks or beads. The 'more' can also be modelled, expected of the child and reinforced during other daily routines such as dinner time, etc., by others who work with the child in school or by the family at home. Good communications are needed by the adults involved in order to ensure a co-ordinated approach to the language intervention by all concerned.

By accepting that the consultative and/or the co-ordinator components are appropriate parts of a speech therapist's role, then one must also accept the need for regular meetings between the speech therapist and others involved with the child. Traditionally, the speech therapist has tried to snatch time with the teacher on returning a child to the class, an unsatisfactory procedure for all concerned. Regular meetings can also present organisational difficulties for schools; however, it is at such planning meetings that objectives and suitable teaching strategies can be identified, and agreed upon and where difficulties that have arisen from previous work can be discussed and hopefully resolved. Priorities on speech therapists' time can also be negotiated. For example, it may be decided that within one particular class a new approach was needed with some children. The speech therapist could commit extra time to this for a while, in order to help the class teacher through the early stages of implementation. A system within each school therefore needs to be established whereby staff members and therapists can have access to each other on a regular and organised basis in order to discuss and plan their work together. Meetings between a speech therapist and children's families also need to be organised in order to facilitate continuity of approach.

Participant

The preceding discussion has, to some extent, assumed agreement on the issue of teamwork and what it means to be part of a team. However, although the virtues of teamwork are extolled by many, the reality is often a series of interventions, separated by professional conflicts and role boundaries with little integration of the programmes carried out by the various professionals. As part of a team, speech therapists may be co-ordinators of the speech and language programmes and be implementing aspects of the programmes; they should also be aware of and implementing other aspects of the curriculum (e.g. overall behaviour management strategies, the stage of gross motor development in need of practice and reinforcement). Earlier, it was suggested that a speech therapist can observe within a classroom in order to discover ways to improve the communications environment. In fact the reverse should also be possible, whereby the speech therapist takes over a group for an activity freeing the teacher to observe the children's language and their interactions in the class. In order to become part of the team in this way, the speech therapist needs to become involved in aspects of the school's routine activities and to work not just in the classroom but in other areas around the school. Taking part in joint workshops and joint courses as suggested by the Warnock committee (DES 1978: para 16. 25-26) can foster understanding and trust between professionals, and becoming a participant in a school enables speech therapists to gain insight into the roles of other members of the team and to keep in perspective their own role and work with individual children. This, of course, has implications for the amount of input to schools from speech therapy services. The therapist who visits a school only once a month cannot hope to become a participant in routine activities or to make a lasting contribution to the curriculum.

One way of attempting to meet the needs of schools and circumvent the lack of speech therapy resources was reported first by Mattocks, Barton and Parkinson (1982) — the use of intensive rotas. The principle of this was that a team of speech therapists provided intensive input to a school for a limited period, usually one term. During this time, they helped establish language programmes for individual children, set up new projects, developed aspects of the curriculum and so on, appropriate to the school. At the end of the term, the intensive team moved on to another school and a monitoring and trouble-shooting service was left in the school being vacated. Such an approach is often greeted with mixed feelings by both speech therapists and teachers. It can be difficult for a school, both in terms of available space and in terms of forming relationships, to have a number of therapists working in a school at the same time. If only a minimal monitoring service is left behind for long periods, then this may be insufficient to deal with problems occurring in this interim period. Furthermore, although the opportunity to work with other speech therapists is both stimulating and supportive, some find that the difficulties of establishing relationships with each new set of children and staff outweigh such advantages. Other pros and cons could undoubtedly be raised, but the division of the larger area health authorities into smaller districts has meant, in many cases, that the intensive team approach has been abandoned. This re-organisation of the health authorities has meant changes for many speech therapy services and has sometimes led to a decrease in available resources. For example, within one of the now smaller districts there may be fewer therapists who have experience of working with children with severe learning difficulties than there were in the previous 'areas'. If, within one district, there are now fewer schools for children with severe learning difficulties, it also means that it is more difficult for a speech therapy department to build up the expertise of its therapists in this field. Nonetheless, some alternation and flexibility of services to schools is still a possibility; that is, extra resources could be provided on a temporary basis to establish a service or to give a therapist some experience in that field, even if such input could not be maintained permanently.

So, finally, we return again to the idea of resource, where the speech therapy service, as well as the individual therapists act as a resource to the special educational sector. The changes that are occurring in education as a result of the Education Act 1981 and within the health authorities as a result of re-organisation require that therapists remain flexible and responsive to demands from their client groups within special education. It also means that the role of the speech therapist is constantly changing in relation to children with severe learning difficulties, although the fundamental role — that of assessing and managing communication disorders — will remain.

References

Bloom, L. and Lahey, M. (1978) *Language Development and Language Disorders*. Wiley.

Bruner, J.S. (1975) 'The ontogenesis of speech acts'. *Jnl. of Child Language*, 2, pp. 1-19.

Craig, H.K. (1983) 'Applications of pragmatic language models for intervention', in T.M. Gallagher and C.A. Prutting. *Pragmatic Assessment and Intervention Issues in Language.* College Hill Press.

Crystal, D. (1982) *Profiling Linguistic Disability.* Edward Arnold.

Crystal, D., Fletcher, P. and Garman, M. (1976) *The Grammatical Analysis of Language Disability.* Edward Arnold.

DES (1972) *Speech Therapy Services* (Quirk report). HMSO.

DES (1978) *Special Educational Needs* (Warnock report). HMSO.

Halliday, M.A.K. (1975) *Learning How to Mean.* Edward Arnold.

Halliday, M.A.K. (1973) *Explorations in the Functions of Language.* Edward Arnold.

Knowles, W. and Masidlover, M. (1979) *The Derbyshire Language Scheme.* Derbyshire Education Authority.

Leeming, K., Swann, W., Coupe, J. and Mittler, P. (1979) *Teaching Language and Communication to the Mentally Handicapped.* Evans/Methuen.

Lowe, M. and Costello, A.J. (1976) *The Symbolic Play Test.* NFER.

Mahoney, G.J. (1975) 'Ethological approach to delayed language acquisition'. *Am. Jnl of Mental Deficiency, 80* (2), pp. 139-40.

Mattocks, D., Barton, L. and Parkinson, G. (1982) 'Intensive speech therapy in ESN(S) schools in Manchester'. *College of Speech Therapists Bull. 359*, pp. 10-11.

McCartney, E., Kellett, B. and Warner, J. (1984) 'Speech therapy provision for mentally handicapped people'. *College of Speech Therapists Bull. 384*, pp. 1-3.

Mittler, P. and Berry, P. (1973) 'Demanding Language', in P. Mittler (ed.). *Research to Practice in Mental Retardation*, Vol. II. University Park Press.

Muma, J.R. (1983) 'Speech-language pathology: emerging clinical expertise in language', in T.M. Gallagher and C.A. Prutting, *Pragmatic Assessment and Intervention Issues in Language.* College Hill Press.

Reynell, J.K. (1977) *The Reynell Developmental Language Scales*, revised edn. NFER.

Roulstone, S. (1983) 'Out of the broom cupboard'. *Special Education: Forward Trends, 10* (1), pp. 13-15.

Snyder, L.K. and Mclean, J.E. (1976) 'Deficient acquisition strategies: a proposed conceptual framework for analysing severe language deficiency'. *Am. Jnl. of Mental Deficiency*, (4), pp. 338-49.

Tomlinson, S. (1981) 'Professionals and ESN(M) education', in W. Swann *The Practice of Special Education.* Open University Press.

THE REMEDIAL THERAPISTS: PROFESSIONS ALLIED TO MEDICINE

Ann Grimley

Remedial therapists are professionals allied to medicine who are concerned with the child with special needs, his family and other professionals from diagnosis and throughout life. Therapists analyse problems in a child and his environment and design physical programmes and management strategies to meet determined and agreed goals set from among the whole team. While consulting with the parent, teacher or others, the therapist explains how to take into account the neurological state and motor malfunctioning in a child and will suggest starting postures for curricular activities or triggers for control or movement functions.

The practical management advice and services given may include: chest hygiene and treatment for acute or chronic productive coughs; skin care; sensorimotor therapies; soft tissue stretching; joint mobilising; deformity prevention or diminution; personal management routines to minimise difficulties in child or carer: lifting, bathing, transfer from bed to chair to car etc.; orthoptic aid and equipment use and care; social skill and leisure activity training, swimming; gym clubs; holiday activities; wheelchair assessment and training; housing and car adaptation assessment and advice; supportive counselling and direction (APCP 1984). The differing professionals assume greater or lesser input and import to the child and his family at different times in his life. Remedial therapists of some denomination or another are members of the health, education and caring teams from birth or diagnosis throughout the life of the individual with special needs.

What is Remedial Therapy?

Remedial therapies can be described as the applications of appropriate general or topical physical or behavioural actions to promote a desirable physical response, learning or behavioural change in a person. Actions may be physical, as applied to the body — for example, heat for pain relief, exercise or massage to ready the muscles for movement activities. The actions of the therapist might also be designed as a stimulus to promote response in a patient to gain self-help skills — for example, chained sequences with physical or verbal prompts applied in prescribed ways to gain self-feeding skills.

Remedial therapeutic activities may be carried out directly by a remedial therapist or indirectly through advising other persons in use of methods and equipment to meet therapeutic aims. These stated aims will be determined following appropriate assessment and problem analysis. Among aims for therapies may be:

to relieve pain;
to promote healing;
to prevent or ameliorate deformity;

to stimulate or improve function to optimum;
to improve or maintain bodily health (in client or carer);
to stimulate or to train specific developmental skills;
to improve self-awareness, required behaviours and life skills;
to rehabilitate following trauma, disease or disabling behaviours;
to provide physical aids and appliances;
to provide verbal and written instructions to other team members on progress and problems in a client;
to give advice on curriculum design and management strategies for individual and group activities.

Which Remedial Therapist For The Child With Special Needs?

Physiotherapists, remedial gymnasts and occupational therapists are the remedial therapists most commonly encountered in the pre-school and primary school health and education services. In the very early life of a child the physiotherapist has the greatest input in the assessment, advisory and clinical service delivery to a child and his family. The remedial gymnast and occupational therapist assume the role with greater input and import towards promoting leisure activities, life and behavioural skills in the older child and adult. As in other multi-professional teams, precise role definition may be difficult to determine, and key therapy worker status can change from time to time.

In the experience of this author, physiotherapists working with children with developmental delays and special needs can be described as natural-link professionals between practitioners in clinical medicine and those in caring and education services. Therapists develop and sustain family contact for support, education, interpretation, encouragement and therapeutic management from cradle to grave. Physiotherapists may be involved with respiratory care and posturing of babes in the neonatal and special care baby units. They advise from diagnosis or suspicion of developmental delay in developmental stimulation and on management strategies and specific therapies throughout life. Active involvement may be maintained in terminal care at home, hospice or hospital. Whyte (1984) demonstrates and discusses with parents the link and active role of the physiotherapist in the Open University video programme on the *Handicapped in the Community* (Whyte 1984).

At differing times in a child's life, the various professionals have greater or lesser importance for the development of the child and to his family. Therapists need to be aware of and sensitive to the needs of the child, his family, classroom peers and staff by taking into consideration the needs, disabilities and abilities of each when determining programmes and practices. Often working in the home as well as classroom, therapists are able to report crisis situations which they have identified. In chronic and debilitating conditions of children, or during family difficulties, the skills of counselling are required of the therapist in supportive as well as practical managements.

Remedial Therapists in Developmental Paediatric Practice

Therapists aim to enable optimum development in a child, leaving him with minimal residual or constraining handicap. They aim to help others concerned with the child to understand his problems and developmental needs, determine realistic goals and manage effectively appropriate therapeutic activities towards agreed goals. Remedial therapists will assess the problems and constraints in the child's development and physical abilities or disabilities. They communicate these findings to all persons concerned in designing and managing the 24 hour programme and care of the child. They aim also to prevent stress and injury to the family and carers of the child (Marks 1985).

The basis of a developmental remedial therapy scheme for a child with developmental delay and/or special needs is the enrichment of sensory motor experiences through activities aimed to prepare the child for an appropriate movement response. The body senses for postural control and reflex integration develop in response to these movement experiences. Activities are aimed to awaken and enhance the child's awareness of himself and increase his repertoire in all possible developmental areas. Descriptive and illustrative examples of differentiation and integration of behaviours in the sensory motor developmental scheme have been given by Cratty (1979), while White (1984) writes on sensory integrative therapies for the cerebral-palsied child.

It is strongly stressed by Hare (1985) that movement skills are hampered when the body is inappropriately placed or organised in relation to the supporting surface. Stability of the body in a position depends upon the evenness of weight distribution. Movements are enabled by weight adjustment of the body over its resting base. Skill activities are not easily performed or postural adjustments made if there is a lack of control by basic postural muscles and of bodily awareness through feedback of weight redistribution for control. Weight transference (shifting one's own position), of the body within its own axis (front/back, side/side, up/down, reaching/withdrawing, pushing/pulling) against, onto or off a surface can be distorted if the body is not correctly placed or readied for action. Remedial therapists will always consider the supporting surface to the body as well as muscle and sensory actions demanded or experienced in a target activity. 'Impairment of trunk function due to postural insufficiency, deformity, fear or pain provides obvious limitation to balance and movement performance and compensatory posturing of limbs and head result' (Hare 1985).

Having noted at assessment whether the child is able to lie, sit, stand or move in space, therapists should state and demonstrate the child's abilities and difficulties or constraints in changing from or into differing positions. To assist balanced hold of a position against a resting surface to enable use of hands, feet, mouth, eyes etc., the remedial therapist will adapt or pad the furniture to the needs of each child. Aids provided must also be designed to fit into the place and lifestyle of the child in the home and classroom! (Kennedy 1984). As well as advising on the equipment and desired starting positions for curricular activities, therapists will suggest ways to prepare the body and muscles for action (Bobath and Bobath 1980). Tools for the task might also be designed or modified to meet the needs of each child: two-handled mug, moulded spoon handles, splints etc. Use of aids and equipment must be explained clearly by the therapist, demonstrated and checked regularly for personal fit, safety and correct use.

When designing a movement or activity programme therapists consider normal developmental sequence and behaviours in children as well as the delays or distortions in the child for whom the curriculum is being designed. Good, upright posture and steady forward movement of a person while walking depends upon the balance mechanisms developed or acquired in the body while seeking the upright against gravity (Cratty 1979). Retention in a child of primitive reflexes and delay in their integration and the development of mature righting and equilibrium reactions leads to problems in development. There are distortions in the development of voluntary control and motor functioning (Stengel, Attermeier, Bly and Heriza 1984). The therapist will assess for level of neuromuscular control, distortions and developments in the learned abilities in the child. Programmes will be designed to encourage as near normal as possible activities to gain use of postural musculatures and reactions. Rotating the body around its midline axis to control the head and for the head and limbs to be controlled independently of activity and the supporting surface encourages and enables a child to experience stimulus and promote reactions according to the integrity of his bodily and mental functioning.

The Remedial Therapist as a Curriculum Design Team Member

Remedial therapists are partners with teachers, parents and other professionals in sharing curriculum design, individual assessment, programme planning and evaluations. While therapists may not always be direct physical handlers of the child, they should be directly involved in the assessment, evaluation procedures and report-back sessions. This is so that they may demonstrate and rationalise suggested changes in prescribed activities or equipment use. Therapists can offer advice on physical methods of intervention and management to reach stated and agreed goals.

The main contribution made by therapists to the priority programme planning and subsequent individual pupil programmes will be towards the initial assessment and regular review sessions. Useful assessments will be of gross, fine and perceptuomotor skills and neurodevelopmental difficulties and deformities.

During assessment, by following a problem-oriented approach, the therapist can determine the clinical patterns underlying the postural deformities (Brown 1985) and positional mouldings in a child, sensory loss or change, muscle strengths or weaknesses, abnormal muscle tone, persistent or primitive reflexes or abnormalities in neurological reactions, joint ranges of motion, bony deformities, soft tissue changes, past or proposed surgery, appliances and aids used or discarded are all areas of investigation by a therapist. They need to be assessed in the light of functional abilities and disabilities in all developmental areas, and in conjunction with family, social and educational needs and objectives.

Regular evaluation of the child's sensorimotor functioning must be carried out as sensory stimulation and response need to become integrated with motor function (Ayres 1974; Rood 1956). Differing levels of sensory ability have differing levels of response for motor action, i.e. hyper- or hypo-sensitive reactions. The quality and quantity of response in a child may not be the only variable to an input stimulation, it can depend upon the presenting physical and neurological arousal state of the child at the time of the stimulus (Opila-Lehman, Short and Trombly 1985).

Therapists must clearly state and explain abilities and constraints of the child's development and make realistic goals and plans for action. Therapeutic management strategies and equipment suggested for use should be simple, realisable, attainable and suitable for home and/or classroom use. One needs to take into account other family or classroom members! In their reports therapists will outline problems which may lead to further secondary physical, social, learning or behavioural problems. These reports may form a foundation for the statement of need to be written as Appendix G in the terms of the 1981 Education Act. A useful guideline document has been compiled by the Association of Paediatric Chartered Physiotherapists (APCP 1985).

The importance of the curriculum development role of the remedial therapist has been described by many, including the researchers and teachers from the Hester Adrian Research Centre, Pre-school project of Manchester University (Sebba 1980); the Child Development Center, University of Tennessee (Connolly 1985); and the British Institute for Mental Handicap (Ricks 1980). It can be seen, therefore, that parents, teachers and remedial therapists must participate together in preparation of curriculum design and content through joint task analyses and discussion of goals and methods to reach them appropriate to each child.

Example.   The teacher or parent may state the desire that the child feed himself. Consultation with the remedial therapist will indicate what level of physical competence would be a suitable entry point into a scheme.

Curriculum area: self help
Goal: feeding
Objective: self-feeding with a rusk

Having agreed the intended goals and objectives, the therapist will assist teacher and parent to specify target behaviour and to analyse the action sequences. Once these are defined, starting positions and equipment needed to enable task completion may be stated. There will most probably be a series of sub-targets of action and sub-action sequences to be learned and finally brought together as a whole activity before the agreed target behaviour can be reached. As stated in Chapter 6 (Hogg) tasks are broken down into their component parts and gradually built up into a whole action as skills are acquired.

Target behaviour: child will be able to eat a rusk, with sucking action
Criterion: holding rusk in two hands fifteen out of twenty attempts
Constraint: strong asymmetrical tonic neck reflex prevents child getting both hands to mouth mid-line
Entry behaviour: pre-requisite skill: child will take two hands to mouth

From the following behavioural analysis, sub-target behaviours can be defined (i.e. an action sequence determined).

Child shall
maintain resting posture
glance at rusk held in mid-line view
fix eyes on rusk
examine rusk with eyes
reach forward with both arms
open both hands and grasp rusk
bring head forward towards hands and rusk
bring hands and rusk towards mouth
mouth opens to receive rusk
mouth closes on rusk
rusk is sucked, bitten
mouth contents are swallowed
head is raised
hands are taken away from mouth
Action sequence repeated

Remedial therapist advice to teacher: prepare the child for action by using individually prescribed (and previously demonstrated on child) facilitatory techniques e.g. tapping, rolling, patting, icing, stretching, and using key body points for movement initiation and control. It is important to use only methods prescribed, demonstrated and understood as some facilitation or stimulation methods may be contra-indicated for certain types of disability.

Starting posture:	side lying (to inhibit the backward and one-side extension thrusting)
Equipment:	side lying board, tilted at 10° forward angle, small, thin pillow under head
	rusk with honey or marmite (child's tastes!) on one edge
Action:	as in usual teaching methods; prepare the child by correct positioning; call name, draw attention to the rusk; present rusk in midline; encourage visual, then manual reach and grasp; encourage visual, olfactory and oral examination of rusk. Facilitate mouth opening, biting and chewing if needed as shown by remedial therapist or speech therapist if deemed appropriate for that child. Give agreed response as reinforcement at attempt, or at completion of task and repeat with addition of next part of the action sequence and so on until the whole activity or behaviour is learned.

All concerned should note that treatment methods of a therapist are designed to meet specific problems and need to be changed or adapted to meet changing needs in a child. Evaluation must be regular with redefinition of aims, objectives and therapy and management methods.

It is important also that all concerned realise that therapy 'treatment' is not an isolated episode once a week or so! It is the therapeutic management over a 24 hour period which is important (Bell and Watson 1985). To this end, and in view of the scarcity of remedial therapists in this speciality area of education, therapists are often best used as co-educators and encouragers of family and classroom personnel. Active movements initiated by the child are to be encouraged in a repetitive manner until accidental movements become well-performed movement skills geared to appropriate developmental goals or functions.

Therapeutic Physical Intervention Programmes and the Child with Special Needs

The therapist not only looks at the core area and task analysis and behavioural approach needed to reach targets but also looks into the pre-requisite functioning in a child from basic postural control so he may have optimum control over the functions of his head and trunk to attempt and control his limbs and hands (Lunnen 1984). In his chapter on 'Motor handicap' Ricks (1980) explains well the distinctive responsiveness of purely retarded children and those with added neurological dysfunction. Together with parents and other involved professionals, problems are determined, aims rationalised and plans and strategies are outlined and developed to reach immediate and long-term goals. The framework provided by the interdisciplinary team process provides for optimum effect and comprehensive intervention with handicapped children and their families (Connolly 1985). Therapists will stress to all that it is important to note that, for children with cerebral palsies, there are no standardised exercises adequate to meet the needs of all children (Bobath and Bobath 1984).

To design a programme of therapeutic and developmental activities, the therapist not only looks at the developmental levels presenting in a child but at the lack of movement from deformities, i.e. limited or stiff joints, unstable or hypermobile joints, spastic or floppy muscles, tight tendons, unequal limb growth. Account is taken of the abnormal movement patterns and problems which might be present in bone and muscle growth. This may be due to muscles acting against their spastic counterparts or antagonists (Brown 1985). Therapeutic handling and stimulation activities should be continued in a 24-hour, seven-day cycle. The advised strategies for management of movement problems and prevention of many deformities is a shared responsibility throughout the life of the child. The repetition of movement sequences and placing in prescribed postures for action can enhance planned learning or curricular activities and physical health (e.g. postural drainage positions for chest clearance).

The basis of the remedial therapists' interaction with other team members aims at enlarging their understanding of motor competence in the child and his problems so they may most appropriately direct their handling and stimulation methods of the child — e.g. resting and activity starting postures; the correct use or possible constraints or hazard advice regarding equipment; lifting and transferring techniques. Therapy treatments when given by therapists or carried out by parents or classroom staff must be coordinated and a balance reached between these and other curricular activities, and classroom/home and family activities and life. The physical needs or constraints of parents or school staff need to be considered — such as bed and bath heights for lifting and transfers.

Referral for Remedial Therapies

Referral for assessment for the need for therapy can be made directly to the therapist by other team members of district handicap teams or through school clinical medical officers, hospital consultants or general practitioners. Health district heads of the remedial services (district physiotherapists, occupational therapists or remedial gymnasts) will receive any referrals and allocate them to the appropriate staff member. Complaints of lack of service should be received by these district therapy service managers at the health authority headquarters.

Summary

Remedial gymnasts, physiotherapists and occupational therapists have an important part to play in the life of the child with special needs. They share their therapeutic aims and expertise with parents and other professionals at school. Together all participate in preparation of curriculum design and content through joint task analysis and choice of goals and methods appropriate to the needs of each individual child. The differing skills and professional abilities are called on to a greater or lesser extent for each remedial professional team member at differing lifetimes and needs of a child, his family or teachers. A sensorimotor training programme is based on an assessment of abilities and disabilities in a child and his family and environment. Movement facilitation techniques are graduated to adjust to an improvement or change in motor response. Motor response develops as a base for later use of more complex perceptual learning schemes. The child with special needs has particular need of early sensorimotor experiences to acquire active body movements and sensory experiences to become aware of the world about him and of himself. Unless children with special needs are correctly assessed, appropriately stimulated and pre-pared for learning activities through physical management pro-grammes they may acquire postural and positional deformities which will further hinder their development and learning and movement skills.

Remedial therapists have a duty to prepare a statement of need to complete the understanding of the needs of each child referred to them. Therapists must contribute to the initial statement and to the subsequent reviews. Their statements must not be subsumed into the medical report but must be attached to the final statement as Appendix G in the form as written by the remedial therapist. The report is for educationalists and for parents and needs to be written clearly, concisely and understandably. Physiotherapists and others are advised to obtain a copy of the '1981 Education act ... guide-lines for paediatric physiotherapists'.

Relevant Addresses

Chartered Society of Physiotherapy,
14 Bedford Row, London WC1R 4ED.

British Association of Occupational Therapists
(The College of Occupational Therapy), 20 Rede Place, London W2 4TU.

Association of Paediatric Chartered Physiotherapists,
Secretary APCP, c/o Chartered Society of Physiotherapy, 14 Bedford Row, London WC1R 4ED.

The Association of Chartered Physiotherapists in Mental Handicap,
c/o Chartered Society of Physiotherapists.

324   The Role of the Linked Agencies

References

Ayres, J. (1974) *The Development of Sensory Integration Theory and Practice.* Kendall-Hunt, Dubuque, USA.

Bell, E.J. and Watson A. (1985) 'Prevention of Positional Deformity in Children with Cerebral Palsy', (Address to Association of Paediatric Chartered Physiotherapists Annual Conference, Edinburgh) *Physiotherapy Practice 1*, no. 2, Churchill Livingstone.

Bobath, B. and Bobath, K. (1980). *Basic Principles of Treatment.* Students' papers 1-2. Acorn Press.

Bobath, B. and Bobath, K. (1984) 'The neuro-developmental treatment', in D. Scrutton (ed.). *Management of the Motor Disorders of Children with Cerebral Palsy.* pp. 6-18, *Clinics in Developmental Medicine* no. 90, Spastics International Medical Publications.

Brown, J.K. (1985) Address to Spastics International Annual Conference. Association of Paediatric Chartered Physiotherapists, Edinburgh.

Connolly, B.H. (1985) *Papers on Early Intervention Program.* Child Development Center, Univ. of Tennessee.

Cratty, B.J. (1979) 'Sensory motor behaviour of infants. Theories, Models and Speculations', in B. Cratty. *Perceptual and Motor Developments in Infants and Young Children.* Prentice Hall.

Eckersley, P. and Kennedy, P. (eds.). (1985) *Guidelines for Paediatric Chartered Physiotherapists on the 1981 Education Act.* APCP.

Grimley, A.M.D. (ed.). (1984) *Evidence of the Service and Constraints by Paediatric Physiotherapists to the British Paediatric Association Working Party on Chronic Childhood Handicap.* APCP.

Hare, N. (1985) Unpublished work and personal communications.

Kennedy, P. (1984) 'Aids to Daily Living', in S. Levitt (ed.). *Paediatric Developmental Therapy.* Blackwell Scientific.

Lunnen, K.Y. (1984) 'Severely and profoundly retarded children', in Campbell (ed.). *Paediatric Neurologic Physical Therapy.* Churchill Livingstone.

Marks, L. (1985) 'Parents: How much help?' *Physiotherapy, 71* (4), pp. 170-2.

Opila-Lehman, J., Short, M.A. and Trombly, C.A. (1985) 'Kinesthetic recall of children with athetoid and spastic cerebral palsy and of non-handicapped children'. *Developmental Medicine and Child Neurology, 27,* (2), pp. 223-30.

Piaget, J. (1952) *The Origins of Intelligence in Children.* International Universities Press.

Ricks, D.M. (1980) 'Motor Handicap', in G.B. Simon, (ed.). *Modern Management of Mental Handicap, A Manual of Practice.* MTB Press.

Rood, M.S. (1956) 'Neurophysical mechanisms utilized in the treatment of neuromuscular dysfunction'. *Am. Jnl. of Occupational Therapy, 10* (4), pp. 220.

Further Reading

Physiotherapy (1985) *71* no. 3.

Mental Handicap (1985) *13* (1).

Binns, Richard (1978) *From Speech to Writing.* The Scottish Curriculum Development Service.

Bobath, B. and Bobath, K. (1975) *Motor Development in the Different Types of Cerebral Palsy.* Heinemann Medical Books.

Cotton, E. (1981) 'The hand as a guide to learning'. *Spastics Society,* 89/4 81/3M

Cratty, B.J. (1979) *Perceptual and Motor Development in Infants and Young Children.* Prentice Hall.

Campbell, S.C. (ed.). (1984) *Paediatric Neurological Physical Therapy.* Churchill Livingstone.

Coates, H. and King, A. (1982) *The Patient Assessment. A handbook for therapists.* Churchill Livingstone.

Cornwell, Morigue (1975) *Early Years.* Disabled Living Foundation.

Finnie, N. (1971) *Handling the Young Cerebral Palsied Child at Home.* Heinemann.

Foster, A.L. and Galley, P.M. (1982) *Human Movement.* Churchill Livingstone.

Goldsmith, B.C. (1979) *Design Date of Wheelchair Children.* The Disabled Living Foundation.

Holt, K.S. (ed.). 'Movement and Child Development'. *Clinics in Developmental Medicine, 55.* Spastics International Medical Publications. Heinemann.

Holle, B. (1976) *Motor Development in Children, Normal and Retarded.* Blackwell Scientific.

Jegard, S. *et al.* (1980) *A Comprehensive Program for Multi-handicapped Children.* Alvin Buckwold Centre.

Levitt, S. (ed.). (1984) *Paediatric Developmental Therapy.* Blackwell Scientific.

Levitt, S. (1982) *Treatment of Cerebral Palsy and Motor Delay,* 2nd edn. Blackwell Scientific.

McCarthy, G.T. (1984) *The Physically Handicapped Child.* Faber.

Tingey-Michaelis, C. (1983) *Handicapped Infants and Children.* University Park Press.

Kephart, N.C. (1971) *The Slow Learner in the Classroom.* Merill.

Presland, J.L. (1982) *Paths to Mobility in 'Special Care'.* British Institute of Mental Handicap.

Robinson, C.M., Harrison, J. and Gridley, J. (1970) *Physical Activity in the Education of Slow-learning Children.* Edward Arnold.

Robins, F. and Robins. J. (1966) *Educational Rhythmics for Mentally and Physically Handicapped Children,* 2nd edn. R.A. Verlag.

Scrutton, D. (ed.). (1984) 'Management of the Motor Disorders of Children with Cerebral Palsy'. *Clinics in Developmental Medicine,* no. 90. Spastics International Medical Publications.

Simon, B.G. (ed.). (1980) *Modern Management of Mental Handicap.* MTP Press.

Simon, G.B. (1981) *The Next Step on the Ladder.* BIMH.

Shennan, V. (1980) *Mental Handicap, Nursing and Care.* Human Horizons Series. Souvenir Press.

Stevens, M. (1976) *The Educational and Social Needs of Children with Severe Handicap,* 2nd edn. Edward Arnold.

Woods, G.E. (1975) *The Handicapped Child.* Blackwell Scientific.

Woods, G.E. (1983) *Handicapped Children in the Community, Medical Aspects for Educationalists.* Wright PSG.

Yorke-Moore, R. and Stewart, P. (1982) *Management of the Physically Handicapped Child.* Pamphlet No. 1 'Guidelines to Handling'. Pamphlet No. 2. 'Guidelines to lifting, carrying and seating'. BIMH.

SUPPORT SERVICES FOR THE HEARING-IMPAIRED

Angela Foulkes and Richard Fitzsimons

The aim of any therapeutic profession must be the reduction of handicap. The therapist's skills are employed to minimise the effects suffered by an individual. When this proves remediable, the therapist's role may be a short-term one. When damage is permanent or recurrent, long-term involvement will be required. The therapist may initiate identification and referral of a problem to medical colleagues or receive referrals from them. In an educational setting therapist, teacher and parents combine forces so that a child is enabled to cope with his damage as well as he can, both at home and at school, and to be as comfortable as possible in doing so. Where aids and equipment are available and appropriate, care is taken that child, family and teacher learn to make optimal use of them, to understand their function and to realise their limitations. In cases of multiple damage the therapist needs to put specific handicap into context, interpreting for teacher and parent the part it plays in the child's behaviour and development.

The support teacher of the hearing-impaired working in a school for children with severe learning difficulties can be seen in all these aspects to have a role parallel to that of the speech therapist or the physiotherapist. The method of work and the focus of concern are, however, very different from theirs because of the nature of the handicap produced by a hearing impairment. Two aspects in particular direct the course of action — deafness as a hidden handicap and as a social handicap.

A hidden handicap: five minutes spent in a classroom would probably suffice for an experienced teacher to pick out among children with severe learning difficulties those with motor problems, fine or gross. Within half an hour one could probably indicate all those with visual difficulties. In contrast, an experienced teacher of the deaf would not expect to identify correctly by observation alone those children who had a hearing impairment. There is no reliable outward and visible sign by which to make accurate judgements about hearing. Only a child suffering a recently acquired hearing loss is likely to make clear his difficulties in understanding the speech of his parent, teacher or friend. Those with chronic or fluctuating impairment may well appear dreamy, inattentive or unco-operative. In the presence of learning disorders it is particularly easy for a hearing loss to be entirely overlooked. A study of an ESN(S) school in Manchester (Foulkes 1985) in which 54 children were tested, revealed 20 unsuspected hearing losses. Of children thought by parents and teachers to have normal hearing, one-third proved to have some impairment; among those considered to have a possible hearing problem, one-half were shown to have normal hearing at the time of assessment. Careful initial testing of all the children was therefore shown to be essential, with provision also for periodic reviews.

A social handicap: just as a faulty telephone line frustrates both transmitter and receiver, so any degree of deafness affects a hearing-impaired person's social contacts as well as himself. Handicap in communications is almost invariably more keenly felt by parent or teacher than by the child with a hearing loss and often precedes diagnosis of mild or moderate impairment. 'He hears when he wants to', 'she ignores me when I am talking to her' are phrases commonly used by parents having a sense of social discomfort but no suspicion that their child's hearing may be imperfect. In schools it is often the teacher's difficulty in communicating with a pupil which leads to the request for a hearing test: what looks like poor ability to listen or lack of social curiosity may prove to be a direct result of hearing loss. If handicap is to be reduced the support teacher must focus, not narrowly — on the child — but as widely as possible upon his social and educational context.

These two aspects of deafness as a handicap underline the necessity for recognition, measurement and interpretation of any hearing problem.

Assessment of Hearing Problems

For more than twenty years stress has been laid on the importance of early diagnosis of hearing loss both for remediable problems to be treated and for compensatory measures to begin when medical treatment is not possible (see Chapter 9). One would expect that any child thought to require full-time, special educational treatment would have had both hearing and vision examined thoroughly before he entered school but, sadly, this does not yet seem to be the case. It is still common for children to arrive in assessment units and schools for pupils with severe learning difficulties without recorded information about tests of sensory function. For this reason the first priority of the support service for the hearing-impaired has at present to be the initial identification of children with hearing problems.

Full implementation of the 1981 Education Act should lead to class teachers being provided from the outset with all information relevant to designing individual learning programmes. Support teachers would help class teachers to interpret data about auditory acuity and middle ear function in terms of educational implications. They would need to assess acuity periodically, examining also children's auditory attention to assist the teacher to provide optimal listening conditions.

The incidence of hearing impairment in schools for pupils with severe learning difficulties is undoubtedly much higher than in the general school population. The study in Manchester showed 29 of the 54 children to have a significant hearing loss (30 db or more). The 20 previously unsuspected losses were spread throughout the age range and included an 18-year-old girl with probable 'glue ear' and a 15-year-old boy with impacted wax. Down's children are known to be particularly at risk, and the study showed 19 of the 23 tested to have impaired hearing.

The testing of children with severe learning difficulties can be entrusted only to people having skill and experience in audiological work with both young and multiply-handicapped children. The Manchester study estimated that the techniques normally practised by those carrying out audiometric screening in schools would have sufficed for only three pupils in the entire school. A team of two needs to be available for assessing hearing in schools for children with severe learning difficulties as it is in a pre-school clinic. One of the team should be the support teacher attached to the school so that information gained from the test may be passed directly to staff caring for the child. Close liaison with medical colleagues is essential as the majority of hearing problems are potentially remediable. No less than 28 of the 29 children with defective hearing in the Manchester school studied had some conductive element in their loss. The ideal situation is a joint clinic with an ENT surgeon and the school medical officer in which results of audiological tests and medical examination can be pooled, necessary treatment or further investigations being instituted immediately.

The Educational Audiologist

The educational audiologist does much more than determine the nature and degree of hearing loss. By training and experience he or she will be able to make value judgements on many areas of need, possibly providing constructs appropriate to the need or indicating the direction of referral for further professional investigation.

For the purpose of children with hearing problems who are in the educational system it is possible to train as an audiologist whose bias is mainly toward the amelioration of the social and educational consequences of hearing loss. It is essential that an audiologist whose function is working with children in an educational setting be specifically qualified to do that. The educational audiologist has, by training and experience, usually three layers of professional expertise which provide complementary strengths: 1. a qualified and experienced teacher of mainstream education; 2. qualifications as a teacher of the deaf; 3. the further study of audiology. To qualify, the educational audiologist will have included most of the following areas of study: the physics of sound; tests of audiological function; speech tests; language development; psychology (normal and abnormal); child development; sociology (family dynamics and advisory work); anatomy and physiology of the hearing mechanism; hearing aids. With this degree of knowledge to hand, together with experience of mainstream and special education, the educational audiologist is well equipped to provide both information and advice regarding children with hearing difficulties.

Testing by the Educational Audiologist

The testing either by comparison of air conduction and bone conduction auditory thresholds or more conclusively by tympanometry can and should be quick, easy and definitive. The use of pure tone audiometry in establishing conductive hearing difficulties tends to be an all or none situation whereas tympanometry is quite capable of differential diagnosis ranging through Eustachian tube dysfunction, serars otitis media, tympanosclerosis, ossicular dislocation, all of which allow for specific medical intervention and remediation. On the known incidence of conductive hearing problems and the researched effects of the condition upon the educational and social development of the child, it is arguable that the facility for determining the condition is imperative and should be in wider use than at present.

The most severe effect of conductive hearing problems is to produce a hearing loss of 60-65 dbs. In the majority of cases the hearing loss is less severe but nonetheless highly significant. As normal conversational speech is produced at about 65 dbs to be received by normal ears capable of detecting all speech sounds in loudness levels less than 10 dbs the effect of a 60-65 dbs hearing loss becomes apparent. It is to reduce the sufferer to complete inability to hear normal speech. Hearing losses less than this reduce the ready ability to discriminate speech. In the classroom such a hearing-impaired child may well totally miss spoken information, even allowing for the fact that few teachers use a normally loud noise but one somewhat raised in loudness. Such a situation would readily recommend itself to the teacher's attention. However a hearing loss of 45 dbs which may fluctuate in time may equally produce listening difficulty and confusions. These are often misapprehended because such children develop defence mechanisms to avoid detection. As stated above the educational audiologist can readily diagnose the condition and explain the significance to the teacher. It is possible to add to the battery of information and at the same time demonstrate to observers the significance of the situation by use of one or more of the available tests of speech discrimination.

These tests are directly related to the ability to discriminate speech; as such, the information is less tenuous to mainstream teachers and provides a benchmark which is readily fixed in teaching techniques. The educational audiologist would choose the test appropriate to the developmental needs and ability of the child. Younger children or those less linguistically or otherwise developed than the norm, may be tested by the use of toy tests such as the Kendal Toy Test. This is a group of toy items chosen because the names contain in total most of the sounds used in speech. In each of the three variations of the Kendal Toy Test there are ten such items together with five additional items used to reduce the chance factor. Once the tester has ascertained that the child does indeed know the names of the items they are randomly spread on a table top; using a voice loud enough to be heard easily, the tester asks the child to identify the test items. By varying the loudness of the voice used the tester can ascertain at which loudness level the child can achieve a 100 per cent score. The normally-hearing child can be expected to achieve such a score when the tester's voice level is down to about 25 dbs as heard at the child's ear. If the child can achieve such a score with the voice at such a quiet level, then, when listening to normal conversation at 65 dbs, he should have no troubles. It can also be seen, when it is necessary for the tester to raise the voice closer to, or even above, the loudness of a normal voice before the 100 per cent score is reached, that the child has definitively demonstrated a marked deviance from the hearing norm. Such deviation can readily be perceived by teachers and parents providing a ready platform of understanding for future action. Similar in nature would be the use of picture cards such as the Manchester Picture Test card. Each card has four items on it, and the child is simply made familiar with the task then asked to identify a specific item on each card.

A more sophisticated speech discrimination test is in the form of words lists such as the Arthur Boothroyd (AB) Word Lists. These are in groups of ten words, each word constructed of three phonemes. Each list is phonemically balanced to represent the spectrum of sounds in normal speech. Such lists may be presented to the listener in closed circuit. That is, through headphones from a tape recorder whose loudness output can be carefully monitored. Conversely in the free field the lists are read directly to the listener who is not allowed to watch the speaker's face. By varying the loudness presented to the subject it is possible to record the increasing or diminishing ability to discriminate the phonemes as the loudness is raised and lowered. The normally-hearing child would be expected to gain 100 per cent scores at about 20-25 dbs. The hearing-impaired child deviates from this according to the degree and nature of the hearing loss. Particularly if the closed mode is utilised, it is possible, not only to demonstrate the presence of a hearing loss and its real significance in the detection of speech, but also to demonstrate any imbalance in hearing between the two ears. It is by no means uncommon to discover children with hearing better in one ear than in the other. Such a condition may cause not only distortions in the perception of speech but create confusion in locating sound sources. Knowledge that the condition exists can be most useful to both parents and teachers. Such awareness allows for a better utilisation of teaching times by building into lesson material checks specific to the affected child.

The use of appropriate tests to establish auditory thresholds of detectability forms a major part of the educational audiologist's role. This area of assessment is often undertaken by an audiometrician who is skilled in child handling and equipment manipulation, but it is the audiologist who is skilled in evaluating the significance of test results and can provide valid constructs for educational, social or medical support. It would appear sensible, where audiometricians are involved, that their work should be overseen by an audiologist. It may also be agreed that the audiometrician should work largely in 'screening' procedures solely to separate the normally hearing and the abnormally hearing child population. The establishing of hearing thresholds in very young children utilises what are, in general, deceptively simple techniques. The apparent simplicity of such testing should not be allowed to obscure the validity of the information obtained. It is essential that testing at this level be explained to observing parents and teachers. This may be done directly following the test or as a commentary during the test session. Such an explanation, involving the relationships between the child's developmental levels and skills, the pitch and loudness of the sounds used as stimuli, receptive and expressive language, anatomical and physiological involvements needs to be handled both in a factual and constructive manner. The level of knowledge and experience needed together with the high skills levels necessary in the test procedure fall quite properly within the remit of the educational audiologist.

Tests such as the distraction test, the co-operative test and the performance test can be used both at the screening level and the diagnostic level for the establishment of auditory thresholds of detectability. They are simple in execution and, if undertaken efficiently, highly definitive having a high correlation with subsequent testing by pure tone audiometry. A limitation is observable insofar as they tap only low- and high-pitch hearing ability leaving the tester to make an assumption regarding the pitches in between. This limitation does not in practice indicate a weakness in the tests as the opposite ends of the sound spectrum utilised in tests represent the essential low-pitched vowel components in speech and the equally essential high-pitched consonant components. An awareness of the acuity in these areas represents vital information when related to the development of speech and language and also in explaining deviations in spoken language. What the child has difficulty in hearing he or she may be expected to have difficulty in expressing. Although many conditions exist which are specific and not related to auditory deficiency it is as well to establish the facts to allow for proper remediation to be utilised by teachers, parents, speech therapists, etc.

The tests mentioned above, although designed specifically to establish auditory function, may well allow the skilled audiologist to make observations about the other areas of development as they affect the hearing test. Children with visual problems, gross and fine motor problems, attention or concentration difficulties, anxiety or lethargy conditions all have to be tested by educational audiologists who, of necessity, become skilled in observing such deviations. Clearly, the audiological assessments can lead on to further assessments undertaken by other professional disciplines.

Post Diagnosis

The parents will, of necessity, become closely involved in the management of the hearing loss. The dynamics of the situation, as it involves professional advisors, parents, siblings and the extended family, are highly complex. It is of the utmost importance that the hearing problem be presented in the most positive manner in order to avoid undue emphasis: it is very easy for parents and teachers to lose sight of the total child and focus upon the area of damage. Few would advocate such a practice but reality often dictates this hierarchy. The educational audiologist, together with his colleagues in the assessment situation, are best placed to set the matter in perspective and to pick up immediately following diagnosis the consequential trail of parent guidance. All experience shows that this immediacy of follow-up is most beneficial in the long term — together with the fact that the test situation, properly handled and explained, provides a firm basis for future work.

The Support Teacher as a Co-ordinator of Information

Many schools favour the provision of a file in which the results of all tests are summarised alongside notes for the teacher describing the child's probable difficulties in class and suggesting strategies which may improve his performance in auditory and linguistic skills.

A report of every test should be sent to the school's medical officer with a copy for the headteacher. When a conductive problem is found, the medical officer arranges for any necessary treatment to be carried out. The 1982 Manchester study showed that a build-up of wax sufficient to impair hearing significantly was a particularly common problem, affecting about a quarter of all the children tested. The school medical officer arranged for treatment to be given and informed the support service when the wax had been cleared.

Through the support teacher re-tests are arranged at the request of parent, class teacher, headteacher or school medical officer. For example Down's syndrome children as a group are so vulnerable to conductive hearing problems that it is felt advisable to arrange an annual review during the winter for any child who initially shows normal hearing. Children placed on the support teacher's case list because of defective hearing are monitored periodically, usually at six-monthly intervals.

Management of Hearing Problems

There is no strict boundary between assessment and management. Recognition and understanding of the child's problem is usually the most important element in its management. A good example of this is monaural deafness which, unsuspected, can produce puzzling inconsistency in behaviour: the child may look vague and inattentive, may require instructions to be repeated, yet not need any raising of level of speech, may even appear wilfully to ignore speech directly addressed to him. Once the hearing loss is recognised and with it his difficulties in localising a speaker, together with the defences he may have built up to contend with it, it becomes easy to compensate for the problem. Advice on management stems directly from assessment of the child's hearing.

Talks and demonstrations can be useful in informing teaching and care staff about hearing and deafness. Advice about facilitating communication with hearing-impaired children, including the use and limitations of hearing aids and lipreading, is best made meaningful by being related to the problems of specific children. In a school catering for severe learning problems it is essential that the support teacher knows individual children well enough to relate their hearing loss to their other difficulties and their stage of development.

Individual teaching sessions, in which the support teacher aims to improve a pupil's auditory attention, speech discrimination and language use, play a smaller part than in mainstream schools. Few children have sufficient ability to transfer and generalise information for weekly sessions of this sort to give them real benefit. The most important aspect of the support teacher's work is informal discussion with the class teacher, usually in the classroom and always related to individual children. The product in terms of educational management may be the modification of an individual learning programme, a strategy to improve listening or even the changing of the position of a child's chair.

The management of individual hearing aids is not easy, and school staff, like parents of deaf children, need support and help in persevering with their use. It is rare for a child to show immediate benefit from an aid, and there is often a lengthy period during which he slowly becomes accustomed to the new experience of sound. He can do so only if those around him continue patiently, and with what must sometimes seem like blind faith, with the chores of checking, adjusting and cleaning the aid. Putting an aid back every time a child pulls it or knocks it out adds considerably to the problems of classroom management.

Verbal communication is a vital area of concern. The hearing-impaired child can often be hindered in the acquisition of language by techniques intended by well-meaning adults to help him — excessive use of gesture, mouthing of speech, use of telegram-style syntax. The support teacher can show how the use of natural language together with contextual clues boosts a child's confidence in communications and the adult's comfort in relating to him.

Summary

The support teacher of the hearing-impaired aims to be viewed not as a visiting 'expert' but as a member of an educational and therapeutic team. The value of the work in assessment and management depends largely on ability to relate and communicate with other members of the team and with parents so that expertise can be pooled for the benefit of children.

Reference

Foulkes, A.M. (1985) 'Hearing losses in a speical school'. National Deaf Children's Society.

Further Reading

Davies, H. and Silverman, S.R. (1984) *Hearing and Deafness.* Holt Reinhart and Winston.

Denes, P. and Pinson, E.N. (1974) *The Speech Chain.* Bell Telephone Laboratories.

Hood, J.D. (1960) 'Principles and practice of bone conduction audiometry'. *Laryngoscope 70,* pp. 1211-28.

Illingworth, R.S. (1980) *The Development of the Infant and Young Child: normal and abnormal,* 7th edn. Churchill Livingstone.

Katz, J. (1978) *Handbook of Clinical Audiology,* 2nd edn. Williams and Wilkins.

Nolan, M. and Tucker, I. (1981) *The Hearing-Impaired Child in the Family.* Souvenir Press.

Tucker, I. and Nolan, M. (1984) *Educational Audiology.* Croom Helm.

SUPPORT SERVICES FOR THE VISUALLY IMPAIRED

Alison Frankenberg

Provision and Prevalence

The visiting teacher for the visually impaired is not a feature of every school for children with severe learning difficulties. There has been no nationwide policy for partially-sighted and blind children, 'normal' or handicapped. Provision varies. Some local education authorities rely on outside help from the RNIB regional advisory teachers or from nearby authorities. Some authorities have special units but no visiting teacher. Others have one or two visiting teachers to cover the whole range of age and ability. A few, like Manchester, have a small team of visiting teachers who, between them, cover the full range of pupils and also assist neighbouring authorities.

Need invariably outstrips provision. Decisions about need are usually based on numbers of children registered as blind or partially sighted with the social services. Some authorities take a more flexible attitude and accept that any child stated by the treating medical personnel to be functionally blind or seriously visually impaired is also in need of educational help. Registration as blind or partially sighted is a particularly unsafe guideline. It usually depends on a decision by an ophthalmologist and also on parental agreement. There may be good medical reasons for delay. Also, some parents, especially of partially-sighted children, are not willing to have their children registered, possibly because of a sense of stigma or non-acceptance of the problem. If LEA policy only allows the teacher of the visually impaired to see registered children, it may be necessary for school heads to lobby for a policy change, or to persuade consultants and social services to register more readily. A further problem is that the number of visually impaired among children with severe learning difficulties tends to be hidden. Even children notified to the handicap register of the community health service may not be listed as blind or partially sighted if that is not their primary handicap: yet this is the largest group of visually-impaired children today.

Cortical blindness is a frequent accompaniment or consequence of brain injury or global retardation. In three years' experience of an assessment team in Liverpool, (Hunt, McKendrick, Poole, Pugh, Rosenbloom and Turnock 1979), the team reported that 15 out of 95 children assessed had 'cortical', or to use their term 'cerebral' blindness. They say, 'This term has been used when the eyes are normal and visual loss appears to be secondary to cerebral malfunction'. They further comment that, 'The majority of children with cerebral blindness, as might be predicted, do not reach schools for the visually handicapped but attend ESN(S) schools ... or reside in hospitals for the subnormal, hence their absence from other surveys of populations of visually handicapped children'. Colborne–Brown and Tobin (1982), in their survey of school placement of blind children, say that 'of the children for whom questionnaires were returned (416) almost half (47%) have a mental handicap in addition to a visual handicap and three-quarters (74%) can be accurately described as additionally handicapped'. They conclude: 'There are likely to be twice or three times as many visually handicapped, multi-handicapped children *outside* the national provision for the visually handicapped'.

Even when the existence of functionally blind or partially-sighted multi-handicapped children is acknowledged, not everyone agrees that they should receive attention specifically from a qualified teacher of the visually impaired. Some administrators assume that only children who need to learn Braille need a specialist teacher, and that children with lesser impairments or general retardation can be coped with by generalist special needs teachers. This view has received some support in the 1984 report of the Advisory Committee on the Supply and Education of Teachers, which considers the requirements for teachers of the visually impaired, as well as other special needs. However, the opposite view appears in the 1984 DES document, 'Proposals for the future provision in special schools for children with visual handicaps', which deplores the use of staff not qualified to teach visually handicapped children. Use of non-specialist staff is a trend which will appeal to administrators in times of economic hardship, but is less likely to appeal to teachers, therapists or parents who usually value the support of someone with specialist knowledge and experience of visual handicap.

Since vision plays an important part in the shaping of human behaviour, and is the sense which integrates other perceptions, visual impairment has a far-reaching effect on all other aspects of development from earliest childhood. According to Reynell (1979), 'Nearly all the early stages of learning are visually dominated, and lay the foundation for many of the higher intellectual processes. When visually handicapped children are able to use intellectual means to transcend the perceptual learning, they can to some extent find ways round the visual difficulties, but by this time they are already one to two years behind their sighted peers in most aspects of learning.' Expert teaching help as well as expert medical treatment is needed in order to assess and minimise the effects of serious visual handicap.

The Specialist Visiting Teacher

The visiting teacher has certain advantages over in-school staff. This is so despite the view of some educationalists that teachers with special responsibility for one aspect of handicap, such as vision, should be fully integrated into the life of the school, so that their specialties can permeate all aspects of school life. This is a reasonable argument in principle. Unfortunately, a more likely outcome in practice is that daily routine will overtake the special interest. The peripatetic specialist, however, has a licence to focus on one aspect of learning and disability, and to spend time observing and assessing individual children. Further, the peripatetic's lack of a fixed place in the structure of the school makes it possible to move more freely between groups: heads, teaching staff, paramedics and parents. In pre-school or home counselling work in particular, it is better that the visiting teacher is not identified with any one school: parents often relate better to someone located impartially with regard to school placement.

Training and Qualifications

There are good reasons why the visiting teacher should have recognised qualifications as a teacher of the blind and partially sighted as well as general teaching qualification. The visiting teacher should have skills to offer which are a worthwhile addition to the class teacher's expertise. A sound knowledge of visually-impaired children in mainstream schooling, and of the implications of visual defects for development, is needed as a baseline and for setting goals.

It is particularly important in the light of the 1981 Act, with the transfer of main responsibility for decisions about school placement from the medical to the educational field, that qualified teachers be available to advise on the needs of individual children. Many health authorities have child development units or assessment centres, either hospital-attached or run by community services. Very often the only educational work in these settings is done by nursery nurses or psychologists. Ideally, each of these establishments should be visited regularly by a local teacher for the visually impaired.

The Role of the Peripatetic

The peripatetic teacher for the visually impaired needs to apportion time to the different groups of pupils; to the teaching of specific skills and adaptation of the school curriculum; and to teaching and advisory roles. The balance of actual teaching and advisory work may be determined by the needs of individual pupils or by the amount of time available to spend in each location. However, enough sample teaching or observation needs to be done with each child for teaching and management suggestions to be meaningful and specific to the child in question. Whatever the amount of time spent, the work of the peripatetic teacher with the child will not be sufficient alone; in order to be effective, work must be done in conjunction with and continued by those who look after the child the rest of the time. Also, written records, teaching suggestions and programmes need to be put into each child's file. It is a matter for discussion among practitioners whether it is better to work within a school in the classroom alongside the group or to withdraw the child to a quiet corner. There is, in fact, value in both; teaching and observation can be done with advantage in the general classroom where others can observe; however some work, particularly performance assessment, needs to be done away from distractions and other sensory cues.

Relationships with Staff and School

In many schools routine meetings are held for planning and for case reviews, but where this is not done the visiting teacher needs to create an informal system for consultation and exchange of ideas. It is advisable for the teacher of the visually handicapped to consult, not only with the head and class teacher, but also with the physiotherapist, speech therapist and any other person working with the children in order to co-ordinate programmes. Parents, too, play a key part in the continuation of teaching and training. The head of the school may be happy for the peripatetic teacher to visit the parents at home, or may prefer home visits to be made in company with, or by, the school's own home-liaison teacher or class-teacher, or to bring the parents into school. In any event, the parents must be part of the planning team for the best hope of success.

While working in any one school, visiting teachers are answerable to the head of that school, although in general they are under the jurisdiction of the director of their own service. As visitors to the school they must adapt to some extent to the school's curriculum and methods, while being clear about the way in which the needs of the visually-handicapped child can be met within that framework. This calls for a knowledge of a wide variety of teaching systems and skill in goal-planning. Objectives should be clear and worked out in accordance with the school's curriculum. Teaching programmes for individual children must be written in a way which is acceptable to the staff who will implement them from day to day.

Assessment and Referral

There are two strands to assessment of visual handicap in children: medical and educational. The former is the province of the ophthalmologist and the orthoptist and leads to treatment; the latter is the field of the teacher and leads to educational planning.

Medical Assessment

Often medical diagnosis and treatment are so successful that no special educational involvement is needed. However, there remain many cases in which treatment is prolonged or the condition is not capable of sufficient improvement, so that the child's learning processes are impeded. In order that teachers know which children should be helped, information needs to pass from doctors to educationalists. Unfortunately, the channels for this are not totally reliable, especially where hospital patients are concerned. It is no-one's responsibility within the hospital system (although consultants will often take the initiative) to make a direct referral unless a child is to be registered with the social services as visually handicapped. The exceptions to this are hospitals with education-linked child development units or assessment centres, where referral is more effective. Referrals before school entry are more likely to come from community medical officers, who maintain a register of handicapped children likely to need special service and who, if the Manchester Health Authority can be taken as an example, are keen to make use of a home visiting and teaching service. After school entry, children are seen by school medical officers who inform the head teacher of special medical problems. However, referral at school entry is too late for a seriously visually-handicapped child: teaching and support for parents should begin at home as early as possible. An open referral system, accepting referrals from doctors, teachers, social workers, health visitors and parents, is the best way of ensuring that no child falls through the net.

A further difficulty often arises over transfer of vital information about the visual problems of individual children from doctors to teachers. This information may be needed to aid decisions about such matters as teaching print or Braille, adaptation of teaching materials and conditions, or to avoid physical risk to the child. Doctors are understandably reluctant to breach medical confidentiality although the registration document itself carries a heading to the effect that information contained in it may be given to persons concerned in the child's care. Orthoptists are often able to bridge the gap between the medical and educational fields, frequently visiting children in both schools and clinics, and being skilled in assessing functional vision. They can explain the medical implications of visual defects to school staff and to parents. They can also check details of treatment, such as the number of hours a squinting eye should be patched and whether a child should wear glasses.

Educational Assessment

The work of the teacher for the visually impaired and that of medical professionals overlaps in the assessment of visual function. The range of visual defects and their implications for education is too wide to be described here. For further information about the diversity in causation and degree of handicap see Robinson (1977) on blindness in childhood, as well as other articles in the same book, or Tallents (1979) on 'Visual handicaps found in a population of mentally and physically handicapped children'. The label 'blind' covers a range from total absence of vision to sufficient vision for recognition of objects but not for reading print. 'Partial sight' may refer to blurred vision, restricted field of vision or innumerable other difficulties. A severely retarded child may have healthy eyes, but faulty mental processing of visual input, causing visual perception difficulties or even cortical blindness.

The specialist teacher builds up a picture of the child's use of vision, or in the case of a totally blind child, of compensatory use of other senses, and monitors change through time. Assessment of this kind aids educational planning. The teacher needs check-lists or tests for repeated observation. Some of these may be simply observation and recording tools designed by specialist teachers themselves to answer questions regularly asked by class teachers and others. From time to time it may be appropriate to use a standardised and widely recognised developmental scale. A useful scale for children under six or with additional handicaps is the Reynell-Zinkin Developmental Scale for Young Visually Handicapped Children (Reynell and Zinkin 1979). Others are the Maxfield-Bucholz adaptation of the Vineland Scale (Maxfield and Bucholz 1957), also for young children, and the Williams Intelligence Test for Children with Defective Vision (Williams 1956), which covers the whole school age-range but is not very appropriate for children with learning disorders. For evaluation and further information on assessment tools see Tobin (1978) and Chapman (1978). There are a few assessment-plus-teaching tools available: notably the 'Look and Think' programme by Chapman, Tobin, Tooze and Moss (1979) and the 'Program to Develop Efficiency in Visual Functioning' (Barraga and Morris 1980). It is also desirable to use check-lists of skill areas such as self-help and motor skills, whether designed by and for the individual teacher or from sources such as the American Foundation for the Blind. These aid goal planning, avoid undetected gaps in learning and help co-ordination where several staff are working together as a team.

Work Areas

Pupils with severe learning difficulties are less likely to learn the more generally recognised skills for the blind such as Braille and independent travel using the long cane. Braille requires good tactile discrimination and sufficient ability to acquire skills and concepts at least equivalent to those needed for print reading and writing. Failing this, signs such as tactile markers for property can be learned by many pupils. Independent outdoor travel may be beyond the competence even of some sighted pupils with learning difficulties, but indoor independent mobility can be taught to any child who can achieve locomotion. Similarly, sophisticated aids to the partially-sighted reader, such as closed circuit television, may not be appropriate, although visual stimulation computer programmes, with switches operated by the child, are a growing and useful resource. In working with special care unit children the main aims are to elicit positive responses to the environment, to discourage maladaptive behaviours and start some purposeful play and explorative processes.

Light stimulation should be available in some form for pupils who are cortically blind or unresponsive, although there is, as yet, little agreement about the chronological or mental age beyond which this is effective. Most research into a critical period for the development of sight seems to have been done with animals (see Gregory 1977), but there is a considerable amount of knowledge about the effects of congenital cataracts and squints on visual development. In Vaughan and Asbury (1980) it is stated that, in the case of severe congenital cataracts 'lens extraction ... should be done in one eye by the age of two months to permit normal development of vision'; and in the case of squint or 'lazy eye': 'If vision has not developed by the age of seven there is no chance that it will develop later'. Bright light stimulation has been used successfully in many centres with visually unresponsive children both in Britain and in other countries (for example, in the Living Light Center, Overbrook School for the Blind, Philadelphia and Melland School for children with Severe Learning Difficulties in Manchester). At the present time, a study is being undertaken by

M. Mabon in Manchester into the use of light stimulation, which should produce some very useful evidence as to the stage of development at which it is effective.

The long-term aim for all pupils is the maximum achievable self-help and independence, for life after school may not be easy. The teacher for the visually impaired should be involved in planning teaching programmes, throughout the pupil's school life, for such skills as eating, handling money, reading social signs, social behaviour and learning to use the environment rather than being concerned only with specific skills for the blind and partially sighted. Opportunities for further training and education for severely additionally handicapped, visually-impaired school-leavers are not readily available, though places in adult training centres may be open to them. Henshaw's School in Harrogate now offers an independence training course for visually-impaired school-leavers with additional handicaps. Hethersett College for Blind Adolescents in Surrey gives vocational guidance and social adjustment training and will accept young people with moderate additional difficulties. Some colleges of further education offer programmes for older pupils with learning difficulties which are also open to the visually handicapped.

Ideally, the same peripatetic teacher or team of teachers would follow a pupil's progress throughout, from pre-school home visiting to further education and on into liaison with post-school placements and careers advisers. The peripatetic teacher for the visually impaired can provide continuity and link all the various agencies concerned with the child, including the family.

Implications of Research and Conclusion

The good peripatetic service is a resource able to lend or demonstrate aids and equipment and disseminate information as well as teach. Staff should be able to study new information and follow, or even undertake, research, in order to plan the most effective use of resources. Access to academic libraries or medical journals is not easy for teachers, but some of the work done in medicine and developmental psychology would be valuable in validating or giving new impetus to teaching programmes. See, for example, Bower's work on the use of echo-location by blind infants (Bower 1977).

In-service research by practising teachers tends to be of the most direct relevance to other teachers, being most often aimed at problem-solving and development of teaching methods, whereas academic research is more likely to be chosen for theoretical interest, suitability of the sample or relevance to an academic programme. It would be a far-sighted policy on the part of an education authority to allow teachers time and facilities for in-service research, but few do, and the number will not increase in times of economic stringency.

Integration

The peripatetic teacher is an agent for integration. Those authorities who have employed visiting teachers for the visually impaired have, in fact, been operating a policy of integration for many years. There are many visually impaired children in neighbourhood mainstream schools in Manchester, Sheffield, Birmingham and elsewhere, maintained in them by a visiting specialist teacher; likewise, children with more than one handicap are able to have help for their visual difficulties while remaining in the school best able to cater for their primary handicap. It would seem to be in line with the intentions of the Warnock Report and the 1981 Act to put more money and resources into specialist peripatetic services.

References

ACSET (1984) *Teachers' Training and Special Educational Needs* (the advisory committee report on the supply and education of teachers).

Barraga, N.C. and Morris, J.E. (1980) *Program to Develop Efficiency in Visual Functioning*. American Printing House for the Blind.

Bower, T.G.R. (1977) *A Primer of Infant Development*. Freeman, pp. 102-5.

Chapman, E.K. (1978) *Visually Handicapped Children and Young People, Special Needs in Education*. Routledge and Kegan Paul, pp. 143-50.

Chapman, E.K., Tobin, M.J., Tooze, F.H.C. and Moss, S.C. (1981) *Look and Think, Schools Council Visual Perception Training Project of Blind and Partially-sighted 5-11 Year olds*, revised edn. RNIB/Schools Council Publications.

Colborne-Brown, M. and Tobin, M. (1982) *Integration of the Educationally Blind: information from questionnaires to parents*. RNIB, Section 5.

DES (1984) *Proposals for the Future Provision in Special Schools for Children with Visual Handicaps*, revised edn.

Gregory, R.L. (1977) *Eye and Brain, the Psychology of Seeing*. Weidenfeld and Nicholson, pp. 189-218.

Hunt, H., McKendrick, O., Poole, J., Pugh, R.E., Rosenbloom, L. and Turnock, R. (1979) 'Visual impairment in childhood: three years' experience of an assessment team in Liverpool', in V. Smith and J. Keen (eds.). *Visual Handicap in Children.* Spastics Internaitonal Medical Publications, p. 45.

Kerr, J.J. (1980) The Living Light Center, Overbrook School for the Blind, Philadelphia.

Mabon, M. *Research Project: use of light to stimulate the visual cortex.* Manchester Service for Visually Handicapped Children and Students, Shawgrove School, Cavendish Road, West Didsbury, Manchester, M20 8JR.

Maxfield, K.E. and Bucholz, S. (1957) *A Social Maturity Scale for Blind Pre-School Children: a guide to its use.* American Foundation for the Blind.

Reynell, J. (1979) 'Mental development', in *Manual, Developmental Scales for Young Visually Handicapped Children.* NFER p. 31.

Reynell, J. and Zinkin, P. (1979) 'Mental development', in *Developmental Scales for Young Visually Handicapped Children.* NFER.

Robinson, G.C. (1977) 'Causes, ocular disorders, associated handicaps and incidence and prevalence of blindness in childhood', in J.E. Jan, R.D. Freeman, and E.P. Scott. *Visual Impairment in Children and Adolescents.* Grune and Stratton, pp. 27-47.

Tallents, C. (1979) 'The visual handicaps found in a population of mentally and physically handicapped children', in V. Smith, and J. Keen. *Visual Handicap in Children,* Spastics International Medical Publications, pp. 68-75.

Tobin, M.J. (1978) *An Introduction to the Psychological and Educational Assessment of Blind and Partially-Sighted Children.* Research Centre for the Education of the Visually Handicapped, University of Birmingham.

Vaughan, D. and Asbury, T. (1980) *General Ophthalmology,* 9th edn. Large Medical Publications. pp. 129, 337.

Williams, M. (1956) *Intelligence Test for Children with Defective Vision.* NFER.

Journals and Bulletins in Britain

The British Journal of Visual Impairment, c/o Faculty of Education, University of Birmingham, B15 2TT.

Computer Assisted Learning for the Visually Handicapped, Newsletter, (Blenkhorn, P. Ed.), RCEVH and CET, RCEVH, Selley Wick House, 59 Selly Wick Road, Birmingham, B29 7JF.

Information Exchange, c/o Education Officer, RNIB, Education Dept, 224 Gt Portland Street, London W1N 6AA.

'In Touch' Bulletin, BBC Publications, PO Box 234, London SE1 3TH

New Beacon, RNIB, 224, Gt Portland Street, London W1N 6AA.

Oculus, Partially Sighted Society, 40 Wordsworth Street, Hove, E. Sussex, BN3 5BH.

Directories and Information Services

Abstracts Service, RCEVH, (Resource Centre for Education of the Visually Handicapped), Selly Wick House, 59 Selly Wick Road, Birmingham B29 7JF.

(Also other information concerning education of the visually handicapped.)

Directory of Agencies for the Blind in the British Isles and Overseas, RNIB, 224 Gt Portland Street, London W1N 6AA.

Directory of Resources for those working with visually handicapped children, Philippa Travis, Dept of Special Education, Faculty of Education, University of Birmingham, PO Box 363, B15 2TT.

Directory of Services for the Mentally/Visually Handicapped (1983) Southern and Western Regional Association for the Blind, 55 Eton Avenue, London NW3 3E7.

Henshaw's Independence Centre, Henshaw's School for the Visually Handicapped, Bogs Lane, Harrogate, HG1 4ED.

Hethersett College, RNIB, 32 Gatton Road, Wray Common, Reigate, Surrey, RH2 0HD.

International Directory of Aids and Appliances for Blind and Visually Impaired Persons, American Foundation for the Blind, 15 West 16 Street, New York, NY 10011.

Optical Information Council, Walter House, 418-422 Strand, London WC2 0PD.

Research Centre for Education of the Visually Handicapped, Selly Wick House, 59 Selly Wick Road, B29 7JF.

RNIB, Reference Library, Braille House, 338 Goswell Road, London EC1V 7JE.

Sources for Equipment, Handbooks or Advice

Active, c/o Toy Libraries Association, Seabrook House, Darkes Lane, Potters Bar, Herts., KN6 2HL: Aids and toys for the disabled.

Light stimulation (advice on):

1. M. Mabon, Manchester Service for Visually Impaired Children and Students, Shawgrove School, Cavendish Road, West Didsbury, Manchester, M20 8JR.
2. R.K. Crisp Feering Educational Developments, Brookfield Cottage, High Road, Swilland, Ipswich, Suffolk.

Low vision aids:

1. Low vision aid clinics, regional eye hospitals.
2. List of opticians from: The Association of Optical Practitioners, Bridge House, 233 Blackfriars Road, London SE1 8NW.
3. Disabled Living Foundation, 380-384 Harrow Road, London W9 2HU.

Parents' telephone service: advice for parents: Tel. 0606 407726.

Resource centres: RNIB, London and local voluntary societies for the blind (see local directories).

Handbooks: RNIB, Education Dept, for handbooks on education of visually handicapped and deaf/blind.

Shawgrove School, Cavendish Road, West Didsbury, Manchester M20 8JR.

1. Handbook of Suggestions for Parents of Young Visually Handicapped Children, Frankenberg, R.A.
2. Programme Planning for Teachers ESNSVH Children, Mabon M.

Sonic aids:

1.   Visionaid Systems, Office No. 7, Enterprise Workshops, Riverside Way, The Meadows, Nottingham.
2.   Wormald International Sensory Aids Ltd, 7 Musters Road, West Bridgford, Nottingham, NG2 7PP.

Further Reading

Adelson E. and Fraiberg, S. (1974) 'Gross Motor Development in Infants Blind from Birth'. *Child Development.*
Anderson, E.S., Dunlea, A. and Kekelis, L.S. (1984) 'Blind children's language: resolving some differences'. *Jnl of Child Language,* (Nov.)
DES (1978) *Special Educational Needs: report of the committee of enquiry into the education of handicapped children and young people* (the Warnock Report).
Eden, John (1981) *The Eye Book.* Penguin.
Fraiberg, S. (1977) *Insights from the Blind.* Souvenir Press.
Harley, R.K. and Lawrence, G.A. (1977) *Visual Impairment in Schools.* Chas. Thomas.
Lowenfeld, B. (ed.). *The Visually Handicapped Child in School.* Constable.
Mills, A.E. (ed.). (1983) *Language Acquisition in the Blind Child Normal and Deficient.* Croom Helm.
Mori, A.A. and Olive, J.E. (1978) 'The blind and visually handicapped mentally retarded: suggestions for intervention in infancy'. *Visual Impairment and Blindness,* (Sept).
RCEVH (1983) *Report on computer hardware in schools and units for the visually handicapped.*
RCEVH (1983) *Some guidelines for evaluating and adapting CAL software with the visually handicapped — using a screen.*
Scott, E.P., Jan, J.E. and Freeman, R.D. (1977) *Can't Your Child See?* University Park Press.
Urwin, C. (1978) 'Early language development in blind children'. DECPBPS, Occasional Papers, Vol. II (2).
Urwin, C. (1984) 'Language for absent things: learning from visually handicapped children'. *Topics in Language Disorders,* (Sept).

THE PERIPATETIC TEACHER FOR THE DEAF-BLIND

Jim Dale

It is thought by many educationalists that the vast majority of deaf-blind children, because of the multiplicity of their handicaps are rightfully placed in schools for children with severe learning difficulties, and that a peripatetic teacher of the deaf-blind would be sufficient help in counteracting the problems created through impairments of sight and hearing. If and when brain damage and additional handicaps are profound, such provision for the deaf-blind child may be realistic, but there is also an increasing number of educationalists (and particularly parents) who believe that a large portion of these children may be misplaced and that peripatetic teachers alone are unable to compensate sufficiently.

From a number of surveys the National Deaf-Blind and Rubella Association (NDBRA, previously the National Association for the Deaf-Blind and Rubella Handicapped, NADBRH) estimated in 1983 that there were 900-1,000 deaf-blind children in the UK between the ages of five and 19 years — this does not include the pre-school or the youngest school intakes. Though there are approximately 75 children in units for the multi-handicapped deaf, there are only 63-65 children in the three units catering specifically for the deaf-blind. Between four and five hundred children are to be found in schools for children with severe learning difficulties. Besides these schools (with the exception of the three units) the peripatetics for the deaf-blind have received requests to visit from schools for the blind/partially sighted, schools for the deaf/ partially hearing and sometimes day nurseries.

Throughout the UK the only agencies providing peripatetic advisory/teaching services for deaf-blind children are the Royal National Institute for the Blind (RNIB), the NDBRA and one local education authority — the Inner London Education Authority (ILEA). The RNIB employ ten advisors for the pre-school visually handicapped. Although not specifically trained for the deaf-blind, they have had extensive experience. The Institute also employs one person to advise on the care and training of deaf-blind people of all ages. The NDBRA have five teachers/advisors for the deaf-blind child. They are based at three residential Family Centres (Ealing, Birmingham, and Newcastle) from where they give a visiting service. From 1972 ILEA employed one teacher to cover all ten divisions, but since January 1985, two extra teachers have begun their peripatetic duties. The service is to concentrate on the needs of deaf-blind children within SLD schools, though official requests from other schools would be considered. Throughout the UK there are only six qualified teachers who are also trained for both the blind and the deaf or who have the Perkins (USA) Diploma for the Deaf-Blind.

When one considers the number of peripatetics, the areas to be covered and the size and complexity of the need, the inadequacy of the services to the deaf-blind is not the least surprising.

Definition

One of the principal reasons for inadequate statistics on the deaf-blind, indifferent attitudes and no co-ordinated policy (NADBRH 1983) is that there has been an insufficiently accurate definition of deaf-blindness. The government's position has little changed since 1974, when an educational category for these children was not accepted by the government as 'one for which special educational provision is provided' (RNIB 1974), despite the NDBRA campaign to have the category recognised.

Why should the definition pose a problem? Deaf-blindness can range from the congenital, totally blind/profoundly deaf (often functioning at a very low educational level) to the adventitious totally blind/profoundly deaf (often functioning at a high educational level). Deaf-blindness can also range from total losses to partial losses and even include children 'who might be described as pseudo-deaf-blind' (Watkins in ICEBY 1971). Though being unable to 'see' a small object and/or give a response to some sound, they are unable to 'conceptualise' visual and auditory inputs as 'normal' children do.

The internationally accepted definition of a deaf-blind child in 1971 (ICEBY 1971) was 'one who has both a visual and auditory impairment to such an extent, when considered conjointly, that he is unable to develop or function satisfactorily in either a regular programme for auditory impaired children or a regular programme for visually impaired children'. It did not say that a programme designed for seeing and hearing children in SLD schools would be satisfactory!

An up-to-date definition from Canada (McInnes and Treffrey 1982) states that 'the deaf-blind are unable to receive non-distorted information from either distance sense and are thus faced with a multiple of complex perceptual, psychological and physiological problems. The combination of impairments make impossible the traditional approaches used to alleviate the handicaps of deafness or blindness'.

There are many causes of deaf-blindness (Illingworth 1963; Kates 1976; NADBRH 1983; Peebles, in ICEBY 1971) most of which bring additional problems, e.g.:

1. syndromes — at least 26 can cause deaf-blindness;
2. meningitis — can cause hydrocephalus and paralysis;

3. birth trauma;
4. retrolental fibroplasia — now rarely through prematurity;
5. venereal disease — has other manifestations;
6. retinitis pigmentosa — can bring mental deterioration;
7. adventitious — can cause frustration and depression;
8. encephalitis — neurological complications rarely include mental defectiveness;
9. unknown — the largest group, rare hereditary diseases and no specific diagnosis;
10. rubella syndrome — the largest single cause, bringing with it (especially if contracted in the first trimester) many medical problems.

The many causes make diagnosis of deaf-blindness that much more difficult, but however confusing the identification and for whatever reasons, it is strongly urged that a far more serious attempt be made to do so.

After so much theoretical emphasis on the benefits of appropriate stimulation in the first year or two of life, no promise is made to help the deaf-blind appropriately. The Education Act (Section 1(4)) says that 'special educational provision for a child under two years is defined as educational provision of any kind'. Nationally, pre-school children may be visited by peripatetic teachers of the hearing *or* visually impaired *or* home-school liaison teachers. The NDBRA estimate that there are 150-250 children in this age group and probably less than 50 receive 'the detailed developmental programmes required to enable them to achieve their capabilities' (NADBRH 1983). Little wonder that the majority will eventually be placed in SLD schools, with the other 400-500 deaf-blind. Perhaps the Individual Reports on Needs will help to identify the deaf-blind child before the dual handicaps take too heavy a toll. At present, nationally, referrals may come to the teacher of the deaf-blind via the peripatetic liaison teachers mentioned above, or social workers, health authorities, the RNIB, day nurseries, schools, parent associations or ILEA.

There is at present no course in this country giving teachers a qualification to work with the deaf-blind. For this one needs to go to the USA. However, a qualified teacher of the blind may become qualified for the deaf and vice versa. There have been a few in-service, short-term training courses, in the Netherlands, at colleges (e.g. Castle Priory), at NDBRA Centres (e.g. Ealing) and provided by ILEA for teachers of children with special educational needs. One may also profit from conferences on the deaf-blind and from teachers already fully qualified.

Even though impairments of the distant senses severely affect the ability to develop and 'traditional' approaches to alleviate the handicaps are considered useless, both the deaf-blind and the pseudo-deaf-blind receive very little help from specialised methods to make better use of residual sight and hearing and alternative teaching to compensate for losses. Perhaps severe brain damage may finally prove that a particular child cannot profit from special programming in units for the deaf-blind child, but he should (for several years) be given the benefit of the doubt. The following quote illustrates discontent with the prevailing system (NADBRH: 1983)

> There is at present NO co-ordinated policy or planning for the deaf-blind in the U.K. Consequently, services for them and their families are completely haphazard. In many parts of the country services are wholly inadequate.

Problems of Development

Besides the causes and additional problems mentioned earlier, when visual and auditory inputs have been non-existent or distorted from birth many aspects of development suffer, e.g. perception, concentration, communication, relationships, loco-motion and motivation. De Long (in ICEBY 1971) suggests that some of these may be the combined result of peripheral sensory defect and impaired maturation (myelination) of the brain.

Loss of vision only will enable the child to develop language and speech. Fraiberg (1968) reports that, of the well-supported blind child, seven out of eight followed language norms for sighted children throughout the first year of life. Loss of hearing only will expose the child to a variety of meaningful visual experiences to receive information from which he can begin to build concepts about his surroundings (ICEBY 1971). He can match shapes (at a distance) study movements and learn to sign.

A non-handicapped child about to perform a task will probably be using one or more of the four codes of 'internal representation' (Open University 1978).

1. A visual code — when the activity is 'internally seen'. There is a visual image of a person, thing or deed.
2. A speech code or an acoustical code — how it is 'heard', sounds provided by memory or from an external source.
3. An action code — from a 'muscular memory' or/and knowledge of a sequence of movements.
4. A semantic code — linking what needs to be done with the memory of something else (e.g. reading pages 7 to 31 would be my age to mother's age).

The amount of representation with a child having insufficient sight and hearing, would probably be nil through a semantic code, very little from speech or an acoustical code and little from a visual code. The major cognitive activity would seem to rely on an action code (touch and movement).

The child could also develop one or more behavioural traits, mannerisms or 'blindisms' for a variety of reasons (e.g. attempting to satisfy demands, or blocking confusing inputs, or to release tension, or to get attention or even to 'occupy' self in an unstimulating environment) (Lowell and Rouin 1977). These could constitute a social handicap, but more importantly, they could become so impelling as to inhibit essential inputs and become a strong brake on any progress. Before attempting to 'extinguish' this type of behaviour one should try to find out why it started and whether there could be a satisfying alternative.

It has often been said that the psychology of deaf-blindness is different from the psychology of deafness or that of blindness and is far more complex than the two combined. Even in the matter of physiotherapy, some standard techniques may need to be modified (Sonksen, Levitt and Kitsinger 1984). Some postures may restrict the child's learning by making him more blind or giving him a greater hearing loss, e.g. lying prone with good sight directed forwards, or on his side with his 'good' ear (or a hearing aid) against the mattress. In addition to the physical impairments, characteristics and problems already mentioned, the child suffers yet another handicap. Insensitivity, fear, lack of consistency, ignorance of methods and many other factors, all contribute to the child's lack of progress.

Assessment and Testing

It is essential that the deaf-blind child be identified as such as early as possible so that parents and educationalists can begin planning the future. Diagnosis and evaluation are not solely to determine the nature and extent of any impairments for possible medical treatment, but also to assist the education authority in deciding the best placement and the teacher as to the most suitable aids, methods and programmes. Even if medical records are sometimes insufficiently detailed, it would be helpful for advisory, peripatetic teachers to have better access and more information from them than is often permitted.

McInnes and Treffrey (1982) are aware that 'In the past, many children who had both visual and auditory handicaps were assumed to be profoundly retarded', and, considering the bulk of the placements, there has been little change in assumptions. Myklebust (1954) and Maiden (1974) warned us of the inadequacies of tests, though social quotients (SQ) as provided by the Adaptation of the Vineland Social Maturity Scale can be helpful. Blea *et al.* (1976) confirm that there were 'no specific tests to measure the intelligence or functioning level of the deaf-blind' nor had adapted testing instruments been studied for reliability or validity. In addition to there being no single suitable material reliably to test a deaf-blind child's capabilities, there are extra problems of assessment, for example:

1. because of the complexities, it would be very difficult to give a thorough assessment in a few days;
2. because of the anxieties of deaf-blindness, the child may be too disturbed to perform at its best;
3. because of lack of experience, psychologists may not be cognisant of the special characteristics that affect the test results of the deaf-blind child;
4. because the child's world is limited, minor illnesses may affect performance;
5. because of lack of experience during infancy, there may be little difference in development (and test result) between a deaf-blind child with a good intellect and one who is severely damaged;
6. because the child is dependent on consistency and is ritualistic, minor changes in test material or method of approach, could cause confusion.

Though testing is so difficult and IQ and SQ scores so doubtful, many authorities (Guidon 1969; Chess *et al.* 1971; McInnes and Treffrey 1982, to name but a few) believe that the child's intellectual capacity far exceeds the limits indicated by his performance. Given sufficient training, the developmental gaps and lags, especially in the child with no (viral?) damage to the brain, will not be permanent deficits.

Teaching

There are a number of models (e.g. developmental, chronological, theoretical, etc.) from which to work with the child. This writer believes that the developmental model may well be the most useful. Several developmental guides provide good opportunities to find answers to several questions.

1. What has he been able to do?
2. When was he able to do it?
3. What can he do now?
4. How well can he do it?
5. What reasons could there be for 'gaps' in the record?
6. What should be attempted next?

The guide should also help build an 'individual programme' for each child, covering all areas of development. One area may be concentrated on more than others and its steps be broken down into finer and finer steps for learning. Such fragmentation will not prevent anyone dealing with the whole child (Funderburg 1978). No developmental guide is fully comprehensive. However, it is helpful to have some tangible base from which to plan and a record a following teacher may continue with.

Deciding and keeping aims and objectives for the deaf-blind child can be quite problematical for a number of reasons.

1. Problems accrue when each teacher has to start afresh due to inexperience (with the deaf-blind) and inadequate transfer of methods, programmes and material.
2. Each person has his/her own aim and objectives, and there is a danger of pursuing them independently. Physiotherapist, speech therapist, teacher, parents and any other

peripatetic service should meet periodically to discuss their respective inputs.

3. People differ in their own interpretation of results.
4. Short-term goals often obscure and neglect long-term aims.
5. Initially progress may be so slow that only very finely recorded steps will give sufficient encouragement to persevere with a method or programme. This may need graphing.
6. Attainment levels in different areas of development may vary greatly. Rate of progress in each area may also fluctuate considerably.
7. One may be uncertain whether to try to fill any gaps in the stages of development or to raise the level.
8. Any break in programme or method (e.g. change of teacher, vacations, etc.) can severely upset progress.
9. The further the teacher-child ratio is from 1:2 the more difficult it is to give adequate individual attention for teaching or detailed recording.

The Role of the Peripatetic Teacher for the Deaf-blind

Besides attempting to overcome the above problems, the class teacher is encouraged by the peripatetic teacher to use certain techniques for the deaf-blind child that she may not otherwise do for the majority of her children. She could:

1. give a set programme of short activities with a recognisable beginning and end;
2. ensure that the work be carefully illuminated and/or initially screened so that other things/activities do not distract the child's attention;
3. try to keep extraneous noise down to a minimum, so that any hearing aid could be put to better use;
4. attempt to synchronise complementary inputs and give more consideration to the times for stimulation and their duration;
5. if strong physical prompts are necessary, work from behind the child so that guidance has a more natural movement (see Chapter 6);
6. to maintain interest in equipment used for training, alter its 'appearance' in subtle ways, e.g. change of colour, texture,

etc. If the changes are too great the task may not be recognised;

7. vocabulary must be planned around the child's likes/
dislikes and used extensively;
8. prevent mannerisms from developing.

There are other facets to the work of the peripatetic advisory
teacher. He/she:

1. needs to proportion attention to the various schools, with
due consideration of distance, number of children in a
school and the number of classes there to be visited. It is
rarely convenient to the school to visit all the classes on the
same day;
2. is able to spread ideas between the schools;
3. is free to assess and observe the child and concentrate on
certain developmental areas and problems;
4. is able to experiment with and lend special apparatus;
5. needs to keep as 'up-to-date' as possible through literature,
meeting with peripatetics for the deaf and for the visually
handicapped, conferences and courses;
6. is occasionally asked to visit the children's home (mainly
after school).

However much time the peripatetic teacher may be able to spend
teaching, most of the work in the week will be done by the family,
the class teacher and aids. Because of this it is essential for all four
elements to have the same aims and methods, and that the 'specialist' teacher operates more on an advisory role.

Aids and Equipment

For many children it might only be possible to tailor-make apparatus and 'toys' that centre round their very limited abilities and
likes. This calls for adaptation and inventiveness. There are also
many children who can profit from a wide range of commercial
apparatus, a few of which can be mentioned.

The use of computer 'games' and ultra-violet light are helping
the child with defective/impaired vision to concentrate more on
what needs to be shown. Vibro-tactile stimuli can be therapeutic
and used to develop skills. Synthetic speech, robotics, and other
control systems will open up the world of the deaf-blind. Perhaps

the future will see a computer fed with facts of a child's abilities, disabilities, age, etc., and able to prescribe the best programmes and methods for development. Even then it may be necessary to devise 'home-made' apparatus that positively rewards and stimulates the child to further effort.

Integration

In 1974, a survey of nine special units for the deaf-blind child (NADBRH) revealed an average staff ratio of 1:2½. Not only does one find an SLD curriculum not geared to the peculiar needs of the deaf-blind child within it, but the staff:child ratio has effectively worsened. The deaf-blind child rarely learns anything when left on his own and is more in need of individual attention than any other.

Integration has, long before the 1981 Act, been an objective worth striving for. The Act gave impetus to such an extent that some became desperate to prove its success without being sufficiently cautious or conscious of failure. When the optimum training has been given to sight and hearing, when certain developmental levels have been reached and when 'unusual' communication is no obstacle to progress within the larger group, integration can be truly beneficial. Even then it has to be gradually made, amply assisted and carefully checked.

Perhaps our aims for the future should respect the reports on International Conferences which show that several countries have decided that residential units/schools specifically for the deaf-blind, provide the best placement.

References

Blea, W.A., Lowell, E.L., Meyer, S., Thielman, V.B., and Rouin, C. (1976) *Learning Steps: A Handbook for Persons Working with Deaf-Blind Children in Residential Settings.* State Department of Education, Sacramento, USA.
Best, C. (1983) *The New Deaf-Blind (National Survey).* National Association for Deaf-Blind and Rubella Handicapped. UK.
Chess, S., Korn, S. and Fernandez, P. (1971) *Psychiatric Disorders of Children with Congenital Rubella.* Brunner/Mazel Inc. New York.
DES (1981) *Education Act* (CH. 60) HMSO.
Fraiberg, S. (1968) 'Parallel and Divergent Patterns in Blind and Sighted Infants'. *The Psychoanalytic Study of the Child, 23,* Yale University Press.
Funderburg, R. (1978) in *Proceedings: Understanding the Needs of Deaf-Blind Children in Isolated Areas.* State Department of Education, Sacramento USA.
Guidon, A.W. (1969) *Report on Number of Multi-Handicapped Children*

Resulting from the 1964-1965 Rubella Epidemic. State Department of Education, Sacramento, USA.

ICEBY (1971) *The Fourth International Conference on Deaf-Blind Children.* Perkins School for the Blind. USA.

Illingworth R.S. (1963) *The Development of the Infant and Young Child: Normal and Abnormal.* E. and S. Livingstone Ltd.

Kates L. (1976) *The Need for Interdependency among Agencies Providing Services to Deaf-Blind Persons.* National Centre for Deaf-Blind Youths and Adults, Sands Point, New York.

Lowell E.L. and Rouin C.C. (eds.). (1977) *State of the Art: Perspectives on Servicing Deaf-Blind Children.* State Dept of Education, Sacramento, USA.

Maiden D. (1974) *The Next Step on the Ladder (Parts 1 & 11).* British Institute of Mental Handicap.

McInnes J. and Treffry, J. (1982) *Deaf-Blind Infants and Children.* Open University Press, UK.

Melzack R. in G. Newton, and S. Levine (eds.). (1970) *The Psychobiology of Development: Early Experience Behaviour,* Charles C. Thomas, Springfield, Illinois, USA.

Myklebust H.R. (1954) *Report of the National Study Committee on the Education of Deaf-Blind Children.* Perkins School for the Blind, Mass. USA.

NADBRH (Council) (1974) *Survey of the Number of Children and Staff in Units for the Deaf-Blind.* (prepared by A. Best) NADBRH.

NADBRH (Council) (1983) *A Programme for Development.* National Assn. for Deaf-Blind and Rubella Handicapped. UK.

NDBRA (1983) *The New Deaf-Blind (National Survey).* National Deaf-Blind and Rubella Association.

Open University (1978) *Cognitive Psychology, Introduction (part 2): Experimental Design and Case Study.* D303 Block 1. Unit 2. Open University UK.

RNIB (1974) *Fifth International Deaf-Blind Seminar.* Royal National Institute for the Blind. UK.

Sonksen P.H., Levitt S. and Kittsinger M. (1984) 'Identification of Constraints acting on Motor Development in Young Visually Disabled Children and Principles of Remediation'. *Child: Care, Health and Development, 10.*

THE DISTRICT AND COMMUNITY MENTAL HANDICAP TEAM

Richard Cotmore

Community Mental Handicap Teams

The concept of the Community Mental Handicap Team (CMHT) was first promoted by two quangos established to monitor and advise authorities on services for the mentally handicapped: the now defunct National Development Group (NDG) and the Development Team for the mentally handicapped (DT). The lack of co-ordination of service provision to mentally handicapped people and their families was of primary concern to these two bodies. The DT stated that, while in many areas professionals were already providing the required advice and help, 'the help is frequently uncoordinated, fragmented and insufficiently related to the needs of the family' (DT 1978: para. 113). Indeed the NDG claimed: 'Only by coordinating the activities of a group of different specialists can the varied overall needs of a mentally handicapped individual be considered' (NDG 1976: para 22). The CMHT was envisaged then as providing a forum for multidisciplinary teamwork, which would facilitate the co-ordination of services. For this reason it was important that the CMHT be seen as 'the first point of contact for parents' (NDG 1977: para 16).

As well as co-ordinating services and access to services, CMHTs were envisaged as providing a direct support service to mentally handicapped people and their families:

The functions of the community team will be to provide the necessary specialised help and support to the mentally handicapped individuals requiring their assistance at home ... This will have the general aim of helping the family to continue to care for the mentally handicapped individual, to make a positive contribution to management and training and should specifically include —

i)   specialist advice, counselling and support for parents. ...
ii)   specialist advice on day to day management. (DT 1978: para 116).

The CMHT's practical support role has since been emphasised: 'We lay particular stress on the domiciliary nature of the service ...' (Mittler and Simon 1978: p. 542).

District Handicap Teams

At the same time as the NDG and DT were recommending CMHTs to improve domiciliary services to families and to provide a more co-ordinated service, the Court Committee on Child Health Services produced its report. The report was critical of the services provided to handicapped children and their families: 'The standard of diagnosis, assessment, treatment and care for children suffering from physical, mental or multiple handicaps whether in the hospital or community does not reach that largely achieved by the health service for the treatment of acute illness ...' (DHSS 1976; para 14.12).

Court was also critical of the lack of co-ordination of services, characterised by overlap, poor coverage and little communication between professionals, with the result that: 'parents fail to obtain the ready help and support for which they constantly and sometimes desperately feel the need' (DHSS 1976; para 4.46). The response of the Court Committee to this situation was to recommend the establishment of multidisciplinary district handicap teams (DHTs). The DHT's clinical functions would include the provision of a 'special diagnostic assessment and treatment service for handicapped children and advice and support for their parents' (DHSS 1976; para 14.22). In addition to its clinical function, the DHT was seen as undertaking 'operational' functions, including the monitoring of services, surveys of need and acting as an information source about handicap.

Government Policy

Faced with two different models for organising services to mentally handicapped children — the CMHT and the DHT — how did the government respond? Although it did not accept all of Court's recommendations it did accept the principle of the DHT, to 'bring the health, education and social services together' (DHSS 1978; para 9). In the same circular, the government accepted the concept of the CMHT. As blueprints there are some obvious differences between CMHTs and DHTs, notably that CMHTs were envisaged as covering mentally handicapped people of all ages and DHTs were intended solely for children. Also CMHTs would deal with mental handicap only and DHTs with all forms of handicap. But who should work with children with a mental handicap?

The Court Committee foresaw DHTs working with all severely mentally handicapped children. It has been argued, however, that the DHT would not be able to meet the needs of all mentally handicapped children, particularly the small number with the 'most severe and complex disorders of development and behaviour' (Mittler and Simon 1978: p. 541). For this reason the CMHT should complement the DHT as a second tier, providing more specialist services. The Campaign for Mentally Handicapped People (CMH) on the other hand, argue that the DHT would be better able to keep mentally handicapped children in touch with generic services, thereby postponing the 'process of segregation'

(Plank 1982: p. 26) and recommend that all handicapped children should be the responsibility of the DHT until school-leaving age, with CMHTs responsible only for mentally handicapped adults.

It would appear that there exist 'inherent conflicts in ideology and government thinking as to who should work with mentally handicapped children' (Gilbert and Spooner 1982: p. 18). It is ironic that two models of team have been recommended, both in an attempt to provide a 'single door' to improve the co-ordination of services.

Teams in Practice

The national pattern of CMHTs and DHTs is constantly changing, as their number continues to rise. There are approximately 110 DHTs and 130 CMHTs in existence at present.[1] Exact figures are difficult to obtain and are soon out of date, but CMH undertook a national survey in 1981 which provides a picture of the operation of CMHTs and DHTs at that time. Of the 158 health districts surveyed, 87 had DHTs in operation and 71 had CMHTs (see Table 12.1)

The national survey found that most health districts had their own variation of DHT; some carried out assessments and co-ordinated treatment programmes; some, in addition, carried out the treatment programme themselves, while other teams had only a co-ordinating function or a planning and monitoring role. CMH concluded: 'There is no typical DHT' and noted the possible implication for parents of such a variety in DHTs: 'The Court Committee intended the system of DHTs to simplify matters for parents, but the present situation means parents are left confused about what exactly a DHT is and what they can expect from it' (Plank 1982: p. 13). Unlike the DHTs which varied greatly in their functions, CMHTs commonly adopted a similar function, that of

Table 12.1: Distribution of Teams in Operation

	DHT	CMHT	Both	Neither	Total
No. of Health Districts	47	31	40	40	158
%	30	20	25	25	100

Source: M. Plank (1982) 'Teams for mentally handicapped people'. CMH Table 1.

'providing a practical support service to families with a mentally handicapped member ...' (Plank 1982: p. 15).

Membership

The core membership of DHTs is summarised in Table 12.2.

The doctors were commonly consultant paediatricians, senior medical officers or community physicians, and most teams had at least two medical members. Seventeen consultants in mental handicap were members of DHTs. A large majority of the psychologists were educational psychologists, and the educationalists included teachers and education department officers.

The core membership of CMHTs was somewhat different (summarised below in Table 12.3). Although most of the CMHTs were assessing the needs and strengths of mentally handicapped people, they were not making the initial diagnosis of mental handicap, as those referred to them had already been labelled thus. CMHTs have undertaken operational functions too. For example, over three-quarters of them recorded the monitoring of local services as one of their functions. More recently, Cubbon has found that many CMHTs have been involved in establishing registers of mentally handicapped people, indeed he considers such registers to be 'natural concomitants' of CMHTs (Cubbon 1983: sheet 5).

CMHTs and Children

The CMH survey found that three-quarters of the CMHTs undertook some work with children. The majority of CMHTs in areas

Table 12.2: Core Membership — DHTs

Profession	No. of DHTs having one or more of each profession	% of total DHTs
Doctor	90	100
Nurse	73	81
Psychologist	73	81
Social worker	72	80
Therapist	50	56
Educationalist	34	38

Source: M. Plank (1982) 'Teams for mentally handicapped people'. CMH Table 10.

without DHTs worked with both children and adults. Where both CMHTs and DHTs existed a number of different arrangements operated. For example, in some areas, CMHTs were involved with adults only; in others the initial assessment was undertaken by the DHT, and the child was referred to the CMHT which co-ordinated the treatment, while in others the 'degree of handicap' determined which team would work with the child. It is interesting to note that few of the CMHTs worked solely with the most severely handicapped people, as envisaged by the DT.

Although there was little involvement by education representatives in the DHTs there was far less in the CMHTs: only nine CMHTs had a teacher or education department official as members and the majority of psychologists were clinical psychologists rather than educational psychologists, as in the DHTs. Eighteen per cent of CMHTs had no medical input, and only five teams had consultant paediatricians as team members. The largest medical output was from consultant psychiatrists in mental handicap.

The CMH survey also found that the social worker and community mental handicap nurse were the 'mainstay' of most CMHTs: 'several teams have only these two professionals, and in many other teams they are the only members employed full time on the team' (Plank 1982: p. 48). This reflected the small size of a lot of CMHTs — the most common size being three or four members. The number of specialist social workers and community nurses in post has continued to rise; for example, the DT found an increase in the number of community nurses in mental handicap

Table 12.3: Core Membership — CMHTs

Profession	No. of CMHTs having one or more of each profession	% of total CMHTs
Social worker	66	81
Community nurse	65	80
Psychologist	54	67
Consultant in MH	52	64
Doctor (other than consultant in MH)	25	3
Therapist	16	20
Educationalist	9	11
Health visitors	4	5

Source: M. Plank (1982) 'Teams for mentally handicapped people'. CMH Table 10.

(CMHNs) from 50 to over 300 in the five-year period up to 1981 (DT 1982: para. 99). As Cubbon points out: 'Generally, CMHTs have not been formed simply by increasing contact between professionals already in post. Usually their creation has accompanied the appointment of professionals with new roles such as specialist social workers and community nurses' (Cubbon 1983: sheet 6).

Plank made the following comment on CMHT membership. 'The CMHTs appear to have made no special provision for dealing with children. The structure of each team remains constant whether concerned with child or adult, and few staff especially trained to work with children are included in the core membership' (Plank 1982: p. 23). Plank also noted that if CMHTs and DHTs are to provide a 'single door' for parents, and co-ordinate services more effectively, they should include all relevant professionals, and yet there are few representatives from education in either sort of team.

CMHT Roles

Potentially, there is a lot of overlap between CMHT members' roles. As a CMH nurse and social worker point out: 'It is clear that many roles in a community mental handicap team are interchangeable. There is no reason why any of the members could not practice behaviour therapy or family therapy given adequate training — social histories and nursing assessments have no particular mystique; and arrangements for short-term care in the ideal community unit could probably be done by any team member' (Gilbert and Spooner 1982: p. 19). This is best illustrated by a detailed consideration of the roles of the two most common CMHT members: CMHN and social worker.

CMHN

There are a number of identifiable roles that CMHNs have been undertaking, including:

1. therapist, whereby they (a) assess the abilities and needs of mentally handicapped people; and (b) undertake training/ teaching programmes in self-help, for example toileting, feeding and dressing;

2. clinical — CMHNs have a clinical nursing role, including the monitoring of medication, offering of advice on physical health and attendance at out-patient clinics;
3. counsellor — several CMHNs have described their counselling role with parents and families, for example: 'Regular, friendly, informal discussion, with parents in particular, often gives them the opportunity to air their views, discuss their grievances and, more important, to talk about their handicapped relative' (Thomson 1980: p. 2007). Such a role can also be a means to an end in helping to establish a trusting relationship between the professional and the family, thereby facilitating the training programme;
4. information bank/liaison — working in the community requires that the CMHN be aware of other agencies and their functions, so that she/he can act as a 'general information bank' for families regarding other resources and facilities (Elliott-Cannon 1981: p. 78). Several CMHNs are based in mental handicap hospitals and have a particular responsibility to form a link between the hospital and parents and, more broadly, between the hospital and the community. Liaison with and support of other resources such as adult training centres (ATCs) and schools is another role adopted by some CMHNs.

The practical nature of the help and support given to families by CMHNs is often stressed, as is their flexibility: 'The most advantageous aspect of the community nurse's role is that she is mobile and flexible. CMHNs are the health service equivalent of the SAS' (Branch 1984: p. iv). It is not surprising then that some community nursing schemes provide a 24-hour crisis intervention service.

CMHNs are becoming involved in an increasingly wide range of support schemes and using their skills in a number of different settings. For example, the CMHN team described by Crook (1984) has become involved in the following schemes for children and their parents:

a hospital toy library, which the CMHNs established and the parents now run themselves;
a local opportunity playgroup for children with social or developmental delays;
the 'Downs early intervention team', the aim of which is to

overcome the trauma and loneliness experienced by the parents;
summer holiday play schemes;
social services short-term fostering care.

With regard to adults, the support offered by CMHNs is not
restricted to mentally handicapped people who live with their
families. For example, some CMHNs support their clients in residential situations such as minimum support group living schemes
and warden-aided complexes. There are also some CMHNs
becoming involved in occupation and employment schemes, by
helping to establish training courses, sheltered workshops and by
placing mentally handicapped people in employment (Waldron
1984).

Social Worker

The DT has specified three areas in which they see a social work
input as appropriate in the mental handicap field:

1. 'Social work where there is mental handicap is essentially
    family work ...' (Simon 1981: p. 38). The basis of this
    claim is the social worker's understanding of family dynam-
    ics: 'the role of the social worker is to assess the family's
    reaction to the handicapped member and, more import-
    antly, to facilitate and help maintain satisfactory adjust-
    ments, which for most families are at times finely balanced
    between health and pathology ...' (Browne 1982: p. 44).
    Browne continues by stating that, in order to support the
    whole family, social workers need to adopt a 'family-
    centred approach' to 'provide a balance to the "official"
    view of handicap which focuses primarily on the needs of
    the mentally handicapped child alone' (Browne 1982:
    p. 51).

    The support commonly associated with social work is
    counselling. For example, Glendinning (1978) found that
    parents thought the resource workers (trained social
    workers) had been most helpful as counsellors, in discussing
    relationships within the family and the parents' own feelings
    and worries;

2. 'The Social Worker's knowledge of the wider range of
    services, statutory and voluntary, that now exist will ensure
    that the family are made aware of services and resources

that are available' (DT 1978: para 117). The social worker should also ensure that the service offered to his client by the other agencies is appropriate and, where it is not, may have to act as the client's advocate;

3. community attitudes. As Browne (1982: p. 40) states succinctly: 'One of the functions of the Social Worker is to interpret to the community the needs of the handicapped and their families and to mobilise all the forces that will encourage and facilitate the handicapped and their families to participate in and contribute to community life.'

There is a lot of agreement that the three functions above fall within the remit of the social worker, but there are other functions, too, which are discussed less often, one of which is 'development work'. There are two aspects to this:

1. the establishment of new or additional resources. Lewis (1982) found the following examples of resources established by specialist social workers; group homes; play-schemes; parents' workshops;
2. to encourage and support day, residential and fieldwork services, both statutory and voluntary, to improve the quality or broaden the scope of their activities. Encouragement of ATC staff to assess every trainee, and to check up on progress following reviews to ensure the implementation of recommendations, were two of the examples found by Lewis.

Frequently omitted in discussions of social work with the mentally handicapped is just that: what is the social work role with mentally handicapped people themselves? Browne (1982: p. 93) suggests: 'direct individual or group work with mentally handicapped people who need help with problems of social functioning'. Examples would include a workshop on sex education and the use of behaviour modification techniques. Browne found, however, an 'expressed lack of knowledge amongst social workers about behaviour modification techniques' (Browne 1982: p. 89). Some social workers do undertake such a 'direct' role with mentally handicapped people, but many feel uneasy about such a role and require more specialist training and preparation before they would consider undertaking it.

Role Overlap

From the role descriptions above, it is clear that there is a lot of potential overlap between the two roles, for example in counselling, therapy/teaching, as an 'information bank' and in 'development work'.

Where CMHNs and social workers work in a team, they have, in some instances, resolved problems of role overlap by adopting different foci in their work — nurses focusing primarily on the needs of the mentally handicapped person, and social workers on the needs of the family (Joinson 1979). Experience of social workers and CMHNs in multidisciplinary CMHTs suggests that it may 'take time' for them to feel comfortable with each others' roles, and that this is facilitated by their being based together. Sines (1983) argues that roles should be defined locally, and not nationally. A CMHN nurse and a social worker working in a CMHT agree; 'Any resulting definition of roles is often worked out on the basis of existing resources and the personnel working in any geographical area' (Ashton and Young 1984: p. iii).

Flexibility of roles between CMHT members has been exhorted often, and Wilson (1979) has claimed that it is the hallmark of a 'mature' team, wherein team members not only know each others' strengths and weaknesses, but are confident of their own roles. Role confidence and mature teamwork may be difficult to achieve, however, because of so much 'role uncertainty' in the field of mental handicap.

Role Uncertainty

The DT has noted the confusion among health authorities concerning the CMHN role and the result that some CMHNs are working without job descriptions. CMHNs themselves have written of the lack of preparation they have received for their move from work in hospitals to work in the community (Branch 1984; Short 1984). A further problem for some CMHNs, as witnessed by Hall and Russell (1979), is the conflict they face in being employed by the health service but in recognising the inappropriateness of the 'medical model' in the field of mental handicap.

In social work, role uncertainty in mental handicap has been found more often among generic social workers in area teams, than among social workers specialising in mental handicap. Browne found role uncertainty among area social workers manifesting itself in a number of ways, for example they were not employing the skills that they employed with their other client groups: 'i.e. "generic" skills were not being applied generically ...' (Lewis 1982: p. 66) and there was a lack of imagination in their work in mental handicap, two examples being little work with volunteers and little encouragement of parents' groups. Browne attributed the role uncertainty she found to the low priority accorded to mental handicap in area offices.

In recent years there has been some role uncertainty with regard to consultant psychiatrists in mental handicap. Several bodies, including the DT and the Royal College of Psychiatrists, have argued that the role of the consultant psychiatrist in mental handicap is to provide psychiatric care to mentally handicapped people and their families. Others have argued however that this is just one aspect of a very broad role, and that it is the breadth of the consultant's role which is unique, since it 'give(s) him a wider and less parochial understanding of human problems than that of other professions' (Harris 1981). Partly as a consequence of this broad overview and partly from tradition consultants are often, or feel themselves to be, the natural leader of a multidisciplinary team.

The delicate issues of leadership and co-ordination bring to the fore problems of role uncertainty and overlap. The debate is not so much at the 'task' level of 'who performs which task?' but at a much broader level, of the scope and the remit of the different professions. Some CMHNs feel, for example, that as a result of their training and experience being exclusively in mental handicap, they should have a broad remit: 'Nursing ... I would wish to interpret as "nurturing" ... Any procedures (activities) which encourage and strengthen self-respect and self-reliance are the legitimate field of the specialist community nurse' (Elliott-Cannon 1981: p. 80).

Critics however, take a narrower view of both mental handicap nurse and consultant roles, arguing that most mentally handicapped people do not require constant medical or nursing supervision and that their medical, psychiatric or nursing needs could be met through services available to the general population, such as the primary health care team. In this view, not only are CMHNs or consultant psychiatrists in mental handicap unnecessary, they are dangerous since they segregate the mentally handicapped from generic services. As this debate continues, an acknowledgement that community multidisciplinary teams should primarily be concerned with 'social rather than medical management' (Browne 1982: p. 94) has led some to conclude that 'social work training and experience provide ... the most appropriate professional background on which a support service for severely handicapped children and their families should be based' (Glendinning 1978: p. 319). The implications of this argument for the co-ordination of CMHTs are that 'the role of co-ordinator might be appropriately allocated to a Senior Social Worker' (Browne 1982: p. 94).

Co-ordination of a team's activities has been facilitated in some teams by adopting the 'key worker' principle, which the Court Report recommended for DHTs and which the NDG and DT have recommended for CMHTs. The key worker is chosen by the team as the most appropriate person to meet the needs of the mentally handicapped person and his family and will have responsibility for the ongoing programme while ensuring that plans formulated at assessments are implemented. In addition, the key worker acts as a 'named person' — the first point of contact for families. CMHTs and DHTs have varied, however, in their adoption of the key worker principle, as the CMH survey showed (see Table 12.4).

Relationships between CMHTs and Schools for Children with Severe Learning Difficulties

Relationships between professionals in the education service and other professionals tend to vary. For example, Glendinning (1978: p. 319) found one resource worker (a specialist social worker) who wished to be attached to a special school, but the other resource workers were less enthusiastic because of the varying reactions they had received from the schools' headteachers. Browne presented a more negative picture: 'On the whole, there seemed to

Table 12.4: Key Workers

	% CMHTs	% DHTs
Always assign a key worker	71	42
Never assign a key worker	17	36
Sometimes assign a key worker	12	21

Source: M. Plank (1982) 'Teams for mentally handicapped people'. CMH Tables 7 and 14.

be an uneasy relationship between the school staff and other professionals who were in contact with the handicapped clients and their families' (Browne 1982: p. 73).

It is worth exploring some of the factors which help to shape the relationships between schools and CMHTs.

Objectives. Because many CMHTs' priorities lie with adults, there are few teachers and educational psychologists incorporated into CMHTs as team members. In some cases, there may be little appreciation of how the schools' and CMHTs' objectives impinge upon each other, with the result that CMHTs have not been invited to school reviews or school-leaver conferences. Hopefully the 1981 Act will stimulate closer links between schools and CMHTs, as a result of the new statutory obligations, including annual reviews.

Organisation. Schools have sometimes found it difficult to understand the complexities of other organisations, particularly social services. It may be difficult to learn which social services area to contact and whom to contact within the area. CMHTs can facilitate such contact by providing a central co-ordinating point, which can 'filter' requests.

Roles and Role Uncertainty. In her study, Browne found that 'the social workers and the teachers felt undervalued by each other ...' (Browne 1982: p. 73). This resulted from teachers thinking that social workers saw schools as 'repositories' and social workers thinking that teachers only used them to 'run messages'. Some schools have been confused by other professionals' roles and the overlaps between these. For example, schools appear to have differed in their interpretations of the CMHN role: some have viewed it narrowly, primarily in terms of clinical nursing functions, while others have viewed it more broadly to include training and counselling.

Terminology. There is a fundamental difference between schools and the education service on the one hand, and CMHTs, health and social services on the other. CMHTs include 'mental handicap' in their title, but this term is no longer recognised by the education service. Mental handicap is a dangerous term, because like many other terms, interpretations vary to such a great extent, with the result that language confuses rather than clarifies. Indeed, one criticism levelled at some CMHTs is that they have not specified what they mean by the term 'mental handicap'.

It is likely that there have been occasions where the 'mental handicap' label has prevented full professional co-operation between the education service and CMHTs. For example there can be some reluctance to involve CMHTs in work with the under-fives, for fear that the parents have not fully accepted the situation and that a professional with a 'mental handicap' tag will add to their anxiety. Another example is the wariness of CMHTs shown by the schools for children with moderate learning difficulties.

Differences in terminology can belie differences in organisational and philosophical preferences. A pertinent issue is that of specialisation; in some areas the education service may have given the CMHTs a lukewarm reception because they see them as a newly-created specialist resource, at a time when 'in the spirit of Warnock' the education service is trying to get more children and teachers into ordinary situations.

Summary

Some of the confusion in both policy and practice with regard to the support of mentally handicapped children and their families has been highlighted. It is important to emphasise that local solutions have varied, in terms of: the establishment of CMHTs and DHTs; the memberships of CMHTs and DHTs; whether or not CMHTs work with children; and in how the professionals have resolved the issue of role overlap. Schools and CMHTs vary in how they work with each other and in the quality of their relationships, and some of the factors determining those relationships have been examined.

Note

1. Research is currently being undertaken into DHTs and CMHTs at the Community Paediatric Research Unit, St. Mary's Hospital, Medical School, London.

References

Ashton, P. and Young, S. (1984) 'Two skills are better than one'. *Nursing Mirror* 2.5.84 CMHNA Supplement, *158*, no. 18, pp. iii-vi.

Branch, R. (1984) 'One way of working'. *Nursing Mirror*, 1.2.84 CMHNA Supplement, *158*, no. 5, pp. iv-v.

Browne, E. (1982) *Mental handicap: the role for social workers.* University of Sheffield.

Crook, P. (1984) 'Setting up a service for the mentally handicapped'. *Nursing Times*, 8.2.84, *80*, no. 6, pp. 49-51.

Cubbon, J. (1983) *The Existence of Mental Handicap Registers in England, Scotland and Wales.* Sheffield City Polytechnic.

Development Team for the Mentally Handicapped (1978) 'First Report'. DHSS.

Development Team for the Mentally Handicapped (1982) 'Third Report'. DHSS.

DHSS (1976) *Report of the Committee on Child Health Services. Fit for the Future* (Court Report). CMND 6684.

DHSS (1978)'Health Services Developments:- Court Report on child health services'. HC (78) 5/LAC (78)2.

Elliott-Cannon, C. (1981) 'Do the mentally handicapped need specialist community nursing care?' *Nursing Times*, 1.7.81, 77, No. 27, pp. 77-80.

Gilbert, P. and Spooner, B. (1982) 'Strength in Unity'. *Community Care*, 28.10.82, no. 435, pp. 17-19.

Glendinning, C. (1978) *Resource Worker Project: Evaluation of a Specialist Support Service for Severely Handicapped Children and Their Families.* University of York.

Hall, V. and Russell, O. (1979) 'Community Nursing for the mentally handicapped: Threat or challenge? Description of a service in action'. *Mental Handicap Studies*, Research Report No. 3. University of Bristol.

Harris, G. (1981) 'The Consultant's challenge'. *Nursing Mirror*, 16.4.81 Supplement, *152*, no. 16, pp. x-xiv.

Joinson, P. (1979) 'Why did Jay ignore us?' *Nursing Mirror* 11.10.79, *149*, no. 15.

Lewis, J. (1982) 'A service for life. An examination of specialist social work for mentally handicapped people'. Clearing House for Local Authority Social Services Research, University of Birmingham.

Mittler, P. and Simon, G. (1978) 'Building support for the mentally handicapped and their families'. *Health and Social Service Journal,* 12.5.78, *88*, no. 4591, pp. 541-2.

National Development Group for the Mentally Handicapped (1976) *Mental Handicap: planning together.* Pamphlet No. 1. DHSS.

National Development Group for the Mentally Handicapped (1977) *Mentally Handicapped Children: a plan for action.* Pamphlet No. 2. DHSS

Plank, M. (1982) *Teams for Mentally Handicapped People.* CMH.

Short, J. (1984) 'From hospital to community'. *Nursing Mirror*, 1.3.84, CMHNA supplement, *158*, no. 5, pp. vi-vii.

Simon, G.B. (ed.). (1981) *Local Services for Mentally Handicapped People.* BIMH.

Sines, D. (1983) 'The role of the nurse in the community mental handicap team'. Talk given at day conference on 27 October 1983.

Thomson, R. (1980) 'Community nursing with mentally handicapped adults'. *Nursing Times*, 13.11.80, *76*, no. 46, pp. 2007-10.

Waldron, J. (1984) 'A worthwhile job'. *Nursing Mirror*, 2.5.84, CMHNA Supplement, *158*, no. 18, pp. vii-viii.

Wilson, D. (1979) 'When is a team not a team?' *Apex, 7* (3), p. 94.

THE SUPPORT UNIT

Jim Buggy

The Role of the Support Unit

The family support unit can take the form of a respite fostering service or, more usually, a purpose-built home/hostel, an ordinary house in the community with qualified residential social work staff, i.e. houseparents.

Some Local Authorities have carers available to actually go into a family's home to allow the parents/family some time off. This latter form of relief is gaining some support, as one of the advantages is that the handicapped person does not have to leave home. The disadvantage is that the family can become 'public property' with the number of professionals involved. The more recognised form of support unit is the purpose-built home/hostel or residential unit whereby the child is admitted for a specific period of time to give the family respite.

Definition of short-term care

In the context of this paper, STC refers to the arrangements whereby a handicapped child is looked after in a place other than his/her own home for a period of time which includes at least one night but does not exceed 2-3 months.

The Philosophy of the Support Unit

The philosophy of the support unit is to provide care for the children and relief to the parents and families of those severely mentally handicapped children. The policy is to treat the child first and the handicap second, to make the transition from home to the support unit as smooth as possible and to make the new living environment of the child as close to the home environment as is feasible. This can only be done by staff getting to know the child well so that a gradual introduction can be made.

Criteria for Admission

These criteria apply to all children who attend special schools, for children with severe learning difficulties and a nominal age range between 2 and 19 years of age. Referrals are sent to a central specialist social work section which is basically a home-finding section for handicapped children. These referrals are received via the family's social worker but can come from special schools, parents, etc. If a child and family are referred from school or from the parents and there is a field social worker involved, then the home-finding section will form a close liaison with that social worker to ensure that no duplication, etc. takes place.

Once the referral is received the child will be visited, either at home or at school, though more usually the initial visit is to the school. An assessment of the child is made: this is as a result of time being spent in the school with the teacher, observing the child and making notes. A written report is then compiled and a copy given to the social worker, the family and the school. A set of papers including the assessment is presented to the residential unit/respite giver, and a visit is usually made to the child by a member of the special unit staff, accompanied by the central specialist social worker. This visit is usually made in the early stages and to the special school. The family are asked to visit the residential unit, if they are able. The central specialist social worker and residential unit staff will then visit the family in the home; and it is also generally preferable if the family and child can visit the residential unit prior to any introductions of the child. Introductions can take the form of a few hours in the unit, perhaps half a day, leading up to a stay over night and eventually a weekend. The residential unit staff compile a written report following the first overnight stay of the child and usually comment on how the child has settled, the suitability of the unit for the child and vice versa. In the initial stages, the central specialist social worker will be called on to assess the compatability of the child in a particular unit. It is not often that a child will have to be changed as a result of incompatability, though if this is necessary, it can be done amicably. When the child is settled and all those concerned agree to placement, the family or field social worker — whoever is the more appropriate — arrange subsequent periods of care, although it is better if one particular person is named as the person who will arrange these periods of care. This is to limit the amount of bureaucracy and confusion and to ensure that a single line of communications is maintained directly with the short stay unit.

The support unit staff continue to pay occasional visits to the child at home and in school. This is to get to know the child better and to determine how best to handle him when in care. It is also done to aid continuity, especially if behaviour modification programmes are required to help maintain the child at a particular functioning level. It also helps to break down the barriers between the residential units and the family. This inevitably occurs from time to time, particularly as a family may feel inadequate as they cannot continue to care for the child and may find a degree of embarrassment each time they visit the residential unit.

There are factors regarding admission which may arise and which one cannot control, for example: family illness; lack of extended family support; the young, single parent still looking for a role in life and who wants more and more short-term care but yet does not want to have the child in care as such; the problem of creating dependence; clients' self-determination who may still want to care for the child in family circumstances; and the pressure of continually caring for that handicapped child that may be taking its toll.

With the development of district handicap teams, specialist social work teams in the community combined with good casework skills, all the agencies involved can have a very important role to play and be effective in helping the family. The support unit can very easily be seen to cure all the family's problems in the form of requesting an increase in short-term care. It takes very close observation and a detailed approach to work with a family, for the social worker to be able to see this and particularly do something about it. Indiscriminate and unthinking use of short-term care can obscure deep-lying emotional problems within the family and require the type of intervention described above. If the family is facing problems it is easy to 'give them more short-term care', and, if they fail to cope, to attribute it to a problem inherent in the family and not among the professionals who have made the services available. In other words, too many professionals can often overlook the real problem in a family by doling out short-term care on an indiscriminate basis. This means that the aim or goal in working with the family should lead to the planning of close co-operation with a clear and well-worked out easily achieved plan for all the family.

Respite Fostering

Another form of family support is the respite foster-parent. The respite care scheme offers relief to parents of mentally handicapped children on an occasional or regular basis, depending on need. Criteria for the use of foster-parents are basically the same as those used when placing a child in the family support unit.

Specially selected foster-parents are available to receive handicapped youngsters into their own home for limited periods, so giving parents some free time, while simultaneously providing the children with an enjoyable and useful experience of living temporarily somewhere other than home. Experience has suggested that a successful single period of respite care frequently develops into a more regular arrangement between natural parents and foster parents, so providing the handicapped youngsters with a home from home while avoiding recourse to residential or hospital care.

The Children

The criteria for placing a child on this are similar to those applied to placing the child in a residential unit for respite, though by and large children on this scheme tend to be younger although the range of handicap is broad. Where there is more than one mentally handicapped child in the family, brothers and sisters can be accommodated together. Most of the children in the scheme live permanently at home but there are also some who are at a residential school for much of the year, for whom some respite care can be offered during holiday periods.

The Foster Parents

The foster parents are formally approved by the Department of Social Services and will have shown particular interest in helping mentally handicapped children. Many have brought up families already, and some have experience of working with mentally handicapped children. Maturity, warmth and resilience are particularly desired qualities in this area of work; age is a secondary consideration.

Advantages of Respite Care

The advantages of respite care are many. The primary one is that the child is able to stay in the parental home for longer. In the past, children were admitted to long-term residential care, whether in hospital or a long-stay residential unit, if an authority had a facility, which meant that only a limited number of people were able to receive some form of support. Now we find a more purposeful plan being drawn up for handicapped children which includes the role of the family support unit. The permutations are many. The child can be left there for a couple of hours while the family do some shopping. The family can call to see the staff and talk about ways of handling a child, perhaps in relation to such aspects as toilet training. This would also include the special school. This makes the family support unit a more acceptable and positive resource for the handicapped child and the family.

One of these permutations offered by the support unit is the playscheme based in the unit during the long school holidays. The playscheme is primarily aimed to give the families respite, in addition to short-term care, during this long period. The play-scheme is aimed at a priority group, the parents who may have to work during the holidays and/or single parents. The Easter, summer and mid-term school holiday periods and weekends are the times when demand is greatest, hence the development of the playscheme to offer a wide range of options.

The playscheme usually has two paid workers and takes six children a day — between the hours of 9.30 a.m. and 4.30 p.m. The children are picked up at home in the morning and returned to the parental home in the evenings. The basic aim is to replicate the school day and provide the child with purposeful experiences and activities during the day. The playscheme is co-ordinated and organised in close liaison with a short-term care unit in the family sup-port unit; this allows approximately twelve children to be cared for at any one time during the Easter and summer holidays. Both schemes have been found to provide a valuable asset to the support of families with severely mentally handicapped children.

Disadvantages

The first thing which comes to mind is separation of the child from the family which, if not done positively and constructively, can be very traumatic. One problem that could arise is that an alternative to the family support unit may not be available, and parents would reluctantly accept the family support unit which, in essence, could cause more problems than it solves. A child may fret for his/her family and separation can cause emotional/behavioural problems, but we have found that if separation is handled sensitively and positively, this can usually be overcome.

Examples of Successful Use of a Respite Unit

Family A — husband and wife, one girl and one boy. The boy, the youngest, is physically handicapped but very active with a moderate/to severe degree of mental handicap. The family coped for four to five years without much assistance. They requested respite and the child was seen, assessed and introductions made and the child placed, but during the process a multitude of problems were uncovered. Mother was reluctant to accept others caring for her child, even though she felt she wanted a break. She eventually did. Father's non-acceptance of the child's handicap, working very long hours, avoiding the issue in the home. Mother looking for someone to talk to. The period of respite helped, but initially caused problems in that the void left needed to be filled positively, coupled with intensive counselling progress was made all round and the support unit has been a magnificent outlet for the boy, even though the family had their reservations about its use in the initial stages. The family now see the unit as their lifeline. The boy plays very well with other children using the unit and has been accepted by all concerned, and he too looks forward to going to the place.

Family B — two mentally handicapped children both at school. Family life revolves around the two children. Children linked with two foster parents, because of the extent of their handicaps, thus allowing the family time to spend with their non-handicapped son. The children are placed at regular intervals with both foster parents — on average, a weekend every four weeks and a week to ten days' holiday during the summer. In fact the family had had their first holiday together last year (1984).

This 'regular' weekend and some time during the school holidays means that the children are still at home with their family, are living as normal life as possible though the pressure is still on the family, simply due to the size of the problem.

Conclusions and Future Trends

Though many local authorities and some health authorities are offering respite care in a traditional hostel, there is a trend developing, and for good reasons, to place handicapped children with respite foster-parents for parental relief and with carers in the community to give relief at home, but we are still a long way from achieving a comprehensive service for mentally handicapped children and their families. The situation has improved very much in the sense that handicapped children are no longer admitted to large subnormality hospitals. To meet their needs authorities are looking towards a variety of local services i.e. small homes/hostels with four to six beds, respite fostering, family carers, playschemes, sitters, paid staff and volunteers. This would go a long way towards servicing a particular community. However, defining the local geographical area, with a workable catchment number could be difficult. Generally speaking, services are improving with certain issues as yet to be tackled, such as integration links between special to mainstream schools, the future role of the traditional adult training centre and generally day care as such. Hopefully with the renewed interest in mental handicap, we may achieve better services for mentally handicapped people in the future.

Legal Assets

Children are admitted to the family support unit on a voluntary basis. The 1977 National Service Act, Section 21, 1B and paragraph 3 of Schedule 8 allows local authorities to carry out prevention, care and after-care for those children as defined in the Act. Children may be admitted under the 1983 Childrens Act but this depends on family circumstances at the time of the pending admission.

Finances

All severely mentally handicapped children under the age of 16 are admitted free of charge if admitted under the above Act. If a child is admitted under Child Care Legislation, which happens from time to time, then an assessment has to be carried out on the family circumstances, and contributions are set according to those circumstances. If a person is over 16 years of age and admitted to care and their circumstances are such that they cannot pay full cost, then a standard minimum charge is levied.

Further information on entitlements and benefits can be obtained from a welfare rights officer based in any local social services department office. Most social services departments produce booklets giving details of their services and general information.

Useful Addresses

City of Manchester Specialist Social Work Section, 102 Manchester Road, Chorlton-cum-Hardy. Tel: 061-881-0911.
Torrington House Hostel, c/o Buckingham County Council Social Services Dept, County Offices, Walton Street, Aylesbury, Bucks HP21 1EZ.
Tel: 0494-776132.
Leeds Social Services Department, Merrion House, 110 Merrion Centre, Leeds LS2 8QA. Tel: 0532-463100.
Dr Barnardo's Chorley Project, c/o Dr Barnardo North West Div. Office, 248 Upper Parliament Street, Liverpool L8 7QE. Tel: 051-709-6291/2.
Exeter Health Authority, the Honeylands Project, Pintoe Road, Exeter, EX4 88D. Tel: 0392-67171.
Dorset Family Support Service (West), (The Leonard Cheshire Foundation Family Care Attendant Programme), c/o Dorset Social Services, County Hall, Dorchester, Dorset DT1 1XJ. Tel: 0305-3131.
The Spastic Society, Beech Tree House North, Meadow Lane, Bamber Bridge, Nr. Preston, Lancs PR5 8LN. Tel: 0772-323131.

Further Reading

Maureen Oswin (1984) *They keep going away* — a critical study of short-term residential care services for children who are mentally handicapped. Obtainable from: The King's Fund Centre, 126 Albert Street, London NW1 7NF.

THE CONSULTANT PAEDIATRICIAN

Ian McKinlay

A consultant paediatrician is a hospital-based specialist employed by the district health authority (population about 250,000). Many paediatricians specialise in some aspect of child health though most are involved in general medicine for children. Thus the consultant with a principal interest in rehabilitation services for handicapped children may not be the doctor most involved in the care of the newborn and is often not the doctor who makes the initial diagnosis of mental or physical handicap.

Doctors have expertise in diagnosis of handicap, its cause, associated medical features such as epilepsy, visual or hearing impairment, genetic counselling aspects, prognosis and potential for medical treatment. They also have a role in the prevention of handicap, promotion of research and teaching. Important health-related questions from parents and professionals can be answered for the majority of mentally handicapped children. However, knowledge is still limited. Up to a third of mentally handicapped children have no known diagnosis, associated factors need to be teased out, genetic counselling may have to be empirical, the prognosis is often uncertain and medical treatment has to be pragmatic. The paediatrician is not equipped professionally to prescribe methods of therapy (physio, speech, or occupational), teaching strategy or sophisticated behavioural management and relies on collaboration with colleagues. Medical knowledge, however, needs to be shared with these colleagues who will often wish to discuss children with the paediatrician or the school doctor who has been advised by the paediatrician. Medical treatment would also be considered 'therapeutic'.

Teachers may not fully appreciate the importance of making a correct diagnosis for a handicapped child — though it will interest them — and it is necessary to know about associated features, e.g. visual/hearing impairment. Each child is assessed for teaching in terms of strengths and weaknesses, whatever the diagnosis. However, parents want to understand how the child's handicap came about — was it anyone's fault, could it happen again in future pregnancies, might their other children have a risk of having an affected child in future? They also ask about the health implications of the diagnosis and its prognosis. If these issues are dealt with, parents can go on to concentrate on helping their child. If they are not adequately dealt with, the uncertainty can distract the parents and can lead to pre-occupation with apparently trivial health problems.

Why are Children Mentally Handicapped?

About two-thirds become handicapped as the result of processes occurring early in pregnancy. A third have chromosomal abnormalities, the commonest of which is Down's syndrome. Chromosomes are the spiral chains of genes present in the nucleus of all cells in the body. Humans have 22 pairs of chromosomes plus two chromosomes determining sex (XX = female, XY = male). Children with Down's syndrome have three number-21 chromosomes instead of two (called trisomy 21). Other trisomies are less common in surviving children, though commoner in miscarried foetuses early in pregnancy. Other handicapped children have additional chromosome fragments (partial trisomies) or lack fragments of chromosomes (deletions). Usually these occur spontaneously in early development of the foetus, but occasionally they may be carried by a healthy parent or by healthy siblings who are at risk of having a handicapped child. About 1:1,000 live born children have a normal number of chromosomes but carry an abnormal X chromosome which is excessively fragile in laboratory conditions. If the child is a girl, this is usually compensated for by the other X chromosome. However, boys cannot do this as they have only one X chromosome. The boys are mentally handicapped while the girls who are carriers are at high risk (1:2) of having mentally handicapped sons (a form of sex-linked mental handicap).

Genes determine physical and intellectual characteristics. These may be active (dominant) or inactive (recessive). If parents both carry one recessive gene and one normal dominant gene, they will be healthy but have a 25 per cent chance of having a child with two recessive genes who is handicapped. Genes cannot be identified directly; their presence has to be inferred from the appearance or the biochemical profile of the child. Some parents carry an unhealthy dominant gene, but show very mild forms of a particular disease. Each of their children has a 1:2 risk of inheriting the gene, and sometimes the gene expresses itself in a more severe way than in the parent. For example, a parent with the gene for tuberous sclerosis may have white patches in the skin and occasional fits. Yet the child may have severe mental handicap and refractory epilepsy.

A woman had three healthy girls by her first union but the first child of the next union was a girl with Down's syndrome. However investigation showed that the mother and the three healthy girls were carriers of the translocation form of Down's syndrome where a chromosome 21 adheres to a chromosome 14. This is only true for 5 per cent of the mothers of Down's babies. However the diagnosis offered the possibility of genetic counselling for the three healthy girls who can have tests in pregnancy to ensure that they need not have a Down's baby.

About 5 per cent of severely handicapped children have suffered from intra-uterine infection with rubella virus, cytomegalovirus or other agents. Congenital rubella is preventable by vaccination of girls before they reach child-bearing age. No safe vaccine is available for cytomegalovirus. A similar proportion of handicapped (or potentially handicapped) children have specific biochemical diseases. These may be treatable, for example, by special diets, but treatment is often not possible. Many of these can be diagnosed in subsequent pregnancies however, and the parents can be offered an abortion if the foetus is affected.

About a fifth of mentally handicapped children have a pattern of physical characteristics ('syndrome') which allows a diagnosis to be made even if the cause of the condition is unknown. The prognosis is usually known, within broad limits, and a recurrence risk can be quoted from previous experience. About a tenth of mentally handicapped children have suffered brain damage during or soon after birth. It is wrong to presume this, however, unless a baby has shown neurological symptoms after a clear perinatal insult or illness. If the cause of mental handicap is not diagnosed the recurrence risk in future pregnancies is 1:10.

Mentally handicapped children carry high risks of other health problems. One-third will develop epilepsy (1:200 in the general population); one-third develop curvature of the spine (scoliosis), foot deformities or other deformities; two-thirds have some visual impairment; and up to a third have a permanent or fluctuating hearing loss. Many of these associated health problems respond to appropriate medical treatment.

The diagnosis of associated impairments requires the collaboration (and co-ordination of services) with ophthalmologists, orthoptists and opticians, audiologists and ear, nose and throat specialists, orthopaedic surgeons, psychologists and therapists. These services are often concentrated in a child development centre which is usually attached to the children's department of the district hospital. (There are 192 health districts in England and Wales.) It may be co-ordinated by a consultant ('developmental') paediatrician or by a senior clinical medical officer. In a few large teaching centres the co-ordinator is a paediatric neurologist who will also be involved in the care of children with brain tumours, neuromuscular diseases and acute neurological diseases, as well as those who are not handicapped in other ways but suffer from complex epilepsy. The centre will keep detailed health records which should be shared with the community child health services.

What is Wrong?

Diagnosis of mental retardation may be possible soon after birth, for example if the baby has Down's syndrome. However, the diagnosis of mental handicap from other causes is often made by increasing suspicion as a child fails to make the expected progress in motor, social, intellectual or language development. Specific immaturities in development have to be considered, and the diagnosis of mental retardation may only be reached by prolonged observation and multi-disciplinary assessment. Care has to be taken that the child is not suffering from a purely physical handicap such as cerebral palsy, visual impairment or deafness.

The discussion between parents and doctors about children with doubtful development is sensitive and individual. Feedback from a social worker or health visitor after home visits will be useful in guiding the doctor as to how much to say and when. If it becomes clear that a handicap is present, the consultation should be carefully planned (Cunningham 1979).

What Does the Future Hold?

Once the diagnosis is clear this should be explained to both parents, together, in the presence of the child, by an experienced physician. The range of health implications should be discussed (e.g. vision, hearing, epilepsy). An account of the range of prognosis should be given together with an explanation of agencies which can help in future. Help should be initiated as soon as possible. The parents should be visited at home by an experienced health professional or social worker, both to ensure that the information given has been understood and to facilitate the parents' formulation of questions. Follow-up sessions are necessary as parents cannot be expected to take in all the information first time.

Could the Handicap Affect Future Children?

Genetic counselling is offered in collaboration with a consultant in clinical genetics. A family tree is worked out. The parents and other family members are examined, and tests may be necessary for them. Further counselling on available resources is available from the social worker and the health visitor.

What Can be Done to Help?

Doctors can put parents in touch with suitable literature, self-help groups, voluntary organisations, peripatetic educational services or appropriate playgroups, nurseries or nursery classes of special schools. Once they diagnose a handicap, doctors are now required by law in the UK to notify the education authority. A doctor may sometimes act as an advocate for a child, explaining the nature of the child's impairments to teachers and suggesting the child's capability to make use of augmented communications systems, for example.

Epilepsy

Treatment for epilepsy is usually by drugs, especially if the fits are frequent or severe. Ideally, a single drug is used, and the dose is adjusted to suit each child. If it doesn't work well, or if side-effects are unacceptable, a change will be made to another drug. Occasionally a special diet will be used ('ketogenic diet'). This has a high fat and low carbohydrate content. After trials of medication it may be concluded that a child is better off on no drugs, even though fits persist. The commonest side effects of drugs are drowsiness, irritability, sleep disturbance, impaired balance and co-ordination and an increased tendency to dribble saliva. Thickening of the gums, loss of hair, excessive weight gain and deficiencies of such vitamins as folic acid and vitamin D also occur. A good diet will usually provide sufficient vitamins for children with epilepsy, but some are fussy eaters. Fits may cease after a time, and if this is maintained for one to two years, discontinuation of treatment is considered.

Some of the anxieties teachers have about the diverse epilepsies of mentally handicapped children could be reduced by clearer explanation by health professionals. Improved access of class teachers to the school doctor or nurse, suitably advised by the paediatrician, would be the best method of achieving this. Sometimes teachers bring pressure to bear on parents to seek better 'control' of the child's epilepsy because of a lack of understanding of the epilepsy and of the limitations of medical treatment. Some guidelines may be helpful. Fits are certainly alarming but rarely dangerous. If the child is unconscious during a fit he should be laid on his side till it ceases. He should be allowed to sleep it off, usually in the classroom, then to resume classroom activities, but should not be sent home. However if a fit lasts longer than ten minutes, or if a child goes from one fit to another without recovery between the fits, medical advice should be sought. An accurate description of fits is useful to doctors in giving treatment advice.

Other Medical Treatments

Medication may also be sought to improve sleeping at night, to improve behaviour or to improve bowel function. Children may be resistant to such medication. Sleep habits and behaviour problems may respond better to behavioural techniques, and bowel function may respond more to a high fibre diet, good fluid intake and increased activity. However drugs have their place so long as their effectiveness is evaluated. For pre-school children, the health visitor acts as the first source of advice and should be the 'named person' for parents in view of her own skills and her link both with general practice and community child health services.

In general, teachers' questions about the health of pupils should be raised with the school medical officer who will make an initial assessment. Sometimes, advice can be given on the spot, but referral to the general practitioner or paediatrician may be necessary. The doctors for special schools in Britain are normally experienced senior clinical medical officers. They are much more accessible than hospital doctors, and their role in complementing hospital and general practitioner services is increasingly important as the result of the 1981 Education Act. Their personal contact with school staff and therapists is an advantage.

Some schools have good facilities for clinics with an adequate room, examination couch and privacy. There is a potential conflict of interest between the need for a private consultation and the wish of school staff to be informed. The presence of the class teacher, head teacher, school nurse and therapists with the school doctor tend to limit discussion. There may be important issues concerning the child or family out of school which are not raised, and additional hospital appointments are sometimes requested. If parents have good contact with the school and confidence in the staff, such problems are minimised. The advantage of such clinics is that misunderstandings between hospital and school staff are reduced. Co-ordinated advice is likely to be in the child's interests.

Schools with clinic facilities will be able to arrange for children to be seen in school by the paediatrician, eye specialist and orthoptist, audiologist and orthopaedic specialist in term-time clinics. In some centres a paediatric neurologist is available, but there are only a few in Great Britain. Neurologists have special expertise in the investigation and treatment of mentally handicapped children and are often used as a 'second opinion' by paediatricians for children with unusual problems. Child psychiatrists have a specialist knowledge of mental illness, and will be involved in the assessment of autistic or psychotic children. They will also offer specialist advice for children with unusual behavioural difficulties or whose families have psychiatric problems. Most specialists in the psychiatry of mental handicap concentrate on services for adults, but in some districts they will be available to give advice for children.

Although health issues are not central to the continuing management of mentally handicapped children and their families, except in the answering of questions about diagnosis, prognosis and treatment, they have an important place in any comprehensive service.

Reference

Cunningham, C.C. (1979) 'Parent Counselling', in M. Croft (ed.) *Tredgold's Mental Retardation*, 12 edn. Balliere Tindall.

Further Reading

Downey, J.A. and Low, N.L. (1982) *The Child with Disabling Illness: principles of rehabilitation*, 2nd edn. Raven Press.

Drillien, C., Drummond, M. (1983) 'Development Screening and the Child with Special Needs'. *Clinics in Developmental Medicine, 86.* Spastics International Medical Publications, Heinemann.

Gordon, N.S. and McKinlay, I. (1985) *The Neurologically Handicapped Child: Treatment and management.* Blackwell Scientific.

Hall, D.M.B. (1984) *The Child with a Handicap.* Blackwell Scientific.

McCarthy, G.T. (1984) *The Physically Handicapped Child. An interdisciplinary approach to management.* Faber.

Thomson, G.H., Rubin, I.L. and Bilenher, R.M. (eds.). (1984) *Comprehensive Management of Cerebral Palsy.* Grune and Stratton.

Woods, G.E. (1983) *Handicapped Children in the Community: Medical aspects for educationists.* Wright.

INDEX

Accommodation 107-8, 115-16, 120
ACE 274
Action and Instrument (Semantic Notions of Leonard) 158
Action and its Training (The Analysis of Action and its Training) 139-50
Action and Mental Handicap 134-9
Action and Object (Semantic Notions of Leonard) 158
Activities and experiences 32-3
Acuity 225
Add-in method 72
Adult digital grip 140, 141
Adult Training Centre (ATC) 366
Aetiology 216
Affective Communication Assessment 165, 167
Age-stage related progression 88
Agent and Action (Semantic Notions of Leonard) 158
Aids and Equipment (for the Deaf-blind) 357-8
Aims, educational 15-17
Ainscow M. (1982) 26; (1984) 14, 22
Ainscow M. and Tweddle D.A. (1979) 20, 297; (1984) 260
Alberto, P; Jones, N; Sizemore, A. and Doran, D.A; (1980) 74
Allport, G. (1924) 195
Amblyopia 226
American Foundation for the Blind 342
Anderson J.R. (1980) 190, 192, 194
Annett J. (1969) 132
Annual reviews 261, 286
Anoxia 216
Anticipation (in mothers) 244
APCP (1984) 313
APRE (Assessment, Programme-Planning, Recording, Evaluation) 25-42
Arthur Boothroyd Word List 331
Articulation 154
Ashton, P. and Young, S. (1984) 369
Assessment 26
Assessment
by the Class Teacher 282-6

by the Educational Psychologist 293-6
of Communication Difficulties 305-8
of Hearing Problems 327-8
of Motor Skills (gross, fine, perceptuo-motor) 317-21
Parents involvement in assessment 255-6
Six Scales of Assessment in Infancy (Uzgiris and Hunt) 113
Thirteen plus (1981 Act) 260, 295, 298
under Section five (1981 Act) 11, 298
Assessment and referral of Visual Impairment 340-3
Medical Assessment 340-1
Educational Assessment 342-3
Assessment and testing (for the Deaf-blind) 354-5
within short term care unit 376
Assimilation 107-8, 117
Association (learning through association) 203-6
Associative networks 192
Asthma 251-2
Astigmatism 225
Athetoid child 92
Atkinson, R. and Shiffrin, R.M. (1968) 200
Attention in the Learning Process 186-94
'Attention deficit' 184, 189
Attribution (Semantic Notion of Leonard) 158
Attwood, T. (1979) 257
Audiological crib 220
Audiometrician 332
Auditory
acuity 328
memory 193
stimulation 65
Ault, R.L. (1977) 101, 120
Authoritarianism (after Muma) 168

391

Autistic 92
 children 94-5, 389
Aversive stimulus 51
Ayres, J. (1974) 318

Backward or forward chaining 47-8
Baer, D.M. (1970) 88
Baer, D.M. and Guess, D. (1973) 156
Baker, B.L., Prieto-Bayard, M. and
 McCurry, M. (1984) 257-8
Bakke, B.L. and Milan, M.A. (1983)
 80
Baldwin, S. (1985) 245
Bandura, A. (1965) 79; (1969) 205;
 (1977) 60
Barkley, R.A. (1983) 186
Barna, S., Bidder, R.T., Gray, O.P.,
 Clements, J. and Gardner, S.
 (1980) 254
Barraga, N.C. and Morris, J.E.
 (1980) 342
Barrett, B.H. and Lindsley, O.R.
 (1962) 65
Bartlett, F.C. (1932) 198
Barton, L. and Coupe, J. (1985) 169
Barton, L. and Moody, S. (1981) 262
Bates, E., Camaioni, L. and
 Volterra, V. (1975) 159, 160
Beasley, W. (1983) 70
Behaviour
 Assessment Battery (Kiernan and
  Jones) 113, 124, 294
 disorders in Visually and Mentally
  Handicapped People 232-3
 Inappropriate behaviours 48-52
 Maintenance of behaviour 57-60
 Modification 45-8
 Modification techniques 184-6
 Parents involvement in
  modification techniques 250-1
 Problems with the deaf 222
Behavioural
 Approach and the child with
  severe learning difficulties
  52-67
 Beyond a Simple Behavioural
  Approach 44-69
 evolution of the behavioural
  approach 45-6
 limits of the behavioural
  approach 64-7
 objectives 22
 overkill 66
Behaviourism 184, 272

Bell, E.J. and Watson, A. (1985) 320
Berger, M. (1982) 64
Bernal, M.E. and North, J.A. (1978)
 259
Berry, I. and Wood, J. (1981) 254
Beswick, J.A. (1984) 75, 76
Beveridge, H. and Hurrell, P. (1980)
 163, 171
Beveridge, S., Flanagan, R.,
 McConachie, H. and Sebba, J.
 (1982) 255, 263
Bevington, P., Gardner, J.M. and
 Cocks, R.P. (1978) 298
Biberdorf, J.R. and Pear, J.J. (1977)
 72
Bijou, S.W. (1966) 71
Binet 87-8
Blea, W.A., Lavell, E.L., Meyer, S.,
 Thielman, V.B. and Rouin, C.
 (1976) 354
Blindness 224-35
 and cortical/cerebral 337, 342,
  343
Bloom, L. (1970) 156; (1973) 157
Bloom, L. and Lahey, M. (1978) 157,
 170, 307
Bobath, B. and Bobath, K. (1980)
 316; (1984) 321
Bond, D.E. (1981) 215
Booth, T. and Statham, J. (1982) 284
Borkowski, J. and Cavannagh, J.
 (1979) 57
Boucher, J. (1981) 257
Boucher, J. and Feiler, A. (1982) 296
Bousfield, W.A. (1953) 190
Bowdler, D. and Collier, D. (1982)
 296
Bowes, T.R.G. (1977a) 112; (1977b)
 92, 98, 112, 344
Bowerman, M. (1973) 156
Bowlby, J. (1951) 98
BPS conference 269
Bradshaw, J. (1980) 246
Bradshaw, J. and Lawton, D. (1958)
 241-2
Branch, R. (1984) 366, 369
Braille 229, 337, 341, 343
Brain damage 385
Brainerd, C.J. (1973) 107
Bray, N.W. (1979) 198
Brazleton, T. (1976) 243
Brearley, M. and Hitchfield, E.
 (1966) 101
Brennan, W.K. (1979) 20

Breuning, S.E., Davis, V.G. and
Lewis, J.R. (1981) 76
Bricker, D.D. (1972) 196
Bricker, W.A. and Bricker, D.D.
(1974) 153
Brinker, R.P. (1978) 169
Bristol Adjustment Guide 222
British Ability Scale 221
British Institute for Mental Handicap
318
Broadbent, D.E. (1958) 105
Brookes, P.H. and McCauley, C.
(1984) 189
Brown, A.L. (1972) 195; (1978) 60,
202
Brown, J.K. (1985) 317, 321
Brown, R. (1973) 156
Brown, A.L., Campione, J.C. and
Murphy, M.D. (1977) 61-2, 203
Brown, F., Holvoet, J., Guess, D. and
Mulligan, M. (1980) 71
Brown, L., Branston, M.B.,
Hamre-Nietopski, S., Pumpian, I.,
Certo, N. and Gruenewald, L.
(1978) 19, 21
Browne, E. (1982) 367-8, 370, 371,
372
Bruner, J.S. (1964) 210; (1973) 111;
(1970) 136; (1975) 159, 263,
303; (1978) 159; (1983) 159
Bruner, J.S., Olver, R.R. and
Greenfield, P.M. (1966) 111
Bryant, P. (1974) 92
Bryuelsen, D. (1983) 253
Buckholt, J.A., Rutherford, R.B. and
Goldberg, K.E. (1978) 163
Burman, L., Farrell, P., Feiler, A.,
Heffernan, M., Mittler, H. and
Reason, R. (1982) 256, 260;
(1983) 30, 297; (1984) 298
Burnham, P.S. (1968) 279

Camaioni and Volterra (1975) 159
Cameron, R.J. (1981) 25, 297;
(1982) 40, 297, 298
Campaign for Mentally Handicapped
People (C.M.H) 361-5
Capie, A.C.M., Taylor, P.D. and
Perkins, E.A. (1980) 257
Carden, N. (1983) 102, 121
Carden, N. and Robson, C. (1985)
102
'Carers' 261
Carey, G.E. (1982) 245

Carey, R.G. and Bucher, B. (1983)
51
Caring for the Carers 245-7
Carnine, D.W. and Becker, W.C.
(1982) 60-1
Castle Priory 351
Cataracts (and Down's Syndrome)
226
'Centres of Causality' 116
Cerebellar lesions 92
Cerebral Palsy 94, 321, 386
and visual impairment 226
cerebral palsied blind 315
Chaining 206
Chapman, E.K. (1978) 342
Chapman, E.K., Tobin, M.J.,
Tooze, F.H.C. and Moss, S.C.
(1981) 342
Chatelanat, S. and Schoggen, M.
(1980) 210
Cheshire Curriculum Statement 16
Chess, S., Korn, S. and Fernandez, P.
(1971) 355
Child Care Legislation 381
Child Development Centre 318
Childrens Act (1983) 381
Childrens Legal Centre 269
Chomsky, N. (1957) 90
Chomskyian 155
Chromosonal abnormalities 384
'Chronic sorrow' 263
Clark, D.B., Baker, B.L. and
Heifetz, L.J. (1982) 258
Clarke, A.B.D. and Clarke, A.M.
(1974) 88
Classical conditioning 45, 185, 203,
204-5
Class inclusion 121
Classification (as a developmental
stage) 121
Classroom assistant 282, 286-8
Classroom Management 70-83
Classroom Teacher 281-6
Cliffe, M.J., Gathercole, C. and
Epling, W.F. (1974) 52
Clustering 191-2, 201, 209
Co-active intervention 149-50
Cochlea 215
substitutes 220
Cocks, R.P. and Gardener, J.M.
(1978) 296
Cognition 85
and Coping Matrix 103
Cognitive Behaviour Modification 206

Cognitive development 85, 88, 102-3,
    135, 137
    A Constructional Approach to
        106-12
    and language development 169
    Cognition and Perception, The
        Development of 101-27
    Cognitive and perceptual skills
        118
    Cognitive processes (automatic
        and deliberate) 188-9
    Cognitive psychologist 184
    Cognitive structures 112
Coin sorting 207-10
Colborne-Brown, M., and Tobin, M.
    (1982) 337
Collins, G. (1984) 76
Collins, M. and Collins, D. (1976)
    254
Collins, A.M. and Quillian, M.R.
    (1969) 191
Colvin, G.T. and Horner, R.H.
    (1983) 145; (1985) 60-3
Communication 85, 97
    A means of 165
    A reason for 164-5
    Development of Language and
        Communication 153-82
    disorders 301-2
    Definitions (relating to Language
        and Communication) 154
    General Guidelines for Promoting
        Communication 164-6
    Pre-communication behaviour 167
Community Mental Handicap Nurse
    365-7, 369, 370
Community Mental Handicap Teams
    359-74
    and Children 363-5
    Membership of 363
    Relationships between CMHTs
        and Schools for Children with
        severe learning difficulties
        371-3
    Roles 365-71
Compounded handicap 214
Conditional association 93
Conditional response (classical
    conditioning) 204
    stimulus (classical conditioning)
        204
Conditioned pleasure/displeasure 93
Connolly, B.H. (1985) 318, 321
Connolly, K. (1973) 136

Conrad, R. (1979) 215, 217, 218
Consultant Paediatrician 383-90
Consultant and Skills Transmitter
    (The Speech Therapist as)
        304-8
Contact-a-family 246
Contingent restraint 50-1
Continuous reinforcement 96
Controlling speech 164
Controlling stimulus 58-9
The Co-operation test 332
Copewell system 20
Corney, M. (1981) 258
Cortical (cerebral) blindness 337,
    342, 343
Coulson, A.A. (1980) 275
Coulson, A. and Cox, M. (1975) 277,
    279
Coupe, J., Barton, L., Barber, M.,
    Collins, L., Levy, D. and
    Murphy, D. (1985) 167
Coupe, J. and Levy, D. (1985) 23,
    113
Court Committee 361, 362
Court Report 371
Craig, H.K. (1983) 308
Craik, F.I.M. and Lockhart, R.S.
    (1972) 200-1
Cratty, B.J. (1979) 315
Creak, M. (1951) 92
Crisp, A.G. and Sturmey, P. (1984a)
    74; (1984b) 70, 76, 77
Crook, P. (1984) 366
Crystal, D. (1976) 155; (1982) 307
Crystal, D., Fletcher, P. and Garman,
    M. (1979) 306
Cubbon, P. (1984) 365
Cullen, C., Hattersley, J. and
    Tennant, L. (1977) 58
Cunningham, C. (1983) 254, 255,
    263; (1984) 242-5
Cunningham, C.C. (1982) 254
Cunningham, C.C. and Jeffree, D.
    (1975) 257, 262
Cunningham, C.C. and McArthur, K.
    (1982) 214
Curriculum 9
    Curriculum Intervention Model
        (CIM) 11-43
    Document 14-25
    Evaluating the curriculum 39-41
Cytomegalovirus 216, 385

Dale, D.M.C. (1984) 224

Deaf-Blind
  Assessment and Testing of, 354-5
  Definition of (and causes of)
    350-2
  Integration of 358
  Peripatetic Teacher of 348-59
  Problems of Development 352-3
  Role of the Peripatetic Teacher of
    356-7
  Teaching the 355-8
National Deaf-Blind and Rubella
  Association (NDBRA) 349
National Association for the
  Deaf-Blind and Rubella
  Handicapped 349
Deafness 214-24
  conductive deafness 215
  hidden handicap 326-7
  sensori-neural deafness 215, 220
  social handicap 326-7
Deletions 384
Demotivation (of the handicapped
  child) 97
Denial (Semantic Notions of
  Leonard) 158
Denial of Special Needs 248-9
DES circulars (1972) 300; (1977)
  275; (1978) 304; (1979) 273;
  (6/81) 11; (8/81) 274; (1/83) 274
DHSS (1976) 360-1; (1978) 361
Deputy Head 277-9
Derbyshire Language Programme
  173, 305
Developmental approach 66, 89
  Developmental Delay (with the
    visually impaired) 227-8
  Developmental models 18-19
  Developmental Paediatric Practice
    (Remedial Therapist in) 315-17
  Developmental team for the
    mentally handicapped (DT)
    359, 360, 364, 365, 367, 368,
    369, 370, 371
Diabetes 251
Differential Reinforcement 51
Differentiation 90, 114-15, 279
Digital grip 137, 147
Directed forgetting 198
Disappearance 157, 169
Discourse analysis 307
Discrimination 6-7, 9, 59, 61, 207
  learning 55, 187
  skills 64
Distraction test 332

District and Community Mental
  Handicap Team 359-74
Doke, L.A. and Risley, T.R. (1972)
  76
Doll, E.A. (1947) 77
Dolman-Delacato Programming 272
Donaldson, M. (1978) 112, 121
Down's Syndrome 91-2, 139, 163,
  384
  and cataracts 226
  and conductive hearing problems
    334
  and deafness 328
  and the effect on the family 342
  and hearing impairment 214
  and motor competence 129
  translocation 385
  and visual impairment 225
  Downs Early Intervention Team
    366-7
Dual Code Theory (after Paivio,
  1971) 194, 196
Duker, P. and Seys, D. (1983) 51

Ear, Nose and Throat surgeon
  (E.N.T) 328
Early Intervention based on
  Pragmatic Functions 167-8
Echo-location 344
Education Act (1981) 2, 6, 11, 12;
  (Section 5) 26, 183, 246, 255,
  260, 286, 289, 293, 295, 298,
  299, 305, 311, 323, 328, 339;
  (Section 1(4)) 351, 372, 389
Educational Assessment (of the
  visually impaired) 342-3
Educational Audiologist 329-34
  Post diagnosis (by the Educational
    Audiologist) 333
  Testing (by the Educational
    Audiologist) 329-33
EDY 31, 45, 207, 296
  scoring procedure 35
Educational Psychologist, The
  291-300
  Assessment by 293-6
  curriculum for children with
    Severe Learning Difficulties
    297
  ratio per child 291
Educational Psychologists, Role of
  with Children with Severe
  Learning Difficulties 293-8
  General Advisory Work 297-8

ESN (S) and (M) Schools 295, 300, 305, 327, 337
Egocentrism, Egocentricity 108-9
Eidetic imagery, memory 195-7
Eisenson, J. (1972) 95
Elaboration (of a task) 208
Elliot-Cannon, C. (1981) 366, 370
Ellis, D. (1978) 230; (1982) 225; (1985) 232; (1986) 226
Ellis, N.R. (1978) 201; (1979) 202
Ellis, N.R., Deacon, J.R., Harris, L.A., Poor, A., Angers, D., Diorio, M., Watkins, R.S., Boyd, B.D. and Cavalier, A.R. (1982) 65
Emotion (The Development of Personality and) 87-100
Encoding 200
English Picture Vocabulary 186, 305
Environmental models and goals 19
Epilepsy 242, 252, 387
   Drugs for, Diet for 387-8
Episodic Memory 194-201
Equal Opportunities Commission 246
Equilibration 108
Equipment moves, the 75-81
Errorless Learning 54-6
Estes, W.K. (1982) 187
'Ethnic classification of idiocy' (after Langdon-Down) 91
Ethological school 90
Eustachian tube 41
Evaluation (Assessment, Programme Planning, Recording and . . .) 37-9
   Evaluating the curriculum 39-41
Existence 157
Experience objectives 22
   Experience and Experiences 157
   Experiential Storage 94
Experimental evidence 6
'Extravert-intravert' 90-1
Extinction 49
Eysenck, H.J. (1981) 87, 90

Facial gestures 116
Failure, A sense of, (with Parents of a handicapped child) 247-8
family centres (for the Deaf-Blind) 349
Family difficulties (amongst families with handicapped children) 241-3
family fund 242, 246
family problems 250-3
family support unit 375-82
Farrel, P.T. (1984) 297; (1985) 296

fathers' difficulties (with birth of a handicapped child) 242-3
Favell, J.E., Favell, J.E. and McGimsey (1978) 71
'feedback concept' 132
Ferguson, D.G. and Cullari, S. (1983) 64
Firth, H. (1982) 257
Fixation 98
Folic acid 388
Fostering (Respite fostering, foster parents) 375-82
Foulkes 327
Fowler, S.A. and Baer, D.M. (1981) 58
Foxen, T. (1975) 113
Foxen, T. and McBrien, J. (1981) 31, 51, 52, 64, 296
Fraiberg, S. (1986) 352
Freud 87-91, 98
Friedman, M., Kropski, A., Dawson, E.T., and Rosenberg, P. (1977) 203
Frostig Psycho-Motor Training 272
Funderburg, R. (1978) 355

Galton (on heritability) 91
Galton, M. and Simon, B. (1980) 70
Garcia, E., Guess, D. and Byrnes, J. (1973) 156
Gardner, J. (1983) 257
Gardner, J. and Judson, S. (1982) 297
Gardner, J. and Murphy, J. (1980) 18, 31
Gath, A. (1978) 292, 293
General Case Programming 62-4
'General management' (after Rushfirth 1984) 321
Generalisation, generalised, generalising 7, 9, 57, 59, 60-1, 71, 98, 107, 108, 137, 139
   of motor skills 142, 143, 145
   Processes involved 61-2
   problems with lack of 166
   problems with small group teaching 72
Genes, (dominant and recessive) 384
Genetic counselling 387
Genetic epistemology 107
Gessell, A. (1948) 89, 90
Gibb Harding, C. (1983) 167
Gilbert, P. and Spooner, B. (1982) 362

Gillham, W. (1979), (1983) 173
Glendinning, C. (1978) 367, 371
Glidden, L.M. (1979) 201
Glossop, C. and Castillo, M. (1982) 254
Glynn, T. (1982) 59-60
Goals (in the curriculum) 17-21
Goal Directed Actions 129, 130-4, 136, 145
  The Analysis of 142-8
Goal directed behaviour 131, 167
Governors, School 274-5, 281
Grasps and Grips 140
Gregory, R.L. (1977) 343
Group engagement 76
Guess, D. and Baer, D.M. (1973) 153
Guess, D., Sailor, W., Rutherford, G. and Baer, D.M. (1968) 156
Guidon, A.W. (1969) 355
Guilt (of parents of handicapped child) 247
Gunstone, C., Hogg, J., Sebba, J., Warner, J. and Almonds, S. (1982) 76

Haber, R.N. and Haber, R.B. (1964) 197
Hailstone, E. (1984) 257
Hall, V. and Russell, O. (1979) 369
Halle, J.W., Baer, D.M. and Spradlin, J. (1981) 59
Halliday, M. (1973) 303; (1975) 160, 306
  Hallidays functions 160, 167
'Handicapped in the Community' (Whyte 1984) Open University video 314
Handicapped Personality 91-3
Hare, N. (1985) 315-16
Hargreaves, D. (1984) 284
Harley and Hill (in Ellis 1986) 231
Harris, J. (1984) 170, 173
Hattersley, J. and Tennant, L. (1981) 257, 258
Head Teacher 275-7
Hearing Impairment 214-24
  Classification of 215
Hearing Problems, Assessment of 324-7
Hearing Impaired, Support Services for 326-36
Hedge, M. (1980), (1981) 162
Held, R. and Hein, A. (1963) 95, 105
Henshaw's school (Harrogate) 344

Herbert-Jackson, E., O'Brien, M., Porterfield, J. and Risley, T. (1977) 70
Her Majesty's Inspectors 19, 280, 284
Hermelin, B. and O'Connor, N. (1974) 95
Herriot, P. (1972) 201
Herriot, P., Green, J.M. and McConkey, R. (1977) 191
Hess, E.H. (1964) 90
Hester Adrian Research Centre 41, 285, 318
Hethersett College for Blind Adolescents 344
Heuristic (*see* Hallidays functions) 160
Hierarchical networks (of memory) 191-2
'High engagers' 79
Hogg, J. (1981) 142; (1982) 129
Hogg, J. and Evans, P.L.C. (1975) 188
Hogg, J. and Mittler, P. (1980) 55
Hogg, J. and Raynes, N. (1986) 295
Hogg, J., Remington, R.E. and Foxen, T.H. (1979) 65, 205
Hogg, J. and Sebba, J. (1986) 135, 150
Holle, B. (1976) 136, 140
Home visiting programmes 253, 254, 255
Honeylands 248
  home therapy scheme 247
  Progress Report 250
  therapy programme 243
Horner, D. (1980) 70
Houts, P.S. and Scott, R.A. (1975)
Hoyle, E. (1969) 279
Hubel, D.H. and Weisel, N. (1963) 105
Hughes, M.G. (1977) 276
Hunt, J. McV. (1969) 88
Hunt, J. McV. and Kirk, G.E. (1974) 206
Hunt, H., McKendrick, O., Poole, J., Pugh, R.E., Rosenbloom, L. and Turnock, R. (1979) 337
Hunter, I.M.L. (1964) 196
Hypopia 225
Hyperactive 91

ICEBY (1971) 350, 352
Iconic sign 219
Illingworth, R.S. (1963) 350

Imagery 207
Imaginative (Halliday) 160
Imitation 149-50, 170
Imitation (Vocal and gestural),
    Development of 115-16
Inclusion tasks 120
Individual Education Plan (I.E.P.) 261
Individual Programme Plan (I.P.P.)
    223
Individual Reports on Needs 351
Individual-structured programming
    125
Individual Tuition, and Small Groups
    70-5
Induction Loop System 221
Informative (Hallidays functions) 160
    Informative speech 164
Inner/Outer Language 217-18
Inner London Education Authority
    (ILEA) 349, 351
Inservice Education (INSET) (from
    Educational Psychologists) 296,
    297, 298
Instrumental (Hallidays functions)
    160
Integration (of the Deaf-Blind) 358
Intensive rotas/teams (of speech
    therapists) 310
Intention, Intentionality 134, 135
    Intentional communication 167
Interactional (Hallidays functions)
    160
Interference theory, interference 197,
    200
Intermittent reinforcing 80
Internalised (language) 217
Internal representation 352
Interpretation
    (transmission-transduction) 216
Intervention 14, 162, 263
    by the speech therapist 302
    early intervention 167
    language 156, 158
    programmes (related to the
        family) 243, 250
    techniques 149
Intervention of the Semantic Level
    168-70
Intervention (on Speech Sounds) 172
Intervention at the Pre-Intentional
    level 166-77
Intervention of the Syntactical and
    Morphological level 170-1
Intrinsic evaluation 39

Intrinsic feedback 132
intrusion 133
IPTA 272

Jan, J.E., Freeman, R.D.,
    McCormick, A.Q., Scott, E.P.,
    Robertson, W.D. and Newman,
    D.E. (1985) 232
Jan, J.E., Freeman, R.D. and Scott,
    E.P. (1977) 226
Jeffree, D. and Cheseldine, S. (1982)
    260
Jeffree, D. and McConkey, R. (1976)
    260
Joinson, P. (1979) 369
Joint assessment (by parent and
    teacher) 260
Johnson, D. and Ransom, E. (1980)
    261
Jones, O.H.M. (1977) 163
'Jugglers curriculum' 140
Junior Training Centres 1, 291, 296

Kagan, J. (1971) 92, 95, 98
Kagan, J. and Klein, R.E. (1973) 92
Kahn, J.V. (1975) 102; (1976) 113
Kates, L. (1976) 350
Kazdin, A.E. (1980) 66; (1983) 60,
    64
Kendal Toy Test 330
Kennedy, P. (1984) 316
Kerfoot, S. and Gray, P. (1984) 260
Ketogenic diets 387
Key, J., Hooper, J. and Ballard, M.
    (1979) 247, 249
Key worker 371
Kiernan, C. (1977) 61; (1981) 57;
    (1984) 173; (1985) 162
Kiernan, C. and Jones, M. (1977) 21;
    (1982) 113
Kiernan, C. and Reid, B.D. (1983)
    169; (1985) 168, 169
Kiernan, C., Reid, B.D. and Jones,
    L.M. (1982) 161, 223
Kintsch, W. (1974) 192
Kirman, B. (1975) 129
'Kith and Kids' groups 254
Kitzinger, M. (1980) 102
Knowledge, Representation of, in
    memory 191-3
Knowles, W. and Masidlover, M.
    (1979) 305
Koegel, F.L. and Rincover, A. (1974)
    72

Kropka, B. and Williams, C. (1979) 214, 219
Kuhn, T.S. (1961) 87
Kyle, J. and Woll, B. (1983) 219

Laing, R.D. 241
Lambert, J.L. (1980) 55, 56
Lamberts, F. (1981) 196
Langdon-Down, J. (1866) 91
Langley (in Ellis 1986) 231
Language Acquisition, Theories of 155-61
Language acquisition device 155
Language and Communication, Development of 153-82
    definitions of 154
    difficulties 161
'Language Development Through Structured Teaching' (Robson 1982) 173
Language Kits and Programmes 172-7
LARSP (The Language Assessment and Remediation and Screening Profile) 170, 306-7
Laslett, R. (1977) 289
Lavatelli, C.S. (1970a), (1970b) 141
LEA 272, 275, 280, 281
    Educational Psychologists within 291-3
    Policy on Visual Impairment of 336-7
Leacroft School (1983) 261
Learning Through Association 203-6
The Learning Process 183-213
Learning Set 111
'Learning Together' 286
Leeming, K., Swann, W., Coupe, J. and Mittler, P. (1979) 153, 161, 302, 305
Leiderman, P.H. (1974) 242, 245
Lenneberg, E.M. (1964), (1967) 90
Leonard, L.B. (1984) 157, 169
Lewis, J. (1982) 368, 370
'Life-plan' (of parent for their handicapped child) 244
Light stimulation 343-4
Linguistic development 90
Linked Agencies, The Role of 291-390
Lipreading 334
Living Light Centre, Overbrook School, Philadelphia 343
Local Authority Advisor 273-4

Location (Semantic Notion of Leonard) 158
Locational integration 4
London Hospital 343
Long term memory 190, 199-200, 201, 207
'Look and Think Programme' 342
'Loose training' 171
Lowe, M. and Costello, A.J. (1976) 305
Lunen, K.Y. (1984) 321
Lysons, C.K. (1984) 217

Mabon, M. 344
Mayer, R.F. (1972) 22
Mahoney, G.J. (1975) 307
Maiden, D. (1974) 354
Makaton signs 229
Management of Hearing Problems 334-5
Manchester Health Authority 344
Manchester L.E.A. (1984) (Published aims for schools) 16
Manchester Picture Card Test 331
Manchester University (Pre-school project of) 318
Mansell, J., Feke, P., DeKock, U. and Jenkins, J. (1982) 76, 79
Marks, L. (1985) 315
Martin, P.J. (1979) 278
Martin, H., McConkey, R. and Martin, S. (1984) 171
Masidlover, M. and Knowles, W. (1977) 173
Matson, J. and McCartney, J. (1981) 44
Mattocks, D., Barton, L. and Parkinson, G. (1982) 310
Maxfield, K.E. and Bucholz, S. (1957) 342
    Maxfield-Bucholz Scales 230
McBrien, J. and Foxen, T. (1981) 44, 207, 296
McBrien, J. and Weightman, J. (1980) 70, 76
McCall, C. and Thacker, J. (1977) 261
McCartney, E., Kellett, B. and Warner, J. (1984) 300
McConachie, H. (1982) 245; (1983) 256
McConkey, R. (1984) 169
McConkey, R. and O'Connor, M. (1981) 173

McInnes, J.M. and Treffry, J.A.
    (1982) 149-50, 350, 354
McIvor, M. and McGrinley, P. (1983)
    56
McNeil, D. (1970) 156
'Means and behaviour' 85
Meichenbaum, D. (1977) 206
Meichenbaum, D. and Goodman, J.
    (1971) 206
Melland School, Manchester 343
Memory
    Long-term 200, 201, 207
    Organisation and 190-1
    Photographic 195, 196, 197
    Sensory 193-4
    Sensory, Episodic and Semantic
        194-8
    Short-term 200
    Visual 195-7
MENCAP 41, 248
'Mental age' 88
'Mental handicap unit' 301
Merrett, F.E. and Musgrove, W.J.
    (1982) 53
Metamemory 202-3, 206
Michael, C.R. (1972) 105
Microcephalics 92
Micro-computer technology, its place
    in cognitive work 125
Miller, G.A. (1956) 191
Miller, J.F. and Yoder, D. (1974) 170
Mindel, E.D. and Vernon, M. (1971)
    217
Minimum Adequate Grammar 172
Mittaug, D.E. and Wolfe, M.S.
    (1976) 73
Mittler, P. and Berry, P. (1977) 153,
    303
Mittler, P. and McConachie, H.
    (1983) 253
Mittler, P. and Mittler, H. (1982) 253
Mittler, P. and Simon, G. (1978) 361
Modality specific coding strategies
    196
Modelling 79-80, 170
    and peer models 74
    as a defined set of semantic roles
        169
    of, by students 71
Models of Memory 198-201
Mogford, K. (1979) 263
Molnar, G.E. (1978) 136
Monaural deafness 334
Mongoloid idiocy (after

    Langdon-Down) 91
Moore, S., Nikolski, I. and Presland,
    J. (1981) 298
Morel (theory of degeneracy) 91
Mori, A. and Olive, J. (1978) 231
'Moro' reflex 95
Morphology 154, 158, 161, 164
Morris (1976) 240
Moss, S.C. and Hogg, J. (1983) 137
Motor
    Behaviour 131, 137
    Competence in Children with
        Mental Handicap 128-52
    Competence/incompetence 130
    development 18-19, 85
    schema 138-9
    skills and behaviour 128-30
Muma, J. (1978) 168, 170
Myelination 94, 352
Myopia 225
Myklebust, H.R. (1954) 354

National Association of Head
    Teachers (NAHT) 277
National Coucil for Special Education
    (NCSE) 41
National Development Group 359,
    360, 371
National Health Service 301
National Service Act (1977) 381
Need (and motivation in motor
    competence) 134
Neigher, N.D. and Scholbuerg, H.C.
    (1982) 70
Nelson, K. (1973) 156
Neonatal reflexes (in cerebral palsied
    child) 94
Neuromuscular system 136
Neuroticism (after Freud) 89
Nomination (Semantic Notions of
    Leonard) 157
Non-existence (after Bloom and
    Lahey 1978; Bloom 1973) 157
Normalisation 271
Normative model 185
Nuffield Maths project 123
Nursery Nurse (NNEB) (The role of)
    287
Nystagmus 226

Oakley, A. (1974) 245
Oates, J. and Floyd, A. (1976) 101
Object Relations in Space, The
    Construction of 117

Object schemes (of Uzgiris and Hunt) 113
Objectives (of the curriculum) 21-5
Objectives framework 14
Observation 93
Observational learning 79
O'Connor, N. and Hermelin, B. (1963), (1978) 196
Occupational therapists 314
Olfactory memory 10
Oliver, R.B. and Scott, T.L. (1981) 71
Ollendick, T.H., Dailey, D. and Shapiro, E.S. (1983) 79
Ollendick, T.H. and Shapiro, E.S. (1984) 79
Ollendick, T.H., Shapiro, E.S. and Barrett, R.P. (1982) 79
Omission (After Reason) 133-4
Open University (1978) 314, 352
Operant conditioning 45
Operant learning 185, 203, 205-6
Operant psychology 184-5
Operations (after Piaget) 118
Operational Causality, Development of 116
Operational period 123
Opila-Lehman, J., Short, M.A. and Trombly, C.A. (1985) 318
Opthalmologist 224
Oral-manual conflict 218
Oralism 218, 223
Ordering 121
Organisation and Memory 190
Orofacial structures 307
Orthoptist 340, 341
Ossicular dislocation 329
Outer ear 215, 216
Over correction 51-2

Packwood (1983) 275
Pairing of Students, Complementary 79
Paivio, A. (1971) 194
Palmar grasp 137, 140
Parental Attitudes to Handicap and Special Educational Needs 239-41
Parent coalitions, groups 246
Parents Contribution to the Education of their Child 253-68
Parents as Partners 239-68
Parental Support (for the visually impaired) 228-9
Parent-Teacher collaboration 260
Parents workshop 257-9

'Pathways to Independence' 260
Paul, J.L. (1981) 253
Pavlov, I.P. (1927) 203
Peabody Mobility Scales 230
Peebles (in ICEBY 1971) 350
Perception 92
Perceptual
    Constructs 114
    Developments 105
    Mechanism 104-6
    Organisation/skills 94
Performance evaluation (of the curriculum) 40
Peripheral vision 225
Perkins' Diploma 349
Permanence of objects 113
Personal construct 272
Personality and Emotion, Development of 87-100
    Study of 87-92
Peters, R.S. (1966) 16
Phonology 154, 307
Physical Intervention Programme 321
Phy6siotherapist, -therapy 314, 322
Piaget, J. 87-91, 98, 101, 102, 103, 106-12, 135, 159, 206, 210, 227, 272
Plank, M. (1982) 361, 362-3, 364-5
Playschemes (offered by support unit) 379
Plowden report (1966) 16, 253
Poling, A., Fugua, r. and Miltenberger, R. (1983) 47
Portage model 250, 253-4, 298
Porterfield, J., Blunden, R. and Blewitt, E. (1980) 70, 75-6
Positive regard 283
Post Lingual deafness 215, 218
Possession (Semantic Notion after Leonard) 158
Pragmatics 154, 156, 158, 164, 167-8
Pratt, M.W., Bumstead, D.C. and Raynes, N.V. (1970) 163-4
Pre-communication Behaviour 167
Pre Lingual deafness 215
Pre-operational 102-3, 157
    The Pre-operational Period 118-23
    LImitations of the Pre-operational Child 121
Presbyacusis 215
Presland, J. (1981) 296
Pre-verbal Communication Schedule 165, 168

Pre-verbal Communication Manual and Checklist 166
Prior, M., Minnes, P., Coyne, T., Golding, B., Hendy, J. and McGillivary, J. (1979) 163
Pro-active interference 197
'Program to Develop Efficiency in Visual functioning 342
Programme Planning 26-30
    Programme Planning 282
Progress Assessment Charts 222
Project TASS 45
PROPH 307
PROP 307
Propositions 192-3, 199
Proto-declarative 160
Proto-imperative 159
Provision and Prevelance (of Support Services for the Visually Impaired) 336-8
Psycholinguistic approach 156
Psychological services (provided by LEA's) 292-3
Psychotic children 389
Pugh, G. (1981) 253, 254
Pugh, G. and Russell, P. (1977) 248
Punishment techniques 49, 52

Quigley, N. (1982) 139
Quilitch, H.R., Christopherson, E.R. and Risley, T.R. (1977) 76
Quirk Committee 300
Quotient of Intelligence 88

Ratio schedules 47
Rayner Commission 273
Reason, A. (1984) 131, 133, 134, 137
Reasoning 120
Recall schema 138
Recognition schema 138
Recording (A.P.R.E.) 33-7, 282
Rectory Paddock (1983) 20, 203
Recurrence (Semantic Notion of Leonard) 157, 169
Reed, M. (1973) 221
Referal (by the Remedial therapist) 322
Refractory epilepsy 385
Rehearsal 200, 203, 207
Reid, B. and Kiernan, C. (1979) 196
Reinforcement 57-8, 78, 93, 170
    and its effect on behaviour 33-7

Natural reinforcers 58, 63
Reinforcement (Positive/Negative) 53-4
    Schedules of Reinforcement 47
Rejection (Semantic Notion of Leonard) 158
Relational and reversal learning 56, 59
Remedial gymnast 314, 322
Remedial Therapy 313
Repetition 133
Representation, (mental, symbolic) 118
Representational art 119
Residential unit 376
Residual vision 232
Respite care, Advantages of 378-9
    Disadvantages of Respite care 379-80
    Respite Fostering 375
    Respite Fostering (The Children, The Foster Parents) 378
Response distortion 61
Retrieval 197-8, 207
Retro-active interference 197
Reverse transverse palmar 140
Review, Reviewing 4, 6, 253
Reynell, J.K. (1977) 305; (1979) 338
Reynell Developmental Language Scales 305-6
Reynell, J.K. and Zinkin, P. (1979) 230, 342
Reynell-Zinkin Development Scales for Young Visually Handicapped Children 342
Rice, H.K., McDaniel, M.W., Stallings, V.D. and Gatz, M.J. (1967) 65
Richards, S.J. and Evans, P.L.C. (1981) 188
Richardson, E. (1975) 275
Ricks, D. (1980) 321; (1982) 251
Riddick (1982) 255
Roberts, K. and Schaefer, R. (1984) 167
Robin, M. and Josse, D. (1984) 244
Robinson, G.C. (1977) 342
Rogers, C. (1967 283
Rogerian 272
Rogow, S.M. (1982) 231
Rondal, J.A. (1978) 163
Rood, M.S. (1956) 318
Room Management 72
    and its variants 75-81

compared with small group and individual teaching 76-9
Rotter, J.B. (1954) 96-7
Roulstone, S. (1983) 304
Routinised tasks 131
Royal College of Psychiatrists 370
Royal National Institute for the Blind (RNIB) 229, 349
Rubella 149, 216, 220, 242, 385
Rubissow, S., Jones, J. and Brimblecombe, F. (1979) 248
Ruder, K.F. and Smith, M.D. (1984) 170-1
Rushfirth (1984) 321
Russell, P. (1983) 253
Rutter, M. (1972) 98
Rutter, M., Birch, M.G., Thomas, A. and Chess (?) (1964) 95
Rutter, M., Maughan, B., Mortimore, P. and Ouston, J. (1979) 284

Salapatek, P. (1975) 93
Salapatek, P. and Kessen, W. (1966) 92
Sameroff, A. (1975) 94
Sameroff, A.J. and Chandler, M.J. (1975) 95
Sandler, A., Coren, A. and Thurman, S.K. (1983) 257-8
Sandow, S. and Clarke, A.D.B. (1978) 254
Sandow, S., Clarke, A.D.B., Cox, M.V. and Stewart, F.L. (1981) 254
Saunders, C.A., Jordan, R.R. and Kiernan, C.C. (1975) 261
Scale Post Holders 279-81, 286
Schaeffer, B. (1980) 219
Schaffer, H.R. (1977) 228
Schema 113, 114, 115, 116, 117, 118
Schmidt, R.A. (1975), (1976) 138-9
Schmidts Motor Schema 148
Schools Council Paper 70 (1981) 17
Schwann cells 94
Scoliosis 385
Scottish Curriculum Publication 286
Sebba (1980) 317, 318
Selectivity (Passive, Active) 104-5
Selective listening 105
Self-help 97
Semantics 154, 164, 307
  Importance of Semantics 156-8
  Semantic code 353
Semantic Notions of Leonard 157-8

Semantic Memory 198
Sense training 272
Sensorimotor 102-3, 106, 157, 159, 318
  development 125
  period 112-18
  Training Programme 323
  understanding 227
Sensori-neural deafness 215, 220
Sensory Handicap 214-35
Sensory Memory 193-4
Sequential sampling 52
Serars otitis media 329
Seriation 121, 136
Setting Events 59-60
Sewell, G. (1982) 70
Sex Education 261
Shaping 206
Shapiro, D.C. and Schmidt, R.A. (1982) 139
Shearer, D.E. and Shearer, M.S. (1976) 254
Shepherd, A. (1976) 143
Shiffrin, R.M. and Schneider, W. (1977) 188
Short, J. (1984) 369
Short Term Care, Definition of 375
Short term memory 199, 200
Sign (developing sign language) 219
Siipola, E.M. and Hayden, S.D. (1965) 195
Simon, G.B. (1981) 367
Sines, D. (1983) 369
Single Code Theory 194
Skills analysis 18-19
Skinner, B.F. (1938) 203; (1974) 46
  Skinneria (Behavioural) 155-6
Slama, K.M. and Bannerman, D.J. (1983) 71
Small group teaching 9-10, 70-5
Smith, B. (1983) 255
Smith, T. (1980) 256
Snellen fraction 225
Snow, C.E. (1972) 156
Snyder, L.K. and MacLean, J.E. (1976) 161, 301
Social influences (their influence in learning) 111
Social Learning Theory 85, 87
Social Quotients (S.Q) 354
Social Worker 367-8, 369
Socialisation 85, 93, 94, 96, 97, 111, 223
  Socio-perception Development in

the Handicapped Child 94-9
Socio-perceptual Development in
  the Young Child 92-4
Sonksen, P.M. (1982) 231
Sonksen, P.M. Levitt, S. and
  Kittsinger, M. (1984) 353
Southend Scheme 248
Spangler, P.F. and Marshall, A.M.
  (1983) 76
Spastic Society 274
Spatial relationship 117
Special needs/care units 112
Specialised resources 237
Specialist visiting teacher 338
Speech, Developing 218-19
Speech discrimination 330-1
Speech Therapist 153, 172, 300-12
  A resource model for 303-4
  as co-ordinator 308-9
  as a participant in school 304
  Intervention by 302
Spence, S. (1980) 219
Spina bifida 241-2, 246
Spitz, H.H. (1979) 191
Sprague, J.S. and Horner, R.M.
  (1981) 63
Standing, L., Conezio, J. and Haber,
  R.N. (1970) 193
Statement of Need 318, 323
Stereotyping (in behaviour) 232
Stengel, Attermeir, Bly and Heriza
  1984 317
Stimulation, auditory, visual 65
Stimulus control 54-5, 61, 63, 65
Stimulus events 59-60
Stimulus shaping 148
Stokes, T.F. and Baer, D.M. (1977)
  57, 60, 145, 207
Storm, R. and Willis, J. (1978) 72-3,
  80
Strabismus 226
Strategies in Learning 201-3
Stratification 279-80
Stress and Rhythm 154
Structural approach 89
Structural model 199-200
Sturmey, P. and Crisp, A. (1984a),
  (1984b) 80
Sturmey, P., Crisp, A. and Dearden,
  B. (1983) 72, 77
Subject Verb (S.V.) (grammatical
  structures) 171
Summerfield Report (1968) 291
Support Services for

the Hearing Impaired 326-36
the Visually Impaired 336-48
The Support Unit 375-82
  philosophy of 375
  role of 375
Sykanda, A.M. and Levitt, S. (1982)
  231
Sylva, K., Roy, C. and Painter, M.
  (1980) 286
Symbolic function (in the
  Pre-operational period) 119
Symbolic Play Test (S.P.T.) 305-6
Symbolic signs 92, 219
Symptom clustering 92
Syntax 154, 158, 164
Synthetic speech 357

Tallents, C. (1979) 342
Target Behaviour 30-1, 47
Task analysis 31-2, 47, 137, 142,
  143
Task independence 73
Task interdependence 73
Taylor Report (D.E.S. 1977) 274-5
Taylor, A.M. and Turnure, J.E.
  (1979) 202
Teams in Practice (C.M.H.T's, D.T's
  etc) 362-3
Technology, Impact of (on the deaf)
  219
Terdal, L.E., Jackson, R.H. and
  Garner, A.M. (1976) 163
Terrace, H.S. (1963) 55
TES 44, 273
Thomas, M. (1985) 296
Thomas, G. and O'Callaghan, M.
  (1981) 46
Thomson, R. (Nursing Times
  13.11.80) 366
Tibbits, J. (1983) 66
Time-out
  Rooms from Positive
    Reinforcement 50
Tizard, B., Cooperman, O., Joseph,
  A. and Tizard, J. (1972) 164
Tizard, B., Hughes, M., Carmichael,
  H. and Pinkerton, G. (1983a),
  (1983b) 256
Tobin, M.J. (1978) 342
Tomlinson, S. (1981) 304
Tonic-neck reflex 95
Touwen, B.C.L. (1976) 136
Trace Decay Theory 197
Transactional relationship 95

Transformational grammar (after Chomsky) 155
Transitivity 122
Translocation (form of Down's Syndrome) 385
Transmission transduction interpretation 216
Trauma (causing deafness) 216
Tredgold, R.F. and Soddy, K. (1949) 91
Trebakoff, M.I. (1977) 231
Trisomy 21, Trisomies (partial) 384
Trout, D. (1983) 244
Tuberous sclerosis 385
Tunnel vision 225
Turnbull, A.P. and Turnbull, H.R. (1982) 256, 262
Turnbull, A.P. and Strickland, B. (1981) 262
'Two Sentences Together' 173
Tymchuck, A. (1979) 247-8
Tympanometry 329
Tympanosclerosis 329

Uslan, M. (1979) 231
Uzgiris, I.C. and Hunt, J. McV. (1975) 61, 85, 113, 118, 124, 294

Van Biervliet, A. (1979) 196
Van Dijk, J. (1977) 149-50
Vaughan, D. and Asbury, T. (1980) 343
Ventral digital 140 (see fig 6:1, p. 141)
Verbalisation 163
Vernon Report (DES 1972) 224
Vibro-tactile stimuli 357
Villiers, de, J. and de Villiers, P. (1978) 155
Vineland
    adapted by Maxfield-Bucholz 342, 354
    Social Age (Doll 1947) 77
    Social Maturity Scale 222, 230
Visual code coding 196
Visual field 225
Visual Impairment 224-35
    Assessment and Referral of 340-3
    Educational Assessment of 342-3
    LEA policy on 336-7
    Medical Assessment of 340-1
    Provision and Prevalence 336-8
    Support Services for 336-48
    Types of Visual Impairment 224-6

Visual Memory 195-7
Visual pursuit (The development of) 113
Vocalisation 159-60
Voicing 154
Volunteer organisations 246
Von Cranach, M. (1982) 130
Vygotsky, L.S. (1978) 206

Wadsworth, B.J. (1984) 109
Wahler, R. and Fox, J. (1981) 59
Waldron, J. (*Nursing Mirror* 2.5.84) 367
Walter, A. (1978) 75
Warburg, M., Fredriksen, P. and Rattlefft, J. (1979) 225
Ward, J. and Gow, L. (1982) 57, 62
Warnock Report, Committee (DES 1978) 6, 12, 42, 52, 240, 246, 253, 255, 256, 271, 291, 295, 304, 310, 345
Watkins (in ICEBY 1971) 350
Watts, J.W. (1980) 275
Weber, M. (1947) 275
Wechsler, D. (1944), (1949) 221-2
Weeks, M. and Gaylord-Ross, R. (1981) 55
Welsh National School of Medicine 241
Wertheimer, M. (1961) 93
Wessels, M.G. (1982) 189
Westling, D.L., Ferrell, K. and Swenson, K. (1982) 72
Westmacott, E.V.S. and Cameron, R.J. (1981)
Whelan, E. and Speake, B. (1979) 20, 102
Wheldall, K. (1982) 57, 66
White (1984) 314
White, O. and Haring, N. (1978) 57
Whitman, T., Scibak, J. and Reid, D. (1983) 44, 50, 52, 62, 65
Whyte (1984) 314
Wikler, L., Wasow, M. and Hatfield, E. (1981) 263
Wilkins, D.A. (1974) 172; (1979), (1982) 245
Williams, C. (1980) 167; (1982) 215
Williams Intelligence Test for Children with Defective Vision 342
Williams, J.L., Schroeder, S.R., Eckerman, D.A. and Rojahn, J. (1983) 51

Wilson, M. (1980) 282
Wilson, M.D. (1981) 14, 17, 19, 39
Wing, J.K. (1966) 94
Winter, S. (1981) 26
Wolfenden (1978) 246
Wolfensberger, W. and Kurtz, R. (1974) 249
Wolkind, S. (1981) 243
Woods, P.A. and Cullen, C. (1983) 76
Woodruff, M.E. (1977) 225

Woodward, M. (1961) 103
Woodward, W.M. (1979) 210
Woodward, R.J., Magim, C. and Johnston, W.A. (1983) 51
Woodward, W.M. and Stern, D.J. (1963) 140

Yule, W. and Carr, J. (1980) 47

Zeaman, D. and House, B. (1963) 187, 195; (1979) 59, 187, 189